CW01262632

CONSUMPTION AND GENDER IN THE EARLY SEVENTEENTH-CENTURY HOUSEHOLD

Frontispiece 1. A copy of the portrait of Sir Hamon Le Strange by John Hoskins, 1617.

DAME ALICE LE STRANGE.
Wife of Sir Hamon le Strange
B. 1585   D 1656.
From a portrait at Hunstanton Hall by John Hoskins

Frontispiece 2. A copy of the portrait of Alice Le Strange by John Hoskins, 1617.

Consumption and Gender in the Early Seventeenth-Century Household

The World of Alice Le Strange

JANE WHITTLE
AND
ELIZABETH GRIFFITHS

OXFORD
UNIVERSITY PRESS

This book has been printed digitally and produced in a standard specification in order to ensure its continuing availability

OXFORD
UNIVERSITY PRESS

Great Clarendon Street, Oxford OX2 6DP
United Kingdom

Oxford University Press is a department of the University of Oxford.
It furthers the University's objective of excellence in research, scholarship,
and education by publishing worldwide.
Oxford is a registered trade mark of Oxford University Press in the UK
and in certain other countries

© Jane Whittle and Elizabeth Griffiths 2012

The moral rights of the author have been asserted

Reprinted 2013

All rights reserved. No part of this publication may be reproduced, stored in a retrieval system, or transmitted, in any form or by any means, without the prior permission in writing of Oxford University Press, or as expressly permitted by law, by licence or under terms agreed with the appropriate reprographics rights organization. Enquiries concerning reproduction outside the scope of the above should be sent to the Rights Department, Oxford University Press, at the address above

You must not circulate this book in any other binding or cover
And you must impose this same condition on any acquirer

British Library Cataloguing in Publication Data
Data available

Library of Congress Cataloging in Publication Data
Data available

ISBN 978-0-19-923353-3

This book is dedicated to Andrew
with love and gratitude from Jane

Preface

This book began as an Economic and Social Research Council-funded research project 'The housewife in early modern rural England' (RES-143-25-0014), which ran during 2003–7 as part of the Cultures of Consumption programme. This provided funding for Elizabeth to work full time on the project for two years, investigating the Le Strange archive, transcribing the accounts into a database and drafting sections of Chapters 1, 2 and 7. The analysis of the database and completion of the rest of the book was undertaken by Jane between 2005 and 2010, interrupted by periods of maternity leave and half-time work and supported by research leave funded by the Arts and Humanities Research Council and Exeter University in 2007–8 and 2010. Elizabeth remained involved throughout this stretch, always willing to look up references and read drafts. We owe thanks to many individuals: particularly all those involved in the interdisciplinary Cultures of Consumption programme for their ideas and enthusiasm, Richard Crangle for crucial help with database design, Clive Wilkins-Jones for sharing his work on the Le Strange library catalogue, and Anne Stobart and Margaret Pelling for their advice on medical history. The book has greatly benefited from comments received at research seminars at Cambridge University, Exeter University, the Economic History Conference, Agricultural History Conference, the Food Standards Agency and workshops on 'Restless interiors', 'Gender and built space' and 'Home and work'.

We aim, in the book, to offer a 'holistic' view of consumption patterns in early seventeenth-century England: that is, to consider all facets of consumption as far as is possible with the surviving documents. In doing so it has been necessary to jump from topic to topic. Many topics of sections in chapters are worthy of books in their own right. Here, we trample over a wide range of specialisms from silverware to medical care, education to architecture, gift-making to taxation. We would like to apologize in advance for errors, but hope that more is gained than lost by putting together this diverse array of activities and objects in a single study, and in attempting to reconstruct consumption as it was experienced in the early seventeenth century by the Le Strange family and their employees.

Jane Whittle
Elizabeth Griffiths

Exeter
2012

Contents

Notes to the Reader	xiii
List of Figures	xv
List of Tables	xvi

1. Issues and Context   1
   History and consumption   2
   Consumption and gender   8
   Consumption and the gentry   14
   The Le Strange family   18
   Methods and chapter plan   23

2. Household Management   26
   Alice Le Strange's accounts   28
   Household and estate management   34
   Gentlewomen as housewives   36
   Two other Norfolk families   43
   Conclusion   48

3. The Acquisition of Goods   49
   Domestic expenditure   50
   Urban shopping   55
   The acquisition of clothing and furnishings   64
   The acquisition of food   72
   Conclusion   84

4. Everyday Consumables   86
   Diet   88
   The meanings of food   97
   Medical care   105
   Household consumables   111
   Conclusion   115

5. Material Culture   117
   Textiles and clothing   119
   Beds and living rooms   132
   Dining ware and kitchen ware   140
   The meanings of goods   145
   Conclusion   153

6. Family Life Cycle and Consumption — 156
Life cycle and expenditure — 157
Births, deaths and marriages — 164
Childhood and childcare — 170
Education and adult children — 174
Conclusion — 181

7. Elite Consumption — 184
Political and legal expenses — 185
Travel and leisure — 191
Literature, music and science — 196
Building and estate improvement — 203
Conclusion — 208

8. The Employment of Labour — 210
Servants — 212
Day labourers — 221
Craftsmen and specialist workers — 225
The Le Stranges and the local community — 228
Conclusion — 236

9. Conclusion — 239

Select Bibliography — 243
Index — 253

Notes to the Reader

MONEY AND PRICES

There were 12 pence (d) to a shilling (s), and 240d or 20s to a pound (£).

Prices are best understood in relative terms with examples:

2d would buy eight wooden trenchers, eleven plaice, an almanac, a yard of the cheapest cloth or a day's work by a child;

6d would buy two chickens, two earthenware pitchers, 4 oz of sugar candy, a yard of black ribbon, or a day's labour by a semi-skilled adult man;

2s would buy a pair of shoes or gloves, an inexpensive book, 2 lbs of almonds or a scythe;

£2 would buy 3 yards of velvet, a second-hand brass cooking pot weighing 60 lb, a cow, or pay for a female servant's annual wage;

£10–15 would buy a suit of clothes for normal wear by the gentry or a coach horse and was equivalent to the annual earnings of day labourer;

£50–100 was the cost of one of the best beds purchased by the Le Stranges, and best suits of clothes purchased by the gentry for weddings; it was also the cost of building a substantial farmhouse;

£2000–3000 was the Le Stranges' average annual expenditure in the 1620s and 1630s and the cost of purchasing a manor; the dowries of Anne Lewkenor and Elizabeth Le Strange were £3500.

THE SPELLING OF LE STRANGE

The surname Le Strange can be spelled Lestrange, Le Strange or L'Estrange. Alice Le Strange refers to her husband as 'Mr Strange' throughout the accounts. Oestmann prefers Lestrange in his study of the family during the sixteenth century. From the 1630s onwards the family adopted the form L'Estrange, which they had not used previously. This form was made famous by Roger Le Strange in the second half of the seventeenth century. We have used the form 'Le Strange' throughout this book as it was the one used by the family at the start of the accounts. It is also the form used in the Norfolk Record Office catalogue.

DATES

The year in the household accounts and in general usage during this period ran from Lady Day (25 March) to Lady Day. This convention is used throughout this study. Where any particular confusion might arise, dates from January to March have been specified as, for example, February 1620/1. In no cases have they been modernized.

ABBREVIATIONS

ODNB: *The Oxford Dictionary of National Biography* online, accessed 2007–10.
OED Online: *The Oxford English Dictionary* online, accessed 2007–10.
TNA: The National Archives.

List of Figures

Frontispiece 1.	A copy of the portrait of Sir Hamon Le Strange by John Hoskins, 1617	ii
Frontispiece 2.	A copy of the portrait of Alice Le Strange by John Hoskins, 1617	iii
Figure 1.1.	The parents and grandparents of Hamon Le Strange and Alice Stubbe	19
Figure 3.1.	Trips from the Le Strange household to London, Norwich and King's Lynn, 1614–28	58
Figure 3.2.	The seasonal distribution of food gifts, 1619	80
Figure 4.1.	The proportion of meat, fish and dairy produce consumed, by edible weight, 1619	89
Figure 4.2.	The seasonality of food consumption in 1619	95
Figure 5.1.	A bed chamber at Hunstanton Hall *c.*1926, showing seventeenth-century furnishings	136
Figure 5.2.	Family portraits *in situ* in Hunstanton Hall *c.*1926; two portraits of Sir Hamon Le Strange (1583–1654) and one of Lady Alice Le Strange hang on the bottom row	138
Figure 6.1.	The Le Strange household, 1610–54	158
Figure 6.2.	Annual expenditure and money borrowed, 1606–53	160
Figure 6.3.	Phases of the boys' education	176
Figure 6.4.	The descendants of Sir Hamon and Alice Le Strange	182
Figure 7.1.	A plan of Hunstanton Hall showing phases of building up to 1650	204
Figure 7.2.	The front of Hunstanton Hall *c.*1926, showing the moat, fifteenth-century gatehouse, and new wings constructed by Sir Hamon Le Strange in the 1620s	205
Figure 7.3.	The front of Hunstanton Hall *c.*1926 seen from the distance, showing the 'upper freestone gates', and the outer wall encircling service buildings to the front of the hall as well as the house itself	207
Figure 8.1.	The annual earnings of three day labourers, 1616–24	223
Figure 8.2.	Land tenure and day labouring in Hunstanton, 1615–24	231

List of Tables

Table 1.1. The estate of Sir Hamon Le Strange of Hunstanton, 1616	22
Table 3.1. Average expenditure per year by decade on domestic consumption by category	53
Table 3.2. Annual expenditure on food and textiles, 1610–25	53
Table 3.3. Who made trips to towns, 1614–28?	59
Table 3.4. Tailors appearing in the disbursement accounts, 1606–25	68
Table 3.5. Second-hand goods purchased at Sir Henry Carvile's in 1625	70
Table 3.6. The nature and frequency of food purchases, 1619	73
Table 3.7. The range of items received as gifts, and the frequency with which they were received, 1613–27	78
Table 4.1. Individual adult consumption per week (assuming twenty-five in the household)	89
Table 4.2. Change in diet during Lent	98
Table 4.3. Consumption at selected feasts in the Le Strange household, 1619–36	100
Table 4.4. A comparison between normal consumption patterns (1619) and consumption when the gentry family were absent (1620)	102
Table 4.5. The cost of medical care per person, 1606–26	105
Table 4.6. Medical practitioners employed by the Le Strange household, 1606–26	107
Table 5.1. Elizabeth Le Strange's four most expensive gowns	126
Table 5.2. Elizabeth Le Strange's other gowns, purchased 1628–37	127
Table 5.3. Clothing accessories, purchased 1610–25	129
Table 5.4. Nicholas' wedding clothes, purchased London 1630	131
Table 5.5. The cost of the black bed, 1620, and the crimson damask bed, 1628	135
Table 5.6. Household linen listed in the 1632 inventory	139
Table 5.7. Dining, cooking and miscellaneous items purchased on a shopping trip to London, 1628	141
Table 6.1. Average expenditure per year	159
Table 6.2. 'Losses in my husband's estate'	163
Table 6.3. Baptisms and payments to the midwife	164
Table 6.4. The cost of the Le Strange children from birth to 1654	181
Table 7.1. Taxes paid, April 1606–April 1626	190
Table 7.2. The cost of a new coach itemized, 1632	193
Table 7.3. Scientific instruments acquired, 1606–30	201

List of Tables

Table 8.1. Servants in the Le Strange household, 1617	214
Table 8.2. The origins of the servants employed, 1613–28	219
Table 8.3. Examples of wage rates, 1610–30	229
Table 8.4. A summary of six tenants' probate inventories	233

1
Issues and Context

This book is a study of consumption in one early seventeenth-century household. Its main source is a set of household accounts kept by Lady Alice Le Strange of Hunstanton between 1610 and 1653 which had been begun by her husband Sir Hamon Le Strange in 1606. The study of consumption is a fragmented field but here the household and the process of accounting provide unity. Alice Le Strange was an exceptionally meticulous and systematic accountant, recording not only all purchases and income but also the food produced and consumed in the household. It is as complete a record of the consumption activities of one historic household as we could hope for. So while, on the one hand, the focus is narrow, illuminating the consumption activities of a single household, on the other it allows an unusually wide-ranging view of consumption. The book examines not just the ownership of goods but how they were acquired and who managed that acquisition. It is concerned not only with durable goods, but with consumables such as food and fuel. It looks not only at goods but also at services provided in the form of labour. The focus is only sometimes on the novel and luxurious but more often on the ordinary and everyday. And the accounts provide not just a snapshot of consumption but also a view of expenditure over the household's lifetime. As such, the book utilizes a range of approaches to consumption. It is concerned with consumption as a process, with gifts and commodities, with material culture and its meanings, with everyday life, and with the construction of identities. It is also a book about gender. Consumption is gendered in three main ways: in terms of who makes the decisions which lie behind consumption practices; in terms of who does the work involved in consumption such as shopping, cooking and cleaning; and in the creation of gendered identities through consumption.

The household was commonly recognized as the woman's proper sphere of influence in the seventeenth century. The housewife had a duty to manage her household and see that all its members were provided with daily necessities. Legal restrictions and convention meant that she was always deputy to her husband, dependent on his wealth and permission to carry out her tasks. Men differed in the amount of freedom and responsibility they gave their wives, but Alice Le Strange was not alone in being given the task of household accounting and other aspects of household management by her husband. With an income of over £2000 in the 1620s, the Le Stranges were members of the upper gentry. Gentry households were not small private family units. They were large and, although centred on the family, family members were outnumbered by live-in employees. The Le Strange household normally contained around twenty-five people. Such households played an important role in the local economy. The Le Stranges were the largest employer in their locality, the largest consumer of locally produced food and also a producer and retailer of wool, timber and various foodstuffs. Study of the gentry has much to offer the history of consumption. The gentry form a neglected link in histories of consumption, connecting London to the provinces, and court lifestyles of high fashion to the modest innovations of parish elites in the countryside. The rest of this chapter provides context for the detailed study that follows, looking in turn at consumption, gender, and the gentry of early seventeenth-century England. It finishes with a brief history of the Le Strange family, an outline of the research methods used and a plan of the book.

HISTORY AND CONSUMPTION

What exactly is consumption? Few historians have been concerned to define the term. Appleby's definition of consumption as 'the active seeking of personal gratification through material goods' is revealingly restrictive.[1] The history of early modern consumption is dominated by studies of the ownership of goods, particularly of new and foreign goods; the act of purchasing, particularly in shops; and the pleasures associated with these activities. These topics have proved fruitful, but together they provide only a partial view of consumption. The concentration on goods and shopping is in part a product of the sources used. Probate inventories, which survive in their tens of thousands for England in the period c.1550–c.1730, list durable goods owned at death.[2] Inventories of merchants, pedlars and shopkeepers list goods available for purchase.[3] Some artefacts, particularly buildings, survive from the early modern period.[4] In comparison the labour involved in providing services was relatively ephemeral. Yet a service like a haircut could be just as vital in shaping personal appearance as a hat, personal cleanliness was as significant in asserting status and morality as fashions in clothing. Goods that were literally consumed, such as food and fuel, disappear from view, attracting attention largely via the durable paraphernalia they left behind such as cooking pots and fire grates.[5] Goods which were consumed but not purchased are also poorly

---

[1] J. Appleby, 'Consumption in early modern social thought', in J. Brewer and R. Porter (eds.), *Consumption and the World of Goods* (London, 1993), 164.
[2] P. Glennie, 'Consumption within historical studies', in D. Miller (ed.), *Acknowledging Consumption: A Review of New Studies* (London, 1995), 169–71; M. Overton, J. Whittle, D. Dean and A. Hann, *Production and Consumption in English Households, 1600–1750* (Abingdon, 2004), ch. 2.
[3] M. Spufford, *The Great Reclothing of Rural England: Petty Chapmen and Their Wares in the Seventeenth Century* (Oxford, 1984); N. Cox, *The Complete Tradesman: A Study of Retailing, 1550–1820* (Aldershot, 2000).
[4] M.W. Barley, 'Rural housing in England', in J. Thirsk (ed.), *The Agrarian History of England and Wales. Vol. IV. 1500–1640* (Cambridge, 1967); R. Machin, 'The great rebuilding: a reassessment', *Past and Present* 77 (1977), 33–56; M. Johnson, *Housing Culture: Traditional Architecture in an English Landscape* (London, 1993); N. Cooper, *The Houses of the Gentry 1480–1680* (New Haven, 1999).
[5] S. Pennell, 'Consumption and consumerism in early modern England', *Historical Journal* 42:2 (1999), 561.

documented. Home production was not necessarily a relic of an earlier economic system but an active choice to ensure quality, freshness and easy availability.[6] Gifts were laden with meanings that could determine how the item was regarded by the receiver and used within the home.[7]

In this study consumption is defined as the acquisition of goods and services and their use within the family and household. The word 'use' is understood broadly, not simply as functional utility but as 'appropriation'—the way in which things are assimilated within the home and attain personal meanings,[8] and in terms of symbolic uses such as denoting status and other aspects of identity. To paraphrase Douglas and Isherwood, commodities are good not only for eating, clothing and shelter but also for thinking and for non-verbal communication.[9] Thus a bed might be slept in and provide warmth and comfort, but its furnishings were chosen to fit a particular scheme of decor determined by personal preferences and the symbolic meanings of pattern and colour, while its size and the quality of materials demonstrate the wealth and status of the family who purchased it. A bed purchased in preparation for marriage embodies hopes of fertility and family longevity, and through time such a bed can become a valued heirloom. These are all aspects of consumption. Most discussions of consumption implicitly treat the consumer as either an individual or a domestic unit—a household. Consumption can take place in different settings: all forms of production consume materials and labour, but here the focus is on the domestic. The Le Strange household accounts combine a record of spending by family members, who were not always resident in the household, with a record of spending on household members, for instance on servants and building workers, who were not part of the biological Le Strange family.[10]

It follows from this definition that consumption is treated as an ongoing process rather than as an act of purchase or a set of objects. Only one of the chapters in this book, Chapter 5, is centrally concerned with durable goods. Chapter 3, on the acquisition of goods, considers purchases as just one of a number of routes by which things could be acquired for the household. Other chapters examine the management of consumption, everyday consumables, variations in expenditure across the family's life cycle, consumption activities and the employment of labour. Fine advocates a 'systems of provision' approach to see consumption in motion and placed in its full economic context, tracing each type of good from design and

---

[6] Overton et al., *Production and Consumption*, 63.
[7] J. Carrier, *Gifts and Commodities: Exchange and Western Capitalism since 1700* (London, 1995), ch. 1; D. Miller, 'Consumption and its consequences', in H. Mackay (ed.), *Consumption and Everyday Life* (London, 1997), 13–63; M. Finn, 'Men's things: masculine possession in the consumer revolution', *Social History* 25:2 (2000), 142–52; F. Heal, 'Food gifts, the household and the politics of exchange in early modern England', *Past and Present* 199 (2008), 41–70.
[8] Miller, 'Consumption and its consequences', 14; Carrier, *Gifts and Commodities*, 10.
[9] M. Douglas and B. Isherwood, *The World of Goods: Towards an Anthropology of Consumption* (London, 1996), 40–1.
[10] We use the modern meaning of family here to mean blood relatives, specifically parents and unmarried children. The early modern meaning of family was synonymous with the household: servants were members of the family.

production through marketing and purchase to use.[11] But there are other ways of viewing the process of consumption. From the consumer's point of view, the process of consumption moves from planning what to acquire, through acquisition and on to various forms of use. It is this process that is central to this book, fulfilling the call for 'greater attention to consumers as much as the consumed'.[12] Douglas and Isherwood point out that periodicity, the frequency with which certain things were acquired or used, is an important dimension of consumption that 'marks rank and creates quality goods'.[13] Household accounts are the most accessible means of documenting the historical periodicity of consumption.[14] Examining consumption over a household's life cycle brings patterns of expenditure, the cost of caring for and educating children, and the celebration of life cycle events, such as birth and marriage, into focus. Seeing consumption as a process reminds us that not only goods but also services, activities and events are consumed.[15] The study of food consumption makes this particularly clear: tracing foodstuffs from production to consumption reveals much about the functioning of the economy, but the full social and economic significance of food needs to be understood in terms of seasonality, status and celebrations.[16]

By viewing, as far as possible, the complete consumption practices of a wealthy household the topics that have received so much attention in existing studies can be set in their full context. Novelty was an important facet of consumption, not only because it is the face of change but also because 'all new goods by virtue of their unfamiliarity offered consumers a lot of interpretative scope'.[17] Yet novelty needs to be seen in the context of older goods and practices with which it coexists and which define it.[18] Novelty could come in a surprising range of forms depending on exactly what was new: new goods could be fitted into old practices, like the turkeys given and consumed at Christmas in early seventeenth-century Norfolk; old goods could be produced in new ways, like the many 'consumer goods' Thirsk describes being commercially produced on a large scale for the first time in England in the late sixteenth and early seventeenth centuries, such as white soap and pins.[19] Some

---

[11] B. Fine, *The World of Consumption: The Material and Cultural World Revisited*, 2nd edn. (London, 2002), chs. 5 and 6.
[12] Pennell, 'Consumption and consumerism', 549. C. Walsh puts this in action in 'Shops, shopping, and the art of decision making in eighteenth-century England', in J. Styles and A. Vickery (eds.), *Gender, Taste and Material Culture in Britain and North America, 1700–1830* (New Haven, 2006), 162–72.
[13] Douglas and Isherwood, *World of Goods*, 84.
[14] See, for instance, L. Weatherill, *Consumer Behaviour and Material Culture in Britain, 1660–1760* (London, 1988), chs. 6 and 7; C.M. Woolgar, *The Great Household in Late Medieval England* (New Haven, 1999), chs. 5–7.
[15] J. Stobart, A. Hann, and V. Morgan, *Spaces of Consumption: Leisure and Shopping in the English Town, c.1680–1830* (Abingdon, 2007).
[16] S. Mintz, 'The changing roles of food in the study of consumption' in Brewer and Porter (eds.), *Consumption and the World of Goods*, 263; Pennell, 'Consumption and consumerism', 561–3; Douglas and Isherwood, *World of Goods*, 44.
[17] Glennie, 'Consumption within historical studies', 180.
[18] Overton et al., *Production and Consumption*, 115.
[19] J. Thirsk, *Economic Policy and Projects: The Development of a Consumer Society in Early Modern England* (Oxford, 1978), 6–7, 53–4, 78–83; Pennell, 'Consumption and consumerism', 553.

goods, such as clothing, had long been subject to fashions of rapidly changing novelty;[20] others, such as tableware, experienced accelerating rates of change between the sixteenth and eighteenth centuries.[21] Truly new consumer products that led to new practices such as tea and tea drinking,[22] or watches and clocks,[23] are relatively rare.

Novelty can also be found in the way goods were acquired. Kowaleski-Wallace notes that the verb 'to shop' appears only in the second half of the eighteenth century, and defines shopping as 'the purchase of what is "desirable but not indispensable"', setting it apart from 'marketing and other forms of buying'.[24] Semantically, shopping had no earlier equivalent: one did not go out 'buying', 'purchasing' or 'spending' in the early seventeenth century, but only to buy certain goods or services. That is not to say that the actual activity did not exist: as Walsh and Peck have shown, the Royal Exchange (opened 1570) and New Exchange (opened 1609) in London were created to allow people to shop, in Kowaleski-Wallace's sense.[25] At this date London had a wide range of luxury shops inside the Exchanges and out, which attracted the wealthy elite from all over the country.[26] Another change was the increasing array of finished articles displayed for sale in shops in the eighteenth century.[27] In earlier periods, ordering bespoke items from craftsmen or buying part-finished goods had been more usual. The multitude of new finished goods did not necessarily signal any increase in choice for those who could afford to pay: bespoke production had offered almost infinite choice.

The new form of shopping coexisted with earlier types of purchasing. Many did not visit London in person but conducted 'proxy shopping' via family and friends. Well documented in the eighteenth century,[28] this was even more dominant in the

---

[20] G. McCracken, *Culture and Consumption* (Indiana, 1988), 6; S. Vincent, *Dressing the Elite: Clothes in Early Modern England* (Oxford, 2003).

[21] M. Johnson, *An Archaeology of Capitalism* (Oxford, 1996), 199–200; Overton et al., *Production and Consumption*, 102–4; M. Berg, *Luxury and Pleasure in Eighteenth Century Britain* (Oxford, 2005) ch. 4.

[22] H. Mui and L.H. Mui, *Shops and Shopkeeping in Eighteenth Century England* (Montreal, 1989); C. Shammas, *The Pre-Industrial Consumer in England and America* (Oxford, 1990); W.D. Smith, 'Complications of the commonplace: tea, sugar and imperialism', *Journal of Interdisciplinary History* 23:2 (1992), 259–78; Mintz, 'The changing roles of food', 261–73; E. Kowaleski-Wallace, *Consuming Subjects: Women, Shopping and Business in the Eighteenth Century* (New York, 1997), 19–36; W.D. Smith, *Consumption and the Making of Respectability 1600–1800* (London, 2002), ch. 6.

[23] C.M. Cipolla, *Clocks and Culture 1300–1700* (London, 1967); E.P. Thompson, 'Time, work-discipline and industrial capitalism', *Past and Present* 38 (1967), 56–97; D.S. Landes, *Revolution in Time: Clocks and the Making of the Modern World* (Cambridge, Massachusetts, 1983); Weatherill, *Consumer Behaviour;* M. Donald, '"The greatest necessity of every rank of Men": gender, clocks and watches', in M. Donald and L. Hurcombe (eds.), *Gender and Material Culture in Historical Perspective* (Basingstoke, 2000), 54–75; Overton et al., *Production and Consumption*.

[24] Kowaleski-Wallace, *Consuming Subjects*, 75, 77.

[25] C. Walsh, 'Social meaning and social space in the shopping galleries of early modern London', in J. Benson and L. Ugolini (eds.), *A Nation of Shopkeepers: Five Centuries of British Retailing* (London, 2003), 52–79; L. Peck, *Consuming Splendor: Society and Culture in Seventeenth Century England* (Cambridge, 2005), 42–61; D. Davis, *A History of Shopping* (London, 1966), 122–6.

[26] Davis, *History of Shopping*, chs. 3 and 5.

[27] Berg, *Luxury and Pleasure*, 257–70.

[28] Walsh, 'Art of decision making', 169–70; A. Buck, 'Buying clothes in Bedfordshire: customers and tradesmen 1700–1800', *Textile History* 22 (1991), 215–19; A. Vickery, 'Women and the world of

early seventeenth century when agents and servants were used to buy luxury products in London.[29] Purchasing luxuries such as fine clothes, accessories, tableware and furnishings might involve pleasurable shopping, but everyday needs such as food, drink, fuel, and basic haberdashery and tailoring were provided in different ways, at least in rural England. Some food items, such as vegetables, barely entered the market at all in rural areas in the early seventeenth century;[30] others, such as bread, might be bought from a local producer, or were retailed on a very local basis, like eggs. Large households like that of the Le Stranges made bulk-buys of coal, wine and dried fruit from the nearest regional town, King's Lynn. The proliferation of small shops in the late seventeenth and eighteenth centuries had little impact on this purchasing system, as it was aimed at people who could not afford to travel or buy in bulk.[31] It is far from clear that the changes in retailing which occurred in the eighteenth century forced people to develop more advanced skills as consumers. Walsh's conclusion to a recent study is circumspect. From the perspective of the eighteenth century she writes:

> Over the course of several hundred years, consumers came to purchase more finished goods rather than semi finished ones or the raw materials for making goods at home, and increasingly they purchased affordable new items rather than second-hand goods. New shopping skills were not needed to cope with this change—shoppers had been used to purchasing finished goods for centuries, but now they spend more time comparing and contrasting finished articles (rather than selecting raw materials), as well as developing their knowledge of these goods and their respective qualities.[32]

Where does this leave McKendrick's 'consumer revolution' of the late eighteenth century?[33] As Glennie has pointed out, 'phrases like the birth of consumer society, emergent modern consumption, and the rise of mass market culture' have been applied to almost every period between the sixteenth century and the mid-twentieth century.[34] These differing chronologies arise from a failure to define exactly what a 'consumer society' is, allowing historians to focus on different types of goods, forms of retailing and classes of consumers, and accordingly come up with very different conclusions.[35] This book is not concerned with identifying any new consumer revolutions. Consisting as it does of a detailed case study of a limited period of time, it has no pretensions to identify significant shifts in consumer behaviour. Nonetheless the full value of any case study lies in situating it properly within its historical context. It provides a fixed point from which we can observe changes

---

goods: a Lancashire consumer and her possessions, 1751–81', in Brewer and Porter (eds.), *Consumption and the World of Goods*, 280.

[29] Peck, *Consuming Splendor*, 33–42.
[30] Cox, *The Complete Tradesman*, 43.
[31] Mui and Mui, *Shops and Shopkeeping*; Shammas, *Pre-Industrial Consumer*, ch. 8.
[32] Walsh, 'Art of decision making', 172.
[33] N. McKendrick, 'The consumer revolution in eighteenth-century England', in N. McKendrick, J. Brewer, and J.H. Plumb, *The Birth of a Consumer Society: The Commercialization of Eighteenth-Century England* (London, 1983), 9–33.
[34] Glennie, 'Consumption within historical studies', 164; McCracken, *Culture and Consumption*, 4.
[35] Glennie, 'Consumption within historical studies', 164; Fine, *World of Consumption*, 156–9.

that had already occurred, and identify those that were yet to come. The early seventeenth century predates a number of shifts in patterns of consumption, most importantly the increase in ready-made or finished goods, the influx of non-European foreign goods and the spread of shop-based retailing.[36]

Yet by the beginning of the seventeenth century a number of important changes in consumption had already happened. Earlier increases in foreign trade brought cheaper spices and sugar and the first goods from the new world. Some innovations in manufacturing had occurred. The Renaissance had widened the cultural horizons of the English elite.[37] The early seventeenth-century Le Stranges ate turkey, washed with English-made white soap, dressed themselves in cloth from the 'new draperies' and owned an extensive library of printed books: all practices which would have been impossible a century earlier. McCracken has argued that the elite of Elizabethan England created a material culture that was quite alien to the rest of society.[38] But it was not just the elite but ordinary people who experienced important changes in consumption in the sixteenth century, as Harrison noted in 1587.[39] De Vries sees change coming from urban households and those of middling wealth in the seventeenth century, and contrasts their 'new luxury' with the 'old luxury' of elite consumption.[40] The idea of a chasm in consumption patterns between the elite and others is perhaps the result of uneven historiographical coverage. Studies of probate inventories have illuminated the material culture of ordinary and middling households. Studies of surviving material objects concentrate on exquisite pieces owned by royalty and the super-rich.[41] The missing piece is the county gentry: people like the Le Stranges of Hunstanton. These families, ensconced in their rural households, had relations at court who provided information about the latest fashions and extravagances of those close to the monarch. But they were also related to London merchants and parish gentlemen who had no such pretensions. Their servants, drawn from households of the middling and lower classes, came face to face with elite consumption habits. These groups then, although distinct, were in contact with each other and inter-mixed. They experienced each other's homes, food and clothing. They did not necessarily emulate one

---

[36] Thirsk, *Economic Policy and Projects*; Spufford, *The Great Reclothing*; Weatherill, *Consumer Behaviour*; Shammas, *Pre-Industrial Consumer*; B. Lemire, *Fashion's Favourite: The Cotton Trade and the Consumer in Britain, 1660–1800* (Oxford, 1991); B. Lemire, *Dress, Culture and Commerce: The English Clothing Trade before the Factory, 1660–1800* (Basingstoke, 1997); Smith, *Consumption*; Overton et al., *Production and Consumption*; Berg, *Luxury and Pleasure*.

[37] Thirsk, *Economic Policy and Projects*; C. Mukerji, *From Graven Images: Patterns of Modern Materialism* (New York, 1983); L. Jardine, *Worldly Goods: A New History of the Renaissance* (London, 1996); C. Muldrew, *The Economy of Obligation: The Culture of Credit and Social Relations in Early Modern England* (Basingstoke, 1998), ch. 1; Overton et al., *Production and Consumption*; Peck, *Consuming Splendor*; J. Thirsk, *Food in Early Modern England: Phases, Fads, Fashions 1500–1760* (London, 2007).

[38] McCracken, *Culture and Consumption*, 14–15.

[39] W. Harrison, *The Description of England* (New York, 1968), 200–20; Shammas, *Pre-Industrial Consumer*; Overton et al., *Production and Consumption*.

[40] J. de Vries, 'Luxury in the Dutch Golden Age in theory and practice', in M. Berg and E. Eger (eds.), *Luxury in the Eighteenth Century: Debates, Desires and Delectable Goods* (Basingstoke, 2002).

[41] Discussed further in the introduction to Chapter 5.

another: there was a strong ethos of consuming according to one's means or risking ridicule. But these contacts offered routes by which novelty and innovation could spread and created a shared culture of consumption.

CONSUMPTION AND GENDER

The association of consumption with housework, housewives and the home means that consumption itself has often been gendered female in Western thought.[42] This book looks beyond these generalizations to examine how consumption and gender relations actually interacted within an early modern household. As we have argued, consumption and gender intersect in three main ways: in terms of who makes consumption decisions and manages the household, who does the work of consumption from shopping to laundry, and how consumption is used to construct gendered identities. Domestic consumption takes place in a household. People within households did not have equal rights of consumption in early modern England. Many, but not all, of these inequalities were a consequence of gender relations. The household head was legally responsible for the other members and this individual had the right to dispose of the household's wealth as he or she wished. Household heads were normally men. It was rare for single women to head their own households, married women were always subordinate to their husbands, and it was only as widows that many women became household heads. As the wife of a head, a woman stood in an intermediate position with regard to power within the household: she had the right to discipline and order her children and servants, she was expected to organize and manage her household, but, in theory at least, she could not control expenditure, make contracts or incur debts without her husband's permission.[43] Children and servants, the other members of the household, had little power and were expected to obey the household head and his wife: they had little or no say in how the household's money was spent, although they might have small amounts of personal spending money.[44] Children, however, as members of the biological family, were given preference in matters of consumption over servants: they wore more expensive clothes and might eat better food.[45] None of these inequalities of power should be overlooked in examining consumption patterns in this period.

Pahl's study of money and marriage in modern Britain argues that the management of household expenses consists of two elements: control of finances and their

---

[42] Carrier, *Gifts and Commodities*, 1; V. de Grazia, 'Changing consumption regimes', in V. de Grazia (ed.), *The Sex of Things: Gender and Consumption in Historical Perspective* (Berkeley and Los Angeles, 1996), 15.
[43] A. Erickson, *Women and Property in Early Modern England* (1990), 24, 100; M. Hunt, *The Middling Sort: Commerce, Gender and the Family in England 1680–1780* (Berkeley and Los Angeles, 1996), 138–42.
[44] P. Griffiths, *Youth and Authority: Formative Experiences in England 1560–1640* (Oxford, 1996), ch. 2.
[45] See Chapter 6: Childhood and childcare, and Chapter 8: Servants.

day-to-day management.[46] In early modern households headed by married couples it is clear that control, the power to make decisions, always lay with the husband. Many men, however, delegated the day-to-day management of finances to their wives. Household accounts provide insight into the power relations of the household on which consumption behaviour rested. Account keeping does not seem to have been strongly gendered. More accounts written by men survive than those written by women, and in elite households this task was often delegated to senior male servants. However, household accounts written by gentlewomen are not uncommon and survive from the sixteenth century onwards. Gentlewomen were educated in arithmetic and household accounting. Such skills were seen as essential to household management, a task every woman was meant to be able to fulfil should her husband wish her to do so. Women's ability and interest in this skill is demonstrated by the frequency with which wealthy widows kept their own accounts. Keeping accounts does not necessarily denote the exercise of power within the household, but it did bring knowledge, and knowledge increased the ability of the accountant to influence decisions. Alice Le Strange's accounts were designed in such a way as to allow Hamon Le Strange to know how much was available to spend on the building and estate improvement projects which soaked up their excess income. Alice's calculations and comments about the level of debt owed by herself and Hamon suggest that she felt a personal responsibility for the household's financial well-being.[47]

More clues to who actually controlled the purse strings in a household are provided by who did the shopping. Shopping, in the sense of the pleasurable activity of visiting shops to buy non-essentials, was regarded as female in its first appearance: the three earliest quotations relating to the verb in the *Oxford English Dictionary* from 1764 to 1845 all refer to women shopping.[48] Berry, writing about 'polite shopping' in the eighteenth century, states that 'For ladies of the metropolis, and in provincial towns, going shopping was a familiar part of the rhythm of their day, an activity undertaken in the morning after breakfast while men went about their business.'[49] While eighteenth-century literary evidence plays down men's shopping, diaries and household accounts reveal men as active shoppers in the eighteenth century.[50] In the early seventeenth century it is evident that much, probably most, pleasurable shopping was done by elite men as such shopping required a trip to London, something men undertook more often than women.[51]

Walsh's study of the gendered nature of shopping in the eighteenth century has concluded that shopping was associated with women because women undertook

---

[46] J. Pahl, *Money and Marriage* (New York, 1989), 57.
[47] See Chapter 2: Alice Le Strange's accounts.
[48] *OED Online*.
[49] H. Berry, 'Polite consumption: shopping in eighteenth century England', *Transactions of the Royal Historical Society* 12 (2002), 380–1.
[50] Finn, 'Men's things'; A. Vickery, 'His and hers: gender, consumption and household accounting in eighteenth century England', *Past and Present* supplement 1 (2006), 12–38.
[51] See Chapter 3: Urban shopping.

the frequent purchases of household foodstuffs. Women were more visible when they went shopping for pleasure because they tended to go out in groups while men usually shopped alone.[52] Women's acquisitiveness and shopping activities drew not only more comment overall than men's activities, but more negative comment. This was true in the early seventeenth century, as in the eighteenth.[53] Criticisms of wealthy women's shopping mirrored attitudes to poorer women's marketing activities. As Roberts has noted, 'marketing women were visible, talkative, and competent', contravening accepted ideals of feminine behaviour. Proverbial wisdom associated market women with malicious gossip and loss of reputation, and contrasted them with good housewives who stayed at home.[54] Wealthy women out shopping were potentially over-stepping another ideal of female behaviour—thriftiness—so shopping could be seen as wasting money, time or both. However, the attention that women's shopping draws in early modern literature does not prove that women went shopping for pleasure more often than men, nor that they spent more money than men. In fact, the gendering of shopping appears to have been remarkably stable over time. Pahl's study of modern Britain found that women were most likely to be responsible for spending money on food and clothes for themselves and their children, while men were most likely to control spending on their clothes, house repairs and privately owned forms of transport. Decisions to spend money on expensive consumer goods were made either by men alone or by couples jointly, but rarely by women alone.[55] This pattern was true for the Le Stranges in the early seventeenth century and is illustrated by Vickery for the eighteenth century.[56]

Everyday purchases were dominated by food, and food purchases were dominated by women. From at least the early sixteenth century women were charged 'to go or ride to market' and 'buy all sorts of things necessary for the household'.[57] Walsh describes the skills of food shopping—'sniffing, pinching, and tasting to choose, not from a standardized range, but from the best of a bad bunch'—as essentially female ones.[58] Finn found that even Parson Woodforde, a late eighteenth-century bachelor who was not averse to buying a nice piece of fish, left the humdrum supplying of everyday household needs to his housekeeper-niece and the female servants.[59] So men might help with food purchases or take an interest, but the ultimate responsibility for ensuring that the household was well supplied with basic provisions was almost always a female one. In very wealthy households, this responsibility was sometimes delegated to a man, in the person of

[52] Walsh, 'Art of decision making', 162–8; Vickery, 'Women and the world of goods', 281.
[53] Peck, *Consuming Splendor*, 67–8; Walsh, 'Art of decision making', 164–6.
[54] M. Roberts, '"Words they are women, and deeds they are men": images of work and gender in early modern England', in L. Charles and L. Duffin (eds.), *Women and Work in Pre-Industrial England* (London, 1985), 153–4.
[55] Pahl, *Money and Marriage*, 144.
[56] Vickery, 'His and hers'.
[57] A. Fitzherbert, *The Boke of Husbandry* (1523); from an excerpt in P.J.P. Goldberg (ed.) *Women in England c.1275–1525: Documentary Sources* (Manchester, 1995), 168.
[58] Walsh, 'Art of decision making', 163.
[59] Finn, 'Men's things', 138.

the household steward.[60] In the Le Strange household, Alice Le Strange took charge of provisioning the household with food. For her this task did not require shopping, but staying at home, overseeing the production and delivery of foodstuffs, and occasionally sending male servants out to buy extra items that were needed.

The careful planning and sheer hard work involved in supplying a household with its everyday needs offers an alternative view to approaches which emphasize the pleasures of consumption.[61] Most purchasing and provisioning was mundane. Even in modern Britain, Miller's study of shopping shows that for most people, most of the time, shopping is a chore not a pleasure. Its primary aims are not individualistic, but to care for others within one's household; and rather than the thrill of reckless expenditure, it is thrift—getting bargains and saving money—that is the primary source of satisfaction.[62] If that is the case now, it seems unlikely that it was less so in the past, when the work of supplying a household was more demanding, and the ethic of thrift in household management stronger.[63] The work of consumption in purchasing, cooking and cleaning is too often overlooked in favour of the pleasures of eating well, fine dress and living in comfort and elegance. These pleasures were not only purchased, they were also created by work within the home.[64]

The *Oxford English Dictionary* still defines a housewife as 'a woman who manages her household with skill and thrift, a domestic economist', but generally the work of housewives has been maligned by historians and others as unchanging in nature and peripheral to the economy.[65] Modern housewifery revolves around the management of the home and family through the work of shopping, cooking, cleaning and childcare.[66] These activities are central to everyday consumption,[67] but have been neglected in consumption studies in favour of more glamorous pleasure-seeking activities. A literature on early modern housewifery exists quite separately from the new history of consumption. These books typically take their structure from early modern advice literature, which demonstrates clearly that, while provisioning the household, cooking, cleaning and childcare have always been important elements of a housewife's work, there have been significant variations over time.[68]

---

[60] See Chapter 2: Household and estate management.
[61] Kowaleski-Wallace, *Consuming Subjects*; Berry, 'Polite consumption', 375–94; Berg, *Luxury and Pleasure*; Peck, *Consuming Splendor*.
[62] Miller, 'Consumption and its consequences', 44–6.
[63] Muldrew, *Economy of Obligation*, 158–65, and introduction to Chapter 2.
[64] J. de Vries, *The Industrious Revolution: Consumer Behaviour and the Household Economy, 1650 to the Present* (Cambridge, 2008), ch. 5.
[65] *OED Online*.
[66] A. Oakley, *Women's Work: The Housewife, Past and Present* (New York, 1976); S. Strasser, *Never Done: A History of American Housework* (New York, 1982); R.S. Cowan, *More Work for Mother: The Ironies of Household Technology from the Open Hearth to the Microwave* (New York, 1983); M.L. DeVault, *Feeding the Family: The Social Organization of Caring as Gendered Work* (Chicago, 1991); D. Miller, *A Theory of Shopping* (Cambridge, 1998).
[67] Oakley, *Women's Work*, 3.
[68] C. Hole, *The English Housewife in the Seventeenth Century* (London, 1953); G.E. Fussell and K.R. Fussell, *The English Countrywoman: A Farmhouse Social History* (London, 1955); C. Davidson, *A Woman's Work is Never Done: A History of Housework in the British Isles 1650–1950* (London, 1982);

The housewife of the seventeenth and eighteenth centuries was assumed to live in a rural household, and was expected to be proficient in providing medical care, distilling, gardening, poultry farming, making butter and cheese, baking bread, brewing ale or beer, spinning and sewing.[69] Early modern housewifery was not detached from the market: women's skills could be used to make money, from wet-nursing and laundry to the sale of products such as fruit, chickens, cheese, beer and yarn. Of course not all women carried out all these activities. Labouring women had less access to resources and were more likely to work for wages; farmers' wives were more likely to be involved in agricultural activities; and urban women were more likely to be involved in services and retail.[70] Gentlewomen had the greatest resources and degree of choice. Country gentlewomen of the sixteenth and seventeenth centuries did not view the skills of housewifery with disdain: instead they participated actively in them. Some gentlewomen offered sophisticated medical care;[71] others prided themselves on the quality of their cheese;[72] some spun their own linen.[73] Alice Le Strange managed the full range of housewifery activities within her household: like many early modern housewives from the gentry she did not carry out much of the physical labour herself, but oversaw the work of her servants, male and female. Yet, more than any goods she owned, it was Alice's role as a housewife, managing production, consumption and care within the household, that seems to have defined her identity.[74]

As Douglas and Isherwood point out, consumer goods not only serve functional uses but also 'are good for thinking'.[75] Consumption activities and goods are used to create and express personal, group and gender identities. Clothing is one of the most obviously gendered types of goods, not only because we look to clothing to signal whether the wearer is male or female but also because men and women seem to have had different attitudes towards clothing. For the eighteenth century, de Vries notes that women tended to spend their disposable income on clothes while men spent theirs on alcohol, while Berg finds that women made bequests of clothing in their wills more frequently than men.[76] This pattern of bequests also

A. Sim, *The Tudor Housewife* (Stroud, 1996); U. Robertson, *The Illustrated History of the Housewife 1650–1950* (Stroud, 1997).

[69] C. Estienne, *Maison Rustique, or The Countrey Farme* (1616); G. Markham, *The English Housewife*, ed. M. Best (Montreal, 1986); see Chapter 2: Gentlewomen as housewives.

[70] J. Whittle, 'Housewives and servants in rural England, 1440–1650: evidence of women's work from probate documents', *Transactions of the Royal Historical Society* 6th ser. 15 (2005), 51–74. On urban housewives and servants, see T. Meldrum, *Domestic Service and Gender 1660–1750: Life and Work in the London Household* (Harlow, 2000), 137–58.

[71] L. Pollock, *With Faith and Physic: The Life of a Tudor Gentlewoman, Lady Grace Mildmay 1552–1620* (London, 1992); see Chapter 4: Medical care.

[72] Lady Neville in an anecdote in N. Le Strange, *Merry Passages and Jeasts*, ed. H.F. Lippincott (Salzburg, 1974), 45.

[73] Recorded in the wills of Lady Phillippa Smith d.1578 and Dame Anne Wentworth d.1575: F.G. Emmison (ed.), *Elizabethan Life: Wills of Essex Gentry and Merchants* (Chelmsford, 1978), 45, 49.

[74] Likewise, Vickery found that the eighteenth-century gentlewoman Elizabeth Shackleton was strongly defined by her good housekeeping: 'Women and the world of goods', 283.

[75] Douglas and Isherwood, *World of Goods*, 41.

[76] de Vries, *The Industrious Revolution*, 141–3; M. Berg, 'Women's consumption and the industrial classes of eighteenth-century England', *Journal of Social History* 30:2 (1996), 415–34.

holds for the early seventeenth century, despite the markedly more flamboyant styles of male dress in that period and roughly equal expenditure by men and women on clothing. Women retained a close association with textiles more generally, through spinning, sewing and laundry, despite the fact that weaving and professional tailoring were monopolized by men. The gendering of other household goods is harder to discern, in part because property laws gave married men rights of ownership to all of a couple's goods.[77]

The importance of consumption to men's identity and its centrality to their assertion of social status is often overlooked. While Alice Le Strange's consumption identity revolved mainly around the business of keeping accounts, provisioning her household, and the range of skills and activities encompassed by housewifery, her husband's activities were rather different. His notebook records the cost and design of coaches, the details of purchasing muskets for personal use and the local militia, the liveries and contracts of his senior male servants, and the hawks he had captured on Hunstanton cliffs.[78] His purchases at London and Norwich typically included beaver hats, books, scientific instruments, weaponry and hawking equipment. While Alice's activities were common to women across a broad swathe of society, if carried out on different scales according to the size and wealth of households, Hamon Le Strange's were exclusive to the gentry. His consumption activities were an expression of the family's social status.[79] This concern for status led men to interfere with women's housekeeping. In so far as gentry status was marked by the offering of hospitality—food, lodgings, and entertainment—gentlemen concerned themselves with ensuring that the quality and quantity of food and furnishings in their households were sufficient.[80] In the late medieval period, elite households with their large numbers of male retainers were so essential to men's political and social status that women were largely excluded from their management altogether.[81] Remnants of this older model of elite housekeeping still existed in the early seventeenth century. Thus, the gendering of consumption activities within the early seventeenth-century household was not straightforward. While early seventeenth-century women, like those of later periods, were assumed to be in charge of housekeeping, housework, provisioning and spending, men also played a significant role. The male household head not only had overall control of all financial affairs but also purchased his own clothes and luxury items: early seventeenth-century men were not averse to pleasure shopping, and as frequent visitors to London and county towns had more opportunities to do this than

---

[77] L. Weatherill, 'A possession of one's own: women and consumer behaviour in England, 1660–1740', *Journal of British Studies* 25 (1986), 131–56.
[78] LEST/Q38.
[79] Discussed in more detail in Chapter 7.
[80] F. Heal, *Hospitality in Early Modern England* (Oxford, 1990), 13; A. Fletcher, *Gender, Sex and Subordination in England 1500–1800* (New Haven, 1995), 138–43.
[81] K. Mertes, *The English Noble Household 1250–1600: Good Governance and Politic Rule* (Oxford, 1998); Woolgar, *The Great Household*.

women. Male servants sometimes kept household accounts, and they often shopped and cooked.

CONSUMPTION AND THE GENTRY

This book is not a history of the English gentry. It is, however, based on the records of an early seventeenth-century gentry household. The records of the gentry reveal much more than the history of that class alone. Gentry households can be usefully understood as business enterprises dotted across the English countryside.[82] They were large-scale employers of servants, agricultural and building labour, craftsmen and specialists. They were producers of grain, wool, meat and timber. Their wealth was spent on a wide array of consumer goods: many drawn from the local economy such as bread, chicken and beef; some from English manufacturers, such as woollen cloth, earthenware and books; some from abroad such as wine, stoneware, raisins and fine linen. Because of their wealth, the gentry reveal what was possible in terms of consumption in rural England in this period.

There was a strong ethos in early modern England that wealth should be spent appropriately, according to one's resources. It was necessary to spend *enough* to display and assert one's status. Gentry who under-spent lost status and faced ridicule and criticism from tenants and fellow gentry.[83] In the early seventeenth century Lady Anne Townshend, living on a small widow's dower after her husband John left their estate heavily indebted, became the butt of jokes for her meagre hospitality: 'Sir John Heydon having dined at the old Lady Townshend, every one askt him what cheare he had, when came home? he told them, very good, for at the first course every man had a T served in upon his trencher; intimating only the marke of the Trencher.'[84] However, to overspend was disastrous. Indebtedness led eventually to the sale of real property, and with property went status. The Townshends were pulled back from the brink by Lady Jane Berkeley, who bought up manors from her spendthrift Townshend sons, John and Robert, and passed them on directly to her grandson Sir Roger Townshend.[85] Sir John Heydon may have poked fun at the Townshends, but he and his brother drove their family so heavily into debt that it declined into obscurity.[86]

---

[82] S. Pollard, *The Genesis of Modern Management: A Study of the Industrial Revolution in Great Britain* (Cambridge, Massachusetts, 1965), 25–30; C. Oestmann, *Lordship and Community: The Lestrange Family and the Village of Hunstanton, Norfolk in the First Half of the Sixteenth Century* (Woodbridge, 1994), 148–51; M. Dawson, *Plenti and Grase: Food and Drink in a Sixteenth Century Household* (Totnes, 2009), 19.

[83] L. Stone, *The Crisis of the Aristocracy, 1558–1640* (Oxford, 1965), 42–4.

[84] Le Strange, *Merry Jeasts*, 27, told by 'Unckle Catline' (Richard Catlyne esq. of Bracondale, Norfolk). Anne Townshend is discussed in Chapter 2: Two other Norfolk families.

[85] L. Campbell, 'Sir Roger Townshend and his Family: A Study of Gentry Life in Early Seventeenth Century Norfolk', Ph.D. thesis (East Anglia, 1990).

[86] H.R. Trevor-Roper, 'The gentry 1540–1640', *Economic History Review* supplement 1 (1953), 19.

Sir Hamon and Lady Alice Le Strange were members of the upper gentry, a status indicated by Hamon's knighthood, the baronetcy purchased for his son Nicholas in 1629, and a rental income of £1720 in the 1620s. As such they were part of England's ruling class, a select group which made up no more than 2 per cent of the population.[87] Internally, this elite was divided by rank into the peerage or aristocracy, the upper gentry of knights and baronets, the middle gentry of esquires, and the lower or parish gentry of mere gentlemen. In 1600 there were sixty-one peers and, as estimated by Thomas Wilson, around 500 knights and 16,000 members of the middle and lower gentry. All were wealthy. Stone estimates an average rental income of £2410 for peers in 1602, while Thomas Wilson thought that 'for the most part' knights had a yearly income or 'living' of between £1000 and £2000, esquires of between £500 and £1000, and gentlemen 'of good reputation' £300 or more in 1600.[88]

As William Harrison put it in the late sixteenth century, any man who 'can live without manuell labour, and thereto is able and will beare the port, charge and countenance of a gentleman' was entitled to be given that title.[89] It was not just the size of income that brought status, but the fact it was derived largely from rents. A rental income allowed the gentry to 'live without manual labour', providing not only wealth but also the time required to take on a governing role. Rents derived from landownership, and landownership brought political power on a local level. Their status, wealth and free time allowed the gentry to monopolize the royal administration of the county, holding unpaid office as justices of the peace, sheriffs, and members of Parliament.[90] Lineage, title, land, wealth and office were defining features of the gentry in the early seventeenth century, but as Harrison noted 'port, charge and countenance' were also vital elements. Each of these words bore multiple meanings then as they do now: 'port' meaning 'behaviour or conduct' as well as 'styles of living, especially a grand and expensive style'; 'charge' meaning 'pecuniary burden, expense, cost' as well as 'a task or duty laid upon one, commission, trust, responsibility'; and 'countenance' meaning 'bearing, demeanour, comportment, behaviour, conduct' as well as 'appearance, aspect and look'.[91] In other words, the gentry were in part defined by how they behaved and looked, by their lifestyle and by how they spent their wealth.

The history of the early seventeenth-century English gentry has generally been written backwards from the Civil War, seeking to identify its causes. The debate over the 'rise of the gentry' and 'crisis of the aristocracy' points to a number of factors causing instability in the relationships among the gentry, aristocracy and

---

[87] Stone, *Crisis of the Aristocracy*, 51; K. Wrightson, *English Society 1580–1680* (London, 1982), 24.
[88] Sir T. Wilson, *The State of England: 1600*, F.J. Fisher (ed.) *Camden Society*, Third Series, vol. 52 (1936), 23–4; Stone, *Crisis of the Aristocracy*, 760, 767.
[89] Harrison, *Description of England*, 114.
[90] Stone, *Crisis of the Aristocracy*, 41; Wrightson, *English Society*, 19–30; M.L. Bush, *The English Aristocracy: A Comparative Synthesis* (Manchester, 1984); F. Heal and C. Holmes, *The Gentry of England and Wales 1500–1700* (Basingstoke, 1994).
[91] All definitions from *OED Online*.

crown in the 100 years leading up to the mid-seventeenth-century crisis.[92] The dissolution of the monasteries allowed a great redistribution of manorial land; monetary inflation led to a revision of traditional terms of tenure and new methods of estate management; and religious differences undermined the power of the established church and led to faction and dissent. Patterns of consumption had a role to play too. Tawney cited 'a new world of luxury and fashion' combined with an ethos of 'conspicuous waste' as undermining the wealth of the aristocracy, something Stone charted in greater detail.[93] Trevor-Roper noted that extravagant spending, such as the construction of grand new houses, was as important in allowing gentry families to 'rise' as in causing the fall of other members of the elite.[94] More recently McCracken has argued that changing consumption patterns among the Elizabethan aristocracy led to them creating a material culture that was alien and separate from the rest of society, increasing the division between court and county society amongst the elite.[95]

The Elizabethan period did indeed see marked changes in elite consumption patterns. Just as debates about luxury formed the focus of contemporary comment about changes in consumption in the late seventeenth and early eighteenth centuries, in the late sixteenth and early seventeenth centuries comment centred on the growing attraction of London as a centre for fashionable consumption.[96] Stone notes that a 'London season', during which most of the aristocracy and much of the gentry were resident in the capital for the winter months or law terms, 'developed with astonishing speed between about 1590 and 1620'.[97] Between 1596 and 1640 seventeen royal proclamations urged 'noblemen, knights, and gentlemen of qualitie' to leave London and return to their proper duties of keeping order and offering hospitality in the country. Unlike many proclamations these were sometimes enforced: in 1633 nearly 250 members of the gentry and aristocracy were subpoenaed for residence in London without due cause.[98] Nonetheless, the fashion for seasonal residence in London continued to grow. The increasing pull of London on the gentry was in part due to well-documented political and legal factors: the presence and increasingly static nature of the royal court at Westminster; increased

---

[92] R.H. Tawney, 'The rise of the gentry, 1558–1640', *Economic History Review* 11:1 (1941), 1–38; Trevor-Roper, 'The gentry'; Stone, *Crisis of the Aristocracy*.
[93] Tawney, 'Rise of the gentry', 8; Stone, *Crisis of the Aristocracy*, 184–9, 547–86.
[94] Trevor-Roper, 'The gentry', 7.
[95] McCracken, *Culture and Consumption*, 14–15; Stone, *Crisis of the Aristocracy*, 749.
[96] F.J. Fisher, 'The development of London as a centre of conspicuous consumption in the sixteenth and seventeenth centuries', in E.M. Carus Wilson (ed.), *Essays in Economic History*, vol. 2 (London, 1962), 197–207; Stone, *Crisis of the Aristocracy*, 385–98; R.M. Smuts, *Court Culture and the Origins of a Royalist Tradition in Early Stuart England* (Philadelphia, 1987), 53–67; F. Heal, 'The crown, the gentry and London: the enforcement of proclamation, 1596–1640', in C. Cross, D. Loades, and J.J. Scarisbrick (eds.), *Law and Government Under the Tudors* (Cambridge, 1988), 211–26; Peck, *Consuming Splendor*; J.F. Merritt, *The Social World of Early Modern Westminster: Abbey, Court and Community 1525–1640* (Manchester, 2005), 140–79.
[97] Stone, *Crisis of the Aristocracy*, 387.
[98] Heal, 'The crown, the gentry and London', 211–12, 222; quotation from proclamation of December 1615 in J.F. Larkin and P.L. Hughes (eds.) *Stuart Royal Proclamations*, vol. I (Oxford, 1973), 356.

litigation in the Westminster law courts; and the growing popularity of the Inns of Court as part of a gentleman's education. Consumption, leisure and business drew the gentry to the capital in the early seventeenth century. However, the many calls for them to return to the countryside noted the vital function they played in the government and economy of provincial England. James I listed the consequences of the gentry's absence from the countryside:

> first, if insurrections should fall out... what order can bee taken with it, when the countrey is unfurnished of Gentlemen to take order with it? Next, the poore want reliefe for fault of the Gentlemens hospitality at home: Third, my service is neglected, and the good government of the country for lacke of the principall Gentlemens presence, that should performe it: And lastly, the Gentlemen lose their owne thrift, for lacke of their owne presence, in seeing to their owne businesse at home.[99]

The idea of hospitality is central to these debates. The provision of hospitality to the poor was considered essential to harmonious social relations in the countryside. Hospitality was an amorphous concept: Heal's important book demonstrates how it could mean entertaining family and friends, entertaining tenants, elite servants and business associates and their families, entertaining strangers, and providing charity to the poor. The key provision was food, and to a lesser extent lodgings. Hospitality for the poor thus consisted of alms in the form of food or perhaps personal gifts of money, but not the regular payment of poor relief. Hospitality meant inviting others to enter your house, sit at your table and consume food prepared in your kitchen.[100] Christmas was a key moment in the annual cycle of hospitality, when gifts of food were received and tenants and kin entertained with feasting.

Tensions between gentry households and the local community had deeper causes than a decline in hospitality, although many are inter-related. A decline in the size of upper gentry and aristocratic households caused by changing political structures weakened their links with the lesser gentry and yeomanry, who had previously provided the majority of male servants and retainers. Inflationary pressures that encouraged the gentry and aristocracy to reform tenures and 'improve' their estates caused understandable ill-will amongst a tenantry faced with higher rents and less security of land tenure. An increasing proportion of money spent on novel, foreign and ready-made goods, mostly in London and county towns, reduced the amount of wealth collected in rents that was spent on locally produced materials and goods. Households that spent part of the year in London were unlikely to run home farms, and their servants might well be recruited in the capital, reducing the amount of wage employment on country estates. All these trends occurred simultaneously, if unevenly, in the late sixteenth and early seventeenth centuries. They become apparent when studying the consumption economy of a gentry household in detail.

---

[99] James I, *The Workes of the Most High and Mightie Prince* (London, 1616), 568.
[100] Heal, *Hospitality*, 3, for a brief definition of hospitality.

THE LE STRANGE FAMILY

The Le Strange family lived at Hunstanton, a coastal parish in the far north-west corner of Norfolk. The heart of the Le Strange estate consisted of a compact group of neighbouring manors located in Hunstanton, Heacham, Ringstead and Sedgeford, and stretching into neighbouring Holme-next-the-Sea. The coastal parishes of Hunstanton, Heacham, and Holme had a mixed economy of the type described by Smith for Stiffkey, which also lies on the Norfolk coast twenty miles to the east.[101] The Wash at Hunstanton is very shallow, and at low tide the sea retreats up to a mile from the shore revealing a long stretch of sandy beach ideal for collecting shellfish and inshore fishing. Sea fisheries at Hunstanton date back to Domesday.[102] The coastal marshland provided ample summer grazing. Hunstanton's inhabitants were able to pursue a range of activities, which included fishing, bird catching and reed gathering as well as more common by-employments, such as dairying, brewing, crafts and textile production.[103] The result was high numbers of smallholders, many of whom owned their own livestock. It created a pool of labour which the Le Stranges could call upon for agricultural work. While some of the coastal soils, such as those in the West Field of Hunstanton where the villagers held most of their land, were very fertile, the inland soils which dominated the parishes of Ringstead and Sedgeford were sandy.[104] Large areas of sandy breck were set aside for the grazing of sheep under the foldcourse system, and only periodically brought into arable cultivation. The Le Stranges owned seven foldcourses: one in Heacham and three each in Ringstead and Sedgeford. From 1625 three of these were kept in hand and four leased out to larger tenants.[105] Foldcourses gave manorial lords or their lessees the right to keep large flocks of sheep which grazed over the tenants' lands when they were not sown with crops; this fertilized the soil but discouraged any enclosure of land. Tenants paid a fee to have their sheep included in the flocks, and large tenants in Ringstead and Sedgeford owned substantial numbers of sheep.[106] Sandy soil favoured the cultivation of rye, although wheat and barley were also grown.

The Le Strange family has been associated with Hunstanton since the early twelfth century, a generation after Domesday, making them one of the oldest and most stable gentry families in Norfolk. The family moved their main residence to Knockin in Shropshire in 1189, but a branch returned to Hunstanton in 1309 when Baron Strange of Knockin enfeoffed his younger brother, Hamon, with the

---

[101] A.H. Smith, 'Labourers in late sixteenth-century England: a case study from north Norfolk [Part II]', *Continuity and Change* 4:3 (1989), 368.
[102] H.C. Darby, *The Domesday Geography of Eastern England* (Cambridge, 1971).
[103] See Chapter 3: The acquisition of food, and Chapter 8: The Le Stranges and the local community; also Oestmann, *Lordship and Community*, 86–131.
[104] T. Williamson, *The Origins of Norfolk* (Manchester, 1993), 9, for map.
[105] LEST/P10; LEST/Q38; LEST/Q37; LEST/DH16.
[106] K.J. Allison, 'The sheep-corn husbandry of Norfolk in the sixteenth and seventeenth centuries', *Agricultural History Review* 5 (1957).

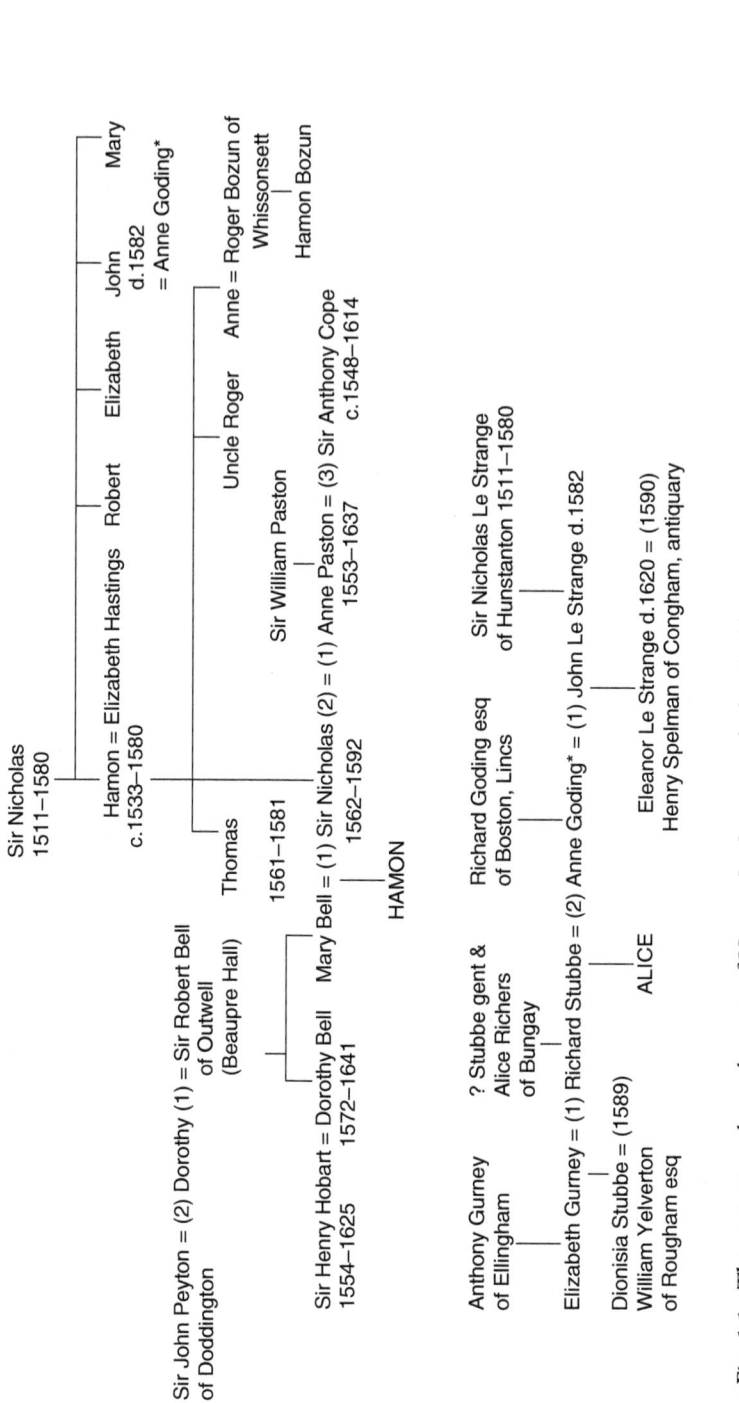

Fig. 1.1. The parents and grandparents of Hamon Le Strange and Alice Stubbe.

manor. It was these Le Stranges who built the original moated house in the fourteenth century that remained as resident lords of Hunstanton until the eighteenth century.[107] The earliest Le Strange of Hunstanton household accounts survive for 1347–8, when a Sir Hamon, a veteran of the Battle of Crecy, returned to live at Hunstanton with his brother-in-law and fellow campaigner, Lord Camoys. These accounts, kept weekly, show a high consumption of butchered meat and fish and the regular brewing of ale, just as in the early seventeenth century. However, the families consumed little sugar, drank wine rarely and for fuel relied on peat, rather than coal from Newcastle.[108] More household accounts survive for the early sixteenth century.[109] Sir Thomas Le Strange (1490–1545) and his wife Anne Vaux (b.1494) set a model that may have been consciously followed by Sir Hamon and Lady Alice almost a century later. Sir Thomas was a Justice of the Peace and sheriff of Norfolk and Suffolk. Despite good court connections, he confined his activities largely to Norfolk.[110] Lady Anne rarely left Hunstanton, where she kept the accounts, managed household and estate affairs and received visitors.[111]

Sir Thomas was succeeded by his son Sir Nicholas (1511–1580), who also took an active role in the county and served the Howards, Dukes of Norfolk (Fig. 1.1). Nicholas survived the fall of the Howards in 1547; accusations of complicity in Kett's Rebellion of 1549, a year when he served as sheriff of Norfolk and Suffolk; and the accession of Queen Mary. He was elected Member of Parliament for Norfolk in 1547 and King's Lynn in 1555. During the 1560s, however, he became involved in the plot for the fourth Duke of Norfolk to marry Mary Queen of Scots, and was arrested and held prisoner from 1569 to 1571. He protested his innocence but never regained his former prominence.[112] The late sixteenth-century Le Stranges experienced demographic misfortune. Sir Nicholas was the great-grandfather of the Sir Hamon Le Strange with whom this book is concerned. He died in 1580, the same year as his son and heir Hamon (c.1533–1580), whose son and heir Thomas (1561–1581) died childless a year later. The estate was inherited by his brother Sir Nicholas (1563–1592).[113]

Sir Hamon Le Strange (1583–1654) was the sole surviving son of Sir Nicholas and Mary, the daughter of Sir Robert Bell of Beaupre Hall, Outwell, Norfolk. Both his parents died young, leaving Hamon an orphan at the age of eight. As a minor, he and his estate passed into the care of his kinsmen Sir John Peyton and Sir Henry Spelman, the antiquarian and jurist, who lived close by at Holme Parsonage.[114]

---

[107] W. Rye, *Norfolk Families* (Norwich, 1913), 477–83; Oestmann, *Lordship and Community*, 12.
[108] H. Le Strange (ed.), 'Roll of household accounts of Sir Hamon Le Strange of Hunstanton 1347–1348', *Archaeologia* 69 (1917), 111–20; C. Hussey, 'Hunstanton Hall', *Country Life* (1926).
[109] Oestmann, *Lordship and Community*; Heal, *Hospitality*, 59–63; B.J. Harris, *English Aristocratic Women 1450–1550: Marriage and Family, Property and Careers* (Oxford, 2002), 67–8.
[110] Oestmann, *Lordship and Community*, 15–17.
[111] Harris, *English Aristocratic Women*, 68.
[112] Oestmann, *Lordship and Community*, 21–4.
[113] Oestmann, *Lordship and Community*, 13, 26.
[114] Sir John Peyton, of Doddington, Cambs, was married to Dorothy, widow of Sir Robert Bell, Beaupre Hall, Outwell, Norfolk, who was Hamon's grandmother. Sir Henry Spelman was married to

In 1602 they arranged the marriage between Sir Hamon and Alice Stubbe, the daughter of Peyton's lawyer, Richard Stubbe, who paid Peyton £1000 for the release of wardship.[115] The negotiations were performed by another uncle, Henry Hobart of Intwood, who remained a trustee until they married in 1604 when Hamon came of age.[116] As a young man, Hamon attended Queen's College, Cambridge, and Elizabeth's court. In 1603, with his friend Sir Robert Carey, he famously rode to Scotland to inform James VI of the death of the Queen, receiving a knighthood in reward. However, he did not pursue a career in royal service, preferring the life of a Norfolk gentleman, holding office at county level, cultivating his mind and running his estate.

Alice Stubbe came from a less elevated social background. Her father, Richard Stubbe, had married as his second wife Anne Goding, the widow of John Le Strange, a younger son of Sir Nicholas (1511–1580), from whom he acquired the manor of Sedgeford just a few miles south of Hunstanton.[117] From a modest gentry family, Stubbe made his way acting as a lawyer and agent to county families, acquiring a scattered estate in Norfolk.[118] With his first wife, Elizabeth Gurney, he had one daughter, Dionisia, who married William Yelverton of Rougham (1558–1631). Alice was some years younger than Dionisia, and the likelihood is that from an early age Alice spent time with her mother's relations, who included the Le Stranges and Spelmans, where she would have met her cousin Hamon. The household accounts show a close relationship between Richard Stubbe and his daughter, with the old man taking a keen interest in Alice and her growing family, lending them money, collecting rents, giving them sheep and offering advice. Alice grew up in Richard Stubbe's house at Sedgeford, and in the 1610s sent her two oldest sons to lodge there with their tutor. The fact that Alice came from the same locality where she later became mistress of a large household gave her an advantage in comparison with many married gentlewomen. She was familiar with the farming economy, including the complex management of foldcourse sheep farming, and knew many of the local families from which the household's employees were drawn. She continued to live among minor branches of her own family such as the Guybons and Spratts, who held leases and worked for the Le Stranges.

At the outset, however, Hamon and Alice struggled financially. As Alice later noted in her account book, 'my husband was left in debt by his fathers

---

Elinor, the daughter of John Le Strange, a younger son of Sir Nicholas (1511–1580). John Le Strange's widow, Anne, was the mother of Alice Le Strange née Stubbe. Marriage settlement of Sir Hamon Le Strange and Alice Stubbe: LEST/AA66-73; *ODNB*; R.W. Ketton-Cremer, *Norfolk in the Civil War*, 2nd edn. (Ipswich, 1985); R.W. Ketton-Cremer, 'Hamon L'Strange and his sons', *Norfolk Gallery* (London, 1958).

[115] Release of Wardship LEST/A73; Settlement 1606 LEST/AA1.

[116] Sir Henry Hobart (1558–1625) married Dorothy Bell, sister of Hamon's mother. See E.M. Griffiths, 'Sir Henry Hobart, a new hero of Norfolk agriculture', *Agricultural History Review* 46, Part 1 (1998), 19–28.

[117] Rye, *Norfolk Families*, and the Le Strange Pedigree in F. Blomefield, *An Essay Towards a Topographical History of the County of Norfolk* (1739–75), Vol. V, 1265. John died in 1582, third son of Sir Nicholas Le Strange (1511–1580).

[118] Rye, *Norfolk Families*, 859.

Table 1.1. The estate of Sir Hamon Le Strange of Hunstanton, 1616

Location	Value
Hunstanton	£331
Heacham Lewis	£226
Hunstanton parsonage	£51
The park and other ground in my own use	£60
Ringstead Great	£111
Ringstead Parva	£114
Calyes (Heacham)	£124
Gressenhall (and Brisley)	£230
Total	£1247

Source: NRO, LEST/Q38.

Executors... £1500, he was left neyther household stuffe nor stock and his chief House halfe built and all his farme houses in such decay. So he hath built most of them out of the ground.'[119] Moreover, Sir Hamon had to pay several annuities, amounting to £296 2s 8d a year, which included £180 to Lady Anthony Cope, his father's second wife, and £100 for life to Richard Stubbe. This reduced his income to £725 a year, not a huge sum for a young man of his status and ambition.[120] Sir Thomas Le Strange (1490–1545) had been in the top rung of the Norfolk gentry. He received between £200 and £300 a year in rents, and made between £75 and £205 a year from direct farming in the period 1536–44. As well as Hunstanton he had held manors in Ringstead, Heacham, Sedgeford, Docking, Fring, Snettisham, Anmer and Godwick in Norfolk; Thorpe and Felsham in Suffolk; and Oakley in Bedfordshire.[121] Only the core of this estate remained when Sir Hamon Le Strange received his inheritance in 1604. From an early date Sir Hamon was concerned to run his estate efficiently. From 1615 he employed surveyors to map the estate, starting with Thomas Waterman's surveys of Hunstanton, Gressenhall and possibly Heacham (1625), and continuing with John Fisher's map of Sedgeford (1630), and an undated one for Ringstead.[122] These maps, combined with a series of field books, rentals and firmals, provide an almost complete picture of the landholding structure and the topography of the estate in the first half of the seventeenth century. Sir Hamon also consolidated the estate: he sold the more distant Fring to purchase neighbouring Heacham in 1609. His landed property and the rental income, as recorded in his notebook in 1616, are shown in Table 1.1.[123] With

---

[119] LEST/P10.
[120] His cousin Sir John Hobart of Blickling 2nd Bt enjoyed an income of £2500 a year in 1625.
[121] Oestmann, *Lordship and Community*, 19, 133.
[122] Hunstanton, LEST/A01; Sedgeford, LEST/OC1; Heacham, LEST/OC2; Ringstead, LEST/OB5, OB6; Gressenhall, NRO, MC 77/1; Hayes and Storr, no. 72.
[123] LEST/Q38.

Richard Stubbe's death in 1619 Hamon and Alice gained Sedgeford as Alice's dowry, adding a further £473 to their income. The receipt accounts show that their income rose at this point to almost £2000 a year, placing the Le Stranges once more amongst Norfolk's 'top rung' as members of the upper gentry of the county.

METHODS AND CHAPTER PLAN

At the core of this book lie the household accounts written by Lady Alice Le Strange of Hunstanton between 1610 and 1654. Her accounting methods and the scope of the accounts are described in Chapter 2. The accounts comprise disbursement accounts, receipt accounts and kitchen accounts. Alice's accounts were preceded by four years of disbursement and receipt accounts kept by Sir Hamon Le Strange from 1606 to 1609. As a set, the accounts stretch across almost half a century; they are systematic and detailed. They represent an enormous body of data relating to the consumption habits of a single household. A mixture of methods are used in this study, some zooming in to focus on particular aspects, others stepping back to view the overall picture. The first twenty years of the accounts, from April 1606 to April 1626, were entered into an Access database, along with the receipt accounts from 1606–12 and 1619–21 and the kitchen accounts from the period 1619–21. This allowed these accounts to be systematically searched for references to particular goods, places and people, and to form the central focus of the book. However, the analysis was not limited to this sample. Where appropriate, a wider view was taken using the whole set of disbursement and receipt accounts. A breakdown of overall expenditure and income across the period 1606–53 is analysed in Chapters 3 and 6. The disbursement accounts for the period 1620–36 have the richest record of clothing, furnishings and material culture, as the Le Strange children grew up and married, and the house was extended and furnished. The accounts from 1626 to 1636 are used in Chapters 5 and 6, as well as to reconstruct patterns of servant employment in Chapter 8. The kitchen books, with their weekly record of food received and consumed, are the bulkiest part of the record. Analysis of food production in Chapter 3 and diet in Chapter 4 is based mainly on the kitchen accounts of 1619–21, which were entered into the database, but other aspects used a wider sample. Food gifts and records of wage labour were extracted from all the surviving kitchen books between 1613 and 1626, along with a comparative sample from the early 1650s. Separate building accounts were kept from 1620 onwards, interspersed with the disbursement accounts. These were not entered into the database, but were analysed in Chapter 8 for the period from 1621 to 1624.

The accounts provide a rich record, but the sparseness of personal detail is often frustrating. Occasionally, Alice broke off from the routine of account keeping to analyse particular aspects of the household or expenditure. She kept a running total of loans and debts from 1630 onwards; she noted the family's losses in the Civil War; and drew up a comparison of the inheritance she and her sister received from their father. She made an inventory of the contents of the bed chambers at Hunstanton Hall in 1632, and of all her linens in the same year. She also wrote an inventory of all the goods inherited by the Le Stranges from her father, extracted from his probate inventory.[124] In 1634 she summarized the performance of her dairymaids over the last seventeen years, noting the amount of cheese and butter produced from the number of cows in the herd.[125] The account books are only part of the Le Strange archive, which is extensive for the whole period from the early sixteenth century to the eighteenth century. Unfortunately it lacks any significant collection of personal correspondence for the early seventeenth century, but there are other documents which make up in part for this absence. These include a notebook kept by Sir Hamon Le Strange that dates from 1613 to 1637;[126] and a series of notebooks kept by Sir Nicholas Le Strange, Alice and Hamon's eldest son. Sir Nicholas also compiled a manuscript jest book in which jests are attributed to particular people (including, often, his mother, Alice) and some of those mentioned also appear in the accounts. There is a catalogue of the extensive Le Strange library dating from *c*.1700. As this records the publication date of each book it is possible to identify those volumes almost certainly owned by Sir Hamon and Lady Alice, which in some cases can be confirmed by purchases recorded in the accounts.[127] Wills survive for Richard Stubbe, Sir Hamon and Alice Le Strange, all of which mention objects and provide some insight into personal priorities, discussed in Chapter 5. There is no complete probate inventory for seventeenth-century Hunstanton Hall. One survives for 1675, but it offers only a partial record. While parts of Hunstanton Hall itself still stand, it was damaged by fire in 1853 and again in 1947.[128] For the wider community of Hunstanton and the neighbouring villages, the Le Strange archive provides lists of tenants, leases and maps. Parish registers survive for early seventeenth-century Hunstanton, Heacham, Ringstead St Andrew and St Peter, and Sedgeford, but in a poor condition and often with gaps. A small sample of local wills and probate inventories of those who had contacts with the Le Stranges was taken and is analysed in Chapter 8.

The first two chapters of the book focus on the process of consumption: planning and management in Chapter 2 and the acquisition of goods in Chapter 3. Chapter 2 looks in detail at the nature of the accounts, Alice Le Strange's accounting practices, and how these fitted in with the activities of Sir Hamon and Nicholas Le Strange. It places Alice's activities in the context of early modern housewifery and the accounting and estate management roles of other gentlewomen in the early seventeenth century. Detailed case studies of women in the Townshend and Hobart families allow specific comparisons to be made. Chapter 3 offers a breakdown of domestic expenditure before moving on to consider where goods were acquired, and in particular the significance of urban retailing in London and Norwich. Clothes and furnishings, and food, are taken as examples to investigate the range of methods by which goods were obtained for the Le Strange household.

---

[124] All the above are in the back of her final disbursement account book, LEST/P10.
[125] LEST/P8.
[126] LEST/Q38.
[127] LEST/NE1.
[128] N. Pevsner and B. Wilson, *Norfolk 2: North-West and South* (London, 1999), 439.

Chapters 4 and 5 examine the types of goods consumed, with Chapter 4 looking at everyday consumables such as food, medicine, fuel and lighting, and Chapter 5 the material culture of clothing, bed chambers and living rooms, and kitchen and dining ware. Chapter 4 explores how the meanings of food were expressed by variations in diet across the year and between social groups. Chapter 5 considers the meanings of durable goods, using evidence of turnover, bequests in wills and gendered attitudes to probe beyond the lists provided by accounts and inventories. Chapters 6 and 7 turn to more exclusively elite forms of consumption. Chapter 6 looks at the household's life cycle of consumption. As the accounts run for almost all of Alice and Hamon Le Strange's long married life it is possible to view the different phases their household and expenditure patterns passed through: these were determined both by their family life cycle and by external events, particularly the Civil War. The treatment of the Le Strange children is viewed through the lens of consumption, stretching from the provision of wet nurses to education and marriage, with comparisons made between sons and daughters. The focus of Chapter 7 is those elite consumption activities which were very largely the preserve of Hamon Le Strange: it examines expenditure on office holding and taxation, horses and coaches, leisure activities, books, music and scientific instruments, and building and estate maintenance. Finally, in Chapter 8 the spotlight is turned onto the hundreds of people who made the Le Stranges' consumption patterns possible: the servants, labourers and craftsmen who worked for the household. Chapter 8 finishes with an assessment of the impact of the Le Strange household on the social and economic structures of the local community.

2

Household Management

...she overseeth the ways of her household and eateth not the brede of idleness[1]

The process of domestic consumption begins not with shopping, but with the rather less romanticized processes of financial planning and household management. Someone had to assess the needs and wants of a household, measure them against its financial resources, and decide how much to spend on what. From the Bible onwards, the male household head was charged with bringing income into the household and his wife with household management. In the words of Robert Cleaver (1598): 'The dutie of the husband is, to get mony and provision: and of the wives, not vainely to spend it.'[2] In the mid-nineteenth century, Mrs Beeton's *Book of Household Management* addressed budgetary advice firmly to the wife, and the housewife is still defined in the *Oxford English Dictionary* as 'a woman who manages her household with skill and thrift, a domestic economist'.[3] In fact, the gendering of these tasks was a great deal more complex. Certainly, household management was an important element of housewifery, the tasks and skills of a married woman in early modern England. Housewifery typically involved overseeing the provision of food, clothing and medical care for the household, but there were other elements of domestic spending, on durables, travel and the structural fabric of the house, which were more likely to be undertaken jointly or by men alone. In most households, neither man nor woman has complete financial control, and the range of domestic money management systems found both historically and in the modern households reflects this.[4]

De Vries describes the internal decision-making system of the historical household as an impenetrable 'black box', but household accounts offer a window into household management.[5] Household accounts survive very largely for the gentry,

---

[1] Sir Hamon Le Strange in the Kitchen accounts, LEST/P8, quoting from the Book of Proverbs.
[2] R. Cleaver, *A Godlie Forme of Householde Government* (1598), 169. See T. Tilney, *The Flower of Friendship* (1573), ed. V. Wayne (New York, 1992), 120, for a very similar passage.
[3] I. Beeton, *The Book of Household Management* (1861) (facsimile edition, London, 1968); *OED Online*.
[4] A. Vickery, 'His and hers: gender, consumption and household accounting in eighteenth century England', *Past and Present* supplement 1 (2006); J. Pahl, *Money and Marriage* (New York, 1989).
[5] J. de Vries, *The Industrious Revolution: Consumer Behaviour and the Household Economy, 1650 to the Present* (2008), 215.

but they nonetheless provide valuable evidence. As long ago as 1965 Pollard argued that expertise developed in managing these large households laid the foundation for business management in the industrial revolution.[6] What Pollard was not aware of was the extent to which these households were managed by women. Historians have recently become more interested in domestic accounting, and particularly its gendered nature.[7] By the eighteenth century, books were published to advise gentlewomen on accounting. There were printed pocket books to enable them to set out their personal accounts, and many large households employed professional female housekeepers. For the sixteenth and seventeenth centuries it has been assumed that elite households were managed by male servants: household and estate stewards. In fact the picture was more mixed: while many of the largest and wealthiest households employed stewards, others, like the Le Stranges, did not.

This chapter describes the documentation and management strategy created by the Le Stranges during their married life from 1602 to 1654, with a particular focus on the accounts of Alice Le Strange. It explores both how typical the Le Stranges were of wealthy households and how typical Alice's activities were for a gentlewoman. It begins by describing the nature of the household and estate records kept by Hamon and Alice Le Strange, which were in fact very largely Alice's work. This leads on to a discussion of the gendered nature of household accounting, and the degree to which account-keeping was a source of power. The second section looks at how household and estate management interacted. It describes the model of management where tasks were delegated to a team of elite servants, and contrasts this with the personal management style of the Le Stranges. The extent to which other gentlewomen extended their management activities to farming and the estate is examined. The third section looks at the idea of 'housewifery' as a set of skills mastered by married women. How far were seventeenth-century gentlewomen 'housewives'? The patterns of gendered management identified in the first two sections are compared with contemporary advice literature on marriage and farming, with particular attention to the advice books owned by the Le Stranges themselves. The final section of the chapter draws comparisons with the management activities of gentlewomen from two other late sixteenth- and early seventeenth-century Norfolk families: the Townshends and Hobarts. This sets Alice Le Strange's activities in context, demonstrating the breadth of management activities undertaken by Norfolk gentlewomen and the restrictions they faced.

---

[6] S. Pollard, *The Genesis of Modern Management: A Study of the Industrial Revolution in Great Britain* (Cambridge, Massachusetts, 1965), 25–30.
[7] R. Connor, *Women, Accounting and Narrative: Keeping Books in Eighteenth-Century England* (London, 2004); B. Lemire, *The Business of Everyday Life* (Manchester, 2005), ch. 7; Vickery, 'His and hers'.

ALICE LE STRANGE'S ACCOUNTS

Hamon Le Strange and Alice Stubbe married in 1602. Their household accounts begin four years later in 1606. These were initially kept by Hamon, recording disbursements or payments, and receipts or income. Alice took over in 1610 and kept the records without break until Hamon's death. The surviving disbursement accounts run continuously from 1610 to 1654 with just a few missing pages. Alice added kitchen accounts to the disbursements and receipts in 1613, and from 1620 onwards started taking control of the estate records. She began with the estate records for Sedgeford, inherited from her father after his death in 1619, but by the 1630s she had taken on the records for the whole Le Strange estate. When Alice took charge of the household accounts in 1610 she transformed their layout and efficiency. She brought clarity to the task and a different approach from her husband. Most obvious is the way that Alice listed every single item whereas Hamon had relied far more on tradesmen, bailiffs and servants submitting their bills. Hamon referenced the bills in numbered files, but this resulted in a lack of detail in the more permanent disbursement accounts. For the years in which Hamon kept the accounts there is no consistent record of the payment of servants' wages or the purchase of food: two major items of expenditure. Alice was more systematic. A particular feature of her approach to accounting was a desire to improve and rationalize her methods. She did this in a number of ways. First, unlike the unorganized payments noted by Hamon, she started to group payments into categories, using brackets and annotating items in the margin: wages to servants, corn and farm labour, expenditure on the various children, food for the household, and building repairs. Second, she siphoned off major expenditure, such as food and building work, into specialist accounts. This enabled her to exert greater control over detail and provided a framework for expansion into new enterprises, which could then be cross-referenced back to the main account. It was the beginning of a fully integrated accounting system covering the household and estate.

The kitchen accounts, or 'household books' as she described them, begin in 1613. They provide a weekly record of the purchase, production and consumption of food for the household.[8] In the first few weeks Alice experimented with the layout, but then arrived at a formula which remained unchanged. Every half-year she started with a stock take. The weekly accounts that followed recorded items used from store, purchased and delivered as gifts from tenants and suppliers. Then for a standard list of staple foods, she noted the amounts received, bought, made, spent, sold and remaining. A limited range of staple foods—beef, bread and corn—was soon increased to include butter, cheese, two types of salt-fish, two types of beer and three types of bread. This provided effective controls over stock and

---

[8] Household Books: LEST/P6: 1st, 3rd, 4th; LEST/P8: 5th, 6th, 8th; LEST/P9: 9th, 10th. The 2nd and 7th books are missing.

expenditure, was easily checked, and could be used to predict consumption and expenditure from year to year. Payments for labour in the farm and garden and small purchases of kitchen, garden and farm equipment concluded the weekly account. The half-year ended with a further stock take which included, from 1616, details of a piggery, with the number of boars, sows and pigs reared for bacon and pork. The dairy, averaging twenty-three cows with followers, appears in the stock take from 1620.

With these refinements, Alice gradually improved her management technique. The receipt accounts which recorded income from the estate, including farm rents, sales of timber, corn, livestock and foodstuffs, were entered at the back of each household book, with half-yearly totals of receipts appearing in the relevant book of disbursements. Separate building accounts appear from 1620 when Hamon's activities extending Hunstanton Hall and carrying out large-scale works elsewhere in the estate gathered momentum. These accounts consisted of two to four pages inserted in each six-month section of the general disbursements, which could be cross-referenced to Hamon's own notebook, where he kept notes of projects, contracts with builders and suppliers, and jotted down his own ideas and designs.[9] With this arrangement, Alice paid the bills and itemized expenditure, while Hamon concentrated on managing the building process. Her accounts meant that he could reliably predict his income stream and plan ahead with a degree of certainty. He could see at a glance the expenses, income and the spare cash that he could allocate to various projects; this enabled him to carry out a rolling programme of building and repairs, which continued without a break, despite the financial setbacks of the 1640s, until his death in 1654.

The inheritance of Sedgeford manor from Alice's father in 1620 increased the value of the estate from £1247 to £1720, but added to the burden of management.[10] Again, the Le Stranges shared the task. Hamon supervised the building work and Alice kept the accounts and managed the sheep flocks. Her sheep and wool accounts are bound with her household accounts. The accounts start in 1618 with 'the children's' accounts of the sheep given to them by their grandfather; references to 'my father's book' indicate how she and her children were trained in estate management. She continued the tradition, later allocating sheep to her own grandchildren.[11] The Sedgeford sheep accounts, which run from 1620 to 1654, show her understanding of the intricate foldcourse arrangements which prevailed in the parish and competence at sheep farming. She quickly purchased more sheep, worked closely with individual shepherds, recorded numbers clipped, the sale of lambs, hogs, wool and skins, and devised grazing schemes to improve the brecks and raise corn yields. Alice drew up field books, and breck books to accompany a survey of three maps of Sedgeford commissioned by Hamon. Hamon supported her enterprises, allowing the purchase of additional parcels of land and rebuilding of Sedgeford Hall and new farmhouses.

From the 1630s the Sedgeford estate accounts appear with those of Hunstanton, indicating a further development in Alice's role.[12] At this stage she

[9] Sir Hamon's notebook: LEST/Q38.   [10] LEST/Q38.
[11] LEST/P10.   [12] LEST/BK7.

progressed to keeping the accounts and field books for the entire estate, starting with Heacham, correcting some of the entries made by Hamon the previous year, followed by Ringstead and Hunstanton.[13] Hunstanton serves as an example of her record-keeping procedures. Traditionally, the estate at Hunstanton was managed through four different types of record. Field books provided a description of the landholding structure. Rentals listed the manorial tenants owing freehold and copyhold rents. Firmals listed those tenants leasing land from the Le Stranges. Bailiffs' accounts gave a brief summary of the holdings, the allowances granted to tenants and the payments received.[14] Before 1630 all these records were kept separately, and it was very difficult to trace what individual tenants owed for their lands, which might be scattered through several parishes, and the type of rent paid. Hamon had commissioned maps of each parish, which gave him a visual image of the geography and the landholding structure, and he made a start on the field books, but much remained to be done.[15] Alice kept the field books, but improved their layout and legibility, so that they can easily be cross-referenced to the survey maps. The rentals, firmals and bailiffs' accounts, she drew together into a single volume, listing each tenant's leasehold and manorial rents, and noting rents paid.[16] Alice continued to refine her methods. In 1636 she placed the tenant's name in a separate column on the left of the page, drawing attention to the holding of each individual. At the same time, she created separate lists of leaseholds and manorial rents. From her work, it is a simple matter to construct tables showing the characteristics of the landholding structure, which is no doubt what she intended. She compiled this combined rental and firmal every four years, noting changes of occupancy. Every year, she entered a summary of the bailiffs' accounts. From 1638, she cross-referenced the receipts from each bailiff back to the household accounts, attaching with a pin, 'a note how this account was received and written in my Booke'; later these receipts were written more securely in the account. In this way, Alice created an integrated system, linking estate and household accounts.

How typical were Alice's account-keeping activities? The Le Strange archives alone contain accounting records left by three other women. A century earlier, Anne Le Strange, wife of Sir Thomas, had set the pattern which Alice later followed. Anne was born in 1494 and married at the age of seven, in 1501. Her eldest son was born some time between 1511 and 1513, and the following two decades seem to have been dominated by child-bearing. However, Harris notes that 'by 1530, Lady Anne was supervising both the Lestrange household and estates and keeping detailed accounts of her cash transactions'. The accounts of 1533–4 show Anne Le Strange receiving rents, tithes and other sources of income; as well as

---

[13] LEST/DI 22 A; LEST/EK5; LEST/BK7.
[14] Hunstanton: LEST/BH1; LEST/BH2; LEST/BK3–9; LEST/BK15. Heacham: LEST/DI 16; LEST/DI 17; LEST/DI 19; LEST/DI 22 A; LEST/DI 22 B; LEST/DI 22 C; LEST/DI 23. Ringstead: LEST/EH4; LEST/EH5; LEST/EH10; LEST/EK4–7; LEST/EK18. Sedgeford: LEST/IC 55; LEST/IC 58; LEST/IC 65; LEST/IB 86; LEST/IB 90; LEST/IB 93. Bailiff Accounts: LEST/R8–R10.
[15] LEST/OA1; LEST/OB5, 6; LEST/OC2; LEST/OC1.
[16] LEST/BK15.

disbursing money 'to pay servants... to buy supplies for the household, to purchase clothes and other necessities for the children, to make repairs, and to reward or reimburse the scores of people who ran their errands and delivered goods and letters'.[17] Alice was aware of this earlier model for her activities: she consulted the sixteenth-century accounts and adopted a similar format for her kitchen books, before adding her own modifications.[18] Variations in handwriting in the accounts from the 1630s suggest that another Anne Le Strange, the wife of Nicholas Le Strange, Alice's son, who was resident in the household, assisted Alice with entries and learned her accounting methods. Catherine Calthorpe, Anne's sister, kept accounts from 1652 to 1662 which remain in the Le Strange collection.[19]

No comprehensive list of surviving household accounts from the sixteenth and seventeenth centuries has been compiled, let alone a breakdown of who kept the accounts. Nonetheless, it is evident that accounts kept by women were relatively common. Forty-three surviving sets of accounts kept by women, dating from 1500 to 1699, can be identified, as well as a further seven kept jointly by married couples.[20] To these can be added examples of women who were renowned for their account-keeping, such as Dame Mary Lowther, but whose accounts do not survive.[21] Gentlewomen's accounts were undoubtedly outnumbered by those kept by men, both gentlemen and household stewards, but the relative frequency with which women's accounts do survive demonstrates that Alice Le Strange was not an oddity. Unlike other tasks in early modern households, account-keeping was not strongly gendered. This gave individual household heads the flexibility to devise their own management strategies. Men might keep accounts as a means of tracking where their income went, and exercising power within the household; women might keep accounts to control and monitor expenditure. A couple might resolve to keep accounts jointly, or to both avoid the task by handing it over to a household steward. Only in the last instance is there a strongly gendered pattern: elite servants such as household stewards were male in this period, with female 'housekeepers' only emerging in the later seventeenth century.[22]

Recent research by Spicksley has argued that arithmetic and account-keeping were more likely to be part of a gentlewoman's education than gentlemen's, precisely because of the role of account-keeping in household management.[23] For example, Lady Frances Hobart (b.1603), 'was taught "to read, to write, and cast

---

[17] B.J. Harris, *English Aristocratic Women 1450–1550: Marriage and Family, Property and Careers* (Oxford, 2002), 67–8.
[18] LEST/P4–5; LEST/P2; LEST/N15.
[19] LEST/P12.
[20] These were identified by searching the Perdita Project's database of women's manuscript writing (http://human.ntu.ac.uk/research/perdita/index.html); Access to Archives with the key phrases 'household accounts' and 'household account' (http://www.a2a.org.uk/); and from our own archival and secondary research.
[21] C.B. Phillips (ed.), *The Lowther Family Estate Books 1617–1675*, Surtees Society, vol. 191 (1979), 62–3.
[22] J.T. Cliffe, *The World of the Country House in Seventeenth-Century England* (New Haven, 1999), 86.
[23] J. Spicksley, 'Women, accounts and numeracy in seventeenth-century England', unpublished paper presented to the Economic History Society Annual Conference, Leicester 2005. Connor, *Women, Accounting and Narrative*, ch. 1.

account nimbly and exactly" at home by a French gentlewoman', while Grace Mildmay (b.c.1552) was 'trained under the watchful eye of Mrs Hamblyn, her father's niece, who, whenever she believed Grace to be "idly disposed" would set her "to cipher" with her pen, "and to cast up and prove great sums and accounts"'.[24] Sir Drayner Massingberd 'stipulated in his will that his daughters should be taught "all sorts of Learning needfull and usefull for them and particularly that they be made perfect in Arithmatick and Casting up Accounts."'[25] Gentlemen, on the other hand, were unlikely to receive such training as part of a university education: arithmetic was seen as 'mechanic' and suitable only as part of a practical apprenticeship in trade. Spicksley notes that Samuel Pepys, 'though educated at St Paul's School in London and Magdalene College, Cambridge, had to obtain his training in arithmetic from Cooper, the ship's mate on the *Royal Charles*'.[26] There were a growing number of advice books on account-keeping in the seventeenth century. Although these were initially aimed at men, by the early eighteenth century advice was being provided specifically for women so that they could keep 'family accounts'.[27]

Account-keeping gave women knowledge of household affairs, but did it actually confer power within the household? Many women kept accounts when they were single or widowed as a means of managing their own affairs. Others kept accounts because their husbands were absent. Alice Le Strange's situation was less usual: keeping accounts while living with her husband in the same household. Account-keeping was not necessarily a source of power. It could enable women's further subordination by allowing the husband to oversee and monitor purchasing activities.[28] In some cases, it may have been a duty pushed onto unwilling women by husbands or other male relatives, saving the expense of a household steward. Gender relations in seventeenth-century England meant that it was the husband's choice, not the wife's, as to who should keep accounts and manage the household. But if a husband did choose to delegate these tasks, as Hamon Le Strange did, there was room for gentlewomen to take on considerable powers of management.

The Le Strange archive demonstrates that Alice's accounting activities were accompanied by a degree of independence and that they conferred on her some control over the household's activities. To the frustrations of the historian (and possibly her husband too) her own personal spending remains almost entirely hidden. She received an allowance each year of £66 13s 4d, carefully noted in the disbursement accounts. How she spent this money is not recorded; Sir Hamon's

---

[24] Spicksley, 'Women, accounts and numeracy', 5, with quotations from Collinges, *Par Nobile. Two Treatises. The one... upon occasion of the Death of the Right Honourable the Lady Frances Hobart... The other... at the Funerals of the Right Honourable the Lady Katherine Courten* (1669), 3–4; L. Pollock, *With Faith and Physic: The Life of a Tudor Gentlewoman, Lady Grace Mildmay 1552–1620* (London, 1993), 26.
[25] Cliffe, *Country House*, 71.
[26] Spicksley, 'Women, accounts, and numeracy', 3.
[27] Connor, *Women, Accounting and Narrative*, 30, 51, quoting *The Ladies Library* (1714).
[28] C. Hole, *The English Housewife in the Seventeenth Century* (London, 1953), 101.

expenses, however, were recorded down to the last penny in the general accounts, allowing Alice oversight. While Alice's arithmetic was not always exact (nor was Hamon's), her organizational skills and attention to detail were impressive and clearly outstripped her husband's. She not only kept the accounts with unerring regularity, but occasionally sat down to analyse what she had recorded. In 'the profits of my dairy' she compared the production rates of cheese and butter by the different dairymaids she had employed between 1617 and 1634.[29] From 1630 onwards she kept a tally of the loans Hamon had taken out, recording both new loans and the running total of money owing each year.[30] She added up the values of the portions she and her half-sister had received from their father in lands, goods and money, noting wryly that her sister, Dionisia, had received £1209 more than her.[31]

The accounts leave only one record of possible disagreement between Sir Hamon and Alice, close to the end of their lives when Sir Hamon was unwell and the household was still struggling with the problems caused by the Civil War. In April 1653, at the foot of half-yearly totals, Alice noted 'I have lost by keeping of my Husbands Reckonings since 1635 beside all the mony in 18 yeares I have spared out of my Owne allowance for my clothes which is 158 li 9s: I have lost over - £280 15s'.[32] The statement is ambiguous: the term 'my husbands reckonings' is her description of the account books. Had Hamon done an audit of the accounts, or had Alice realized the mistake herself? Alice's reaction to this error is characteristic: first, she allows various expenses which she had paid out of her own allowance over the years, not only clothes but also the purchase of lead for building work and of sheep, reducing the sum to £176 17s 9d;[33] then she began to pay back what she owed from her own allowance. She deducted £30 from her half-yearly allowance that April and the following November, with a careful note in the account that she had been 'paid short' and for what reason. By April 1654, however, she was paid her normal allowance. Hamon died in that June. However the problem had arisen, it was resolved before his death.

The accounts were a tool for gaining control of the household and estate, a tool used by both Alice and Hamon Le Strange. Hamon, on the whole, seems to have recognized his good fortune in having such an active and capable wife. On the front page of her Fifth Household Book, romantically concealed under a flap, he took a quote from the Book of Proverbs, writing, 'who shall finde a virtuous woman for her price is above pearls, the very heart of her husband trusteth in her...she overseeth the ways of her household and eateth not the brede of idleness';[34] and in his will he thanked Alice for 'her ever incessant industry in straynes of knowledge above her sex, to the just, faithfull and laudable advantage and advancement of myne estate'.[35]

---

[29] LEST/P8.   [30] LEST/P10.   [31] LEST/P10.   [32] LEST/P10.
[33] The precision of these calculations suggests that she kept her own personal accounts of expenditure from her allowance which do not survive.
[34] LEST/P8 (1621–5).
[35] LEST/AE8: the will of Sir Hamon Le Strange, 1654.

HOUSEHOLD AND ESTATE MANAGEMENT

With an income of over £2000 a year from the 1620s the Le Stranges were members of the upper gentry. Yet their management strategy was that of the lesser gentry. Hamon and Alice managed their estate and household directly, without the aid of elite servants: they employed no receiver and no stewards. A list of the servants employed in 1617 records a clerk, falconer, cook, butler, coachman, horsekeeper, bailiff of husbandry, scullion, two servants in husbandry, a dairymaid, backhouse maid, washerwoman and two chambermaids.[36] None of these staff had a senior managerial function, a fact reflected in their pay: apart from the cook and falconer, none received more than £3 a year. Elite servants normally received around £20 a year at this date.[37] On the estate manorial bailiffs, who were also tenants, collected and paid in the rents and other revenues from particular manors, as was traditional on such properties. The receipt of income from the bailiffs and all expenditure, as we have seen, was managed by Alice Le Strange along with the home farm.

Sir Hamon Le Strange's interests and activities are discussed in detail in Chapter 7. He was an active Justice of the Peace and held other political offices such as sheriff, Member of Parliament and Deputy Lieutenant. He was a bibliophile, music lover and had interests in science. He enjoyed hunting and hawking. His involvement in domestic affairs is best illustrated by his general notebook, which dates from 1613 to 1637.[38] The notebook demonstrates a degree of overlap between Alice's and Hamon's roles. Hamon agreed terms of employment with new male servants, and purchased their liveries, while Alice employed the female servants and recorded all the wages paid in the disbursement accounts. Alice kept the estate documents, but it was Hamon who played the hands-on role of an estate steward.[39] He leased out land, sold timber and wool, conducted law suits, and invested in improvements. Hamon oversaw the enlargement of Hunstanton Hall in the 1620s and much of his notebook is concerned with work to improve land and buildings on the estate, with diagrams, instructions and agreements with craftsmen for work and materials: payments arising from these activities were carefully recorded in Alice's accounts.

In 1630 the Le Stranges' eldest son, Nicholas, married and with his wife took up permanent residence in his parents' household. Nicholas, like his father, kept notebooks which have survived, allowing us to see how he combined aspects of both his parents' skills and shared their interests in the estate.[40] The notebooks display his father's academic interest in science, technology and natural history,

---

[36] LEST/Q38, fol. 11.
[37] L. Stone, *The Crisis of the Aristocracy 1558–1641* (Oxford, 1965), 292–3. Cliffe, *Country House*, 114.
[38] LEST/Q38.
[39] D.R. Hainsworth, *Stewards, Lords and People: The Estate Steward and his World in Later Stuart England* (Cambridge, 1992).
[40] LEST/KA6, LEST/KA9–10 and KA24.

while replicating his mother's methodical style of record. Despite his parents' extensive management activities, Nicholas found a specialist area where he could exercise his interests. He developed plans for draining, cultivating and improving the marshes at Hunstanton and Heacham, before taking on further projects of land improvement at Sedgeford. These activities were costed and analysed using mathematical tables and almanacs. Payments for labour and materials do not appear in Alice's accounts, so we can assume that this aspect was run independently by Nicholas and his wife, Anne, out of their own allowance, which in turn suggests that they kept their own accounts, which have not survived.

Direct management was an unusual strategy for gentry of the Le Stranges' wealth and status. They had the advantage of a very compact estate: all of their manors neighboured their home parish of Hunstanton, with the exception of Gressenhall, which was only twenty-four miles away in mid-Norfolk. This geographical concentration allowed them to dispense with the elaborate management structures preferred by the aristocracy and those with large, scattered properties. Yet it was also a matter of choice. Their strategy had a number of advantages: it saved expenditure on elite servants' wages; it gave Hamon and Alice greater control and knowledge of their finances; and it allowed them to build closer personal bonds with tenants and suppliers to the household, thus adding to their status in the local community. The major costs were time, and a degree of immobility. They could not afford to be absent from Hunstanton for extended periods. Gentry who attended court or chose to spend much of the year in London could not behave like the Le Stranges.

Given the amount of work involved, the Le Stranges' direct management strategy was only made possible by Alice's willingness to take on significant responsibilities in running the estate. Harris argues that it was quite normal for women to be involved in estate management in the period 1450–1550. She suggests that most wives became their husband's junior partner in managing the family's assets, and that when wives 'had proved their competence, the majority of men delegated considerable power and control over their resources to them'. She notes that, while aristocratic households employed professional and semi-professional officials to assist them, 'no substitute existed for competent wives who shared their husbands' interests and on whose loyalty they could count'.[41] Widows were even more likely to manage property themselves.[42] By the seventeenth century wives were more likely to spend time with their husbands in London and at court, but Cliffe still concludes that 'what is particularly striking about the business activities of gentlewomen is the extent to which they become involved in estate management'.[43] He gives the example of Bulstrode Whitelocke, who wrote, 'I found none so good stewards as my wives', and Blanche Lingen, who managed her husband's estate and repaid his debts for nine years when he was declared

---

[41] Harris, *English Aristocratic Women*, 64–5. These views are supported by Rowena Archer, '"How ladies...who live on their manors ought to manage their households and estates": Women as landholders and administrators in the later Middle Ages', in P.J.P. Goldberg (ed.), *Women in English Medieval Society* (Stroud, 1997), 150.
[42] Harris, *English Aristocratic Women*, 145.
[43] Cliffe, *Country House*, 72.

lunatic.[44] Women not only managed estates but also took a direct interest in farming. Harris notes a number of gentlewomen from the earlier period managing large sheep flocks in Norfolk, just as Alice Le Strange did in the seventeenth century: 'Dame Eleanor Townshend never kept less than 8,000 sheep during her widowhood' in the late fifteenth century, while in the 1550s, 'Dame Elizabeth Spelman left one of her younger sons, Erasmus, 200 sheep and over 1,000 to her grandson Thomas'.[45]

Estate management and farming were clearly not out of bounds to gentlewomen. Pollock observes that, while the formal education of gentlewomen did not prepare them for these tasks, the education received by gentlemen was equally unhelpful.[46] We should not imagine that all gentlewomen proved themselves competent: Francis Shirley of Staunton Harold in Leicestershire (d.1571) was reputedly ruined by taking no interest in estate management and leaving it to his wife.[47] Time spent at the Inns of Court gave gentlemen basic legal knowledge useful to the management of estates, but women's upbringing gave them other advantages. They were more likely to spend time at home during adolescence and young adulthood, allowing them to observe first hand how farm and estate were run. Indeed, Alice Le Strange's father, Richard Stubbe, as both a lawyer and the manager of his own Norfolk estate, almost certainly provided her with a useful practical education which formed the background to her later activities.

GENTLEWOMEN AS HOUSEWIVES

The ideal model in early modern society expected a wife to be subject and obedient to her husband and at the same time to be capable and competent, a good housewife and able to take on whatever tasks around the household that her husband thought appropriate. Pollock has explored how these contradictions manifested themselves in the education of elite women of the period: girls were taught not only how to keep accounts and manage a household or even an estate, but also to be modest and obedient. She argues convincingly that the two roles were not necessarily in contradiction: a woman's subordination to her husband took precedence over any skills she might possess.[48] The extent to which a wife developed and exercised responsibilities and skills within marriage depended on her husband's permission. The two roles assigned to married women are clearly evident in late sixteenth- and early seventeenth-century advice literature for married couples. Two distinct genres of advice took very different standpoints: marriage advice literature, which drew heavily on the Bible, emphasized women's subordination, whereas husbandry manuals outlined the wide range of skills which were

---

[44] Cliffe, *Country House*, 73–4.
[45] Harris, *English Aristocratic Women*, 148.
[46] L. Pollock, '"Teach her to live under obedience": The making of women in the upper ranks of early modern England', *Continuity and Change* 4:2 (1989), 237.
[47] F. Heal and C. Holmes, *The Gentry in England and Wales 1500–1700* (Basingstoke, 1994), 98–9.
[48] Pollock, '"Teach her to live"', especially 249, 252.

considered integral to 'housewifery'. The Le Strange library catalogue shows that Hamon and Alice Le Strange owned both types of book.[49]

Housewifery, or huswifery to give it its seventeenth-century form, is a word that has now largely fallen out of use.[50] It was the set of skills pertaining to a good housewife or married woman. Although husbandry was occasionally used as its male equivalent, the duties and skills of a good husband,[51] more often husbandry referred to farming or agricultural work. Thus husbandry was an occupation for men of a particular level of wealth in a particular sector of the economy while housewifery was universal for women. All married women were expected to be good housewives, although their actual portfolio of tasks varied according to their wealth, location and inclination. Gentlewomen, as well as women lower down the social scale, were described as being good housewives or skilled in housewifery. For instance, John Smythe of Nibley wrote that 'country housewifery seemed to be an essential part' of Lady Anne Berkeley's activities,[52] while Sir William Stonhouse described the profits his wife, Dame Elizabeth, built up from running a dairy business, as 'all that stock of monie which by her carefull good huswiferie shee hath acquired by my allowance'.[53] Sir Edmund Molineux sent his two daughters to a cousin to be brought up 'in virtue, good manners and learning to play the gentlewoman and good housewives, to dress meat and oversee their households',[54] while Ralph Verney advised his god-daughter in 1652 to learn French because 'there were "many admirable books" in that language which would inform a girl about "all manner of good housewifery"'.[55] It has been argued by Davies that 'great ladies' would not have identified with the housewives of marriage advice books, which were descriptive of the urban bourgeoisie.[56] In doing so she overestimates the bureaucratization of gentry households and underestimates women's involvement in household management. Housewifery was not considered beneath the status of elite women and the presence of marriage advice books in gentry libraries indicates that they were read.

The Le Stranges owned four marriage advice books published before 1630. The earliest was Heinrich Bullinger's *The Christian State of Matrimony* translated by Giles Coverdale (1575). Originally published in 1546, it was typical of early works of this type, very largely concerned with the legality of marriage and moral behaviour.[57] Robert Cleaver's *A Godly Forme of Houshold Government* (1598) and William Gouge's *Of Domesticall Duties* (1622) are both longer works which give detailed consideration to the working relationship between husband and wife. All three of these books are primarily religious texts, setting out the Christian ideal of

---

[49] LEST/NE1.
[50] *OED Online*.
[51] For instance, Cleaver, *A Godlie Forme of Householde Government*, 61–2.
[52] Quoted in Harris, *English Aristocratic Women*, 148.
[53] Cliffe, *Country House*, 72.
[54] Pollock, '"Teach her to live"', p. 236.
[55] Pollock, '"Teach her to live"', 241.
[56] K. Davies, 'Continuity and change in literary advice on marriage', in R.B. Outhwaite (ed.), *Marriage and Society: Studies in the Social History of Marriage* (London, 1981), 77.
[57] Davies, 'Continuity and change', 61–2.

marriage and quoting frequently from the Bible.[58] Richard Brathwaite's *The Good Wife: or a Rare One amongst Women* (1618) was written in verse, taking the form of advice from a father to son on the choice of a wife. While non-religious in approach, Brathwaite is still more concerned with the moral and social behaviour of the wife than her practical skills.[59] Christian texts on marriage, such as those by Bullinger, Cleaver and Gouge, were unanimous in asserting that the wife was subject to her husband and owed him complete obedience.[60] Wives' subjection was justified both in biblical terms using the creation myth[61] and in practical terms. Cleaver states 'if shee bee not subject to her husband, to let him rule all houshold, especially outward affaires: if shee will make heade against him, and seeke to have her own wais, there will bee doing and undooing. Things will go backeward, the house will come to ruine...'.[62] Brathwaite adds a further reason: he warns the son not to choose a wife who is 'self-singular', as it 'disvalues a man that's subject to a woman'.[63]

Yet despite this insistence on the wife's inferiority to her husband, even the religious texts acknowledged that the wife also had responsibilities, particularly within the house. She was charged with the education of her young children and daughters, and with the direction of maid servants.[64] More significantly for our discussion, she was expected to 'keep house', be a good housewife and help in the provisioning of the household. The phrase 'keeping house' was a double-edged one, implying both that a woman had a responsible role in running affairs within the household and that she should stay at home, leaving outside affairs to the husband. All four writers emphasized this. Bullinger states, 'Whatever is to be done without the house, that belongeth to the man, and the woman to study for things within to be done, and to see saved or spent conveniently, whatsoever he bringeth in'; while Cleaver writes, 'The dutie of the husband is, to travell abroad to seeke living, and the wives dutie is to keepe the house. The dutie of the husband is, to get mony and provision: and of the wives, not vainely to spent it.' Gouge is also clear that 'affaires abroad do most appertaine to the man, and are especially to be ordered by him: that which the wife is especially to care for, is the business of the house: as the Apostle laieth downe as a rule for wives... that they keep at home, and governe the house'. Brathwaite agrees, advising the son to 'chuse thee no gadder (for a wife should bee | In this respect (I'm sure) like to a Snaile,) | Who (hous-wifelike) still in her house we see; | For if her care or providence do faile, Her howse-affaires will go disorderlie'.[65]

---

[58] Davies, 'Continuity and change', 80, for more details about these three authors.

[59] The four books were accessed on EEBO. References are to the editions owned by the Le Stranges, as recorded in LEST/NE1, with the exception of Cleaver, where the catalogue cited a 1596 edition but the 1598 edition was used instead.

[60] Bullinger, *Christian State*, fol. 2v and fol. 64v. Cleaver, *Godly Form*, 82. Gouge, *Domesticall Duties*, 269, 286.

[61] For example, Bullinger, *Christian State*, fol. 2v.

[62] Cleaver, *Godly Form*, 82.

[63] R. Brathwaite, *The Good Wife: or, a Rare One amongst Women* (1618), fol. B3.

[64] Cleaver, *Godly Form*, 53, 85. Bullinger, *Christian State*, fol. 92, Gouge, *Domesticall Duties*, 259, 367.

[65] Bullinger, *Christian State*, fol. 78. Cleaver, *Godly Form*, 168–9. Gouge, *Domesticall Duties*, 255. Brathwaite, *Good Wife*, fol. B2v.

In keeping her house, the wife was be 'huswifely', exercise 'good huswiferie' and be a 'good housewife'.[66] Unfortunately the writers are not always specific about what these terms actually mean, although the excerpts given above imply a responsibility for saving and spending in order to provision the household. Gouge provides a clear if rather limited summary: 'it appeareth that the businesses of the house appertaine, and are most proper to the wife: in which respect she is called the hous-wife.... 1. To order the decking and trimming of the house. 2. To dispose the ordinary provision for the family. 3. To rule and governe the maid servants. 4. To bring up children while they are young.'[67] Bullinger says that mothers must teach daughters 'huswifely working with theyr hands', which included spinning, sewing and weaving; and that fathers should not promise their daughters in marriage until 'he hath good experience of her huswifery, and the governing of a house'.[68] Brathwaite emphasizes the time it takes to become skilled in housewifery, advising the son to choose a wife 'Nor yong nor old, but has yeares enow | to know what huswife means.' Cleaver, too, emphasizes the housewife's skill: 'Shee that will be a good saver, must not be a slender Huswife, but skilfull in all points.... She must not let her maides have their own waies, for want of skill, but she must be able to direct and prescribe, what & how, in every businesse.' One of the housewife's skills was careful management: 'Shee must have a good forecast, to contrive & dispatch things in due time, and good order, that necessaries bee not wanting when they should be used, and confusion doo not make more labour then is needfull.'[69]

Cleaver, Brathwaite and Gouge all suggest circumstances in which wives might assist their husbands in their duty of providing for the household. Cleaver writes, 'The care and burthen to maintaine their family is common to them both: yet so, as properly the husband is to get it, and to bring it in, and the wife to order & dispose it. Howbeit the dutie of the wife, or of the husband, doth not so exempt either of them, but that shee also according to her abilitie and power, must helpe her husband to get it...'. Gouge agrees that the wife is 'joint governour with the husband of the familie' and thus 'ought to be an helpe in providing such a sufficiencie of the goods of this world, as are needfull for that estate wherein God hath set them'. For him, a good wife could by 'her industry and providence... preserve and increase' her husband's goods. Brathwaite is more straightforward: for the husband, the ideal wife was 'such a one as may supplie thy place when th'art from home'.[70]

English husbandry manuals are more explicit and detailed in their descriptions of housewifery, although not necessarily comprehensive. The Le Stranges owned three extensive guides to husbandry: Conrad Heresbach's *Foure Bookes of Husbandry*, translated by Barnaby Googe (1586), Charles Estienne's *Maison Rustique, or The*

---

[66] Bullinger, *Christian State*, fol. 53. Cleaver, *Godly Form*, 62. Gouge, *Domesticall Duties*, 254.
[67] Gouge, *Domesticall Duties*, 367, echoing Cleaver, *Godly Form*, 175.
[68] Bullinger, *Christian State*, fol. 92–92v. Cleaver also mentions spinning, *Godly Form*, 88.
[69] Brathwaite, *Good Wife*, fol. B3v. Cleaver, *Godly Form*, 84–5.
[70] Cleaver, *Godly Form*, 179, fol. N5. Gouge, *Domesticall Duties*, 253–4. Brathwaite, *Good Wife*, fol. B3v.

Countrey Farme, translated by Surflet (1616), and a collection of Gervase Markham's works in nine books: *Whole Art of Husbandry* (1631), which included *The English Husbandman* and *The English Housewife*. Heresbach, a German writer, who borrowed from classical literature on farming, is generally uninformative about who should carry out particular tasks on the farm, although he does mention a maid servant 'so skilfull in huswyferie, that she may well be my wyues suffragan'.[71] The work is aimed at elite gentlemen who wanted to understand the business of farming, but employed a bailiff and other servants to carry out the day-to-day management of the farm.[72] The wife is assumed to be uninvolved. The works of Estienne and Markham, in contrast, say a great deal about the role of the housewife. This is in part because their books are not confined strictly to agriculture, but also discuss the processing and sale of farm products, medicinal remedies for people and animals, and, in Markham's case, cookery.

Estienne's *The Countrey Farme* was a work on French agriculture, but the 1616 English edition was 'newly reviewed, corrected, and augmented, with divers large additions' by Gervase Markham, the prolific author of English self-help books. The title page claimed that these additions meant not only that the book now covered the 'husbandrie of France, Italie and Spaine' but also that it had been 'reconciled and made to agree with ours here in England'.[73] Markham drew heavily on the content of *The Countrey Farme* when composing his own works, *The English Husbandman* and *The English Housewife*, originally published in 1613–14 and 1615. *The Countrey Farme* contained seven books or sections and runs to over 700 pages. It is organized according to different aspects of the farm: the farmhouse and workers, the gardens, orchard, meadows, arable grounds, the vineyard, and the warrens, woods and park. It covers everything from how to design a farmhouse to distilling cider and raising peacocks. Its structure means that details of the housewife's work are scattered throughout; for instance, bread-making appears in the chapter on arable farming. However, chapter 11 of book 1 deals specifically with 'the condition and state of a huswife'. The opening of this chapter is informative, and worth quoting at length:

> I doe not find the state or place of a Huswife or Dairie-woman to be of lesse care and dilligence than the office of her Husband, understood alwayes, that the woman is acquited of Field matters, in as much as shee is tyed with matters within the House and base Court (the Horses excepted) as the husband is tyed to doe what concerneth him, even all the business of the Field. Likewise, according to our custome in France, Countrie women looke unto the things necessarie and requisite about the Kine, Calves, Hogges, Pigges, Pigeons, Geese, Duckes, Peacocks, Hennes, Fesants, and other sorts of Beasts, as well for the feeding them as for the milking of them: making of Butter and Cheese: and the keeping of Lard to dress the labouring men their victuals withall. Yea,

---

[71] C. Heresbach, *Foure Bookes of Husbandry* (1586), 3. See J. Thirsk, 'Plough and pen: agricultural writers in the seventeenth century', in T.H. Aston et al. (eds.), *Social Relations and Ideas: Essays in Honour of R.H. Hilton* (Cambridge, 1983), 297–9.

[72] A. McRae, *God Speed the Plough: The Representation of Agrarian England 1500–1660* (Cambridge, 1996), 138–9.

[73] Estienne, *Countrey Farme* (1616), title page.

furthermore they have the charge of the Oven and Cellar: and we leave the handling of Hempe unto them likewise; and also the care of making Webs, of looking to the clipping of Sheepe, of keeping of the Fruits, Hearbes, Rootes, and Seeds: and moreover, of watching and attending the Bees. It is true that the buying and selling of Cattell belongeth unto the man, as also the disposing and laying out of money, together with the hyring and paying of servants wages: But the surplusage to be employed and layed out in pettie matters, as in Linnens, Clothes for the household, and all necessaries of household furniture, that of a certainetie belongeth unto the woman.[74]

It then continues by outlining her moral and Christian outlook, while the following chapter lists 'the remedies which a good huswife must be acquainted withall, for to helpe her people when they be sicke'.[75]

In compiling *The English Housewife*, Markham drew together the scattered advice contained in *The Countrey Farm*, adding material from elsewhere, and adapting it for an English readership.[76] Although the Le Stranges did not acquire this work until 1631, well after Alice had mastered many of the processes described, it provides another, more securely English, summary of the skills expected of a housewife. In the introduction to *The English Housewife*, which was a sequel to *The English Husbandman*, Markham described the contrasting roles of husbandman and housewife in a familiar fashion:

> Having already... passed through those outward parts of husbandry which belong unto the perfect husbandman, who is the father and master of the family, and whose office and employments are ever for the most part abroad, or removed from the house, as in the field or yard; it is now meet that we descend in as orderly a method as we can to the office of our English housewife, who is the mother and mistress of family, and hath her most general employments within the house...[77]

These 'employments' included preparing and administering medicinal remedies; growing herbs and vegetables; cookery; distilling medicines, such as aqua vitae, and foodstuffs, such as vinegar; preserving wine; processing of wool, hemp and flax into cloth; running a dairy and making butter and cheese; making malt; brewing beer and ale; and baking bread. The book describes all these processes in some detail.[78]

The husbandry manuals say little about women's managerial functions, such as keeping accounts or running an estate, nor do they dwell on women's roles within the family bringing up children and directing servants, as the marriage advice books do. It is not always clear what type of woman is being addressed. *The Countrey Farme* includes the tell-tale phrase that the housewife should 'give good account unto the Mistress or Lord', indicating that the woman envisaged is an elite servant,

---

[74] Estienne, *Countrey Farme*, 38.
[75] Estienne, *Countrey Farme*, 39.
[76] M.R. Best, 'Introduction', in G. Markham, *The English Housewife*, ed. M.R. Best (Montreal, 1986), xi–lviii.
[77] Markham, *English Housewife*, 5.
[78] For a more detailed analysis of *English Housewife*, see M. Roberts, '"To bridle the falsehood of unconscionable workmen, and for her own satisfaction": what the Jacobean housewife needed to know about men's work, and why', *Labour History Review* 63:1 (1998), 15–25.

perhaps the wife of the bailiff managing the home farm.[79] *The English Housewife* is more indeterminate. As Wall notes, 'Markham writes for the wife of a large landed estate, but assumes her to have yeoman's values.'[80] Some of the advice, such as elaborate cookery recipes, is clearly aimed at elite women; others, such as how to make pottage, less so. This need not concern us greatly, however. The gentlewoman could accept advice on keeping pigs and milking cows in the same way a gentleman read advice on ploughing and keeping cattle: the expectation was not that he or she should do the work themselves, but that they should understand the processes which lay within their sphere of responsibility, and be able to direct the employees who did the work in a competent and informative manner. It is as evidence of these spheres of responsibility that both marriage advice books and husbandry manuals are so useful.

The advice books describe an ideal: how far did Alice Le Strange conform to this depiction of the ideal housewife? Her areas of responsibility fit closely with the list of skills provided by Estienne and Markham, indicating that the tasks listed in these books were not an old-fashioned 'fantasy' of self-sufficiency that commentators such as Wall have assumed.[81] Alice was reputed to be 'skilled in surgery' and purchased both medicinal ingredients and ready-made medicines for the household.[82] The kitchen accounts demonstrate that she oversaw both garden and kitchen. The Le Stranges employed a male gardener and a male cook, although an anecdote in Nicholas Le Strange's *Book of Jests* describes Alice and her daughter-in-law Anne skinning rabbits in the kitchen, showing that food preparation was sometimes undertaken by the women themselves.[83] Alice owned at least three limbecks, which would have allowed her to distil aqua vitae and vinegar, although aqua vitae was also purchased ready-made. Hemp seed was purchased and labourers were employed to process hemp into rope for use in the farm and household. Alice oversaw the production of textiles by local workers, providing them with wool to card and spin, and then giving yarn to knitters and weavers to make hose and cloth for the household.[84] The dairy was one of Alice's areas of special interest. The household brewed its own beer every fortnight: the actual work was done by the coachman, but, again, the kitchen accounts indicate that it was Alice who oversaw this process. Bread was baked in the Hall's kitchens, with grain produced on the home farm and elsewhere on the estate. The kitchen accounts reveal Alice's management of the piggery, to supply bacon and pork for the household. It is clear that Alice Le Strange, like Lady Anne Berkeley, was an accomplished 'country housewife'. Alice Le Strange also demonstrates how the two strands of a wife's ideal behaviour, subjection and capability, were not necessarily contradictory. There is

---

[79] Estienne, *Countrey Farme*, 38, and McRae, *God Speed the Plough*, 138–9, on the intended elite readership of the book.
[80] W. Wall, *Staging Domesticity: Household Work and English Identity in Early Modern Drama* (Cambridge, 2002), 37.
[81] Wall, *Staging Domesticity*, 40.
[82] See Chapter 4: Medical care.
[83] N. Le Strange, *Merry Passages and Jeasts*, ed. H.F. Lippincott (Salzburg, 1974), 80.
[84] See Chapter 3: The acquisition of clothing and furnishings.

little evidence of her being anything other than obedient to her husband's will. He, as the marriage advice literature advised, gave her the freedom to run her house with little interference. She did so with housewifely efficiency, using the account-keeping skills that many gentlewomen were proficient in. He recognized her abilities and gradually delegated more tasks to her, relating to the estate as well as the house.

Did Alice keep to the house, as well as keeping house? Neither Hamon nor Alice took part in a London season. Her trips to the capital were infrequent, although she travelled to Norwich once or twice a year. The very extent of her accounting, farming and estate management responsibilities kept her at home, although not literally within the house. The insistence on the division between inside and outside in female and male spheres of action and responsibility, universal in the advice texts examined, was problematic for women of all levels of wealth, and always seems to have been interpreted with flexibility.[85] Lower down the social scale, the farming and food-processing activities under women's care were predominantly located in or near the house, but women were also needed in the fields at time of peak labour demand, and frequently made trips to market to sell produce such as butter and eggs.[86] For gentlewomen responsibility for the house seems often to have extended to the estate, or at least those parts of the estate that were located near the family's home. Gentlemen did indeed tend to take on those responsibilities that required 'being abroad', that is, away from home altogether in London, or elsewhere. From the perspective of the gentleman, the more home-bound wife was the obvious person to oversee the day-to-day running of aspects of the estate as well as the household. In short, Alice was an ideal housewife by early seventeenth-century norms.

TWO OTHER NORFOLK FAMILIES

Not all gentlewomen had the opportunity to develop the range of activities undertaken by Alice, because, as we have stressed, it depended on choices made by the husband as to both the lifestyle the couple led and the degree of responsibility he chose to afford to his wife. This can be illustrated by offering a number of comparisons with Alice Le Strange's experience, drawn from two other late sixteenth- and early seventeenth-century Norfolk households: the Townshends and Hobarts. The Townshends of Raynham were friends of the Le Stranges: Sir Roger Townshend (1595–1637) was a close friend of Sir John Spelman, Hamon's friend and cousin, who married Roger's sister Anne Townshend. The Hobarts of Blicking were wealthy relations of the Le Stranges.

---

[85] A. Flather, *Gender and Space in Early Modern England* (Woodbridge, 2007).
[86] M. Roberts, '"Words they are women and deeds they are men": images of work and gender in early modern England', in L. Charles and L. Duffin (eds.), *Women and Work in Pre-Industrial England* (London, 1985).

Jane Stanhope (d.1617/18) married Sir Roger Townshend of Raynham Hall in 1566 with an unusually generous dower agreement. The couple had two surviving sons and spent much of their time at court rather than in Norfolk. When Sir Roger died in 1590 Jane received a life interest in most of his lands, giving her an income of around £1000 a year. She remarried in 1597 to Henry Lord Berkeley, but seems to have continued to lead a life independent from her new husband. She kept her own accounts and her surviving personal account book for 1597–1606 demonstrates that she had complete control of all her landed property. This was substantial. Not only did she hold the lands left her by her first husband, but she also purchased lands from her sons when they became heavily indebted (partly because her dower restricted their income). She bought two Norfolk manors from her son and heir John Townshend for £2000, and the Wivenhoe estate in Essex from her second son Robert for £2272. Despite having possession of Raynham Hall she built herself a new house at Walton-on-Thames between 1602 and 1607, which she later sold to purchase a house in Kensington. She also owned a house at the Barbican in London. By the time of her death her income exceeded £2500 a year. She settled the majority of her property on her grandson and ward, Sir Roger Townshend (1595–1637), the son of her son John, as well as giving his sister Anne £2000 for her marriage portion. Her will reveals that like many Norfolk gentlewomen she owned extensive flocks of sheep, 800 of which were left to her steward and the rest to Sir Roger. Lady Jane Berkeley was a formidable and shrewd business-woman. Her particular forte seems to have been property dealings, many with close family members, demonstrating a thorough understanding of the law and a willingness to be ruthless on occasion. She was notable in retaining the independent lifestyle of a widow despite a second marriage which also brought her increased status and wealth.[87]

Her daughter-in-law, Anne, was less fortunate. Anne was one of the three daughters and heiresses of Nathaniel Bacon of Stiffkey. She and her sisters were well educated, first by a schoolmaster at home and later at the school of Mr Sayers and his wife at Dickleborough. She was married to Sir John Townshend in 1593 at the age of twenty. The couple had two sons and a daughter but the marriage was not happy. Anne had a sheltered upbringing in Norfolk, much like that of Alice Le Strange, while her husband was a courtier and military man. Sir John became increasingly heavily indebted. The couple initially had no house of their own as Raynham Hall had been leased out. Their marriage agreement stipulated that they would reside with Anne's parents at Stiffkey for the first two years, but this broke down after a disagreement between Nathaniel and John, leaving the couple to lodge with friends at Melton Constable. They stayed there until 1597, when the lease on Raynham finally fell in. Life at Raynham was possibly no happier, as in 1603 Sir John seems to have been planning to let the house out again and go abroad, leaving his wife and children with no support, much to Anne's alarm. Before this plan could be carried out he was killed in a duel, dying in August 1603. Anne's troubles

---

[87] L. Campbell, 'Sir Roger Townshend and his Family: A Study of Gentry Life in Early Seventeenth Century Norfolk', Ph.D. thesis (East Anglia, 1990), 5–10, 133–6, 200–9.

did not end at this point. Her modest jointure was reduced from £333 to £250 by legal action from her mother-in-law, the result of Sir John's indebtedness. Lady Jane Berkeley also purchased the wardship of Anne's son, her grandson, Roger Townshend, who was then eight years old, removing him legally from his mother's control.

Despite this, Anne remained on respectful terms with Lady Berkeley and does seem to have retained contact and influence over her son. She lived quietly at Heydon on one of the Townshend's properties. After 1616, when Roger came of age, she received her full dower and more, as a valuation of 1618 notes that she had property worth £555 a year. Despite her restricted means she seems to have managed what she had well, taking an interest in farming and estate management, and was trusted by her son to manage his affairs on the Raynham estate when he was absent.[88] She managed her estate directly but audited her servants' accounts rather than keeping them herself.[89] She died in 1622. Anne, therefore, represents a woman who might have blossomed into the competent manager of a large household and estate in the model of Alice Le Strange, but was thwarted by circumstances: an unhappy marriage, indebted husband and over-bearing mother-in-law. Instead, she was left to make a modest success of her widowhood.

Dorothy Bell, Sir Hamon Le Strange's aunt (his mother's sister), married Sir Henry Hobart in 1590. They had eight surviving sons and three daughters. Unlike the Le Stranges or Townshends, Sir Henry was a self-made man, the younger son of a minor gentry family. He received no inheritance in land, trained as a lawyer, and slowly accrued great wealth through public office, service at court and a highly successful legal career. His wife brought him a modest dowry of £500, and he purchased no landed estate until 1596, soon after his appointment as Steward of the City of Norwich. Between 1596 and his death in 1625 he assembled a Norfolk estate worth £5000 a year, and succeeded Sir Edward Coke as Lord Chief Justice and Sir Francis Bacon as Chancellor to the Prince of Wales. Sir Henry Hobart's upwardly mobile career required constant modification of his lifestyle and living arrangements.[90]

In 1597 he established his family at Intwood Hall, a few miles south of Norwich, but in 1609 acquired Chapelfield House, as a gift from the corporation of Norwich. Then in 1616 he purchased the prestigious but dilapidated Blickling Hall from Lady Agnes Clere. The process of rebuilding Blickling was still under way at the time of his death. In addition he also purchased a London property, Highgate House, in 1624. Initially Sir Henry Hobart seems to have exercised close control over his affairs, relying on trusted family members, attorneys and servants to perform particular tasks. However, his plans to rebuild Blickling coincided with his appointment as Judge of Assize for the Midland Circuit and led to a more formal structure of household and estate accounting. A comprehensive series of

---

[88] Campbell, 'Sir Roger Townshend', 1–15, 120–45, 209–16.
[89] NRO, Bradfer Lawrence, MS vii b(i).
[90] E.M. Griffiths, 'The Management of Two East Norfolk Estates in the Seventeenth Century, Blickling and Felbrigg', Ph.D. thesis (East Anglia, 1988). For acquisition of the estate, see 78.

personal and household accounts for 1621–5 survives from this period, as well as a full account for the Norfolk Estate, and building accounts for Blickling Hall.[91] The personal and household accounts were kept by a servant, Richard Glover, who acted as receiver-general for the household and estate.

In the accounts Glover provided information on income and expenditure, and balanced the accounts every three months. By this date Hobart's income from rents alone exceeded £6000 a year, and was augmented by interest on loans, legal fees and income from offices. Annual allowances were paid to family members. In 1622 Lady Dorothy Hobart received £200 for herself, with £80 a year each for her two younger daughters. Her older sons received £400, £120, and £100 respectively. The house steward, Mr Trench, received £100 a quarter, with further household expenditure itemized in the account. In 1622, Trench was dismissed after Glover found that he had defrauded the brewer's bills, and Sir Henry gave responsibility for household expenditure to Lady Dorothy. She proved unequal to the task, and exceeded her allowance of £1200 a year. Sir Henry made her repay the extra money from her allowance at a rate of £25 a quarter, and appointed a new household steward in 1625. It is unclear why Lady Dorothy was unsuccessful in managing the extra responsibility allotted to her in 1622: did she lack the experience, was she overburdened with other tasks such as caring for her children, was the household too complex, or was her husband too demanding? Certainly the household had none of the stability that allowed Alice Le Strange to build up her administrative systems over a period of years with gradual improvements. The sums of money and multiple houses involved made it a much more difficult business to manage.

Sir Henry and Lady Dorothy Hobart's son and heir, Sir John Hobart (1593–1647), was the chief beneficiary of his father's accumulated wealth. He married twice, both times to aristocratic brides: Phillipa Sydney, the daughter of the Earl of Leicester, in 1616 and Frances Egerton, the daughter of the Earl of Bridgewater, in 1622. After his first marriage, his father allowed him £400 a year. This figure proved inadequate, leaving Sir John with debts of £1650, which were repaid by his second wife. On his father's death in 1625 he inherited an estate worth £2500 a year. Unlike his father he had no significant income other than from his lands, yet he aimed to maintain the lifestyle of a leading county gentleman. He finished the rebuilding of Blickling Hall, furnished it and improved the surrounding park, as well as maintaining houses at Highgate in London and Chapelfield in Norwich. His political interests as an MP in the 1620s and 1640s meant that the family spent long periods in London. Unlike Alice Le Strange, Lady Frances Hobart travelled with her husband and thus spent much of her time away from the family home at Blickling. Despite the deaths of four younger brothers in the 1630s and of Lady Dorothy in 1641, which increased Sir John's income to over £4000 a year, the couple struggled to make ends meet and became increasingly indebted.[92]

Fortunately, Lady Frances Hobart was a better financial manager than her mother-in-law. A biography written by her chaplain, John Collinges, notes that

---

[91] NRO, Box T68A; NRO, 10191 25A1.
[92] Griffiths, 'Two East Norfolk Estates', 40–1, 246–53.

she was renowned for her beauty, education, good works and strongly held religious beliefs. The eldest of eight daughters, she received an education 'proper to her noble station' from French governesses, who taught her to sing, dance and play the lute in preparation for a life at court. Interestingly, however, she was also taught more practical skills: to 'cast accounts nimbly and exactly and to use her Needle and order the affairs of the Household', things which, her chaplain noted, 'were to her and to her dear husband of extraordinary advantage'. Like Alice Le Strange, she not only attended to household affairs 'within doors', but also to those that were 'ordinarily no women's employment. . . . Perceiving her husband ingaged in great debt, she undertook the management of his whole estate, auditing all his account and that to so good a purpose that she shortened his debt by £6000.'[93] Lady Frances instigated new accounting systems for the estate and the household, and initiated schemes of estate improvement. However, despite her managerial control of the couple's financial affairs, her lifestyle did not permit her to take day-to-day responsibility for the accounts and supervision of the estate in the manner of Alice Le Strange. These routine tasks were still delegated to an array of household servants. Being away in London for much of the time, nor was it possible for her to initiate and oversee the home-production of food and drink as Alice did. Like many women, Lady Frances was only able to exercise her full management talents as a widow, although on a reduced income. She retired to the Chapelfield House and, according to Collinges, cared for her 'family of servants' and worked on her 'receipts and disbursements' until her death in 1665. She managed her jointure with skill, bequeathing to her nephew a well-modernized estate.[94]

These case studies demonstrate the varied models of management undertaken and allowed to gentlewomen in seventeenth-century Norfolk. Alice's history stands out for its unusual stability: in part, merely a demographic accident of her and her husband's long lives, but also a choice made by Hamon, to remain at home in the country and allow his wife many responsibilities. Alice's upbringing, as a modest and practical country gentlewoman, allowed her to take full advantage of this lifestyle to develop her talents in household, farm and estate management. Anne Townshend might have been another woman in this mould, had her husband not been so difficult and unappreciative. By contrast Dorothy Hobart was perhaps overwhelmed by her husband's increased income, itinerant lifestyle and their numerous children: when offered more managerial responsibility, she found the task difficult. Jane Berkeley and Frances Hobart were rather different women, moving as they did in aristocratic circles. Both seem to have been well educated and very able, at times even dominating their husbands. Jane Berkeley displayed a formidable legal knowledge: aided by contacts at court, and at the expense of some of her own family, she excelled in property transactions. Frances Hobart pulled back her husband from severe indebtedness by acting as his receiver-general.

---

[93] Collinges, *Par Nobile*.
[94] Griffiths, 'Two East Norfolk Estates', 323–6.

CONCLUSION

It was the lifestyle chosen by husbands, to reside in London, rural Norfolk or elsewhere, which set the overall stamp on patterns of consumption in gentry households. Provisioning a stable rural household like that of the Le Stranges with food was a different, and easier, proposition from provisioning a household which spent much of each year in London rather than at home in Blickling, like the Hobarts. On the other hand, the Hobarts' mobile lifestyle gave them better access to and knowledge of luxury goods, in both London and Norwich, the acquisition of which was more complicated for the Le Stranges. Husbands also had the power to determine the division of managerial labour within the household. It was common for gentlewomen to have responsibility for keeping accounts and managing consumption, but not all gentlewomen were given this opportunity, and not all had the necessary ability or inclination if they were. Often this job was performed by professional male stewards. However, the most able women, if given the freedom by their husbands, extended their activities beyond household management into the related areas of farming and estate management. Historians have perhaps underestimated the degree to which gentlewomen's education and upbringing prepared them for these roles. Advice literature was unequivocal in asserting women's subjection and obedience to their husbands: in other words, the husband's right to make the final choice in any management decision concerning the couple's wealth and lifestyle. However, the same literature is also consistent in suggesting a wide range of responsibilities and skills that were suitable for women: the care of children, supervision of servants, housekeeping and housewifery. Husbandry guides demonstrate the extent to which country housewifery involved practical farming activities as well as food processing, cookery, medicine and textile production. Marriage advice literature, despite its conservatism, saw a role for housewives to create and manage income as well as expenditure. It seems unlikely that Alice Le Strange would have perceived herself as a radical or unusually assertive woman when taking on her account-keeping and management activities. Instead, she and Hamon could look back at precedents like Anne Le Strange in the sixteenth century and feel comfortable in the knowledge that, according to the books in their library, Alice was fulfilling the role of an ideal housewife, under her husband's benevolent and appreciative control.

3

The Acquisition of Goods

> ...*paid to Lock the tailor for apparel and £6 for a debt due unto him from my uncle Roger Le Strange: £22 10s*[1]

The process of domestic consumption outlined in Chapter 1 involves planning, acquisition and then use. Why use the term acquisition and not shopping or purchases? As Kowaleski-Wallace has pointed out, the term 'shopping' first came into use in the second half of the eighteenth century to describe the pleasurable experience of browsing and purchasing in urban shops.[2] The building of the London Exchanges in the late sixteenth and early seventeenth centuries demonstrates that this was not an eighteenth-century innovation, even though it was not described as shopping in the earlier period.[3] Purchasing, in the sense of buying goods and services for money, has a much longer history, stretching back at least to the Roman period. But acquisition is a broader term, it encompasses the full range of means by which items could be obtained for the household. In the case of the Le Stranges this meant home production; gifts; the commissioning of items from craftsmen, sometimes with materials provided, sometimes not; and the purchase of ready-made items new and second-hand. There are two influential models of how methods of acquisition have changed over time. One, dominant in economic history and peasant studies, traces the transition from home production and self-sufficiency to reliance on commodities purchased in the market.[4] The other, found in anthropology, describes the transition from gifts to commodities as the dominant means of exchange.[5] Both of these models imply a dualism that misrepresents the complexity of historical experience. The two extremes of complete home production and complete reliance on the market are, in fact, extremely rare. Even in modern, market-orientated societies, many households engage in forms of

---

[1] Alice Le Strange, disbursement accounts (1611), LEST/P6.
[2] E. Kowaleski-Wallace, *Consuming Subjects: Women, Shopping and Business in the Eighteenth Century* (New York, 1997), 75, 77.
[3] L. Peck, *Consuming Splendor: Society and Culture in Seventeenth-Century England* (Cambridge, 2005), 42–5.
[4] R. Britnell, *The Commercialisation of English Society 1000–1500* (Cambridge, 1993); E. Wolf, *Peasants* (London, 1966), ch. 2; T. Scott (ed.), *The Peasantries of Europe: From the Fourteenth to the Eighteenth Centuries* (London, 1988).
[5] J. Carrier, *Gifts and Commodities: Exchange and Western Capitalism since 1700* (London, 1995), ch. 1; M. Osteen, 'Gift or commodity', in M. Osteen (ed.), *The Question of the Gift: Essays across Disciplines* (London, 2002); A.E. Komter (ed.), *The Gift: An Interdisciplinary Perspective* (Amsterdam, 1996).

home production, such as growing vegetables, knitting or, most commonly, preparing food and drink.

The transition from home production to market purchases occurred early in England. By the late thirteenth century many households in rural England did not own enough land to support themselves independently and relied on various forms of exchange and commerce. The poorest households were often the most market dependent, reliant on selling labour and purchasing basic foodstuffs as well as other goods.[6] It was large wealthy households that persisted longest in producing a significant proportion of their foodstuffs and some textiles at home, or at least on their own estates. This pattern is observed in the eighteenth century and is evident in the Le Strange accounts a century earlier.[7] However, these activities were combined with the purchase of a wide range of goods produced in England and abroad. Gift exchange remained a significant element of elite households' food economy. This chapter uses a number of approaches to illuminate the process of acquiring goods in the early seventeenth century. First it examines expenditure: the amount the Le Stranges spent and the proportion spent on different types of goods. Second, it looks at purchases from towns, particularly London. Although the accounts only occasionally record where particular items were bought, it is possible to count the number of trips made to London, Norwich and King's Lynn by the Le Stranges and their servants. These trips can then be linked to clusters of luxury items recorded in the accounts. Later sections look in detail at acquisitions in two significant areas of consumption: clothing and furnishings, and food and drink. They illustrate the multiple routes by which these items were acquired. The first demonstrates the key role played by craftsmen in providing finished articles for the Le Strange household; the second emphasizes the importance of home production and the gift economy, alongside purchases.

DOMESTIC EXPENDITURE

Household accounts record patterns of expenditure. Not everything in the Le Strange household incurred expense when it was acquired; for instance, some furnishings, and Hunstanton Hall itself, were inherited, and some food was received as gifts. But the great majority of consumption activities did. Even home-produced food generated costs in terms of equipment, labour and the purchase of livestock, which were recorded in the kitchen accounts. This section analyses the Le Stranges' pattern of expenditure on 'domestic consumption'. The Le Strange household can be imagined as a large business, which was primarily concerned with the maintenance of the estate as a source of income and status, and of the family's political and dynastic ambitions. Spending on these areas is here

---

[6] C. Dyer, *Standards of Living in the Later Middle Ages: Social Change in England c.1200–1520* (Cambridge, 1989), ch. 5.
[7] M. Girouard, *Life in the English Country House* (New Haven, 1978), 217; P.A. Sambrook and P. Brears (eds.), *The Country House Kitchen 1650–1900* (Stroud, 1997).

regarded as 'non-domestic', and is discussed more fully in Chapter 6, which examines expenditure and loans across the life cycle of Hamon and Alice Le Strange. This section focuses on those categories which can been defined as domestic: food, clothing, furnishings, travel, wages, childcare and education and medical care.

Alice Le Strange attempted a degree of categorization herself within the accounts. From 1613 she recorded expenses relating to food in separate 'household books' or kitchen accounts. From 1620 she separated building accounts into distinct sections within the disbursement accounts. The household books include expenditure on domestic fuel, agricultural labour and kitchen equipment—that is, the expenses of food production—as well as actual foodstuffs. We have not attempted to disaggregate them, as these totals are closer to the cost of the foods consumed than food purchases alone. Even for the late seventeenth and early eighteenth centuries, Weatherill found that a significant proportion of expenses went on food production as well as purchases in rural households.[8] The building accounts mix expenditure on the extension, improvement and upkeep of the Le Stranges' own house and farm buildings at Hunstanton Hall, which might be considered domestic consumption, with the expenses for building and improving houses and farm buildings elsewhere on the estate. As a result they are excluded from our current discussion.[9] Servants' wages are easy enough to place in a 'wages' category of expenditure, but the wages of other employees have been categorized according to their activities: agricultural labourers under food, building labourers under building work, tailors, weavers and shoemakers under textiles and clothing, and so on.

Gross expenditure by the Le Strange household averaged below £1000 a year in the 1610s, rising to over £2000 in the 1620s, reaching a peak of over £3500 in the 1630s, and falling back to below £3000 in the 1640s. The gross totals include the repayment of loans and some large land transactions in which manors were bought and sold with little net gain. With these payments removed, expenditure followed a similar pattern of change over time, but averaged at £2200 a year in the period 1620–50, corresponding closely with the Le Stranges' income. With the exception of the 1610s, when Alice and Hamon did not yet have the benefit of their full estate, expenditure categorized as non-domestic outweighed domestic expenditure. Family allowances, maintaining and improving the estate, political and legal expenses, and building work took up the majority of expenses. Domestic expenditure is broken down into a number of categories in Table 3.1. 'Household' was consistently the largest, varying between 31 per cent and 51 per cent of the average total domestic consumption expenditure across the four decades from 1610 to 1649. The household category includes all the expenses recorded in the kitchen accounts relating to food purchases and production, as well as fuel and lighting, and other purchases of small household items such as storage containers and kitchen utensils, some of which were recorded in the disbursement accounts. In the years

---

[8] L. Weatherill, *Consumer Behaviour and Material Culture in Britain 1660–1760* (London, 1988), 133–4.
[9] See Chapter 7: Building and estate improvement.

1610–12 household expenses made up only 5–15 per cent of the total, probably because of poor recording. This rose to a more believable average 43 per cent for 1613–19, once the kitchen accounts were begun.[10]

Textiles and clothing were the next most costly category, followed by 'London, luxury and lifestyle'. These two categories are closely related. The London category includes the cost of trips to London, as well as luxury items which were clearly purchased on trips to the capital. This includes some clothing and textiles. 'Luxuries and lifestyle' encompasses items specific to the gentry lifestyle and consumption patterns, including expensive furnishings and luxury household ware such as silverware and glass, paintings, armour, books, scientific instruments, hawks and hawking equipment, and money lost at bowls and cards. Many of these items were purchased in London, although this is not always clear in the accounts, and some came from Norwich. The 'horses and travel' category also contains characteristically elite expenditure on multiple horses and coaches, as well as the cost of transporting goods and letters. 'Miscellaneous bills' includes all those entries which noted bills but lacked sufficient detail for further categorization: these declined over time as Alice became more rigorous in her accounting practices.[11] Childcare and education and medical care are both small but distinctive categories of expenditure. Although there was some overlap between medicines and foods, medicines were normally recorded in the disbursement accounts and food in the kitchen accounts.

The categories used in Table 3.1 are exclusive: they do not overlap. Table 3.2 provides a more detailed examination of the sixteen years between 1610 and 1625, using inclusive categories for food and for textiles and clothing. For food it uses the totals from the kitchen accounts alone. For textiles and clothing it uses a category from the database, which contained all items defined as textiles and clothing. In 1620 the Le Stranges' average yearly domestic expenditure jumped from around £550 to around £800, reflecting their increased income. Interestingly the proportion spent on the different categories shows no obvious shift before and after that date: the proportion spent on food rose slightly, while that spent on textiles remained almost exactly the same.[12] More significant were the considerable annual variations, with expenditure on food varying from 19 per cent to 50 per cent, and that on textiles and clothing varying from 8 per cent to 30 per cent.

The earliest estimates of domestic expenditure on a national level were calculated by Gregory King in the late seventeenth century. In 1695 he estimated per capita expenditure on diet, clothing and other expenses for the whole of the English population divided into bands of total expenditure.[13] He expected expenditure on

---

[10] This artificially inflates the proportion spent on textiles in 1610–12: see Table 3.2.
[11] Bills form a large proportion in the accounts of 1606–9, which were kept by Sir Hamon Le Strange.
[12] Comparing 1613–19 and 1620–5, the proportion of expenditure recorded in the household books (food) rose from 36.5 per cent to 38.4 per cent while that on textiles fell from 17.1 per cent to 16.7 per cent.
[13] G. King, 'The LCC Burns journal', in P. Laslett (ed.), *The Earliest Classics* (New Jersey, 1973), 210; G.S. Holmes, 'Gregory King and the social structure of pre-industrial England', *Transactions of the Royal Historical Society* 5th series 27 (1977), 41–68; N.B. Harte, 'The economics of clothing in the late seventeenth century', *Textile History* 22:2 (1991), 277–96.

Table 3.1. Average expenditure per year by decade on domestic consumption by category

	1610–19	1620–9	1630–9	1640–9	1610–53
(a) In £s					
Household	183	349	454	410	352
Textiles and clothing	112	108	170	35	99
London, luxuries and lifestyle	41	129	116	90	87
Wages	52	71	87	92	76
Horses and travel	44	79	87	73	69
Miscellaneous bills	75	95	25	14	52
Childcare and education	8	52	46	40	33
Medicine and medical care	8	11	8	4	8
Total	523	894	993	758	776
(b) Percentages					
Household	35	39	46	54	45
Textiles and clothing	21	12	17	5	13
London, luxury and lifestyle	8	14	12	13	11
Wages	10	8	9	12	10
Horses and travel	8	9	9	10	9
Miscellaneous bills	14	11	3	2	7
Childcare and education	2	6	5	5	4
Medicine and medical care	2	1	1	1	1
Total	100	100	102	102	100

Source: Le Strange disbursement accounts, 1610–53; LEST/P6, P7, P10.

Table 3.2. Annual expenditure on food and textiles, 1610–25

	Kitchen accounts, £	Textiles and clothing, £	Total domestic consumption expenditure, £	Kitchen accounts, % of total	Textiles and clothing, % of total
1610	–	130	336	–	38.7
1611	–	115	306	–	37.6
1612	–	196	622	–	31.5
1613	198	53	522	37.9	10.1
1614	187	110	418	44.7	26.3
1615	189	62	574	32.9	10.8
1616	222	87	572	38.8	15.2
1617	183	103	672	27.2	15.3
1618	219	134	574	38.2	23.3
1619	214	115	540	39.6	21.3
1620	162	256	846	19.1	30.3
1621	268	146	842	31.8	17.3
1622	355	133	704	50.4	18.9
1623	413	131	837	49.3	15.7
1624	338	78	827	40.9	9.4
1625	327	63	790	41.4	8.0

Source: Le Strange disbursement and kitchen accounts, 1610–25; LEST/P6, P7, P8.

food to decline from 69 per cent to 24 per cent as overall wealth rose. In doing so he anticipated 'Engels Law', the nineteenth-century theory which states that, because the need for food is relatively inflexible compared with other wants, expenditure on food declines proportionally as wealth increases.[14] King expected expenditure on clothing to follow a 'U'-shaped curve, according to levels of wealth.[15] The poorest individuals were only able to devote a small proportion of expenditure to clothing. Those who spent just under £27 a year in total devoted the largest proportion to clothing: 28 per cent. Wealthier groups spent proportionally less, with King estimating that those who spent £500–1000 a year devoted 15 per cent of expenses to clothing.

However, when compared with concrete examples of expenditure taken from household accounts, such as those of the Le Stranges, those tabulated by Weatherill for the late seventeenth and early eighteenth centuries, and King's record of expenditure for his own household, King's national estimates can be shown to be misleading in a number of ways.[16] First, total wealth (or total expenditure) caused less variation in overall patterns of expenditure than King predicted. Second, King underestimated expenditure on food, partly as a result of overestimating expenditure on clothing. Twenty per cent of expenditure in King's own household went on clothing and household textiles, compared with King's estimate of 35 per cent on apparel alone for his wealth band.[17] In the accounts studied by Weatherill, which date from the 1690s to 1740s, no household allotted more than 16 per cent of expenditure to clothing. The poorest household she analysed, the Lathams, with an annual expenditure of £17, spent only 11 per cent on textiles, rather than the 22 per cent predicted by King for individuals (not households) spending around £7 a year.[18] The Le Stranges spent the predicted proportion, but only if we include household textiles as well as clothing: as is shown in Chapter 5, household textiles made up a significant proportion. Rather than a 'U'-shaped curve, these figures suggest that spending on clothing and textiles was quite flat, increasing in proportion to overall spending.

The households analysed by Weatherill spent between 72 per cent and 43 per cent on food purchases and production.[19] The need to include food production costs, which were also partly the costs of commercial farming, may inflate these figures somewhat. Nonetheless, the wealthiest household she studied, that of Lady Griselle Baillie, whose household did not produce food, still spent 45 per cent of her £630 expenditure a year on food, compared with the 24–27 per cent anticipated by King.[20] This accords well with the Le Stranges' pattern of spending,

---

[14] C. Shammas, *The Pre-Industrial Consumer in England and America* (Oxford, 1990), 122.
[15] Harte, 'Economics of clothing', 291.
[16] Weatherill, *Consumer Behaviour*, 133; King, 'Burns journal', 250 (also printed in Harte, 'Economics of clothing', 283).
[17] King, 'Burns journal', 250.
[18] Weatherill, *Consumer Behaviour*, 133.
[19] With the exception of Rachel Pengelly 1700–8, where Weatherill notes the existence of a maintenance agreement which is not clearly recorded; *Consumer Behaviour*, 126–7.
[20] Weatherill, *Consumer Behaviour*, 133; King, 'Burns journal', 210.

shown in Table 3.2. Their expenditure on food did not decrease as a proportion of overall expenditure when overall expenditure increased: in fact, it increased slightly. It seems that in early modern England expenditure on food, like that on other categories, increased with wealth. One response to increased wealth was to employ more servants, another was to entertain larger numbers of guests at social events based on the consumption of food; both increased the food expenditure recorded in household accounts. Even individual food expenditure was actually quite flexible. As is shown in Chapter 4, the gentry ate more meat, more varieties of meat, fish, fruit and vegetables, and more imported products than ordinary households. They spent money accessing food that was very fresh, out of season, or preserved in sugar. Food, despite being a necessity, could also be a luxury. Engel's law was developed in the mid-nineteenth century by observing the impact of falling food prices on working-class expenditure. Rather than being a law, it is culturally specific: it does not seem to apply to early modern England.[21]

URBAN SHOPPING

Studies of elite consumption in Elizabethan and early seventeenth-century England all point to the crucial role played by London. Fisher's pioneering article described London as the gentry's 'centre of conspicuous consumption'.[22] Stone listed 'the pleasures and vanities of London' as one of 'the four main forms' of conspicuous consumption that drove English aristocracy into debt and argued that the London season developed rapidly between 1590 and 1620.[23] McCracken places the draw of court and of London at the centre of 'a spectacular consumer boom' amongst the nobility in Elizabethan England.[24] Royal proclamations ordered the gentry and nobility to leave London so they could keep order in the provinces and offer traditional hospitality in their country houses.[25] The draw of London to the English elite, as a place of regular and protracted stays, dates from the middle of Elizabeth's reign.[26] By the first three decades of the seventeenth century it was well established. Its causes were various. The royal court and its culture became more firmly fixed in London. New patterns of education turned London's Inns of Court into finishing schools for country gentlemen. Increased litigation at the

---

[21] Shammas, *Pre-Industrial Consumer*, 131.
[22] F.J. Fisher, 'The development of London as a centre of conspicuous consumption in the sixteenth and seventeenth centuries', in E.M. Carus Wilson (ed.), *Essays in Economic History*, vol. 2 (London, 1962).
[23] L. Stone, *The Crisis of the Aristocracy 1558–1641* (Oxford, 1965), 186, 387. See also Fisher, 'The development of London', 113–14.
[24] G. McCracken, *Culture and Consumption: New Approaches to the Symbolic Character of Consumer Goods and Activities* (Indiana, 1988), 11–12.
[25] F. Heal, 'The crown, the gentry and London: the enforcement of proclamation, 1596–1640', in C. Cross, D. Loades, and J.J. Scarisbrick (eds.), *Law and Government under The Tudors* (Cambridge, 1988), 211–26.
[26] F.J. Fisher, 'London as an engine of economic growth', in P. Corfield and N. B. Harte (eds.), *London and the English Economy, 1500–1700* (London, 1990), 186.

central legal courts required more frequent trips to London. Additionally, private coaches made travel to London less arduous, and more accessible to women, allowing whole families to make the journey. Private coaches were rare before the 1590s, but quickly became common for the gentry.[27] London's economy boomed in this period. London's population grew faster than the country's as a whole, reaching 200,000, (or 5 per cent of England's total population) by 1600 and doubling in size again by 1650.[28] It was England's premier international port, the first place where many new imported products became available. London was a producer of luxury products, with demand spearheaded by the royal court.[29] It was also the first English town where something recognizable as 'shopping', pleasurable browsing of non-essential commodities, came into being.[30] London was the centre of other pleasures and pastimes with the golden age of English drama based on its commercial theatres, first established in the late 1570s.[31]

The government feared that the gentry's presence in London was causing a dangerous decline in the traditional social bonds of the countryside. It relied on the gentry's presence in the regions to keep order: organizing militias, putting down rebellion, and administering local and county courts. It was keen for the gentry to 'keep hospitality', entertaining their tenants and smoothing social tensions on country estates.[32] By 1632, proclamations even recognized the raw economic realities of the situation: money spent in London was impoverishing the rural economy.[33] There was a gendered dimension to this outcry. James I, in a speech to Parliament, singled out women for blame:

> One of the greatest causes of all Gentlemens desire, that have no calling or errand, to dwell in *London*, is apparently the pride of the women: For if they bee wives, then their husbands; if they be maydes, then their father must bring them up to *London*; because the new fashion is to bee had nowhere but in *London*: and here, if they be unmarried, they marre their marriages, and if they be married, they loose their reputations, and rob their husbands purses.[34]

---

[27] Fisher, 'The development of London'; R.M. Smuts, *Court Culture and the Origins of a Royalist Tradition in Early Stuart England* (Philadelphia, 1987), 54; J.F. Merritt, *The Social World of Early Modern Westminster: Abbey, Court and Community 1525–1640* (Manchester, 2005), 141; J. Crofts, *Packhorse, Waggon and Post: Land Carriage and Communications under the Tudors and Stuarts* (London, 1967), 109–24.
[28] J. Boulton, 'London 1540–1700', in P. Clark (ed.) *The Cambridge Urban History of Britain*. Vol. II. *1540–1840* (Cambridge, 2000), 316. National population totals from E.A. Wrigley and R.S. Schofield, *The Population History of England 1541–1871* (Cambridge, 1981), 208.
[29] Merritt, *Early Modern Westminster*, 154.
[30] Merritt, *Early Modern Westminster*, 156–9; Peck, *Consuming Splendor*, 42–5.
[31] A. McRae, *Renaissance Drama* (London, 2003), 3.
[32] Heal, 'The crown, the gentry and London'.
[33] J.F. Larkin (ed.) *Stuart Royal Proclamations*. Vol. II. *Royal Proclamations of King Charles I 1625–1646* (London, 1982), 351.
[34] James I, *The Workes*, 567–8 (italics in original). See also Heal, 'The crown, the gentry and London', 214, for James repeating this argument in his poetry.

Early seventeenth-century drama and literature criticized and ridiculed women as spendthrift shoppers, echoing proverbial hostility to marketing women, and anticipating similar attacks on women as shoppers in eighteenth-century literature.[35] According to these views, women, unlike men, had no excuse for being in London other than to spend money.

Despite all this discussion, the impact of London on the consumption habits of the provincial gentry remains unclear.[36] This section explores the Le Stranges' pattern of interaction with London between 1610 and 1628. It examines which members of the Le Strange household travelled to London, how long they stayed, what was bought, and how much was spent. The role of London is contrasted with that of Norwich and King's Lynn. The rise of the county town as a centre of gentry sociability and leisure is normally associated with the late seventeenth and eighteenth centuries. For Norwich the development occurred earlier. Not just a county town but a provincial capital for the whole of East Anglia, Norwich was England's second largest city with a population of 12,000–13,000 in 1600, reaching 30,000 by 1700.[37] Pound describes sixteenth-century Norwich as 'becoming increasingly a centre of conspicuous consumption—a lesser London'.[38] It was an important centre of the textile industry but had a diversified economy with over 100 different trades by the Elizabethan period.[39] Coach travel benefited centres such as Norwich as well as London, encouraging whole families to travel to the county town when previously only gentlemen had attended for the quarter sessions and assizes. By the late seventeenth century Norwich has 'its own winter season, a copy in miniature of that of London', as well as a 'summer Assizes week' with balls, theatre and shows.[40] The 'genteel custom of public promenading in Chapel Field' dated from at least the sixteenth century.[41] King's Lynn, the closest town to Hunstanton, was much smaller, with a population of *c.*7000 by the 1680s, which had risen from below 3000 in the early sixteenth century. It was nonetheless a busy international port with two weekly markets.[42]

---

[35] Merritt, *Early Modern Westminster*, 156; Peck, *Consuming Splendour*, 67–8; I. Warren, '"Witty offending great ones"? Elite female householders in an early Stuart Westminster parish', *The London Journal*, 32: 3 (2007), 212–13. On market women, see M. Roberts, '"Words they are women and deeds they are men": images of work and gender in early modern England', in L. Charles and L. Duffin (eds.), *Women and Work in Pre-Industrial England* (London, 1985), 153–4; for the eighteenth century, see C. Walsh, 'Shops, shopping, and the art of decision making in eighteenth-century England', in J. Styles and A. Vickery (eds.), *Gender, Taste and Material Culture in Britain and North America, 1700–1830* (New Haven and London, 2006), 164–6.

[36] Although see I. Warren, 'London's cultural impact on the English gentry: the case of Worcestershire, c.1580–1680', *Midland History* 33:2 (2008), 156–78.

[37] P. Corfield, 'A provincial capital in the late seventeenth century: the case of Norwich', in P. Clark (ed.), *The Early Modern Town: A Reader* (London, 1976), 233.

[38] J.F. Pound, 'The social and trade structure of Norwich 1525–1575', in Clark, *The Early Modern Town*, 138.

[39] D.M. Palliser, *The Age of Elizabeth* (London, 1983), 242.

[40] Corfield, 'A provincial capital', 254–5.

[41] A. Dain, 'An enlightened and polite society', in C. Rawcliffe and R. Wilson (eds.), *Norwich since 1550* (London, 2004), 194.

[42] A. Metters, '"Mixed enterprise" in early seventeenth-century King's Lynn', in C. Rawcliffe and R. Virgoe (eds.), *Counties and Communities: Essays on East Anglian History* (Centre for East Anglian

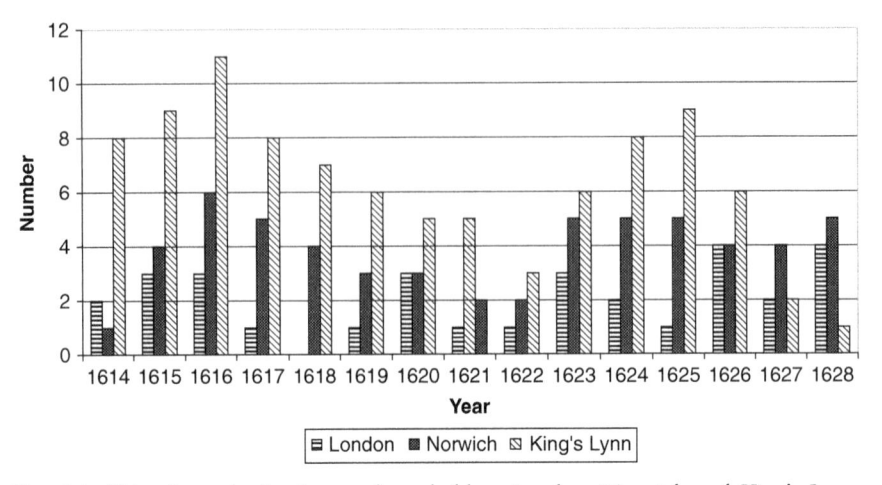

[Figure: Bar chart showing number of trips per year 1614-1628 to London, Norwich, and King's Lynn]

Fig. 3.1. Trips from the Le Strange household to London, Norwich and King's Lynn, 1614–28.
Source: Le Strange disbursement accounts, 1614–28; LEST/P7.

Trips to London, Norwich and King's Lynn by members of the household can be identified in the accounts: they incurred expenses for horsemeat, meals and accommodation at inns. When the Le Stranges stayed with friends they made tips to the servants of that house. The male members of the household travelling alone went on horseback. Servants took carts if boxes needed to be collected. Alice Le Strange and other members of the family travelling with her went by coach. The Le Stranges purchased their first coach in 1606, another in 1617 and a third by 1623.[43] Trips to all these towns were significant ventures; even King's Lynn was eighteen miles away, a return journey requiring an overnight stay or, at the very least, the purchase of food for the horses. Norwich was forty-seven miles away: a one-way journey by coach required at least one overnight stay, and the Le Stranges often did it with two, staying with friends along the way. London was over 120 miles from Hunstanton: a one-way journey by coach required three overnight stays. Figure 3.1 shows the frequency of trips made by members of the Le Strange household to London, Norwich or King's Lynn in the fifteen years from 1614 to 1628. On average, someone from the household visited London twice a year, Norwich four times a year, and King's Lynn six times. There was considerable variation: in 1618 no trips to London were made, while in 1626 and 1628 there were four trips. Boxes and parcels arriving from London quite separately from any trips made are also noted in the accounts. These averaged two a year. Taken

---

Studies, 1996), 225–40; C. Muldrew, *The Economy of Obligation: The Culture of Credit and Social Relations in Early Modern England* (Basingstoke, 1998), 39, 55–7, 69; P. Slack, 'Great and good towns 1540–1700', in Clark (ed.), *Cambridge Urban History*, vol. II, 352.

[43] See Chapter 7: Travel and leisure.

Table 3.3. Who made trips to towns, 1614–28?

	London		Norwich		Total	
	No.	%	No.	%	No.	%
Male servants alone	17	55	29	48	46	50
Hamon or Nicholas Le Strange and male servants	9	29	14	23	23	25
Alice and Hamon Le Strange with others	5	16	18	30	23	25
Total	31	100	61	101	92	100

Source: Le Strange disbursement accounts, 1614–28; LEST/P7.

together this evidence shows that there was no year in the period 1614–28 when goods purchased in London did not arrive at the Le Strange household. Trips to London were most commonly made in early summer: June was the peak month, with 26 per cent of all London trips in 1614–28 made in that month. It was least common to travel up to London in January to March. Trips to Norwich and King's Lynn were more evenly spread throughout the year, but with a dip in the months of February and March, when winter travel conditions and Lent combined to discourage journeys and purchases.

Only male servants travelled alone. Sir Hamon Le Strange or his sons travelled accompanied by male servants. Alice Le Strange travelled only with her husband, as far as can be discerned. Table 3.3 shows that the majority of journeys to London were made by male servants rather than the Le Stranges. The male Le Stranges travelled to London more than twice as often as Alice. Alice Le Strange went to London only five times in the fifteen years from 1614 to 1628. Her first visit to London recorded in the accounts was in June 1617, when she and Hamon stayed for around three weeks and had their portraits painted. Alice made a second three-week trip to London in 1620, when she and Hamon took their two eldest sons to Eton for the first time. Alice and Hamon made another trip in January 1620/1, the longest recorded in the accounts, staying for seventeen weeks. This coincided with Hamon's attendance at Parliament and legal business arising from Alice's father's will, but the probable reason for the length of Alice's stay was that she became pregnant while in London and waited until the early stages of pregnancy had passed before travelling back to Norfolk.[44] There was another short visit in 1626 when Hamon junior enrolled at Lincoln's Inn, followed by a substantial eight-week visit in 1628. The 1628 trip seems to have been carried out mainly for the purpose of shopping, although they also spent £14 8s 8d on 'law charges'. For each of these visits rooms were rented by the week. In 1620–1 their weekly charges were £1 10s for chamber rent for a suite of rooms, and £3 12s in board for a household of nine people: Hamon and Alice Le Strange, their two young children, Elizabeth and

---

[44] Miscarriage is more likely in early pregnancy. Her last child, Mary Le Strange, was born in October 1621.

Roger, a gentlewoman, a maid servant and three male servants. The cost of travel both ways, 'for diet, horsemeat and money given away' was £18 7s 8d in 1620. Overnight stays at Barton Mills (just outside Mildenhall in Suffolk), Cambridge and Ware were typical of the London journeys. The long stay in London in 1620–1 cost a total of £163 8s 10d in board, lodgings and travel; the shorter three-week trips cost around £35.

The pattern of visits to Norwich was rather different. A smaller proportion of the trips were made by male servants alone. Hamon went to Norwich regularly to attend the assizes and on other business: of the years surveyed only 1614 provided no evidence of Hamon travelling to Norwich. Unlike trips to London, Alice more often than not went with him. From 1615 onwards the Le Stranges had friends living at Sprowston Hall, just outside Norwich, who they visited once or twice a year.[45] These visits had a distinctive seasonal pattern and were made most commonly in July/August or December, coinciding with the assizes. While such visits had a social function, they were also used to make purchases. In contrast, visits to King's Lynn were overwhelmingly made by the household's male servants: 84 per cent were specified as such. Many of these journeys were specifically to collect things, such as trunks, which had been shipped from London or elsewhere. Only six journeys to Lynn in the period 1614–28 are specified as made by 'Mr Strange', and none at all show evidence of having been made by Alice. It seems that the Le Stranges had little reason to visit Lynn in person. Thus, the Le Strange accounts show that most trips to towns were made by men, most often male servants but also male gentlemen. Female servants from the Le Strange household did not travel to towns to make purchases. Alice Le Strange had limited opportunities to shop. From 1616 onwards she normally travelled to Norwich at least once a year. Her visits to London were infrequent and irregular, and certainly did not constitute attendance at a London 'season', although the Le Stranges did treat Norwich in this way.

Identifying what was bought on particular trips is more challenging. Entries in the accounts do not normally state where items were purchased. Bills were not necessarily paid at the time items were chosen or ordered, nor were goods necessarily taken home immediately. When large purchases were made in London, they were shipped home separately by sea to King's Lynn, and arrived at Hunstanton some time after the person who had purchased them. The accounts reveal the complexity of making purchases. Routine purchases had to be planned in advance and male servants sent to town with clear instructions about what to buy from whom. It was only the most senior male servants who were trusted with such trips: men who could be relied on to handle money, make choices, and ensure they were not cheated. In the years 1617–20 William Guybon was the favourite used for these purposes. He was the eldest son of Alice's cousin, Francis Guybon of Sedgeford, from a parish gentry family of some wealth. Errands that simply required collecting goods that had already been chosen and paid for were done

---

[45] It is not clear what the exact link is. Sprowston Hall was owned by the Corbett family. Miles Corbett, who died in 1607, was married to a Spelman widow.

by lesser servants. For London, the Le Stranges also used Frank Gurney, a London merchant who was related to Alice's family, and another relative, 'cousin Grinell', to carry out their business and make purchases when they could not attend themselves. This use of London agents or proxies was a common strategy in the early seventeenth century.[46] On the whole, however, the Le Stranges seem to have preferred to go to London in person to make purchases. Sir Hamon was quite capable of making independent purchases relating to his own interests: books, instruments, hawks and coaches. He had complete control of buying his best clothing and an eye for fashion. He also designed and ordered the livery of the elite male servants of the household. There is no evidence of him buying clothing for Alice, or his daughter Elizabeth, although it is possible (and likely) he did do so but that they were either gifts or were paid for out of Alice's annual allowance, and therefore do not appear in the accounts. Nonetheless, Sir Hamon Le Strange did not make large purchases of furnishings for the house, such as new beds for the best rooms, without Alice.

The Le Stranges made their most spectacular London shopping trip of this period in 1628. Purchases cover nine sides of entries in the accounts, or 308 individual entries. During this eight-week stay they spent £492 10s 8d. Their most expensive purchases were a new 'crimson damask' bed and matching furnishings for their best bedroom at a cost of £84 14s 4d (see Table 5.5), and five second-hand arras tapestries for £41 14s 6d; a couch and upholstered chairs for their dining room were less expensive. They bought two new dresses for their fourteen-year-old daughter, Bess, at a cost of over £20 (see Table 5.2). There were two new beaver hats at £2 7s and £2 5s and two pairs of Spanish leather boots for Sir Hamon Le Strange, as well as knives, spurs, scabbards, powder horns, powder, shot, musket corks, bullet bags and other small items such as '7 new chess pawns'. They made extensive purchases of household stuff including glassware, basketware, earthenware, brassware and silverware, which seem to be listed in the accounts shop by shop, as they were purchased (see Table 5.7). There were also many small purchases of stockings, linen, shoes, gloves, lace, points and paper. The 1620 trip was the next most significant in terms of purchases. Around 120 separate purchases were made, including the new black bed for over £50, £5 worth of books, and gloves, hats, stockings, lace, boots, spurs, cloth, earthenware, brass and ironware, silverware and a new upholstered couch. In total they spent £185 5s 6d, including accommodation and diet. None of the other journeys to London on which Alice accompanied Sir Hamon led to the same quantity of purchases. There were around forty items obviously purchased in London in 1617, thirty in 1620–1 despite the length of the stay, and a similar number in 1626.

Hamon's trips to London on his own never resulted in such extensive purchases. Nonetheless his more frequent visits are a regular feature of the accounts. For example, in June 1616, Hamon bought a number of items for himself: silk stockings, two pairs of gloves, a dozen points, a ruff and two pairs of cuffs, a girdle with

---

[46] Peck, *Consuming Splendor*, 37; Merritt, *Early Modern Westminster*, 155; Warren, 'London's cultural impact', 165–6.

hangers, boot hose and a feather; as well as two bits and a pair of reins for the coach horses, a book, a voider for sweetmeats and eight Venice glasses in a box. He collected a new suit from the tailor and paid almost £4 to Hodgetts the book binder. Back in London in September Hamon spent £4 at the saddler and £5 at the hatter, had a pair of stockings dyed, and purchased a pair of knives, boot hose, a feather, a pair of stag's leather gloves, a girdle, a hawk's hood and a silver toasting fork, as well as having a tooth pulled. Later that year the Le Stranges paid a bill for £3 11s 7d to Frank Gurney for sweetmeats and two boxes arrived at Lynn containing cloth for the servants' liveries, all sent up from London. Once they reached adulthood, Nicholas and Hamon junior's purchases followed a similar pattern to their father's. When in London in 1626 they bought a falcon, falcons' hoods and bells, powder, shot, bullets, boot hose, a girdle, a ring, 'a brass candlestick to write by', 'a pair of green spectacles', an inkhorn, 'a book of instructions for musters' and three almanacs. However, they also seem to have bought things for the rest of the family, collecting a kirtle, stomacher, sleeves and lace for their twelve-year-old sister, Bess, from the tailor, and purchasing 'a fan with a silver handle', a rebater wire and French roll, also for Bess. There was a hat for ten-year-old Roger, 'a box with nine Indian dishes' and 5 yards of pentado, which were perhaps for their mother.

Norwich, as a centre of the textile industry, was an excellent location to buy cloth and haberdashery. But the Le Stranges did not limit their purchases in Norwich to these items. They frequently bought books there, and purchased scientific instruments and a clock from a Norwich goldsmith, Edward Wright. Thus, on a trip in April 1616, Alice and Hamon purchased lengths of broad diaper, diaper towelling, baize and frieze, as well as lace and sewing silk. They spent £3 on books, and paid bills to Sappe the shoemaker and to two different tailors for making clothes for Nicholas and Hamon junior. They had a looking glass mended and bought two brushes and a dozen points. Later in the accounts, when they had more money to spend and more children to clothe, the lists of Norwich purchases become more extensive. For instance, in November 1619 they purchased nineteen pairs of gloves, two cauls, a headdress and ribbons for seven-year-old Jane and three bands (collars) for Roger, who was almost three years old. Cloth and other items were purchased to make clothes for Nicholas, Hamon junior and Jane: lengths of sempeterny, baize, fustian, sarsenett, canvas, frieze and stuff, along with silk lace, silver lace, buttons, sewing silk, 'silver twist', binding and yarn. In addition, they bought a horn book, two ells of cambric, a ream of paper, a quire of gilt paper, cards and dice, a hat, viol strings, a hawk, two hawk's hoods, shot, arrows, bow strings and a quiver. The shopping trip ran to at least sixty-two entries in the accounts.

Purchases made at Lynn were more mundane and less distinct in the accounts. Certainly the more basic types of fabric and haberdashery were sometimes bought there, as well as supplies of paper, coal, wax candles, shot and gun powder, apothecary stuff, dried fish, wine, dried fruit and other imported groceries. Some of these items may also have been purchased elsewhere at smaller market towns and villages closer to home. Hamon Le Strange made regular trips to Walsingham and Fakenham, where quarter sessions were held. Walsingham had a mercer in the

1620s, and there was a woollen draper even closer to Hunstanton at Burnham Ulph at the same date.[47] The earliest household accounts kept by Hamon Le Strange from 1606 to 1609 are more informative about where items were bought, and record him purchasing apothecary stuff and saddlers' wares at Walsingham, and hawking gloves from Sanders the glover of Snettisham.[48] Goods could also have been brought to the house by pedlars, although this is not explicitly mentioned in the accounts. Pedlars, selling linen, haberdashery and other small items, were an established part of rural retailing by the mid-sixteenth century.[49] Nicholas Le Strange's jest book contains a jest told by Philip Calthorpe, which records a gentlewoman's delight at the pedlar's visit: 'A gentlewoman that lov'd to bable away her mony in Bone-laces, pinnes, and such toyes, often usd this short Ejaculation; God love me, but as I love a Pedlar.'[50] Fairs were only used occasionally. The accounts from 1606–25 mention five fairs. Gaywood fair, Massingham fair and Stanton fair were all held in October and were used by the Le Stranges to buy and sell horses. Fring fair, held later in the year, was mentioned once, when £1 13s was 'laid out' there. Lynn mart, a January fair, appears twice.

Much of what was normally bought at Lynn could also be purchased in Norwich. Norwich offered many things that were also purchased in London, such as books, hawking equipment, fine fabrics, clothing accessories, glassware, watches and clocks. This makes it difficult to estimate the proportion of domestic consumption expenditure that was laid out in particular places. The categories used for Table 3.1 reveal that the Le Stranges spent 9–10 per cent of domestic consumption expenditure from 1620 onwards on travel, accommodation, purchases and expenses in London. However, this does not represent a full measure of spending in London. The 'London and luxuries' category used to make these calculations is an exclusive one, and many items that were definitely or probably bought in London were placed in other categories: 'bills' includes tailors' and hatters' bills, many of which were from London, 'luxuries and lifestyle' includes many London purchases that could not definitely be identified as such, while 'textiles and clothing' also includes some items purchased in London. 'Childcare and education' includes the expenses of sending all three sons to the Inns of Court, and of supporting Roger while he was in prison in London during the Civil War. The coaches bought by the Le Stranges all came from London and are included in the 'horses and travel' category. Some non-domestic expenditure also ended up in London, most significantly taxes, and a portion of family allowances. A rough

---

[47] Wills of William Hubbard of Burnham Ulph (now Burnham Market), woollen draper, 1626, and Philip Browne sen. of Walsingham, mercer, 1626: both NRO, NCC wills. Also J. Patten, 'Changing occupational structures in the East Anglian countryside, 1500–1700', in H.S.A. Fox and R.A. Butlin (eds.), *Change in the Countryside: Essays on Rural England 1500–1900* (London, 1979), 108–9.
[48] George Sander of Snettisham, glover, made his will in 1621: NRO, NCC wills.
[49] M. Spufford, *The Great Reclothing of Rural England: Petty Chapmen and their Wares in the Seventeenth Century* (Oxford, 1984), 6; T.S. Willan, *The Inland Trade* (Manchester, 1976), 55.
[50] N. Le Strange, *Merry Passages and Jeasts*, ed. H.F. Lippincott (Salzburg, 1974), 44.

estimate is that money spent in London accounted for around 20 per cent of domestic consumption expenditure, and 10 per cent of overall expenditure.

London played a smaller part in the Le Stranges' life than we might have expected. Members of the household made regular trips to the capital, but, despite owning a coach and having considerable wealth at their disposal from 1620 onwards, they did not partake in a London season. Alice Le Strange visited London much less often than her husband, and was never resident there like her adult sons. That said, two visits by Alice to London did result in extensive and expensive purchases for the house. It is likely that it was these gargantuan shopping trips by members of the country gentry that led Londoners to believe country gentlewomen came to London to fritter away their husbands' wealth. Yet these shopping trips were large precisely because gentlewomen visited London infrequently, and it was not purely women's expenditure. The items were bought by the Le Stranges mainly for their house, which had been newly enlarged and needed extra furnishings. The enlargement of the house was Hamon's project and it seems likely that he had a strong say in how the best rooms, where guests were entertained and accommodated, were decorated. It was this that incurred the cost. Rather than attending a London season, Alice and Hamon Le Strange regularly went to Norwich in the summer and at some point over Christmas, as part of their social calendar. As a result, much of their luxury shopping was conducted in Norwich rather than the capital. The local town of King's Lynn served a much more functional purpose.

THE ACQUISITION OF CLOTHING AND FURNISHINGS

The history of early modern retailing has concentrated on the types of outlets where goods were bought, chronicling the decline of markets and fairs and the rise of the retail shop.[51] Yet the set of choices faced by a consumer and documented by household accounts was rather different. The early modern consumer chose not only where to buy things but how they should be made. Production and consumption were closely linked. Similar choices are still made by modern consumers for particular types of goods: curtains are a good example. In the early twenty-first century curtains can be bought ready-made in standard sizes, or they can be made-to-measure to your requirements. They can be acquired second-hand, as gifts from friends or relatives, or as purchases. Alternatively, the fabric can be purchased separately, and the curtains made at home or taken to a curtain-maker. These last two strategies can also be used to alter ready-made and second-hand purchases. The Le Stranges used all these routes to acquire clothing and furnishings in the early seventeenth century. There were two main differences between their patterns of acquisition and those found in the modern economy. The first is that in early modern England items were only rarely purchased ready-made. The rise of the

---

[51] D. Davis, *A History of Shopping* (London, 1966); F. Braudel, *Civilization and Capitalism 15th to 18th Century: The Wheels of Commerce* (London, 1985), 26–80; N. Cox, *The Complete Tradesman: A Study of Retailing, 1550–1820* (Aldershot, 2000), ch. 2.

retail shop and specialist producers of consumer goods in the late seventeenth and eighteenth centuries gives the illusion that consumers in that era were offered new and unprecedented levels of choice. In fact, they were being offered an increased range of ready-made items. When self-made and made-to-order goods dominated, as in the early seventeenth century, the choice was almost infinite for the wealthy consumer. The second difference is that home production of raw materials was also a viable choice for some items, a route that is very rare in the modern economy. We might make wooden furniture at home or knit jumpers, but we are unlikely to have grown the tree that provided the wood or raised sheep for the wool. This section explores the range of routes or strategies used by the Le Stranges to acquire their clothing and furnishings. It becomes clear that for the Le Stranges social interaction with the actual producers of their consumer goods was a significant part of acquiring goods, unlike the impersonal interactions experienced by modern consumers.

Gervase Markham included in his *English Housewife* (1615) a chapter 'Of wool, hemp, flax and cloth' which described how to prepare, dye, card, spin and weave woollen cloth, and how to grow hemp and flax, and process, spin and weave it for linen. He stated that 'Our English housewife, after her knowledge of preserving and feeding her family, must learn also how, out of her own endeavours, she ought to clothe them'.[52] In fact, even Markham did not expect housewives to carry out the whole cloth production process, but rather to prepare the raw materials and spin them into yarn, which could then be 'delivered up to the hands of the weaver'.[53] Styles has shown that even in the eighteenth century many households in northern England spun wool to knit their own stockings, or linen yarn which was 'woven on commission by a local jobbing-weaver'.[54] Using evidence from late sixteenth- to early eighteenth-century probate inventories, Shammas notes that, although many households show evidence of spinning, it was extremely rare for a single household to carry out the whole cloth production process of raising sheep, processing the wool and weaving it into cloth.[55]

The Le Stranges had sheep on their home farm and foldcourses. Between 1622 and 1625 they were receiving over £100 a year for the sale of wool, although this enterprise operated on a smaller scale for much of the accounts. Each year Alice Le Strange recorded the washing and clipping of her 'kitchen sheep', which were kept primarily for mutton, and the amount of wool they produced. The purchase of wool cards shows the household organized the preparation of wool for spinning. Carding and spinning may have been done by household servants. Other people were also paid to do this work. For instance in 1613 a spinner was paid 10d a week for four weeks' spinning, and a carder 7d a week for three weeks' work. Entries of this type are intermittent in the accounts: there are only two purchases of wool

---

[52] G. Markham, *The English Housewife*, ed. M.R. Best (Montreal, 1986), 146.
[53] Markham, *English Housewife*, 152.
[54] J. Styles, *The Dress of the People: Everyday Fashion in Eighteenth-Century England* (New Haven, 2007), 139–46, quotation from 140.
[55] Shammas, *Pre-Industrial Consumer*, 31–3, 37.

cards, two entries relating to carding and sixteen relating to spinning in the sixteen years of accounts from 1610 to 1625. The wool spun in this way was then sent either for knitting into boot hose or for weaving. The Le Stranges did not produce linen. They grew hemp to make rope, but purchased linen yarn to be knitted or woven in the same way as their wool.

Entries relating to weaving and knitting are more frequent. There are forty-seven entries between 1610 and 1625 recording cloth being woven to order. The pieces woven were typically large, on average 34 yards long. The cost of weaving varied according to the width and type of the cloth: in 1610, they paid 3d per yard for 'ell broad cloth'; in 1612, 2d per yard for 'yard broad cloth' for napkins. Other commissions varied from 1.5d per yard up to 7d per yard for one lot in 1625. These textiles, which appear to have been both woollen and linen, were used only for household purposes, most commonly for sheets but also for coverings, napkins, tablecloths, towels and ticking: they were not used for clothing. Five weavers were named, all men, but most were not named. Stockings and hose were knitted from linen or woollen yarn. These standard garments, worn by both men and women, were most commonly acquired by the Le Stranges providing local knitters with yarn. There are seventy-five entries in the accounts from 1607 to 1625 relating to this process, many of which are payments for multiple pairs of hose. The cost varied from 3d for babies' hose to 3s 8d for a fine pair of men's hose. As with weaving, most of the entries are anonymous, but occasionally knitters are named. They were normally women and included the wife of Ralph the tailor, the wife of Wix the thatcher, the daughter of Widow Banyard a tenant, and the sister of Kettwood the Le Stranges' butler, as well as one man, Mr Dixon.

At the other extreme were those items purchased ready-made. These were less common and largely restricted to small things: silk stockings, Spanish leather shoes and boots, gloves, hats and some table napkins. Silk stockings were imported from continental Europe and bought ready-made at some expense, costing between £1 5s and £2 10s a pair. It is likely that boots and shoes made of Spanish leather were also imported ready-made: unlike other footwear the Le Stranges purchased, no shoemaker is named. Spanish leather boots for Sir Hamon Le Strange cost £1 a pair. Gloves of all types were always purchased ready-made, and were bought in large quantities (see Table 5.3). They ranged from fine gloves for Sir Hamon, such as the 'pair of gloves laced with black silk and silver' for £1 2s or beaver gloves for £1 8s, to cheaper and plainer versions for everyday wear by the gentry, such as '2 pairs of white gloves' for 2s 6d, down to harvest gloves for agricultural workers costing 5d, and young children's gloves for 3d. Hats were also ready-made but were then often lined and decorated to order. The hats recorded in the accounts were primarily for Sir Hamon and were often luxury items. For instance a 'sad coloured beaver hat with a cypress band' was purchased for £3 5s in 1610, and then 'dressed and lined' at a further cost of 3s. This was the most expensive hat purchased, but hats were in general quite costly. Of the forty-seven hats recorded, eleven cost more than £1 and seven more than £2.[56] Hatters were mentioned six times, two by name, which

---

[56] The most expensive ones were made of beaver.

suggests a somewhat more personal relationship than with glovers, who were named on only one occasion. The two named hatters, Sommers and Rust, were both based in London.

Some items of furniture were bought ready-made. In 1621 the Le Stranges bought an 'oyster table' and a little folding table in London. They bought a livery cupboard in 1625, and bedsteads on various occasions. The bedstead for their expensive Black Bed was purchased in London for 26s, but was then painted, gilded and provided with four 'knobs' to their own orders at a much greater cost of £7. Table napkins, although sometimes woven to order, were also bought ready-made by the dozen. Alternatively, linen cloth was purchased and napkins cut and hemmed at home.

The two most common strategies for acquiring clothing and furnishings were either to purchase materials and then have items made by local craftsmen or to have things made to order. Those who made items to order were often trusted craftsmen who had a longstanding relationship with the Le Stranges. They included Broadhead the joiner, Rust and Sommers the hatters, Sappe the Norwich shoemaker, and two London tailors, Mr Lock and Lawrence Michael. Sappe made shoes for Sir Hamon and the children, and probably Alice too, appearing frequently in the accounts from 1608 to 1620. The two high-status tailors used regularly by the Le Stranges were based in London. They had much in common. Both acted as money lenders, and took payments from the Le Stranges for investment in the East India Company, as well as making clothes. Mr Lock's position seems to have been usurped by Lawrence Michael in 1618, although Lock was still used occasionally after that date. Some payments were described as 'for apparel' and others 'for money borrowed of him' but many entries were less clear. Payments for apparel were often round numbers, such as £30, indicating that a tab was kept for expenses relating to clothing, which blurred the line between payment for clothes and borrowing money in any case. Lawrence Michael seems to have found favour with the family after Sir Hamon paid £8 for John Spratt to be bound apprentice to him in 1616. Spratt was probably the son of Edward, Alice's cousin, who was a trusted family servant for much of the period of the accounts.

As they were always paid by bill, the details of the clothes made by Lock and Michael are not given. However, their location in London and the large sums paid to them indicate that they were responsible for the fashionable outer garments worn by Sir Hamon and probably Alice too, although no details of her clothes purchases were recorded in the accounts. Such tailors must have advised their clients on changes in fashion and occasionally constructed clothes to written orders using measurements kept on record rather than relying on the client to visit in person for each new garment. An anecdote in Nicholas Le Strange's *Merry Jeasts*, told by Alice Le Strange and relating to Nicholas' wife Anne, describes the possible consequences of this system:

> My Daughter writing to a new Taylor at London, (yet not so new, but that he had her measure, and had made her one garment a little before) hastily subscribd her Name for Anne LeStrange, An: Lestr. He more rashly apprehending it, and working to one Mrs

Table 3.4. Tailors appearing in the disbursement accounts, 1606–25

Name	Location	Times mentioned	Dates
Mr Clarke	Poss. Lynn	3	1619–20
John Davison	?	30	1610–25
Dye	Sedgeford	1	1617
Edwarde	Holme	1	1606
Foster	?	1	1621
Gascoine	Norwich	4	1610–12
Fothergay	Lynn	1	1607
Mr Goldman	?	1	1616
Mr Lock	London	41	1606–24
Lawrence Michael	London	47	1616–25
Peirt	Norwich	1	1616
Nicholas Powle	Ringstead	38	1606–16
Ralph	?	5	1617–19
Smith	Norwich	1	1615
Thomson	?	4	1612–16
Willson	?	4	1618–22

Source: Le Strange disbursement accounts, 1606–25; LEST/P6, P7.

Lester, made her Gowne by her Mould, and so sent it downe with a direction to Mrs Anne Lester.[57]

These elite London tailors were used alongside a number of others, as shown in Table 3.4. Some were from Norwich and Lynn, others were more local. John Davison was paid 6d a day, the same rate as the thatcher and skilled agricultural labourers. He did basic work, mostly on household items such as cushions, coverings, hangings, blankets and beds, but occasionally clothes for the children. The other men paid by the day—Ralph, Willson and Dye—were also likely to have been local.[58] They were all engaged to make children's clothes. Nicholas Powle was local too, living in neighbouring Ringstead, but seems to have been of somewhat higher status. He was normally paid by bill and made items for Sir Hamon as well as the children.

The detailed records in the later accounts of Nicholas Le Strange's wedding clothes and Elizabeth Le Strange's gowns demonstrates that tailors at all levels were paid separately for labour and materials, which were carefully itemized. It is likely that high-status tailors in London and Norwich purchased the materials themselves. The local tailors paid by the day were provided with cloth, trimmings and thread by the Le Stranges. While tailors are frequently named in the accounts, the drapers, mercers and haberdashers who sold cloth and other items are not named, with one exception. A Mr Anguish supplied lace, loops, buttons and fabric to the household

---

[57] Le Strange, *Merry Jeasts*, 114.
[58] Dye almost certainly came from Sedgeford, where a Robert Dey, tailor, made his will in 1640: NRO, NCC wills.

between 1607 and 1617 and sometimes sent bills, although only eight entries refer to him by name. A Christopher Anguish was employed as a servant by the Le Stranges from 1616 to 1623, indicating an extra link with this one supplier. Upholsterers worked on a similar basis to tailors. Upholstered furniture was a luxury item in this period and all the specialist upholsterers used by the Le Stranges were located in London.[59] In 1612, Gillbert the upholsterer was paid for making twelve stools and four chairs covered with red Russian leather, and also for packing them and 'laying them into the ship' to be transported to Norfolk. In 1626 an upholsterer was paid 'by his Bill for frames; feathers; girtweb; tick; nails; leather; and making them ready for the outsides; and Matt to pack up this suit of Chairs and Stools for a lodging chamber: £3 15s'.

For both tailors and upholsterers the cost of labour was a small proportion of the overall cost of the items they made. Nicholas Le Strange's wedding suits cost over £87 in fabrics and trimmings, but only £18 16s in tailoring; while Elizabeth Le Strange's most expensive dress, which cost over £60 in total, cost only £1 4s to make.[60] The upholsterer who helped make the Black Bed, which cost over £50, was paid £2 9s 10d for his work. Occasionally, saddlers were used rather than upholsterers to cover chairs and stools with leather: in 1628 'the saddler' was paid £1 10s for '30 days making chairs and stools' and 8s for the red leather skins used. The best beds were made by London upholsterers and joiners, or, in the case of the Red Damask Bed purchased in 1628, a bed frame was imported from France and purchased in London. Ordinary beds were made by the local Norfolk joiner. Feathers and down for mattresses and pillows were also purchased in Norfolk. Like other items these were sometimes bought ready-made (for instance a pair of 'new down pillows' which cost 14s in 1622), but were more often constructed at home. A 'featherbed' or mattress was constructed like a large version of a pillow. In 1618, 24 yards of Milan fustian was purchased to make a tick or case for a down bed at a cost of £4. A 'featherbed driver' was employed for three and a half days, presumably to stuff the tick and sew it together, at 2s a day.

Not all the furnishings in Hunstanton Hall were purchased new. Some were inherited, others purchased second-hand. A few were home-made by members of the household. Bequests of furniture appear in the wills of Richard Stubbe, Hamon Le Strange and Alice Le Strange.[61] Alice received a significant bequest of furnishings from her father in 1619, described in the codicil of his will and again in an excerpt of his probate inventory copied by Alice into the accounts. This included the complete furnishings of five bedrooms and a dining room, as well as brewing equipment.[62] However, inherited items were often remade with new textiles, which constituted the majority of the cost for items such as beds. Sales of used furnishings created a second-hand market, and the Le Stranges were not above buying items

---

[59] G. Beard, *Upholsterers and Interior Furnishing in England 1530–1840* (New Haven, 1997).
[60] See Tables 5.1 and 5.4.
[61] See Chapter 5: Beds and living rooms; bequests are discussed in Chapter 5: The meanings of goods.
[62] LEST/P10.

Table 3.5. Second-hand goods purchased at Sir Henry Carvile's in 1625

Items purchased	Price paid	Price for new goods
6 old needlework cushions	15s	–
A brass pot weighing 60 lb at 8d/lb	£2	15–16d/lb
A brass pot weighing 48 lb at 8d/lb	£1 12s	15–16d/lb
A brass ladle	2s 6d	–
A little ladle	8d	–
A chafing dish	5s 6d	–
A chest	£1	–
A table	16s	–
A livery cupboard	10s	10s
An old bedstead with four curtains	10s	5s 6d–12s
3 pairs of blankets	15s	12s 6d–14s/pair
A pair of new down pillows	15s	£1 3s 9d
A turkey cupboard cloth	£1	£2–3
A broad fish pan weighing 12 lb at 10d	10s 4d	–
A copper kettle weighing 13 lb at 14d	15s 2d	14–16d/lb
A dripping pan	4s	–

Note: Price for new goods taken from the accounts, 1610–25.

Source: Le Strange disbursement accounts; LEST/P7.

second-hand, if only from households of similar status. They purchased a set of Arras tapestries second-hand in 1628, and spent £10 on 'a Turkey Carpet of 4 yards long and 2 carpets for side board and cupboard' from 'my Lady Tasborough' in 1629. In 1625 a set of furnishings and kitchen ware were purchased 'at Sir Henry Carvile's', as shown in Table 3.5. As Sir Henry Kervile of Wiggenhall St Mary, south of King's Lynn, made his will in 1624, it seems likely that this was a 'probate inventory sale'.[63] It is notable that, in all these cases, Alice recorded who the items had previously belonged to. Soft furnishings were bought at a considerable discount second-hand, and, interestingly, brass pots too, but wooden furniture cost much the same whether new or second-hand.

Clothing, like furnishings, was sometimes inherited. Alice Le Strange bequeathed her best dresses to poorer relatives and everyday items to servants. People lower down the social scale must sometimes have purchased these items second-hand, although there is no evidence that the gentry bought clothes this way. However, they were not above having their clothing altered and remade. The teenage Elizabeth Le Strange had her gowns 'mended' on a number of occasions or adjusted to her growing height with extra lengths of cloth. Another anecdote from Nicholas Le Strange's jest book told by Alice Le Strange indicates that it was not unacceptable, although nonetheless worthy of jest, for adults to have old clothes reworked into new styles. The jest relates to her parents' generation in late Elizabethan England: 'The Lady Cary seeing Sir John Heydon in a metamorphosed

[63] TNA PROB 11/144.

suite, accosted him thus; how now Sir John? what an old payre of Breeches new printed? by God Madame, says he, if it were not for printing and painting your face and my Breeches had beene out of fashion long since.'[64]

The employment of tailors did not preclude clothing being made at home, although this is poorly recorded. The most likely items to be home-made were embroidery of various types and linen underclothes, shirts and smocks, which are rarely itemized in the accounts despite the large quantities of fine linen cloth purchased. Women, including gentlewomen, were expected to be skilled in plain sewing and able to hem table cloths and napkins, and make the family's linen underclothes and their own aprons.[65] There are many entries in the accounts such as those for 1635 which record '8 ells of Holland at 4s 6d for 4 smocks for Besse', '6 ells of Holland for 4 aprons', 'an ell of fine Holland for cuffs and neckcloths' and '6 yards of bone lace', which have no associated payments to tailors. This type of work must have been done by Alice and Elizabeth Le Strange or their female servants. Gentlewomen also did fine embroidery. The accounts record large quantities of cruel and silk thread being purchased but no payments to embroiderers. Alice inherited cushions worked with embroidery by her mother. Cushions, carpets and tablecloths decorated with embroidery of this type were considered worthy of some of the best rooms in the house.[66] Alice was painted wearing an embroidered caul, perhaps her own work, in her portrait of 1617. A surviving bed in early twentieth-century Hunstanton Hall displays the needlework of Ann Woodhouse, who was Lady Le Strange from 1686 to 1696.[67] Embroidery was an important creative outlet for high-status women.[68] Only the wealthiest individuals, royalty and members of court, paid to have their clothes embroidered and such work was extraordinarily expensive.[69]

Acquiring fashionable, attractive and well-made clothing and furnishings in early seventeenth-century England was not a straightforward matter. Households such as the Le Stranges' utilized a wide range of strategies to meet their needs. They inherited things, made things at home or had servants make them; they had things made to order and altered by local craftspeople with basic skills, and by skilled craftsmen further afield; and they purchased things ready-made and second-hand. They relied on workers in Hunstanton and the neighbouring villages, in Lynn, Norwich and in London. The accounts reveal subtle differences in the way people involved in these transactions were treated. Skilled craftsmen were always named and paid by bill. Local craftsmen such as the joiner or tailors who were employed frequently by the Le Stranges to do specific work to order were also named but

---

[64] Le Strange, *Merry Jeasts*, 24.
[65] S. Vincent, *Dressing the Elite: Clothes in Early Modern England* (Oxford, 2003), 54; A. Vickery, 'His and hers: gender, consumption and household accounting in eighteenth century England', *Past and Present* supplement 1 (2006), 29–31.
[66] See Chapter 5: Beds and living rooms; The meanings of goods.
[67] See Figure 5.1.
[68] G.W. Digby, *Elizabethan Embroidery* (London, 1963).
[69] P. Wardle, 'The King's embroiderer: Edmund Harrison (1590–1667): II. His work', *Textile History* 26:2 (1995), 142; L. Stone, *The Crisis of the Aristocracy 1558–1641* (Oxford, 1965), 564–5.

usually paid by the day. Local people who carried out less specific tasks such as spinning, knitting and weaving were paid by task but only occasionally named. Most striking is the fact that retailers who did not produce their own goods were, with one exception, never named in the accounts. Thus, it seems that ordering goods from a producer was seen as a personal matter, a social interaction, whereas buying goods from a middleman was not. In this way, most purchases in this period were a social act. As ready-made goods became more common in the late seventeenth and eighteenth centuries, the social nature of consumption was gradually reduced and replaced with anonymous interactions. This attitude towards retailers is also illustrated in the purchase of food.

THE ACQUISITION OF FOOD

The Le Stranges acquired food by three main routes. As well as making purchases, they produced food on their own estate and received frequent gifts of food. Table 3.6 shows the range of food items purchased in a single year, 1619, and the frequency with which they were purchased. While imported groceries make up a significant element of purchased items, many were products of the local economy. Two items, eggs and manchet bread (fine white bread), were purchased every week, while beef and tongue were purchased almost every week apart from during Lent. Fresh fish, sowse and feet, and chickens were regular purchases. Weekly purchases of fresh food indicate deliveries by local traders, particularly the butcher and baker. The baker seems also to have sold eggs, which are always recorded next to the bread purchases. Despite the regularity of these purchases the names of these tradesmen are never recorded in the accounts. Village bakers were common in sixteenth- and seventeenth-century Norfolk, as were butchers, although not every village had one. There was a baker in neighbouring Sedgeford, Thomas Akers, to whom the Le Stranges sold wheat in 1620.[70] Goodwife Akers sent them a gift of six chickens in 1622, so it possible that this was the Le Stranges' supplier. The only client-type relationship between the Le Stranges and a food producer that can be identified in the accounts was with Matthew Gittings, who leased the Le Stranges' rabbit warren. He paid £8 annually for the warren, and in return Alice could buy rabbits whenever she needed them. During 1619 she bought 302 couples of rabbits at a cost of £10 13s 4d from Gittings, more than covering his lease.

The regularity with which butchers' meat, eggs and manchet bread appear in the kitchen accounts make it certain that they were being delivered by professional suppliers. Other purchases, although frequent, were less regular, indicating goods brought to the door by a host of local producers, an assumption supported by the pattern of food gifts discussed below. Domestic poultry and pigs were raised by many local farming households. Fresh seafood was also locally available, with

---

[70] The will of Thomas Akers of Sedgeford, baker, 1628–34: NRO wills of the Peculiar of the Dean and Chapter of Norwich.

Table 3.6. The nature and frequency of food purchases, 1619

53	Eggs	2	Nutmegs
53	Manchet bread	2	Pears
44	Beef	2	Peascods
42	Tongue	2	Prunes
36	Fish, fresh	2	Salad oil
24	Sowse and feet	2	Vinegar, kitchen
22	Chickens and capons	2	Wethers
14	Birds, wild	1	Apples
13	Oatmeal	1	Barley, French
12	Veal	1	Bread, household
11	Oysters	1	Breedshead and suet
9	Currants	1	Caraway seed
9	Lamb	1	Cheeks and bocedes of neat
9	Raisins	1	Cheese
8	Pigs	1	Cheese, Holland
8	Salt	1	Crabs
7	Pigeons	1	Damsons
7	Rice	1	Figs
5	Mace	1	Fowl
4	Bread, brown	1	Ginger
4	Ducks	1	Herring, fresh
4	Ducklings	1	Hops
4	Goslings	1	Isinglass
4	Sugar	1	Liquorice
4	Wine	1	Onions
3	Aniseed	1	Pepper
3	Butter	1	Salmon pie
3	Cinnamon	1	Salmon, salt
3	Geese	1	Saltfish
2	Almonds	1	Sanders
2	Herring, red	1	Shrimps
2	Mustard seed	1	Walnuts

Notes: The table records the number of weeks in which particular items were purchased during a fifty-three-week accounting year from April 1619 to April 1620.

Source: Le Strange kitchen accounts, 1619; LEST/P6.

fishermen resident in Hunstanton and Holme.[71] Fresh fruit, vegetables, butter and cheese were purchased only rarely, largely because the Le Stranges had their own supplies. Groceries, spices and imported foodstuffs were occasional purchases. Wine and large purchases of dried fruit were bought in King's Lynn. For instance, in 1619 Alice Le Strange paid William Guybon for his charges at Lynn 'when the wine came home', and again 'when he bought the fruit' before Christmas. The frequency of purchases is not always a good guide to the amount bought or the regularity of consumption. For instance, salt fish was purchased in bulk and

---

[71] For instance, wills were made by Thomas Geyton of Hunstanton, fisherman, 1629, and Nicholas Baker, fishermen, of Holme-next-to-Sea, 1615: NRO, NCC wills.

consumed at a steady rate of three fish a week, rising to ten during Lent. One purchase lasted well over a year.

The size of gentry households and lack of local retailers for many products made it difficult, and certainly expensive, to supply a gentry household in the early seventeenth century without some recourse to home production. This is demonstrated by the account books of the Le Stranges' cousins, the Hobarts, dating from the late 1620s onwards.[72] Resident much of the year in London and paying long visits to friends elsewhere, they lived at their house in Blickling for only part of the year. On arrival at Blickling they had to scour the locality for supplies of barley, straw, oats, meat, bread and coal. This was disruptive to the local economy as well as costly. The Hobarts struggled with mounting debts during this period. The Le Stranges' continuous residence at Hunstanton allowed them to take a very different course. For them, home production was not a relic of a bygone age, but a practical strategy taken to ensure quality, regular supply and reduced cost. Brown bread, beer, butter, cheese, bacon, pork, mutton, venison, honey, fruit and vegetables were all produced on the estate, in and around Hunstanton Hall. Production took place on a large scale, with 340 loaves of bread and 177 gallons of beer produced and 52.5 lbs of home-made cheese consumed in an average week in 1619. This food and drink fed not only the family and resident servants but also a varying number of agricultural and building labourers. It required investment in buildings and equipment as well as labour.

In 1610, as one of their first building projects, Sir Hamon and Alice Le Strange spent £130 on building a new dairy and altering the brew-house at Hunstanton Hall. In the autumn of 1612, nine cows were purchased, and over that winter the dairy was kitted out with equipment in preparation for the following summer's milk production. They bought nineteen large milk bowls for 30s; three cheese vats, two great 'tunnells' (funnels) and a sile dish for 20s; a churn for 7s; and a butter keeler for 3s; another keeler and funnel for 2s; and a cheese tub, bucking tub and rinsing tub for £1 10s. Three copper kettles, a brass kettle and a pewter cistern were also purchased that winter at a cost of over £7, for the dairy or brew-house, as well as other small purchases such as '4 long trays' and '3 stone jugs' and '3 earthen pans'. It is not coincidental that the first kitchen accounts begin in April 1613 just as the dairy was up and running, and that in 1613 the number of servants employed by the Le Stranges increased from seven to twelve. That summer the dairy produced 297.5 pints of butter and 178 cheeses. In 1633, Alice Le Strange wrote up a year-by-year 'reckoning of the profit of my dairy' at the back of one of her kitchen account books. For every year since 1617 she noted the name of her dairymaid, the number of cows, the maximum amount of butter made in a week, the amount of salted butter barrelled up for the winter and the weight of cheese produced.[73] The level of production had more to do with weather conditions than the skill of the dairymaid: milk production depended on a good growth of grass, so dry summers and cold springs and autumns reduced the amount produced. Variations were

---

[72] NRS, 18147 33A3; NRS, 18145 33A3; NRS, 14649 29D2; NRS, 12278 27C4.
[73] At the end of LEST/P8.

considerable. In the bumper year of 1628, Anne Haymish managed to produce 70 pints of butter in one week from twenty-three cows, store 17 firkins of butter for the winter, and make 295 stone of cheese. In the poorest year, 1632, the maximum amount of butter produced in one week was 30 pints, only 6.5 firkins of butter were stored for the winter, and 188 stone of cheese made.

This level of production allowed the household to be self-sufficient in butter and cheese, only buying extra butter in early spring when supplies were scarce, and usually selling a small surplus of both butter and cheese each year. Dairying was an exclusively female pursuit and one with which gentlewomen concerned themselves.[74] The consumption of cheese in England had increased since the fifteenth century and became more fashionable amongst the upper classes in the late sixteenth century.[75] Although the actual work was done by female servants, Alice's accounts show the type of detailed management gentlewomen engaged in. As well as her overview of profits, she noted dairy production and the state of her herd in regular half-yearly stocktakes in the kitchen accounts. Thus, at the end of the half year from April to October 1626 she wrote:

Butter: Remayne half a firkin of salt butter: sold 7 score and 10 lbs of fresh butter: remayne 9 firkins of salt butter.
Cheese: Remayning 5 score and one cheese half weighing 85 stone 12 lbs. Made 8 score and 16 cheese: spent all that remayned: and 49 of the new cheeses weighing 37 stone 9 lbs so spent this half year 7 score and 11 cheese weighing 6 score and 3 stone half: Remayne 88 cheses half weighing 5 score and 10 stone 3 lbs and 38 cheeses unweighed.
Cowes: Remayning 21 milch cowes: a bull: and 5 heyfers of 2 years olde: a bull and 5 heyfers of a year old: killed a heyfer of 2 yeare old: and dried to fatt 3 cowes: remayne 18 milch cowes a bull and 4 heyfers of 2 year half olde: and a bull and 5 heyfers of a year half old: and 6 calves bought up wherof one a bull calf.

That gentlewomen took pride in their cheese, and served it to elite guests at the dinner table, is indicated by another of Nicholas Le Strange's merry jests, this one recounted by his wife, Anne Le Strange:

The Lady Nevill would needs carve a peece of cheese, with superlative commendations, to a good witty merry gentleman then at the Table, and when he had tasted, askt his opinion; Madame says he, the cheese it seemes is your owne, and therefore you have some reason to like it, but I professe, for my part, I would never desire to eate worse; she rashly apprehending the worse sense, grew very angry, till he explained his meaning.[76]

The household's dairy economy is particularly well documented because it was self-contained and under Alice Le Strange's direct management. Grain production was closely entwined with the wider estate economy, making it more difficult to discern

---

[74] P. Brears, 'The dairy', in Sambrook and Brears (eds.), *Country House Kitchen*, 164; M. Dawson, *Plenti and Grase: Food and Drink in a Sixteenth Century Household* (Totnes, 2009), 101.
[75] See Chapter 4: Diet.
[76] Le Strange, *Merry Jeasts*, 45–6.

what was specifically for home consumption. From at least 1632, when Alice reorganized the estate documentation, the Le Stranges held sixty-five acres of pasture and 146 acres of arable in hand for their own use at Hunstanton. The farmland seems to have been under Alice's direct management from the start of her accounts in 1610.[77] A summary of grain sown in 1618, written in Alice's hand at the start of one of the kitchen accounts, suggests around fifty acres of arable were sown that year: twenty acres of mixtlyn (a mixture of wheat and rye), twenty-three acres of barley, six acres of rye and a small amount of peas.[78] The pasture closes were used for grazing by the dairy herd and for the kitchen sheep. The wider estate economy produced much larger quantities of grain. A summary noted, again by Alice, in the receipt accounts for 1620 lists the grain received and how it was used.[79] That year, the Le Stranges received 321.5 combs of barley, 45.75 combs of wheat, 3.5 combs of rye, 23 combs of oats and 12.5 combs of peas.[80] Twenty combs of barley, nine of wheat and all of the rye came from tithes, while 36.75 combs of wheat came from the home farm. The wheat, rye, oats and peas were all used by the Le Stranges. The large quantity of barley came chiefly from leasehold rents. This was a commercial proposition and just over half of it (52 per cent) was shipped out to be sold elsewhere. A further third (32 per cent) was sold to five local men. The remaining 16 per cent was used by the Le Stranges: 20 combs had already been consumed, 13 combs were laid up for future use and 18 combs were set aside as seed.

The household used grain to make two basic foodstuffs, bread and beer, as well as for feeding livestock. Cheat bread, a medium quality loaf, and household bread, or wholemeal, was baked in the household each week using a mixture of wheat and rye at a ratio of 1:3.[81] Beer was brewed using malted barley and hops. In the 1610s Alice paid for her barley to be malted at a cost of 7d a comb. Sixty combs of barley were malted for use in brewing each year. The Le Stranges first grew their own hops, the other vital ingredient for beer, in 1622, when a 'hop man' was paid 5s 6d 'for roots and setting 60 hills of hops'. The brew-house was renovated at the same time the dairy was built, and beer was being brewed at home when the first kitchen accounts begin 1613. The large quantities required by the household made home-brewing the most practical solution to ensuring a supply. Both bread and beer were made by male servants: the cook baked and the coachman brewed, a pattern typical of elite households in the sixteenth and seventeenth centuries.[82]

As well as dairy products and grain, the Le Stranges produced much of their own meat, also on a large scale. Every six months Alice added up the red meat consumed 'of store', that is, from her own farm. Thus, in April 1619, she noted the consumption of three beef cattle and two veal calves, eleven swine for pork and

---

[77] LEST/BK15.
[78] LEST/P6, in a section after the disbursement accounts and before the kitchen accounts.
[79] At the end of LEST/P6.
[80] One comb contained 4 bushels. Bushels are measurements of volume, so they vary in weight between grains. A bushel of wheat weights 53 lb.
[81] See Chapter 4: Diet.
[82] Dawson, *Plenti and Grase*, 69, 80, 199–203.

two for bacon, four deer, and forty-three sheep, as well as the beef which was purchased each week. The management of sheep and pigs was a complex business, like that of the dairy, with animals of different ages and sexes being raised for different purposes: this was all carefully recorded in the kitchen accounts. In 1619, the Le Stranges were keeping a flock of sixty-nine kitchen sheep and a large piggery with thirty-eight swine. While cattle and sheep were fed on pasture and hay from the estate, pigs were fed on waste from the household and dairy and were fattened with barley.[83] Barley was also fed to the poultry: in summer 1619, Alice spent 16 combs of barley 'in fowls, swine and doves'. No attempt was made in the kitchen accounts to record the turnover of poultry and game birds on the farm. The numbers consumed were large, and they were frequently purchased and received as gifts. Birds were often exchanged live, so they could be kept and fattened until it was convenient to eat them. Frequent purchases of hens and eggs indicate that Alice did not attempt self-sufficiency in poultry.[84] Possibly she saw purchases of these small items, which were easily produced by her tenants and were typically the province of women, as a way of supporting their household economies. Chicken was consumed largely by the wealthy rather than by ordinary households, making poultry a useful 'cash crop' for farming housewives of poor and middling households.

Poultry were also an important element of the gift economy. As Heal has pointed out, food gifts were a distinctive element of the economy of great households in the period before the Civil War, and 'critical to the maintenance of bonds in early modern society'.[85] Food made a useful gift because its consumability justified repeated giving. Alice Le Strange carefully recorded the food gifts she received in the kitchen accounts, alongside purchases and products of the home farm and estate. While the people who sold food were never named in the early accounts, the givers of gifts were always recorded.[86] For the twelve full years for which kitchen accounts survive between 1613 and 1627 there were almost 1500 entries recording gifts in the kitchen accounts, presented by 317 different people and encompassing 126 different types of items. Table 3.7 shows the range of items received and the frequency with which they were given. Everyday foodstuffs such as grain products, beef and most vegetables were only rarely given. Poultry were the most common gift; fruit, wild birds and fish also appear frequently. Groceries were less common, and only some seem to have been acceptable: sugar loaves and wine appear with some frequency but not dried fruit or spices. Cakes were given, but very rarely pies. Christmas was the peak time to give and receive gifts, as shown by Figure 3.2, although gift-giving was not restricted to this period. The Le Stranges feasted their tenants at Christmas, so it is possible that some of these gifts were returned to the

---

[83] J. Broad, 'Regional perspectives and variations in English dairying', in R. Hoyle (ed.), *People, Landscape and Alternative Agriculture, Agricultural History Review*, supplement 3 (2004), 95.
[84] See also Dawson, *Plenti and Grase*, 101.
[85] F. Heal, 'Food gifts, the household and the politics of exchange in early modern England', *Past and Present* 199 (2008), 44.
[86] The kitchen accounts from the 1650s do record the names of local people selling food.

Table 3.7. The range of items received as gifts, and the frequency with which they were received, 1613–27

Chickens	284
Capons	184
Turkey	179
Pigeons	107
Pigs	100
Apples	69
Hens	51
Pears	51
Soles	51
Codling	46
Curlew	46
Salmon	45
Brettcocks	44
Pease	38
Teal	38
Ducklings	37
Skulls	35
Green plover	32
Larks	28
Veal	28
Stints	24
Wardens	23
Dotterel	22
Lumps	22
Brett	21
Eggs	21
Geese	21
Goslings	21
Plovers	20
Damsons	19
Duck	19
Oysters	19
Plaice	18
Mallard	16
Sugar loaf	16
Sturgeon	15
Swans	14
Crayfish	11
Grey plover	11
Lamb	11
Redshanks	11
Eels	10
Cherries	9
Cockerels	9
Knots	9
Mead	9
Buttspragge	8
Cakes	8
Crab	8
Quinces	8
Widgeon	8

Medlars	7
Salmon trout	7
Trout	7
Barberries	6
Lemons	6
Pullets	6
Snipes	6
Butts	5
Carp	5
Cockles	5
Partridges	5
Raspberries	5
Walnuts	5
Brawn	4
Herrings	4
Oranges	4
Plums	4
Sack	4
Woodcocks	4
Conger eel	3
Grapes	3
Mackerel	3
Peacock	3
Peahens	3
Pheasants	3
Sucket	3
Wine	3
Artichokes	2
Bustard	2
Cod	2
Green geese	2
Green ginger	2
Ling	2
Maydes	2
Peaches	2
Peascods	2
Pickerel	2
Pippins	2
Salmon pie	2
Sandlings	2
Sea bream	2
Sinetts	2
Sprats	2
Whiting	2
Apricots	1
Beef	1
Bullaces	1
Cheese	1
Chicks	1
Filberts	1
Gall	1
Haddock	1

Continued

80   Consumption and Gender

Table 3.7 *Continued*

Honeycomb	1
Horsemeat	1
Hippocras	1
Marmalade	1
Mullet	1
Nuts	1
Onions	1
Rabbits	1
Saffron	1
Salt salmon	1
Seal	1
Sheldrake	1
Shrimps	1
Strawberries	1
Tarragon roots	1
Thornback	1
Turkey eggs	1
Venison	1
Verjuice	1
Vetches	1
Vinegar	1
Wash balls	1

Note: This records the number of times items were given, not the total number received.

Source: Le Strange kitchen books, 1613–27; LEST/P6, P8.

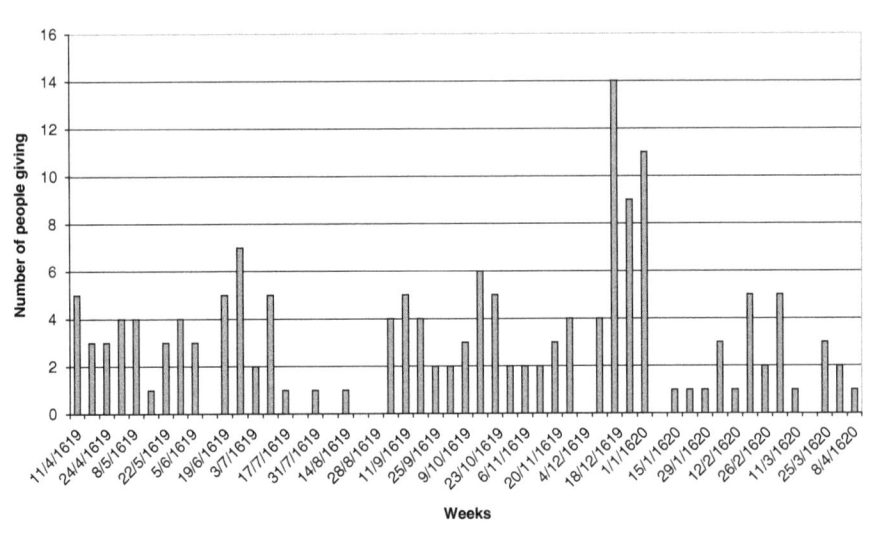

Fig. 3.2. The seasonal distribution of food gifts.
Source: Le Strange kitchen books, 1619; LEST/P6.

givers almost immediately, as cooked food presented in the mode of traditional hospitality.

Turkeys were more valuable and less common than chickens, and a relative novelty, although well established in Norfolk by this date. They were given by those of slightly higher status: large leasehold tenants and lesser gentry. People of this status also gave pigeons and other more unusual domestic or semi-domestic birds such as swans, peacocks, peahens, pheasants and partridges. Apples and pears were commonly given, but cherries, quinces, barberries, grapes, apricots, strawberries and walnuts were more unusual and again were generally given by wealthier households. Heal found that wild birds were luxuries of similar status, while sea fish were rare as gifts.[87] Here, location makes a difference. Sea fish and wild birds were common gifts at Hunstanton: many of the wild birds were coastal waders such as plovers, curlew and dotterel. They were offered to the household by the full range of gift-givers, from humble tenants to the lesser gentry. Food gifts produced or gathered outside the local economy were in the minority. Sugar loaves were the most frequent, a gift characteristic of the urban economy.[88] Eight different men gave sugar to the Le Stranges, of whom only one can be identified as a tenant. It seems likely that these were local traders of various kinds who valued the Le Stranges as customers.

Although outnumbered by purchases and home-produced items, gifts were far from insignificant in the household economy. Some items were only received as gifts, most notably turkeys, but also partridges, peacocks, pheasant, swan, cockles, crayfish, sturgeon and various wild birds and fruit. Even for chickens, which were a frequent purchase, gifts received accounted for a third of those consumed. Gifts were not without cost. At least two-thirds of gifts were immediately reciprocated with payments which Alice Le Strange described as 'rewards'. Such rewards have been interpreted as tips, given to whoever brought the gift, usually a servant or child in return for delivering it.[89] Closer examination of the payments suggest that this was not the case. The Banyards were Le Strange tenants in Hunstanton and frequent gift-givers. Gifts of chickens and capons from the Banyards were rewarded with sums varying from nothing at all to 3d, 4d, 6d, 8d and 12d: payments of 6d were most common. It seems unlikely that a servant or child would be paid 6d for making a delivery from the neighbouring village, which was less than a mile away from Hunstanton Hall, given that an adult man was paid 4d for a day's hard labour in the same accounts. Instead, the reward seems to relate to the cost of what was given. A gift of six chickens was typically rewarded with a payment of 6d, half the normal cost of chickens recorded in the accounts. Fat capons were purchased for 1s each, and gifts of two capons were rewarded with payments of between 4d and 12d. Yet the relationship between the value of the gift and the size of the reward was only a loose one: for instance, a fresh salmon, which cost 2s 8d to purchase, was met with rewards varying between 6d and 1s 6d.

[87] Heal, 'Food gifts', 55–6.
[88] Heal, 'Food gifts', 45.
[89] Heal, 'Food gifts', 48, 62.

Anthropological studies of the nature of the gift argue that gifts were given with the expectation of receiving something in return, but that the return gift should be delayed in time.[90] The payment of a 'reward' on receipt breaks this rule: presenting a gift and receiving 6d in return neither allowed the full gift to stand nor equated to the real monetary value of what was given. However, there is no indication that it was regarded as insulting in early seventeenth-century England, as many people made multiple presentations of food to the household for reward. The same people also sometimes made full gifts for which no reward was given. In the conventions of gift-giving, the presentation of a reward appears as an assertion by Alice Le Strange of her household's social superiority and her right to give and choose favours, even in the face of a gift. Alice Le Strange would have expressed it differently, perhaps as a careful measurement of the current balance of favours and needs between her household and the household of the gift-giver.

The people who gave food gifts to the Le Stranges were almost always of lower social status. People of high status rarely appear. The Le Stranges received no food gifts from their cousins the Mordaunts or Hobarts, despite frequent house visits, nor from their friends the Knivetts, whose christenings they attended, nor the Townshends, who acted as godparents to their children. Sir Ralph Hare, an old friend of Sir Hamon, never sent gifts. Their cousins the Bozouns, with whom they had many other interactions, sent a gift of pheasants once, Alice's sister Yelverton a gift of carp once, while Hamon's maternal uncle, Uncle Bell, sent gifts only twice, and the Spelmans only once. Lady Sidney, with whom the Le Stranges stayed frequently at Walsingham, sent three gifts, all unusual: seeds, artichokes and apricots, suggesting a shared interest in gardening rather than anything else. Clearly, food gifts held little significance in holding together the social bonds between these families. The only exception to this pattern was Alice's father, Richard Stubbe, who sent gifts with some regularity: salmon, salmon pie, beef, venison and larks. Here the relationship was different: it seems that his household in neighbouring Sedgeford was treated almost as an extension of Hunstanton Hall, and when he had surplus food he sent it on to his daughter and son-in-law, with whom he maintained a close relationship. It is likely they did the same.

The most frequent gift-givers instead came from groups of slightly lower social status who were nonetheless wealthy by local standards: the lesser gentry, wealthy yeoman and clergymen. People with sixteen different surnames appear thirty or more times presenting food gifts to the Le Stranges in the twelve years for which kitchen accounts survive between 1613 and 1627. All were tenants of the Le Stranges, and at least ten were leaseholders. Two, Mr Burwood and Mr Hocknell, were local clergyman.[91] Two more, the Guybons and Warners, were 'cousins' related to the Le Strange family: the Guybons were the largest landholders in Sedgeford and the Warners were bailiffs of Gressenhall. Four of the other families,

---

[90] See P. Bourdieu, *Outline of a Theory of Practice* (Cambridge, 1977), 5; C. Levi-Strauss, 'The principle of reciprocity', in Komter, *The Gift*.
[91] Mr Burwood was the rector of Hunstanton; Mr Hocknell was at Ringstead St Andrew. See the will of Lawrence Hockenhull, clerk, registered 1626: NRO, NCC register Mittings, 76.

the Bastards, Cremers, Banyards and Segons, also acted as bailiffs for the Le Stranges between 1610 and 1625. The most frequent givers of gifts were the Read family, making ninety-seven gifts between them: this family included not only two tenants but also prominent local officials: both John Read and Christopher Read were collectors of the subsidy, while William Read was a hundred official. All these families were closely intertwined with the Le Stranges, who they relied on for legal protection and economic and social favours.

Not all tenants gave gifts to the Le Stranges. A comparison between gift-givers and a 1621 list of Hunstanton tenants (free, customary and leasehold) for the manor of Hunstanton and Mustrells reveals that, of the fifty-nine tenants listed, between thirty-one and thirty-six gave the Le Stranges food gifts at some point between 1613 and 1627 whereas between twenty-three and twenty-eight did not.[92] Larger tenants were more likely to give than smallholders: twenty of the twenty-six tenants who paid more than 20s rent a year to the Le Stranges gave gifts compared with eleven of the thirty-three who paid less than 20s. Day labourers employed by the Le Stranges for agricultural and building work rarely gave gifts. Of the nineteen men employed by the day during 1619 only eight gave food gifts, often on a single occasion. Many of the Le Stranges' most regular workers never gave gifts.

The presentation of food gifts was an aspect of the local economy in which women played an active part. Of the 317 people who gave or sent food gifts to the Le Stranges between 1613 and 1627, 30 per cent were women. In many instances, both husband and wife sent gifts on different occasions, but Alice Le Strange carefully recorded exactly who the gift came from, even if it was delivered by a third party such as a servant, child or grandchild. Many of the items sent by women were the products of their own labour or management. The gifts presented by women were dominated by poultry and fruit. Despite making up only 30 per cent of gift-givers, the majority of chickens and half the gifts of apples and pears were given by women.[93] In contrast, other types of food, such as game birds, wild birds and seafood, were only rarely given by women. Some women specialized in particular gifts. Widow Mason made half the gifts of mead presented between 1613 and 1627, and she also gave honeycomb on one occasion. Through the record of gifts it is possible to glimpse into a wholly female network of support and patronage. Alice Le Strange's midwife, Goodwife Crisp, made gifts on nine occasions between 1613 and 1627: four of these gifts were made just before or after the birth of one of Alice's children, but the gifts continued long after Alice's childbearing years. Four wet nurses used by the Le Stranges, nurses Longstraw, Cobbes, Costen and Lane, all married women in local families, also made gifts.

The tradition of making gifts of food, so vibrant in Alice Le Strange's earliest kitchen accounts, was nonetheless in decline. In the first five full years of surviving kitchen accounts, dating from 1613 to 1619, the household received an average of

---

[92] List of tenants taken from LEST/EH 5. For five names it was not possible to make an exact fit as the first name was not recorded in the kitchen accounts.
[93] Based on an analysis of the gifts given between April 1617 and April 1619.

186 food gifts per year.[94] By 1622–6 this had fallen to 125. The first kitchen account which survives after the turmoil of the Civil War records a mere thirty-two gifts in 1650. The Le Stranges' strong Royalist stance had reduced their political power and ability to offer patronage. Tenants became more assertive. Chickens and other local products were now typically purchased from tenants instead, and the names of those making sales recorded. Purchases of turkeys, formerly the archetypal Christmas gift, now outnumbered the handful received as gifts.

CONCLUSION

The Le Strange household accounts do not record a static pre-industrial mode of consumption, but a moment in the constantly changing society and economy that was early modern England. The importance of London was increasing, food gifts were on the decline and home production for large gentry households was holding steady. Pleasure shopping may have existed in the early seventeenth century, but it is barely in evidence here. Hamon Le Strange was partial to picking up hats, gloves and books, but only travelled to London or Norwich when politics, law or social commitments drew him there. Alice Le Strange's visits to London suggest why satirists may have poked fun at country gentlewomen's shopping habits: she visited only rarely, and so, when she did, had extensive purchases to make. She was not acquiring personal fripperies, but purchasing furnishings and equipment for the household in consultation with her husband. The gendered pattern of purchasing revealed by the Le Strange accounts accords closely with what Vickery has observed for the eighteenth century. Men bought their own clothes, weapons, books, horses and coaches, and scientific instruments; women bought clothes for themselves and their children, textiles for the home and food. More expensive furnishings were bought by men and women together. Pahl's study of money and marriage in Britain in the 1980s suggests that these patterns persist to the present day.[95]

The history of retailing barely scratches the surface of the multitude of ways in which things could be acquired in the early modern economy. Fairs, markets and pedlars hardly feature in the Le Stranges' household accounts; instead, it is the close links to producers that loom large. There were purchases from anonymous retailers and foreign goods bought ready-made, but many purchases involved specific social links. Clothing and furnishings were typically made to order by trusted craftsmen: either urban specialists or local workers paid by the day. Home production provided employment for local families as day labourers or servants within the Le Strange household. Food gifts demonstrate the degree to which the Le Stranges' consumption was intertwined with local politics, society and economy. All of this serves to emphasize the complexity of consumption in this period. It was not just a matter of planning what was needed in advance, so that it could be ordered from distant retailers and craftsmen in response to detailed instructions or produced in

---

[94] Measured per person making a gift, rather than per item received, which would be much higher.
[95] J. Pahl, *Money and Marriage* (New York, 1989), 143–4.

sufficient quantity at home. It was a matter of balancing local patronage, so as not to offend friends, tenants and economic contacts, and to support rather than disrupt the local economy. It was also a matter of spending wisely and to maximum effect. Patterns of expenditure show that money was spent on textiles and food in proportion to overall spending, which in turn was closely related to income. To overspend would lead to indebtedness and ridicule; to underspend would reduce the status of the family. Food and textiles, the two dominant categories of domestic expenditure, were not only basic necessities but also luxuries which displayed the family's status. Despite input from her husband, the majority of this business of managing consumption was in the hands of Alice Le Strange.

4

Everyday Consumables

Meate rem[aining]: 7 Collers and 3 Sheildes of Brawne; a Tongue; a Boare Pye and 2 Apple Tartes[1]

Food, drink, medicines, fuel and cleaning products constitute consumption in its most literal sense: those things that were used up—consumables. In most cases, they were not just used, but used daily. As Mintz writes: 'anything *that* everyday must be quite special. Our tastes and habits in other spheres of consumption ... do not approach food in significance'.[2] Douglas and Isherwood observe that variations in food consumption are used to mark both the passage of time, through daily, weekly and annual routines, and differences in social rank.[3] Styles of eating, heating and cleanliness were both everyday experiences and important indicators of status. Consumables remain the poor relation in studies of early modern consumption, just as they do in contemporary sociology.[4] Pennell notes that the lack of studies 'exploring daily and extraordinary food habits as a prism for attitudes to consuming' in early modern England is especially surprising given the high proportion of expenditure which went on food.[5] Studies of early modern food and drink have concentrated on a number of changes that were evident from 1660 onwards and gathered pace in the eighteenth century. The introduction and spread of tea-drinking with sugar brought profound changes in the ordinary British diet, as well as new ways of socializing, and an array of new accessories such as tea pots, tea cups and sugar spoons.[6] The replacement of the single large cooking pot with saucepans, the increasing use of forks and the larger numbers of plates all point to new ways of cooking and dining.[7] Cookery books show an increased French

---

[1] Alice Le Strange, kitchen accounts (May 1619); LEST/P6.
[2] S. W. Mintz, 'The changing roles of food in the study of consumption', in J. Brewer and R. Porter (eds.), *Consumption and the World of Goods* (London, 1993), 262.
[3] M. Douglas and B. Isherwood, *The World of Goods: Towards an Anthropology of Consumption* (London, 1996), 43–4.
[4] J. Gronow and A. Warde, 'Introduction', in J. Gronow and A. Warde (eds.), *Ordinary Consumption* (London, 2001), 3–4.
[5] S. Pennell, 'Consumption and consumerism in early modern England', *Historical Journal* 42 (1999), 561. Expenditure on food is discussed in Chapter 3: Domestic expenditure.
[6] C. Shammas, *The Pre-Industrial Consumer in England and America* (Oxford, 1990), ch. 5; Mintz, 'The changing roles of food', 261–73; W. D. Smith, 'Complications of the commonplace: tea, sugar and imperialism', *Journal of Interdisciplinary History* 23:2 (1992), 259–78.
[7] L. Weatherill, *Consumer Behaviour and Material Culture in Britain 1660–1760* (London, 1988); S. Pennell, '"Pots and pans history": the material culture of the kitchen in early modern England',

influence, representing, it is argued, the first significant break with medieval ingredients and techniques.[8] The early seventeenth century predates this period of change. Had food culture really been static since the medieval period? Thirsk's recent study suggests not: she argues that the English diet was subject to 'fads and fashions' from at least 1500 onwards, with a steady stream of changes in foodstuffs and cooking techniques.[9]

Food, medicines and household consumables were all concerned with bodily needs. Food and medicine were closely connected, using many of the same ingredients and preparation techniques. Some items, such as sugar candy and rose water, were both medicines and foodstuffs. Popular dietary regimens, such as Thomas Elyot's *The Castle of Health* (1595), sought to promote health through diet. Warmth and cleanliness were essential elements for maintaining health and caring for the sick. In the early seventeenth century, food, medical care and cleanliness were all elements of housewifery: their provision for the household was assumed to fall to women in the first instance. Laundry was exclusively undertaken by women, but food preparation and medical care could be full-time male occupations and those considered to be expert practitioners, high-status cooks and physicians were men. The Le Stranges employed a male cook and relied on the services of specialist male healthcare providers. This chapter begins with a detailed examination of the diet of the Le Strange household, covering the type and quantity of food and drink consumed and the seasonality of that consumption. It is followed by a section looking at the meanings of food consumption: patterns of feast and fast, the impact of status and fashion on food consumption, and comparisons between actual diet and recipe books. Next, there is a section on medical care. Despite Alice Le Strange's reputed skill in surgery and ability to produce medicines at home, much of the Le Stranges' medical care, both advice and medicines, was purchased. The household accounts enable the care provided for different members of the family, the types of practitioners who were employed and the range of medicines bought to be examined. The final part of the chapter opens up a neglected topic: household consumables such as candles, fuel and soap. Domestic fuel was undergoing a significant shift from wood to coal in the period under consideration here, whereas standards of cleanliness, as Thomas has noted, differed according to both rank and gender.[10]

Journal of Design History 11:3 (1998), 201–16; N. Cox, '"A flesh pott, or a brasse pott or a pott to boil in": changes in metal and fuel technology in the early modern period and the implications for cooking', in M. Donald and L. Hurcombe (eds.), *Gender and Material Culture in Historical Perspective* (Basingstoke, 2000), 143–57.

[8] S. Mennell, *All Manners of Food: Eating and Taste in England and France from the Middle Ages to the Present* (Oxford, 1985), 88–9.

[9] J. Thirsk, *Food in Early Modern England: Phases, Fads, Fashions 1500–1760* (London, 2007).

[10] M. Spufford, 'Chimneys, wood and coal', in P.S. Barnwell and Malcolm Airs (eds.), *Houses and the Hearth Tax: The Later Stuart House and Society* (York, 2006); K. Thomas, 'Cleanliness and godliness in early modern England', in A. Fletcher and P. Roberts (eds.), *Religion, Culture and Society in Early Modern Britain* (Cambridge, 1994), 70–2.

DIET

Despite a research agenda set by Appleby some years ago, surprisingly little is known about what people were actually eating in England in the period between 1500 and 1660.[11] Thirsk's *Food in Early Modern England* builds on pioneering research by Wilson and Mennell, and, like them, she draws much of her data from cookery books and medical texts.[12] Both Wilson and Thirsk use household accounts, but Dawson's recent study of the late sixteenth-century Willoughby family is the first to offer a detailed study of food based on accounts as a source.[13] In doing so, he builds on a rich vein of late medieval studies using similar techniques, carried out by Dyer, Harvey, Woolgar, and Threlfall-Holmes.[14] These medieval studies provide both a point of comparison and a set of techniques for analysing household accounts. In comparison with the modern diet, wealthy households of medieval and early modern England enjoyed a wide range of food in the types of meat, fish and plants eaten. In other ways, however, the diet was monotonous. It was high in meat, bread and alcohol. Bread was overwhelmingly dominant as the main form of carbohydrate, beef as the form of meat and beer as drink. This trio of foodstuffs was even eaten for breakfast.[15] Figure 4.1 shows the proportion of meat, fish and dairy produce consumed, by edible weight. Beef accounts for exactly one-third of consumption, while together beef, cheese, mutton, pork and the Le Stranges' favourite fish, plaice, make up more than three-quarters of the weight consumed. Individual patterns of consumption in the household are estimated in Table 4.1, assuming an average of twenty-five people per day were being fed.[16]

The bread came in three grades: highest quality manchet bread, which was white bread made from wheat flour; middling quality cheat bread, which contained some bran and which could be made from wheat or a mixture of grains; and household or brown bread, which was wholemeal.[17] In the Le Strange household, manchet bread

---

[11] A.B. Appleby, 'Diet in sixteenth-century England: sources, problems, possibilities', in C. Webster (ed.), *Health, Medicine and Mortality in the Sixteenth Century* (Cambridge, 1979), 97–116.

[12] A.C. Wilson, *Food and Drink in Britain from the Stone Age to Recent Times* (London, 1973); Mennell, *All Manners of Food.*

[13] M. Dawson, *Plenti and Grase: Food and Drink in a Sixteenth Century Household* (Totnes, 2009), a study of the household accounts of the Willoughbys of Wollaton Hall in Nottinghamshire and Middleton Hall in Warwickshire.

[14] C. Dyer, *Standards of Living in the Later Middle Ages: Social Change in England c.1200–1520* (Cambridge, 1989); B. Harvey, *Living and Dying in Medieval England 1100–1540* (Oxford, 1993); C.M. Woolgar, *The Great Household in Late Medieval England* (New Haven, 1999); M. Threlfall-Holmes, *Monks and Markets: Durham Cathedral Priory 1460–1520* (Oxford, 2005); C.M. Woolgar, D. Serjeantson, and T. Waldron (eds.), *Food in Medieval England: Diet and Nutrition* (Oxford, 2006).

[15] N. Le Strange, *Merry Passages and Jeasts*, ed. H.F. Lippincott (Salzburg, 1974), 40–1, describing scholars having breakfast at an inn.

[16] For the size of the household see Chapter 6: Life cycle and expenditure.

[17] W. Harrison, *The Description of England*, ed. G. Edelen (New York, 1968), 133–5; G. Markham, *The English Housewife*, ed. M. Best (Montreal, 1986), 209–10.

Everyday Consumables 89

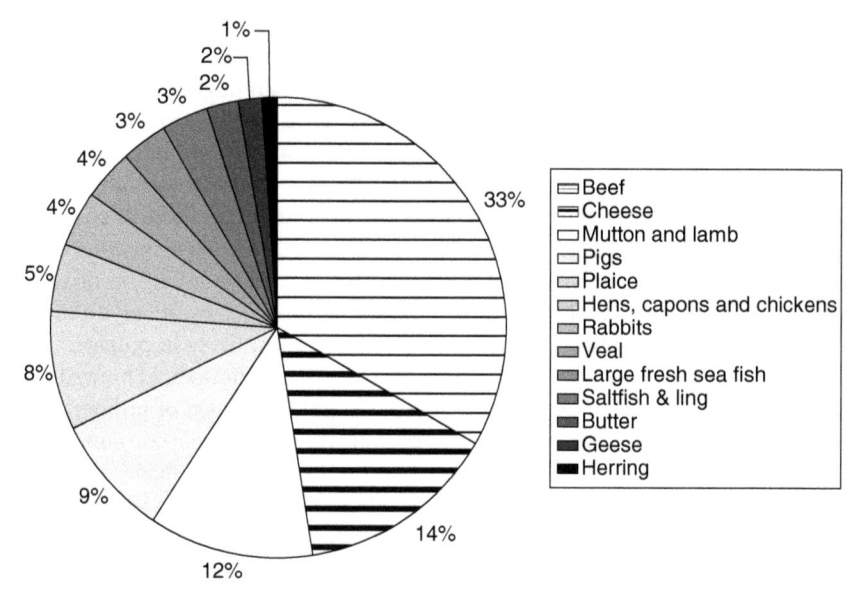

Fig. 4.1. The proportion of meat, fish and dairy produce consumed, by edible weight, 1619.
Notes: Edible weights of meat and fish from particular animals taken from Harvey, *Living and Dying*, pp. 226–30. Different weights are used for adults and young, as given in Harvey. For disagreement with Harvey's estimates, see Dawson, *Plenti and Grase*, pp. 85 and 119. Large fresh sea fish includes turbot, thornback, sole, codling and others, estimated to have an average edible weight equal to cod. A pint of butter is assumed to be equivalent to a pound. Rabbits are assumed to be young rather than mature.
Source: Le Strange kitchen accounts, 1619; LEST/P6.

Table 4.1. Individual adult consumption per week (assuming twenty-five in the household)

	Weekly	Daily
Manchet bread	1.4 batches	0.2 batches
Cheat and household bread	1.3 batches or 8.4 lbs of wheat and rye	0.2 batches or 1.2 lbs of wheat and rye
Beer	6.8 gallons	7.8 pints
Beef	5.2 lbs	11.9 oz
Mutton and pork	3.0 lbs	6.9 oz
Fish	2.4 lbs	5.4 oz
Cheese	2.1 lbs	4.8 oz

Source: Le Strange kitchen accounts, 1619; LEST/P6.

was purchased, while cheat bread and household bread were made at home from a mixture of wheat and rye, baked at least once a week. Alice Le Strange measured the consumption of bread in 'casts' or batches, but does not note the number of loaves each cast contained. She does record the quantity of wheat and rye used each week, however: over the whole year, 74.5 bushels of wheat and 219 of rye were used.

According to Campbell, a bushel of wheat weighs 53 lb and rye 51 lb.[18] These were used to make 1712.5 casts of cheat and household bread: thus, a maximum of 8.8 lb of grain was used to make each cast or batch of bread, although 8 lbs seems more likely, once we account for other uses of grain and loss as bran. Harrison writes that 40 casts of manchet bread were made from 'the flour of one bushel'.[19] This statement, supported by evidence from Stone for the medieval period, suggests that casts of manchet bread were much smaller and lighter than those of cheat and household bread, weighing 0.86 lb.[20] On an average day, an average member of the Le Strange household ate cheat and household bread made from 1.2 lb of wheat and rye at a proportion of 1:3, and 0.2 casts of manchet bread of unknown weight.[21] Oatmeal was also eaten in small quantities, most likely in pottage.

The other major use of grain in the diet was for beer. The household brewed beer every two weeks. Over the year 168.5 hogsheads (9099 gallons) of ordinary beer (known as buttery beer after the room in which it was stored) were consumed, and 6 hogsheads (324 gallons) of stronger cellar beer. The beer was made using 400 bushels of barley malt. In the medieval period 8 bushels of malt made 50–96 gallons of ale.[22] Beer, brewed with hops as well as malt, gradually replaced ale as the most common English drink during the fifteenth and sixteenth centuries. Beer keeps better than ale, but its other great advantage was that 'beer drew more alcohol from the grain'.[23] In fact, legislation at York in 1601 assumed twice as much beer as ale could be produced with the same quantity of malt.[24] Harrison, citing direct observation of his wife's brewing techniques in the late sixteenth century, noted that 20 gallons of beer could be produced from 1 bushel, or 160 gallons from a quarter of malt.[25] The Le Strange household made just over 196 gallons from each quarter, including the strong cellar beer, so their ordinary buttery beer must have been quite weak.[26] The household consumed beer in large quantities: about 8 pints a day for each adult, a typical per capita consumption in late medieval and early modern England.[27] Wine was also drunk by some members of the

---

[18] B.M.S. Campbell, *English Seigniorial Agriculture 1250–1450* (Cambridge, 2000), 215.
[19] Harrison, *Description of England*, 134.
[20] D.J. Stone, 'The consumption of field crops in late medieval England', in Woolgar et al., *Food in Medieval England*, 14, 16.
[21] Dawson, *Plenti and Grase*, 70–1, discusses the weight of bread that could be obtained from a weight of grain.
[22] Dyer, *Standards of Living*, 58.
[23] J. Bennett, *Ale, Beer, and Brewsters in England: Women's Work in a Changing World, 1300–1600* (Oxford, 1996), quotation from 79.
[24] R.W. Unger, *Beer in the Middle Ages and the Renaissance* (Philadelphia, 2004), 136.
[25] Bennett, *Ale, Beer and Brewsters*, 86; Harrison, *Description of England*, 137–8.
[26] This is similar to the amount quoted by P. Sambrook, *Country House Brewing in England, 1500–1900* (London, 1996), 111; see also Dawson, *Plenti and Grase*, 78.
[27] Harvey, *Living and Dying*, 58: the monks of Westminster had a basic allowance of a gallon of ale a day; the same allowance is found in the household of Alice de Bryene in Suffolk 1412–13. A.L. Martin, *Alcohol, Sex, and Gender in Late Medieval and Early Modern Europe* (Basingstoke, 2001), 9; and as the ration in the English Navy in 1565, Unger, *Beer*, 129; while John Haynes of Exeter purchased enough beer for each member of his household to consume 1.75 gallons a day in 1634. C. Muldrew, *The Economy of Obligation: The Culture of Credit and Social Relations in Early Modern England* (Basingstoke, 1998), 65–7. For lower estimates see Martin, *Alcohol, Sex, and Gender*, 129.

household, with 203 gallons purchased for the whole year in 1619–20. It is likely that wine consumption was concentrated around Christmas and other feasts, with only a few senior members of the household maintaining a small amount of steady consumption at other times. In the fifteenth century, monks received an allowance of between 0.25 and 1.4 pints of wine a day, as well as their ale, while Dyer estimates 'superior members' of wealthy medieval households consumed two-thirds of a pint a day.[28]

The Le Stranges ate a wide range of domestic and wild animals, a pattern found in other wealthy households of this period.[29] The large quantities of beef were mostly bought from the butcher, along with regular purchases of tongue and 'souse and feet' (pickled pigs' ears and feet).[30] The accounts carefully distinguish between the meat of young animals, such as veal, lamb and pig (or piglet), and mature animals, such as beef, mutton, pork and bacon. To these standard domestic animals were added two forms of semi-domesticated game from the estate: occasional deer and frequent rabbits. The rabbits came from the Le Stranges' own warren, and deer from the 200-acre park which surrounded Hunstanton Hall.[31] Birrell calculates that an average deer park of 100–200 acres could support 50–100 deer, of which 9 per cent could be culled each year.[32] The monotony of hunks of red meat was livened up with a wide variety of bird meat, which, although not as significant in terms of weight, must have made the diet more pleasurable. Five types of domestic poultry were consumed: chickens, ducks, geese, pigeons and turkeys. Young chickens and adult hens and capons were the most popular birds, accounting for 50 per cent of the edible weight of poultry consumed. Geese and turkeys accounted for 17 per cent each, and were mostly eaten around Christmas. Pigeons, although the most numerous, accounted for 9 per cent, just a little more than ducks, at 8 per cent.[33] Herons were also taken 'of store' either from a heronry on the estate or wild from the nearby marshes.[34] A few partridges were eaten. Added to these were three types of wild bird. Larks were eaten in large numbers—Wilson describes them as 'the favourite small birds' of this period, 'much commended by physicians'.[35] Coastal wading birds also seem to have been relished by the Le Stranges: in 1619–20 the household ate 130 stint, thirty-eight snipe, thirty-seven plovers, twenty-six dotterels, twelve knots, nine redshanks and seven curlew. Three types of wild duck were consumed—mallard, teal and widgeon—most of which were

---

[28] Threlfall-Holmes, *Monks and Markets*, 67–9.
[29] Thirsk, *Food*, 45.
[30] Wilson, *Food and Drink*, 90: 'Not only were the hindparts of a hog or boar put into pickle on occasion, but also its ears, cheeks, snout and trotters, the whole mixture was known as souse.'
[31] An inventory for Hunstanton Hall in 1675 records 'the hay of the meadow for the deer: £8'; NA PROB 4/3988.
[32] J. Birrell, 'Procuring, preparing and serving venison in late medieval England', in Woolgar et al., *Food in Medieval England*, 187.
[33] Edible weight of chickens, hens, ducks and geese, from Harvey, *Living and Dying*, 228–30. Edible weight of pigeons estimated at 0.3635 lb per bird, and turkeys at 8.5 lb per bird.
[34] On heronries, see D.J. Stone, 'The consumption and supply of birds in Late Medieval England', in Woolgar et al., *Food in Medieval England*, 158–9.
[35] Wilson, *Food and Drink*, 122.

killed by Hamon Le Strange or his senior servants out hawking and wildfowling in the marshes of Hunstanton and Heacham.

Fish, cheese and eggs provided further variation from red meat, and were the mainstay of the diet on 'fish-days' and during Lent. A steady intake of salted cod or 'salt fish' and higher quality salted ling was supplemented with a plentiful supply of fresh sea fish.[36] Plaice was relatively cheap at Hunstanton, costing on average 1d for five and a half fish, and eaten in very large numbers. Other larger and more expensive fresh sea fish were also consumed. The most expensive were brett or turbot, costing between 40d and 10d, of which nineteen were eaten in 1619–20, and fresh salmon at a similar price, of which they had five, mostly as gifts. Others, costing between 2d and 6d each, were butt or flounder, codling, lump, sole, thornback and the unidentifiable brettcocks and skull.[37] Herring was eaten only during Lent, when it was consumed in large amounts, with pickled white herring preferred to red or smoked herring. Oysters were bought in large numbers when they were available. Other seafoods, such as cockles, crabs and crayfish, appeared only a few times a year. Eggs were also purchased on a weekly basis. The accounts record cost rather than the number: Rogers notes 1619 as an unusually expensive year for eggs, with 100 costing 3s 6d.[38] If this was also the price in rural Norfolk, the Le Stranges' average weekly expenditure of 25d would have purchased at least fifty-nine eggs.

The flavouring for grain, meat, fish and dairy produce was provided by dried fruit and spices, mostly imported from outside England, and by fresh herbs, fruit and vegetables, which came almost exclusively from the garden. Currants and raisins, sugar, salt and mustard seed were used in large quantities, along with vinegar, where purchases possibly supplemented a homemade supply. Almonds, aniseed, caraway, cinnamon, ginger, liquorice, mace, nutmeg, pepper, salad oil (olive oil) and walnuts were used sparingly.[39] Saffron was not purchased, but was a speciality crop in Norfolk, and was grown by the Le Stranges. Other exotic foods were only very occasional purchases. No cloves, dates, oranges, olives and capers were purchased by the Le Stranges in 1619–20, although they do appear in small amounts in the accounts of 1620–1 and/or 1621–2.

The final element of the diet was locally grown fresh fruit and vegetables. The consumption of these items was not recorded in the kitchen accounts, although gifts and purchases of seed, plants and fruit occasionally were, along with the gardener's wages. Occasionally entries give more detail: the kitchen accounts for May 1623 record a purchase of seeds for 'wallflowers 4d: garlick 4d: fennell 2d;

---

[36] Wilson, *Food and Drink*, 35, on the superior nature of 'ling'.
[37] Fish names, unlike bird names, were often local and have changed over time, making identification difficult.
[38] J.E. Thorold Rogers, *A History of Agriculture and Prices in England*. Vol. V. *1583–1702* (Oxford, 1887), 374. If anything eggs would have been cheaper in rural Norfolk.
[39] In comparison, the fourteenth-century Le Stranges at Hunstanton purchased pepper, almonds, galingale, walnuts, ginger, oil, sugar, cinnamon, saffron, liquorice, cumin and aniseed: C.M. Woolgar, 'Diet and consumption in gentry and noble households: a case study from around the Wash', in R.E. Archer and S. Walker (eds.), *Rulers and Ruled in Late Medieval England: Essays Presented to Gerald Harriss* (London, 1995), 29.

purselin 2d: cardus 2d:[40] cucumbers 2d: melons 2d; Alexanders 3d: stockgillflowers 3d: cabbages 4d'. Apples, pears and damsons were frequently received as gifts of food, suggesting that they were commonly grown locally. Plums, wardens, quinces, medlars, bullaces, peaches, apricots, raspberries, barberries, grapes and cherries also appear as less common gifts. The Le Stranges purchased cherry trees, strawberry sets and '8 score gooseberry standards' in 1622, while in 1635 a new orchard was planted after the purchase of eleven pear trees, nine apple trees, eight plum trees, two Portugal quinces and two peach trees: a melacoton and a nectarine.[41] In 1619–20 the only fresh vegetable recorded in the kitchen book was peas, which were purchased and received as gifts when newly ripe in June and July. Both peas and beans were grown on the home farm, mainly for animal fodder, but they could also have been used in the kitchen. Onions and garlic were occasionally purchased, probably when the household ran out of its own supply.

Markham's *The English Housewife* (1615) and Elyot's *The Castle of Health* (1595), both books owned by the Le Stranges, list the types of plants that were grown in gardens and eaten in this period. Many of these were very common in England by this date: such as leeks, lettuce, spinach, rocket and cress, and herbs, such as parsley, thyme, sage and hyssop.[42] There is direct evidence that the Le Stranges acquired rosemary seed, fennel seed, seed of sweet marjoram and tarragon roots; nonetheless, we can expect a much wider range of plants than this to have been present in their garden. There is less certainty about the new and exotic plants listed by Markham and Elyot, and painted by Nathaniel Bacon, the Suffolk gentleman, artist and gardener, in his *Cook Maid with Still Life of Fruit and Vegetables* (c.1620–5).[43] Cabbages, melons, cucumbers and artichokes all appear in the accounts as seeds, plants or gifts, but there is no mention of pumpkins, tomatoes, parsnips, carrots, turnips, radishes or potatoes. Carrots do appear in one of Nicholas Le Strange's *Merry Jeasts*, as a novelty in beef stew. The jest was told by Sir William Spring, who married Elizabeth Le Strange in 1636, so probably dates from the 1630s or 1640s.[44]

While the accounts record the ingredients of the meals consumed in the household, they say very little about how they were cooked and served. The employment of a male cook as one of their best paid servants with a wage of £5 a year indicates that the Le Stranges cared about cookery. Alice, and later her daughter-in-law Anne, also prepared food in the kitchen at least occasionally. Another merry jest, recounted by Nicholas Le Strange, begins 'my mother was cutting up a plumpe fatt Rabbit, and my wife satt by her....' in the kitchen.[45] The kitchen accounts provide a list for each week of the 'meat remaining'—cooked dishes that were

---

[40] A carduus is a thistle, possibly a globe artichoke.
[41] Disbursement accounts; LEST/P7, fol. 111, winter 1635. The trees cost £3 10s in total, plus 7s 6d for the gardener to collect them.
[42] See C.C. Dyer, 'Gardens and garden produce in the later middle ages', in Woolgar et al., *Food in Medieval England*, 34; and Thirsk, *Food*, 8.
[43] K. Hearn, *Nathaniel Bacon: Artist, Gentleman and Gardener* (London, 2005).
[44] Le Strange, *Merry Jeasts*, 121–2.
[45] Le Strange, *Merry Jeasts*, 80.

being stored ready for consumption. The most common item was collars (pieces of neck) and shields (shoulder) of 'brawn', or pickled pork,[46] followed by joints of mutton, pork and veal, and various game birds. There were a wide variety of pies: pies of tongue, lamb, apple, boar, salmon, pear, venison, warden, pheasant, pigeon, goose and bustard are all recorded.

The consumption of particular foodstuffs was rarely spread evenly throughout the year. Food consumption followed an annual routine that was affected both by seasonal variations of the availability of foods and by cultural norms that dictated some foods were eaten at certain times and avoided at others. Figure 4.2 depicts the seasonality of food consumption in the Le Strange household.[47] Young animals and fresh dairy produce were a feature of the summer; mature animals, wild and domestic, of the early winter. Pigeons, partridges, larks, wild duck and oysters all had well-defined seasons. The natural cycle created a 'hungry gap' from January to April, when little fresh produce was available. At this time, food that stored well became the mainstay: salted and pickled fish, cheese, apples, dried fruit and, of course, grain for bread and beer. Yet the kitchen accounts make it clear that a wealthy household like that of the Le Stranges was not held hostage by the seasons. Poultry, pork, bacon and veal were all consumed in late winter and early spring. Beef and tongue were eaten all year round except during Lent, despite variations in price. Not all wild foods were strongly seasonal: the Le Stranges ate wading birds and large fresh sea fish in all seasons.

The impact of local availability and personal taste is also evident. The sandy soil of north-west Norfolk encouraged the cultivation of rye and rabbits.[48] The location of Hunstanton on the edge of the North Sea meant that fresh sea fish, and particularly flatfish of various types, were easily available, as were oysters.[49] Medieval household accounts from Hunstanton show that using rye flour for bread and plaice as a staple fish were longstanding patterns of consumption for the Le Stranges.[50] Other foods were relative novelties: turkeys received as gifts at Christmas show that East Anglia was an established centre of turkey rearing less than a century after the birds had been introduced from the New World.[51] Types of fish were particularly susceptible to local variations. Conger eel was commonly eaten along the south coast, but it does not appear at all at Hunstanton.[52] At

---

[46] On brawn, see Harrison, *Description of England*, 313–14, Wilson, *Food and Drink*, 88–90, and Dawson, *Plenti and Grase*, 102.
[47] Similar to the pattern noted in C. Dyer, 'Seasonal patterns of food consumption in the later middle ages', in Woolgar et al., *Food in Medieval England*.
[48] Wilson, *Food and Drink*, 256, notes that 'rye bread was still universal in Norfolk' in the early modern period.
[49] Post-medieval earthworks reveal the presence of oyster beds on the coast near Hunstanton Hall, whether these were active in the early seventeenth century is unclear: B. Cushion, 'Heacham: Earthwork vestiges of Norfolk's oyster industry?', *Norfolk Archaeology* 43:2 (1999), 346–50.
[50] Dyer, *Standards of Living*, 57; Dyer, 'Seasonal patterns', 202; a more detailed discussion of the fourteenth-century Hunstanton accounts can be found in Woolgar, 'Diet and consumption'.
[51] Turkeys were introduced to England in 1523–4: Wilson, *Food and Drink*, 128–30; Thirsk, *Food*, 254; Dawson, *Plenti and Grase*, 111.
[52] D. Serjeantson and C.M. Woolgar, 'Fish consumption in medieval England', in Woolgar et al., *Food in Medieval England*, 108–9; Woolgar, 'Diet and consumption', 25–7.

	Early and Late Summer Duckling (100%) Pigeon (93%) Lamb (100%) Fresh butter (81%) Young pigs (90%) Chickens (89%)		
Early Summer and Late Winter Veal (83%)	**Early Summer: Mid-April to Mid-July** Veal (61%) Chicken (59%) Lamb (69%) Heron (100%) Gosling (100%) Peas	**Late Summer: Mid-July to Mid-October** Young pigs (67%) Partridge (70%) Oysters (54%) Pear damson and plum	**Late Summer and Early Winter** Mutton (74%) Duck (86%) Lark (98%) Venison (100%) Partridge (96%) Oysters (86%)
	Late Winter: Mid-January to Mid-April Pickled herring (100%) Plaice (72%) Stockfish (45%)	**Early Winter: Mid-October to Mid-January** Mature pigs (59%) Venison (88%) Rabbit (42%) Geese (61%) Turkey (66%) Wading birds (58%) Wild duck (71%)	
	Early and Late Winter Capons and Hens (94%) Gifts of apples (100%) Currants and raisins (76%) Wild duck (100%) Mature pigs (88%) Turkey (100%)		

Fig. 4.2. The seasonality of food consumption in 1619.

Source: Le Strange kitchen accounts, 1619; LEST/P6.

Note: Shows the percentage of each foodstuff that was consumed during each season in 1619.

Westminster Abbey, the monks' diet in the late fifteenth and early sixteenth centuries was dominated by fish from the cod family, accounting for 49 per cent of edible weight in fish consumed, compared with just over 20 per cent at Hunstanton, while plaice accounted for only 4 per cent compared with Hunstanton's 51 per cent. The large fresh sea fish eaten at Hunstanton, where they made up 20 per cent of fish consumption, barely figured at all at Westminster.[53] The Le Stranges ate very little freshwater fish, unlike the sixteenth-century Willoughby household in the north midlands.[54] Nor did they eat any of the rarer large

---

[53] Harvey, *Living and Dying*, 48, 226–7.
[54] Dawson, *Plenti and Grase*, 131–5.

marshland birds such as crane, spoonbill or bittern, despite the areas of marsh on their estate. No hare was eaten, perhaps because of the abundance of rabbit. Some patterns of consumption can be put down to personal preference. Either Hamon or Alice seems to have been partial to tongue and 'souse and feet', neither of which were particularly high-status foodstuffs but which were regularly purchased from the butcher along with the beef.

How did the early seventeenth-century diet of a wealthy household differ from that of the medieval period? Beer had replaced ale. Novelties had appeared such as turkeys, cherries, peaches and artichokes, but none of these dominated the diet.[55] Turkey, like beer, was easily adopted because it fitted existing patterns of consumption, adding to the repertoire of poultry that were consumed at Christmas. Other novelties from the new world, such as the potatoes and tomatoes which now dominate our diet, required a more significant shift in ways of cooking and eating, and were not adopted at this date. There were strong continuities with the medieval period: comparisons with Woolgar's analysis of medieval household accounts show that the proportion of red meat from cattle, sheep and pigs was very similar.[56] There is no evidence at Hunstanton of a higher consumption of mutton, which Thirsk argues appeared in the sixteenth and early seventeenth centuries, despite the Le Stranges' involvement in sheep farming.[57] Comparison with the more detailed analyses offered by Dyer and Harvey show that the Le Stranges ate more poultry and rabbits than two early fifteenth-century East Anglian households or the monks of Westminster Abbey between c.1495 and c.1525.[58] Dawson argues that increased rabbit consumption was a national trend, evident in the late sixteenth-century north midlands as well as Norfolk.[59] The early seventeenth-century Le Strange household also consumed a great deal more dairy produce. Woolgar notes that 'in 1341–2, the household of Thomas de Courtenay, at South Pool, with about twenty servants, consumed during the year 227 lb of cheese, [and] 48 lb of butter'. The Le Stranges consumed 2730 lbs of cheese and 411 lbs of butter, roughly ten times as much. The great household of Humphrey Stafford, first Duke of Buckingham, kept six milk cows to supply his household in 1452–3. The much smaller Le Strange establishment was supplied by twenty milk cows. Monastic allowances provided 2.5 oz of cheese on days when dairy produce was eaten (238 days of the year); the Le Stranges provided an average of 4.8 oz per person for every day of the year.[60] Cheese eating increased across England in the fifteenth century, as a result of a more pastoral economy. Fifteenth-century household accounts show that cheese made most headway into female-headed households,[61] perhaps as a

---

[55] Thirsk, *Food*, 71, 298.
[56] C.M. Woolgar, 'Meat and dairy products in medieval England', in Woolgar et al., *Food in Medieval England*, 93.
[57] Thirsk, *Food*, 237.
[58] Dyer, *Standards of Living*, 59; Harvey, *Living and Dying*, 51–3. Thirsk notes increased rabbit consumption in the early modern period, *Food*, 247–8.
[59] Dawson, *Plenti and Grase*, 108–9.
[60] Woolgar, 'Meat and dairy products', 99–100.
[61] Woolgar, 'Meat and dairy products', 99; Woolgar, *The Great Household*, 128.

result of women's close association with both making and eating dairy products. In contradiction to Harrison's assertion that cheese was 'reputed as food appertinent only to the inferior sort', Thirsk notes the increasing fashionability of cheese consumption in the late sixteenth century.[62] The Le Stranges' diet may have been influenced by Alice Le Strange's enthusiasm for dairying, but the household accounts of other gentry families, such as the Willoughbys of Leyhill, Devon, and the Cokes of Much Marcle, Herefordshire, also reveal dairying on a similar scale.[63]

THE MEANINGS OF FOOD

Cultural conventions were just as important as the seasons in determining the food consumption patterns of the wealthy. In medieval England the church had proscribed not only the period of Lent, the six and a half weeks before Easter, but also three 'fish-days' each week as periods of abstinence when no flesh was consumed.[64] The Reformation could have removed these restrictions on diet, but, instead, many of them were re-imposed by Royal Proclamation. The nature of the Lenten fast was relaxed in 1538, allowing the consumption of 'milk, butter, eggs, cheese and all other white meats', but the government remained keen to enforce fish-eating. In 1548 a proclamation sought to enforce 'abstinence' on Fridays, Saturdays and during Lent, when people should 'spare flesh and use fish for the benefit of the commonwealth and the profit of his majesty's realm'. The three reasons cited were the moral good of forbearing pleasures; the prevention of a shortage of red meat; and the support of the fishing industry, whose boats and manpower were vital for the Navy. This legislation was frequently re-enacted by Elizabeth, with Wednesday added as an extra fish-day from 1564 onwards.[65] James I continued the tradition with three proclamations 'forbidding the eating of flesh in Lent, or on fish-days' in 1619 alone.[66] The restrictions remained in force until the Civil War, when they were abandoned. One interpretation of the frequent re-issues of these proclamations was that few people were bothering to restrict their diet as instructed, but the Le Stranges seem to have observed them fully.

The most striking change in diet during Lent was that beef, eaten in large quantities at all other times of the year, disappeared, as did mutton (Table 4.2). It was replaced with white herring, which was not eaten at all at other times of the year. The amount of other fish eaten—plaice, salt fish and large fresh sea fish—also

---

[62] Harrison, *Description of England*, 126; Thirsk, *Food*, 38; see also Dawson, *Plenti and Grase*, 82.
[63] For the Willoughbys, see T. Gray (ed.), *Devon Household Accounts 1627–59*, Part 1 (Exeter, 1995); for the Cokes, see British Library, Add 6987–6.
[64] For diet during late medieval Lent, see C.M. Woolgar, 'Group diets in late medieval England', 192–4, and Dyer, 'Seasonal patterns', 202, both in Woolgar et al., *Food in Medieval England*.
[65] P.L. Hughes and J.F. Larkin (eds.), *Tudor Royal Proclamations*, Vol. 1 (New Haven, 1964), 260–1, 413–15; P.L. Hughes and J.F. Larkin (eds.), *Tudor Royal Proclamations*, Vol. 2 (New Haven, 1969), 293–4; P.L. Hughes and J.F. Larkin (eds.), *Tudor Royal Proclamations*, Vol. 3 (New Haven, 1969).
[66] J.F. Larkin and P.L. Hughes, *Stuart Royal Proclamations*, Vol. 1 (Oxford, 1973), 413–16, 424–6, 450–4. Interestingly these proclamations cite only economic and political reasons: maintaining the supply of red meat and the strength of the Navy.

Table 4.2. Change in diet during Lent

Foodstuff	Measure	Pre-Lent total	Pre-Lent average (per week)	Lent total	Lent average (per week)
Beef	Stone	53.5	8.9	0	0
Veal	Number	1	0.2	3	0.5
Muttons	Number	8	1.3	0	0
Mature pigs	Number	3	0.5	1	0.2
Geese	Number	7	1.2	0	0
Hens and capons	Number	72	12	15	2.5
Turkey	Number	9	1.5	2	0.3
Wading birds	Number	20	3.3	36	6
Butter	Pints and lbs	1.5	0.25	19	3.2
Cheeses	Number	17	2.8	35	5.8
Eggs	Cost, d.	170	28.3	191	31.8
Ling	Number	3	0.5	3.5	0.6
Salt fish	Number	17	2.8	62	10.3
Plaice	Number	110	18.3	1240	206.7
Large fresh fish	Number	6	1	54	9
Herring, white	Number	0	0	710	118.3
Beer, buttery	Hogsheads	16.25	2.7	18	3
Bread, manchet	Cast	217	36.2	166	27.7
Bread, cheat	Cast	140	23.3	155.5	25.9

Note: The table compares the six weeks preceding Lent (16 January to 26 February 1619) with the six weeks falling completely within Lent (5 March to 15 April 1619). Easter fell on 16 April 1619.

Source: Le Strange kitchen accounts, 1619–20; LEST/P6.

increased significantly. Rations of cheese more than doubled. The interpretation of 'white meat' was quite generous, including veal and poultry, although these were eaten in moderation. In comparison, the accounts of Sir Richard and Lady Lucy Reynell of Forde near Teignmouth in Devon from 1628 to 1631 show a more relaxed attitude to Lent.[67] Like the Le Stranges, they ate plenty of fresh fish along with poultry and veal, and, presumably because of their easy availability in the area, lobster and shellfish during Lent. However, they also ate mutton, both from their own animals and purchased, and rabbit. Their only apparent concession to Lent was to stop purchasing beef, perhaps because butchers were abiding by the statutes and not selling any, but they did occasionally kill their own oxen.[68]

In sharp contrast to Lent, Christmas and New Year were periods of excessive meat consumption. Feasts were held during a two-week period from 25 December to Twelfth Night, 6 January. The foods consumed at Christmas, and at other celebrations in the Le Strange household, are shown in Table 4.3. Both the quantity and quality of food consumed increased at Christmastime. Increased quantity was very largely a consequence of the number of people being entertained.

---

[67] Gray, *Devon Household Accounts*, Part 1.
[68] Two oxen were killed during Lent 1630. Beef was also purchased two days before Easter in 1631 on 8 April.

The gentry traditionally provided hospitality for their kin and tenants.[69] Increased quality is demonstrated not only by the consumption of high-status food such as venison but also by the fact that low-status foods such as cheese and salt fish were consumed in smaller quantities than usual despite the larger number of people. Some foods, such as geese and turkey, were Christmas traditions, then as now. Expenditure on food was actually below average during the two Christmas weeks because food was purchased in advance, received as gifts and taken from the home farm for this special period.[70] Cooking required extra labour, with a boy paid for twelve days' work 'turning the spit' to roast meat.

One of the most spectacular feasts in the whole period covered by the account books was that held to celebrate the wedding of Elizabeth Le Strange in October 1636, shown in Table 4.3. By the 1630s average food consumption in the household had increased, reflecting its growing size, but, even with this taken into account, the wedding feast was impressive. The consumption was spread over two weeks in the kitchen accounts, so the feast lasted for at least two days and probably more. The quantity of manchet consumed gives a rough indication of the number of extra people who were being fed. The food for the wedding feast seems to have been lighter than the typical Christmas fare, with more emphasis on poultry and rabbits and less on beef and pork. We can imagine the swans providing a centre piece. Although the quantity of food was similar to a Christmas feast, the cost was higher, approximately £50 more than a normal fortnightly spend on food in this period. Special luxuries such as sweetmeats, including a 'bride cake' for 3s and dried fruit, were purchased, and some expensive fish, including sturgeon. As with Christmas, extra labour was needed: Willden, the cook, was paid £1 'for 8 days helping my cook at the marriage of my daughter Elizabeth to Mr Spring', as well as 2s to a boy for six days turning the spit and 4s 8d to Alice Chant for fourteen days helping the cook.

Christenings were also marked by feasts. They had a distinctive selection of foods characterized by sugary delicacies known as 'banqueting stuff' and quantities of wine.[71] In the first twenty years of the accounts, 'comfits', sweetmeats made with sugar, were only purchased by the household for christenings. At Mary Le Strange's christening in 1621 there were comfits of cinnamon, almond, orange, aniseed and coriander, violet and musk. Other special foods purchased included white sugar candy, muscadines (a sweetmeat flavoured with musk), candied stuff, dried paste, dried sucket (fruit preserved in sugar), quince marmalade, marzipan, macaroons, wafers and biscuit bread. This was washed down with sack and claret wine. The feast was not restricted to sweetmeats and wine. The consumption of bread, meat

---

[69] F. Heal, *Hospitality in Early Modern England* (Oxford, 1990), 73–4.
[70] The average expenditure in each of the two Christmas weeks in 1619–20 was £2 6s 8d, compared with average weekly expenditure of £4 1s 2d during that year. In contrast, Heal, *Hospitality*, 71–2, finds increased expenditure at Christmas in various sixteenth-century accounts from gentry households.
[71] A.C. Wilson (ed.), *'Banquetting Stuff': The Fare and Social Background of the Tudor and Stuart Banquet* (Edinburgh, 1991).

Table 4.3. Consumption at selected feasts in the Le Strange household, 1619–36

Foodstuff	Average weekly consumption, 1619	Christmas and New Year, 1619[a]	Christmas and New Year, 1620[b]	Mary's christening feast, 1621[c]	Elizabeth's wedding feasts, 1636[d]	Christmas and New Year, 1636[e]	Average weekly consumption, November 1636[f]
Manchet bread[g]	36	96	112.5	69	143	177	63
Beer[h]	3.5	5.75	7.75	5.25	6.75	7.25	3
Fresh butter[i]	7.75	0	2	18.5	41.5	8.5	21
Hens and ducks[j]	12.5	47.5	68	50	137	80	25
Rabbits	11	37	40	24	49	33	26
Beef (pieces)	12	34	43	20	23	35	13
Muttons	1.7	4	4	5	6	5.5	3.5
Swine	1.4	4.5	3	3	3.5	4	3
Geese	1.3	8.5	12	0	6.5	17	7
Turkeys	0.7	9	10	2	10.5	24	6.5
Swans and peacocks[k]	0	0.5	0	1	3	0.5	0
Deer	0.15	2	1.5	2	1.5	1	0

a. Weekly average of two weeks, 26 December to 8 January 1619.
b. Weekly average of two weeks, 24 December to 6 January 1620.
c. Consumption in the week 7–13 October 1621.
d. Weekly average of two weeks, 16–29 October 1636.
e. Weekly average of two weeks, 25 December to 7 January 1636.
f. Weekly average of four weeks, 6 November to 3 December 1636.
g. Number of casts.
h. Buttery and cellar beer in hogsheads.
i. In pints or lbs, which are assumed to be equivalent.
j. Capons, chickens, hens, ducks and ducklings.
k. One peacock was consumed Christmas 1619; the other birds were swans.

Source: Le Strange kitchen accounts: LEST/P6, P9.

and beer during the week of Mary's christening was equivalent to that in a Christmas week.

Most households would not have been able to afford the quantity and variety of food and drink consumed by the Le Stranges. Between 1500 and 1650 wage rates failed to keep pace with the rising price of grain and other foodstuffs, resulting in falling real wages for labouring families. This was particularly acute from the 1590s onwards, with the cost of living remaining high until the mid-seventeenth century.[72] The situation was ameliorated somewhat in rural England by the fact that many workers received food and drink as part of their wage payments, cushioning them from high prices. The board and lodging received by young men and women who worked as live-in servants accounted for as much as 77 per cent of their wage payment.[73] Servants were employed by households of all levels of wealth, but gentry and yeomen farmers employed them in the largest numbers. One of the perks of working as a servant in a wealthy household was to receive adequate quantities of good quality food.[74] Day labourers also received food and drink as part of their work payment. A Norfolk wage assessment for 1610, which set the legal maximum wage for agricultural workers, specifies wage rates with and without food. The value of food and drink made up an average of 48 per cent of the payment received, ranging from 67 per cent for the lowest paid workers to 43 per cent for the best paid.[75] The wage rates in the account books indicate that Alice Le Strange almost always paid her workers with food and drink as well as cash.

Did the Le Stranges' servants and labourers eat the same food as their employers? Normally, it is impossible to differentiate between diets within the household. However, from mid-January 1620 Sir Hamon, Alice, their two youngest children, a gentlewoman, a maid and three male servants all stayed in London for nine weeks.[76] As the two older children were away at school, this means that a period of nine weeks can be observed when none of the Le Strange family was resident. In Table 4.4 this is compared with the same period in the previous year, when they were at home. Some things disappeared completely from the household's menu during the family's absence. No manchet bread, butter, mutton, turkey, chicken, duck, rabbit, currants, fresh fish or salted ling were consumed. The consumption of eggs and beef was much reduced. The beef that was eaten seems to have been purchased for one meal just before the start of Lent, a traditional feast day. In the family's absence, cheaper smoked red herring were purchased for Lent rather than

---

[72] C.G.A. Clay, *Economic Expansion and Social Change: England 1500–1700*, vol. I (Cambridge, 1984), Table IIIa, 50. Thirsk, *Food*, 60.

[73] J. Whittle, 'Servants in rural England c.1450–1650: hired work as a means of accumulating wealth and skills before marriage', in M. Agren and A. Erickson (eds.), *The Marital Economy in Scandinavia and Britain 1400–1900* (Aldershot, 2005), 96.

[74] D. Woodward, 'Early modern servants in husbandry revisited', *Agricultural History Review* 48:2 (2000), 144.

[75] Analysis of data from J.C. Tingey, 'An assessment of wages for the county of Norfolk in 1610', *English Historical Review* 13 (1898), 522–7.

[76] See Chapter 3: Urban shopping. Chamber rent indicates that Alice and Hamon stayed in London for seventeen weeks from January 1620. The kitchen accounts indicate nine weeks: some household members must have returned in mid-March, Hamon and Alice later.

Table 4.4. A comparison between normal consumption patterns (1619) and consumption when the gentry family were absent (1620)

	Manchet bread	Cheat bread	Household bread	Beer	Cheese	Butter	Sheep	Pigs	Geese
1619	32.7	22.7	5.6	2.8	3.6	0.6	0.9	0.4	1.1
1620	0	14.3	4.1	1.8	3.4	0	0	0.6	0.7

	Turkeys	Hens and ducks	Rabbits	Beef	Eggs	Currants and raisins	Fresh fish	Salt fish	Ling
1619	1.2	8.2	2.1	18.0s	2.4s	2.4s	1.6s	5.7	0.6
1620	0	0	0	0.7s	0.1s	0	0	5.6	0

Note: This table compares average weekly consumption patterns in a nine-week period from January to March in 1619 and 1620. Beef, eggs, dried fruit, and fresh fish are measured by cost rather than quantity.

Source: Le Strange kitchen accounts, 1619–20; LEST/P6.

the usual pickled white herring. Otherwise, the diet consisted of cheat and household bread, beer, cheese, pork or bacon, goose and salt fish. Given that the complement of servants was reduced during this period, the fact that the quantities of cheese, pork or bacon, and salt fish consumed remained stable or slightly increased demonstrates that these foodstuffs were being used to replace the wider variety of meat and fish that were normally consumed. This in turn suggests that the servants and labourers would normally eat some of the same food as the family although not in the same quantity, perhaps as leftovers.[77] When the family was absent, it was not thought appropriate to slaughter or purchase these foodstuffs for the servants alone.

An early seventeenth-century list of menus that survives for the Townshends of Stiffkey in Norfolk shows the senior servants being given plainer dishes than the high table with less roast beef and more mutton, although they were still very well fed by contemporary standards.[78] The small amounts of beef and eggs, the absence of butter and the large quantities of fish consumed by the Le Stranges' workers in 1620 were partly a consequence of the time of year. In other respects, the diet is very similar to that given to the servants of Robert Loder, the wealthy yeoman farmer from Berkshire.[79] This diet, which was heavy in bread, beer, bacon and cheese and supplemented by other types of meat and fish when available and appropriate, was that of middling households. It lacked the variety of meat and quantity of beef, dried fruit and spices enjoyed by the Le Stranges. Labourers such

---

[77] Harrison, *Description of England*, 129, notes servants eating leftovers in the households of gentlemen and merchants.
[78] Thirsk, *Food*, 84–5.
[79] G.E. Fussell (ed.), *Robert Loder's Farm Accounts 1610–1620*, Camden Society Third Series, vol. 53 (London, 1936), analysed in Whittle, 'Servants in rural England', 96.

as harvest workers in fifteenth-century Sedgeford and those employed by the Le Stranges in the early seventeenth century enjoyed this diet when at work.[80]

Much writing on early modern food has relied on evidence from cookery books. Despite their extensive library, the Le Stranges do not seem to have owned any cookery books apart from a chapter in the works of Gervase Markham, which was almost certainly purchased for other reasons. Nonetheless, Markham's collection of recipes in *The English Housewife* provides a good example of those current at the time, ranging as they do from grand dishes designed for feasts to everyday meals such as pottage. Thirsk argues that he was a 'writer and farmer who also observed food on the family table of ordinary folk' and that 'his recipes and instructions for food in *The English Housewife* are precise, and plainly spring from a sound personal knowledge'.[81] Best argued that the book was intended not only for the gentry but also for 'the more "general" reader, possibly the wife of a wage earner'.[82] However, a comparison between the ingredients required for the recipes and the foodstuffs purchased and consumed by the Le Stranges shows that many of Markham's recipes were over-ambitious and extravagant even for the wealthy gentry.

The book lists 156 recipes. These were compared with the foods consumed by the Le Stranges in a thirty-month period from April 1619 to October 1621. Only 40 per cent of the recipes could have been cooked on a regular basis in the Le Strange household. Of the remaining recipes, 29 per cent contained foods the Le Stranges never, or only very rarely, purchased or consumed, so were almost certainly not cooked in the household; a further 31 per cent could only have been prepared occasionally as they contained large quantities of items the Le Stranges purchased or ate in only small quantities. It was not only spectacular dishes such as the 'compound salad usual at great feasts', which contained quantities of almonds, capers, olives, oranges, lemons, pickled cucumbers and red cauliflower, as well as raisins, currants, sugar and salad oil; 'best tansy', which was based around the difficult to acquire item of 'walnut tree buds'; or olla podrida, a Spanish stew that required potatoes,[83] that were beyond the Le Stranges' repertoire. There appears to be a significant mismatch between the standard flavourings used and the Le Stranges' eating habits. Many fritters and puddings listed by Markham required large quantities of spices such as cloves, mace, cinnamon and nutmeg. Many of the recipes for boiling meat and making sauces and pies required prunes, dates, oranges and lemons. In the recipes, roast meat was commonly stuck all over with cloves. Fruit for tarts was boiled in white wine. The banqueting stuff, which previous writers have singled out as elite foods,[84] were in fact no more difficult to achieve than many of the other dishes, requiring large quantities of almonds, quinces, caraway comfits, ginger and other spices.

---

[80] C. Dyer, *Everyday Life in Medieval England* (London, 1994), 83.
[81] Thirsk, *Food*, 91.
[82] Best, 'Introduction', in Markham, *English Housewife*, xxvii.
[83] Although see Thirsk, *Food*, 84, for evidence of this stew being cooked in England in 1630.
[84] Best, 'Introduction', in Markham, *English Housewife*, xxvii.

Between April 1619 and October 1621, the Le Stranges bought 8d worth of oranges (probably just a few fruits), nine lemons, which cost 8d each, and 1.25 lb of dates at 2s a lb.[85] Only prunes were cheaper and purchased in larger quantities: 60 lbs of prunes were purchased during the period at 2d a lb. Of the spices that were so common in the recipes, they purchased 1.5 lb of cloves at 6s a lb, surely not enough to stick all over the roast meat they consumed in such large quantities; 2.75 lb each of mace and cinnamon, the mace costing 8s a lb, and the cinnamon 3s a lb; and 7 lb of nutmeg at 3s a lb. They also purchased 10 lb of aniseed at 10d a lb, an ingredient not frequently required by the recipes. The Le Stranges purchased 16 lb of almonds, which cost 1s a lb for small almonds and 16–18d a lb for large Jordan almonds, 3 lb of ginger at 14d a lb as well as green ginger worth 21d, and an occasional pint of white wine.[86] Comfits were purchased for christening feasts but not at other times. Quinces were grown locally. Markham does not provide quantities in his recipes and Best suggests that most spices were used in only small quantities, while Thirsk notes that they had become cheaper over time.[87] But the quantities purchased by the Le Stranges were simply not adequate to prepare the majority of these recipes on a day-to-day basis. This was an issue of taste rather than price: the Le Stranges could have afforded more had they wished to buy them. While Markham's book does contain some plainer recipes, there are also noticeable gaps. There is no recipe for brawn, which was almost constantly present in the Le Stranges' larder, or for sea fish or salt fish. We must conclude that many gentry households subsisted on plainer food than that described by Markham and did so out of preference. Cookery books, then as now, presented a fantasy world of richness and variety that was not matched in reality and are not a good guide even of elite cooking practices.

It might be argued, of course, that the Le Stranges were unusual among the gentry for their plain eating habits. However, they cared enough about their food to employ a well-paid male cook. Dawson argues that heavy flavouring with spices was falling out of fashion, so it is possible it was Markham's cookery book which was lagging behind the times.[88] The accounts provide evidence that the Le Stranges kept up with some of the latest fashions in foodstuffs. They ate large quantities of cheese and butter, purchased salad oil and cabbages, and planted trees to grow cherries, nectarines and peaches, as well as slips to grow globe artichokes. They consumed large quantities of sugar, purchasing 333 lbs of sugar in thirty months during 1619–21, as well as home-produced honey.[89] They purchased seven different varieties of sugar comfits for a christening feast in 1621.[90] In all these activities they were moving with the times and partaking in fashionable food consumption. The differences in diet between the gentry and their servants, its susceptibility to fashion and the use of food to mark significant life cycle events all emphasize that

---

[85] They purchased three lemons, and received another six as a single gift.
[86] It is possible that some unspecified wine was white; most of the wine is described as claret.
[87] Best, 'Introduction', in Markham, *English Housewife*, xxxvi; Thirsk, *Food*, 52, 92.
[88] Dawson, *Plenti and Grase*, 168.
[89] Thirsk, *Food*, 31, 35, 38, 48, 71, 75, 80, 94, 324–6; Dawson, *Plenti and Grase*, 161.
[90] Norwich admitted its first comfit maker as a freeman in 1604, Thirsk, *Food*, 325.

food, as well as being an everyday necessity, was an important element in the construction of the gentry's identity.

MEDICAL CARE

Medical care formed a small but distinctive category of expenditure in the household accounts. Although foods and medicines overlapped, they were clearly distinguished from 1613 onwards when foods were recorded in the kitchen accounts and medicines in the general disbursements. In many entries Alice recorded for whom the medicines or care had been purchased, allowing us to compare the health of different family members and identify particular periods of illness (Table 4.5). Modern Hunstanton is a seaside resort, but up to the nineteenth century it was a malarial hotspot. Malaria was endemic but localized in early modern England: the mosquitoes that spread the disease particularly favoured areas of salt marsh, such as those found on the coast of north-west Norfolk close to Hunstanton Hall.[91] Half of Alice and Hamon's eight children failed to reach adulthood: a high rate of mortality even by early modern standards.[92] There is no firm proof in the accounts that the family suffered from malaria, but it seems likely that they were affected. Men hunting wildfowl in the marshes, a favourite pastime of both Sir Hamon and Nicholas Le Strange, were particularly vulnerable.[93] The accounts show that both Sir Hamon and Nicholas had regular bouts of ill-health.

Between 1606 and 1626 Nicholas Le Strange suffered most, and required the highest expenditure on medical care. He had at least six periods of sickness which

Table 4.5. The cost of medical care per person, 1606–26

Person	Number of entries	Cost of medical care
Hamon Le Strange	22	£32 0s 0d
Nicholas	30	£41 9s 8.5d
Hamon junior	5	4s 8.5d
Jane	5	£3 6s 4d
Elizabeth	6	£2 9s 2d
Roger	7	£8 15s 8d
Total medical entries	331	£172 4s 3d

Source: Le Strange disbursement accounts; LEST/P6, P7

---

[91] M.J. Dobson, *Contours of Death and Disease in Early Modern England* (Cambridge, 1997). Maps on pp. 348 and 178 show, respectively, that malaria was still present in Hunstanton in the 1860s and that north-west Norfolk in the same period suffered from particularly high infant mortality.
[92] E.A. Wrigley and R.S. Schofield, *The Population History of England 1541–1871* (Cambridge, 1981), 249.
[93] D. Defoe, *A Tour through the Whole Island of Great Britain* (Penguin, 1971), 53, describing London men who hunted in the Essex marshes.

required the personal attendance of a paid medical practitioner. During the most severe, in September 1617, he was carried by two household servants to Dr Rant's house, and a payment of £13 4s was made 'to Doctor Rant for Nicholas when he lay sick at his house 6 weeks: himself and a maid for their chamber and diet and the Doctor his pains'; as well as a further £4 8s to the apothecary for medicine, and 12s in tips to Rant's servants. There is no strong seasonal pattern in Nicholas's illnesses, making it impossible to confirm whether he suffered from malaria or another persistent infection. His ill-health stands in stark contrast to his brother Hamon junior, who did not require the doctor once in the whole period. Jane was ill at the same time as Nicholas in 1614 and 1616, but otherwise had no serious bouts of illness until she died, presumably quite suddenly as the doctor was not called. Elizabeth was also relatively healthy during her childhood. Roger, on the other hand, needed the doctor three times in this period: in 1620; in 1622 when Dr Rant came and stayed for five days to treat him; and again in 1623.

Sir Hamon Le Strange had a collection of medical books, and in his later life at least carried out a protracted correspondence with a number of doctors.[94] He suffered from periods of ill-health, like his son Nicholas. There are twenty-two entries in the accounts up to 1626 specifically relating to medical care for Hamon. All these are from 1620 onwards, suggesting that Alice changed her accounting practices and started allocating medical expenses specifically to her husband at this point; anonymous expenses in the earlier period could well be for him too. Hamon was sick in 1620 at the same time as Roger and Elizabeth, but his treatment was more extensive. A surgeon let his blood, and he paid £17 12s to a Dr Harvey, almost certainly William Harvey, the royal physician, for a consultation.[95] He was ill again in 1623, but less seriously, having his waters 'cast', and purchasing 'apothecary things' on two occasions. In 1624 he required the doctor again, but this was a shorter visit, costing only £3 6s. Alice herself leaves no record of whether she suffered from illness.

The Le Stranges employed a range of medical practitioners: sixteen medical men are named in the accounts between 1606 and 1626, as well as a midwife and a horse doctor, as shown in Table 4.6.[96] The family had two regular physicians: Mr Nicholls, the physician whom they used from 1606 to 1613, and Dr Rant, who they relied on after that date. William Rant (1564–1627) was one of only a few Norfolk physicians at that date with a medical doctorate.[97] However, a number of other doctors were employed on occasion both at home and when away from Norfolk in London. The advice from these men was supplemented with guidance and medicines from apothecaries. Dr Rant had his own apothecary, who dispensed

---

[94] Thirty-one letters survive in the Le Strange collection dating from 1641 to 1654 and relating to Hamon Le Strange's health and medical care: LEST/P20. A few are printed in G. Keynes (ed.), *The Letters of Sir Thomas Browne* (London, 1931), 310–17.

[95] R. French, 'William Harvey (1578–1657)', *ODNB*.

[96] Edmund Parker, the horse doctor, was also a farrier and former servant of the Le Stranges: not all the entries related to medical consultations.

[97] M. Pelling and C. Webster, 'Medical practitioners', in Webster, *Health, Medicine and Mortality*, 210.

Table 4.6. Medical practitioners employed by the Le Strange household, 1606–26

Name	Skill	Number of entries	Date of entries	Location
Dr (Duncan) Burnett	Physician	1	1624	Norwich
Goodwife Crisp	Midwife	8	1612–21	Sedgeford
Mr (Richard) Curtis	Physician	3	1613–23	King's Lynn
(Robert) Dey	Apothecary	1	1621	Norwich
Mr Fletcher	Physician	5	1610–13	
Dr (John) Gifford	Physician	1	1625	London
Mr (Roger) Harris	Apothecary	1	1620	London
Dr (William) Harvey	Physician	1	1620	London
(William) Makins	Apothecary	9	1610–17	King's Lynn
(Giles) Michell	Bonesetter	2	1609–12	South Creake
Mr (John) Mingay	Apothecary	2	1615–20	Norwich
Mr Mosely	?	1	1610	
Mr Nicholls	Physician	15	1606–13	
Edward Parker	Farrier and horse doctor	74	1606–25	
Dr (William) Rant	Physician	24	1614–24	Norwich
Mr Sillett	Apothecary	4	1610–13	
Wilson	Surgeon	1	1608	King's Lynn
Dr (Edmund) Willson	Physician	1	1625	London

Sources: Le Strange disbursement accounts; LEST/P6, P7. Checked against Margaret Pelling's biographical index of medical practitioners; see Pelling and Webster, 'Medical practitioners' for details of her sources. First names in brackets are from Pelling's index.

the treatments he recommended.[98] A further five appear in the accounts, some used regularly, some only once or twice. Only one man described as a surgeon appears in the accounts: Wilson, who was called from Lynn to examine baby Dorothy Le Strange's eye in 1608. Michell, who was paid for curing a servant's leg, was an unlicensed bonesetter from nearby South Creake.[99] As with the general pattern of purchases in the accounts discussed in Chapter 3, the Le Stranges drew on medical help from London, Norwich and King's Lynn, as well as closer to home. The Le Strange accounts confirm the picture conveyed by Pelling and Webster's survey of medical practitioners in Norfolk during 1550–1600: there was no shortage of people to call on for expertise and advice, but getting help for an emergency in rural Norfolk was more difficult.[100]

The range of medical practitioners consulted, for servants as well as for the family,[101] was in addition to the care provided by Alice Le Strange herself. A chance reference reveals that Alice 'did great service to the poor in the way of surgery'.

---

[98] He appears as 'Dr Rant's apothecary', but may also have been one of the other apothecaries who is named in the accounts.
[99] He was prosecuted in 1597 for practising without a licence, see Pelling and Webster, 'Medical practitioners', 231.
[100] Pelling and Webster, 'Medical practitioners', especially 225–7.
[101] There are at least three cases in the accounts of doctors or surgeons being called to treat servants.

Challoner's eighteenth-century *Memoirs of Missionary Priests* records the story of Thomas Tunstal, a Catholic priest who was sent to England in 1610 and who spent a number of years in prison before escaping from Wisbech Castle. In doing so he injured his hands, and when staying with friends near Lynn was recommended to seek help from Lady Le Strange. Alice 'received him kindly, dressed his wounds, and promised him her best assistance for making a cure'. However, she also mentioned her patient to Sir Hamon Le Strange, who, as a Justice of the Peace, realized that 'this must be the popish priest lately escaped out of Wisbeach, for whom he had that day received orders to make diligent search'. Hamon committed Tunstal to Norwich gaol, where he was brought to trial and condemned at the next assizes.[102]

Medical care was an important and accepted strand of a housewife's skills in the sixteenth and seventeenth centuries.[103] As Gervase Markham puts it in his *English Housewife* (1615), knowledge of physic was:

> one of the most principal virtues which doth belong to our English Housewife; you shall understand that sith the preservation and care of the family touching their health and soundness of body consisteth most in her diligence, it is meet that she have a physical kind of knowledge; how to administer many wholesome receipts or medicines for the good of their healths... [104]

He devotes the first chapter of the book to 'her general knowledge both in physic and surgery, with plain approved medicines for health of the household, also the extraction of excellent oils for those purposes'.[105] There are numerous examples of aristocratic and gentlewomen who took this role seriously: for example, Lady Grace Mildmay (1552–1620); Lady Margaret Hoby (1571–1633); Ann Howard, Countess of Arundel (1557–1630); Elizabeth Grey, Countess of Kent (1582–1651); Alethea Talbot, Countess of Surrey (c.1583–1654); Mary Sidney, Countess of Pembroke (1561–1621); Margaret Clifford, Countess of Cumberland (1560–1616); Dame Frances Powlett (d.1599); Margaret Boscawen (d.1688); Bridget Fortescue (1666–1704); and Elizabeth Freke (1641–1714).[106] These women not only administered medical care and prepared their own medicines

---

[102] R. Challoner, *Memoirs of Missionary Priests* (London, 1741–2), 111–13.
[103] D.E. Nagy, *Popular Medicine in Seventeenth-Century England* (Ohio, 1988), ch. 5; L. Hunter, 'Women and domestic medicine: lady experimenters, 1570–1620', in L. Hunter and S. Hutton (eds.), *Women, Science and Medicine 1500–1700* (Stroud, 1997); M.E. Fissell, 'Introduction: women, health and healing in early modern Europe', *Bulletin of the History of Medicine*, 82:1 (2008).
[104] Markham, *English Housewife*, 8.
[105] Markham, *English Housewife*, 5. C. Estienne, *Maison Rustique, or The Countrey Farme* (1616), devotes most of its advice to the housewife to medicinal remedies.
[106] L. Pollock, *With Faith and Physic: The Life of a Tudor Gentlewoman, Lady Grace Mildmay 1552–1620* (London, 1993), 97–109; M. Hoby, *The Diary of Margaret Hoby 1599–1605*, ed. D. Meads (London, 1930), aqua vitae 180; visiting sick 86; dressing wounds 72, 100, 168, 170, 186; surgery on baby 184; J.T. Cliffe, *The World of the Country House in Seventeenth-Century England* (New Haven, 1999), 71; Hunter, 'Women and domestic medicine'; M.P. Hannay, '"How I these studies prize": the Countess of Pembroke and Elizabethan Science', in Hunter and Hutton, *Women, Science and Medicine*; F.G. Emmison, *Elizabethan Life: Wills of Essex Gentry and Merchants* (Chelmsford, 1978), 37; A. Stobart, 'The Making of Domestic Medicine: Gender, Self-help and Therapeutic Determination in Household Healthcare in South-west England in the Late Seventeenth Century',

but also experimented with remedies and occasionally conducted surgery. They often passed their medical expertise, books and recipe collections on to their daughters. More general evidence of the widespread interest of elite and middling women in medical care is provided by the large number of medical receipt or recipe collections written by women which survive from this period. The Perdita Project has collected 114 manuscript recipe books compiled by seventeenth-century women, the great majority of which combine medical and cookery receipts.[107]

Medical expertise was seen as 'naturally' falling to women in the first instance, not only because of the caring role involved but also because of the close relationship between cookery and preparing medicines.[108] A woman accomplished at brewing, dairying, cooking and gardening would not be daunted by the demands of medical preparations: selecting ingredients, infusing and distilling. Grace Mildmay prepared medicines on a commercial scale and dispensed them charitably.[109] There is no evidence that Alice Le Strange did this, but there are indications that she prepared some of her own medicines. One piece of equipment needed was a still or limbeck, which could be used to produce alcohol, vinegar and perfume.[110] Alice owned a still by at least 1610, when a basket was purchased to carry it. A limbeck was purchased for 15s 7d in 1612, and another still in 1615 for 10s. That year the glazier was paid for work on 'the stillhouse', and in 1618 and 1620 repairs were carried out on the 'three stills', while a superior 'purse limbeck with a brass bottom' was purchased for £1 19s in 1624.

A wide range of medicines and medical ingredients were purchased: ninety-one different types are listed in the accounts from 1606 to 1626, ranging from alcermes to zeduary roots. Some were distinctly exotic, such as mummy and a bezoar stone, while others were much more mundane, such as liverwort water and oil of bays.[111] Thirty-nine, or 43 per cent, were 'raw' ingredients, in the sense of plant products and minerals that had not been pre-processed into medical preparations. Of these, twenty-nine were derived from plants, eight were mineral and two were animal products. The minerals were often administered to animals rather than people; for instance, verdigris and arsenic were purchased 'for the horse' in 1623, and quick silver (mercury) and brimstone (sulphur) for the dogs. Some basic medicinal preparations were carried out in the household; for instance, on two occasions the separate ingredients for a 'purging drink' were purchased. The majority of purchases, however, were of ready-prepared medicines. These included products such as aqua vitae, syrup of lemons and conserve of roses, which could have been produced at home, as well as preparations such as mithridate, 'Dr Mundford's

---

Ph.D. thesis (Middlesex, 2009); E. Leong, 'Making medicines in the early modern household', *Bulletin of the History of Medicine* 82 (2008).

[107] http://human.ntu.ac.uk/research/perdita/catindex.htm.
[108] A. Wear, *Knowledge and Practice in English Medicine, 1550–1680* (Cambridge, 2000), 52, 170.
[109] Pollock, *With Faith and Physic*, 97, 102–3.
[110] Markham, *English Housewife*, ch. 3, 'Of distillations and their virtues'.
[111] Mummy was supposed to be exactly that—small quantities of Egyptian mummies. Bezoar stone was a concretion found in the stomach of some animals, particularly the wild goat of Persia and various antelopes. It was thought to be an antidote to poison, see *OED Online*.

water' and 'powder for worms'. Leong, in her study of Elizabeth Freke's notebooks and inventories of medicines, found that Freke made medicines at home in large quantities for household use and purchased ready-made products, combining a 'need for commercially available medical advice and products with a strong interest in home-based medicine'.[112] In fact, some of her home-made medicines used ready-prepared items such as rosewater and fennel water as ingredients.[113] It seems likely that Alice Le Strange did the same.

The catalogue of the Le Strange library demonstrates the type of medical books Hamon and Alice would have referred to.[114] It lists thirteen medical books in English published before 1626: Thomas Moulton, *The Mirror or Glass of Health* (1580); Levinus Lemnius, *An Herbal for the Bible* (1587); William Clever, *The Flower of Physic* (1590); Thomas Elyot, *The Castle of Health* (1595); Robert Record, *The Urinal of Physic* (1597); William Langham, *The Garden of Health* (1598); Thomas Cogan, *The Haven of Health* (1584–1612); Philip Barrough, *The Method of Physic* (1610); Petrus Pomarius, *Enchiridon Medicum* (1612); Charles Estienne, *Maison Rustique* (1616); Christof Wirsung, *The General Practice of Physic* (1617); Gervase Markham, *Markham's Masterpiece* (1610–); and Joannes de Mediolano, *The Englishman's Doctor* (1624). Following Slack's classifications of Tudor vernacular medical literature, six of these were books of remedies, four were regimens, two were herbals, one was specialized, one contained a plague tract, and one advice on surgery.[115] It seems that the Le Stranges' medical books were largely a practical collection bought with an eye to avoiding illness and diagnosing and treating ailments. The 'regimens' offered an outline of medical theory, but in an applied sense, adapted as guides to healthy living and good diet. Elyot's was a much republished classic of this genre; Cogan's was also popular, while Clever's was more obscure and intellectual.[116] The earliest book of remedies in the library was Moulton's. Originally a plague tract, the 1580 edition had a general list of remedies tacked onto the back. Later, a whole series of books on remedies was purchased: Barrough's and Wirsung's were both extensive guides, while Markham's dealt with the diagnosis and treatment of horses. *Maison Rustique*, the English edition of which was also partly Markham's work, while not primarily a medical book, contains extensive descriptions of remedies for both humans and domestic animals. Record's *Urinal of Physic* had general application in a period when the examination of urine was commonly used to diagnose other ailments.[117] Lemnius' *Herbal for the Bible* is the least empirical medical book owned, perhaps purchased more for its theological interest than as a true herbal, whereas Langham's *Garden of Health* was encyclopaedic and practical, with plants discussed in alphabetical order and an index to ailments that might be treated at the end.

---

[112] Leong, 'Making medicines', 150, 167.
[113] Leong, 'Making medicines', 160.
[114] LEST/NE1.
[115] P. Slack, 'Mirrors of health and treasures of poor men: the uses of the vernacular medical literature of Tudor England', in Webster, *Health, Medicine and Mortality*, 243.
[116] Slack, 'Mirrors of health', 249–50.
[117] Wear, *Knowledge and Practice*, 120–1.

The Le Strange family had persistent health problems which were treated by Alice Le Strange herself and by a range of medical practitioners. The servants were also cared for in this way. The preparation of medicines was a significant element of early modern housewifery, practised by many elite women. It used many of the same skills as processing and preserving foodstuffs. The strategies used by the Le Stranges for healthcare mirror those used for the provision of clothing and food: they called on experts in London and Norwich but also used skilled locals; medicines were made at home but also purchased ready-made; the products used were a mixture of those grown or collected in the locality and purchases of English and exotic products.

HOUSEHOLD CONSUMABLES

As well as food and medical care the maintenance of the household required other commonplace consumables to provide light, heat and cleanliness. The Le Strange household used large quantities of candles, fuel and soap. As each of these has a quite separate historiography, lighting, heating and cleaning are considered in turn in the following section. The period after 1660 saw a minor revolution in the lighting of elite houses. Wall mirrors were increasingly used to reflect the light from chandeliers, girandoles and sconces holding multiple candles.[118] Evidence from the Le Strange household and elsewhere demonstrates that, before this change, wall mirrors were rare and lighting other than daylight was provided by single candles, normally held in portable candlesticks. There were three main types of artificial lighting in early seventeenth-century England: luxury wax candles, cheaper tallow candles, which were made of mutton fat, and the cheapest of all, rush lights. Unlike wax candles, tallow candles needed frequent trimming to keep them alight and they gave off an unpleasant smell.[119] Hole thought that tallow candles 'were chiefly used in the servants' quarters or in the lesser bedrooms. For the better rooms wax candles were prepared from beeswax.' She assumed candles were made at home.[120] The Le Stranges purchased tallow candles in large quantities and did not make them at home. Wax candles were bought on only three occasions between 1610 and 1626. The Le Stranges occasionally sold wax from their beehives, so it is possible that some wax candles were made in the household. Up to 1621 the Le Stranges purchased 100–200 lb of tallow candles a year, rising to around 400 lb a year from 1623 onwards when the house was enlarged. They cost between 4d and 6d a lb, and came mainly from one tallow chandler, William Crisp. The tallow produced in the Le Stranges' kitchens was exchanged with the chandler: in 1614–20, they sold between 70 and 170 lbs of tallow a year for 1d a lb. After 1621, both their consumption of candles and production of tallow increased, and they began to use

---

[118] J.E. Crowley, *The Invention of Comfort: Sensibilities and Design in Early Modern Britain and Early America* (Baltimore, 2000), 122–31.
[119] Crowley, *Invention of Comfort*, 112–13.
[120] C. Hole, *The English Housewife in the Seventeenth Century* (London, 1953), 112–13.

two other tallow chandlers as well as Crisp, relying on direct exchange to offset the cost of large purchases. This leads to some complex entries in the account book. For instance, in March 1625 Alice recorded 'received of William Tuck for 12 stone of tallow at 8 pound half of candle for every stone: 5 score and 2 pound in all; to him for 200 pound of candle beside 100 pound before: £4 10s.'[121] Tallow candles received in part exchange for home-produced tallow were also used in middling households such as that of Robert Loder in Berkshire.[122] Robert Loder estimated that his household used 2 lb of candle a week, and paid the same price as the Le Stranges, 4d a lb in 1612. The amount of candles used by the Loders and the Le Stranges in 1612 was very similar at 104 lbs and 105 lbs respectively. However, by 1625, the Le Stranges were using four times that amount, 402 lbs, reflecting their larger house. Nonetheless, even this consumption is comparatively modest. Westminster Abbey allotted individuals 24 lbs of candle a year, enough for one candle a night.[123] Thus, 400 lbs would have provided sixteen candles a night for a large house containing twenty-five or more people. Poorer households that could not afford tallow used home-made rush lights, made by dipping rushes in animal fat.[124]

At least four different types of fuel for heating and cooking were used in the Le Strange household: coal, charcoal, faggots or bundles of wood, and whin or gorse faggots, reflecting the range of fuels normally available in England at this date. Different fuels had different qualities in terms of the heat and fumes given off. For instance, the Le Stranges used coal to burn lime for the building work, but faggots of wood to burn bricks. Faggots of gorse were recommended for baking bread because they gave off a hot, clean heat; straw was recommended for drying malt, although gorse was also acceptable.[125] The early modern period saw an important transition from wood to coal as a domestic fuel. Hatcher notes that 'it is probable that more than half of all the coal which was produced in Britain before 1700 was burnt in the home', while Spufford suggests that 'in the 1560s and 1570s there was a turning point when coal became much more commonly used in vernacular houses'.[126] The transition from wood to coal was not a simple one: coal fires require different hearth furniture and, more significantly, different shaped chimneys from wood fires.

Cox's analysis of Gloucestershire inventories shows that coal was used in the kitchen and service rooms, while wood was used in living rooms and bedrooms.[127] It was easier to control the heat of a coal fire for cooking, but coal was considered too smelly and dirty for the living rooms. On the other hand, for cooking processes where the food came into close contact with smoke, charcoal or wood was preferred

---

[121] Disbursement accounts; LEST/P7.
[122] Fussell, *Robert Loder's Farm Accounts*, 45, 152.
[123] Harvey, *Living and Dying*, 202.
[124] Hole, *The English Housewife*, 114–15; D. Woodward, 'Straw, bracken and the Wicklow whale: the exploitation of natural resources in England since 1500', *Past and Present* 159 (1998), 68.
[125] Woodward, 'Straw, bracken and the Wicklow whale', 52; Markham, *English Housewife*, 189–90.
[126] J. Hatcher, *The History of the British Coal Industry*, Vol. 1 (Oxford, 1993), 409; Spufford, 'Chimneys, wood and coal', 23; see also Woolgar, *The Great Household*, 140.
[127] Cox, 'A flesh pott', 149.

because it gave a more pleasant flavour.[128] Charcoal and coal appear in the Le Stranges' kitchen accounts as well as the disbursement accounts, indicating that they were both used in processing and cooking of food, as were the faggots of wood and whins. The Le Stranges used coal for heating some rooms in the house, as they purchased two grates in 1618 and another in 1620—grates were only needed when coal was being burnt in a fireplace.[129] They were not alone amongst the East Anglian gentry in using coal for domestic heating at this date: Hatcher cites the case of Sir Thomas Kytson of Hengrave Hall near Bury St Edmunds owning an iron cradle for burning coal in his hall in 1603.[130] The enlargement of Hunstanton Hall in the 1620s would have allowed chimneys suited to coal fires to be built. Coal is a dirtier fuel than wood, and as a result chimneys needed to be cleaned more often. The chimneys of Hunstanton Hall were swept at least once a year in 1619–21: again, this is recorded in the kitchen books, perhaps because the kitchen chimney required most attention.

The four fuels had quite different origins. Charcoal, wood and gorse were all made or collected on the Le Stranges' estates. Wood and gorse came from Hunstanton and the neighbouring manors. Gorse was a managed crop. The kitchen accounts record it being sown at Barrett Ringstead and Sedgeford, as well as being dug up and made into faggots. The faggots of whin and wood were made by the Le Stranges' usual day labourers, who were paid 12d for making 100 wood faggots in 1611, rising to 14d by 1619. The more specialist gorse faggots were sold for 2s 2d a 100. Charcoal came from the Le Stranges' manor at Gressenhall in central Norfolk, which contained woodland. Coal was readily available in King's Lynn, brought by sea from north-east England.[131] The Le Stranges' coal, which came from Scotland as well as the north-east, was purchased at Lynn and then transported by sea to be 'landed' at Hunstanton.[132] Coal was bought by the chalder, or more rarely by the ton. It was purchased in large quantities: an average of 23.5 chalders and 1 ton of coal each year between 1610 and 1625, costing on average 12.7s per chalder and 13.8s per ton. This was not all for domestic use—some was used in their building work and some sold on to tenants and workmen.

The idea that people in early modern England were dirty and smelly arises from a number of misconceptions. It is true that people rarely took baths or washed their outer clothing. However, outer clothes made of wool, fur and other luxurious fabrics were brushed rather than washed. The hands and face were washed regularly, and the body and outer clothing were kept clean by changing linen underclothes. The gentry marked their status with higher standards of cleanliness, which was made possible by their employment of servants, better water supply and washing facilities, and larger quantities of linen. Cleanliness was also gendered:

---

[128] Thirsk, *Food*, 15, 108, 184.
[129] M. Overton, J. Whittle, D. Dean, and A. Hann, *Production and Consumption in English Households, 1600–1750* (Abingdon, 2004), 98.
[130] Hatcher, *British Coal Industry*, 416.
[131] Hatcher, *British Coal Industry*, 503, 579–85; J. Lee, *Cambridge and its Economic Region 1450–1550* (Hatfield, 2005), 161.
[132] It is possible that some was brought directly to Hunstanton.

women were expected to have higher standards of personal cleanliness than men, and almost all the work of cleaning was done by women.[133] In the late fifteenth and early sixteenth centuries, the only female servants employed by Cambridge colleges were laundresses.[134] Cleaning was an important part of housewifery.[135] However, the technical challenges of laundry also stimulated male interest in the late sixteenth and early seventeenth centuries, with Hugh Plat, Leonard Mascall and John Partridge all publishing work on how to remove spots and stains and keep clothes smelling sweet.[136] The production of soap and starch, two everyday products that were used in large quantities, was among the fashionable economic schemes of the period.[137]

The great majority of evidence for cleaning relates to laundry. Hunstanton Hall and other large houses on the estate were provided with separate wash houses: a service room with its own water supply. At Hunstanton a new well was dug and pumps fitted to ensure a convenient water supply in 1610. An inventory of Hunstanton Hall from 1675 records the wash-house containing three leaden cisterns for holding water, as well as two tables and three keelers (shallow wooden tubs).[138] Alice purchased a bucking tub and rinsing tub in 1611, and another two in 1615. Bucking tubs were for washing large quantities of linen using lye, a strong alkaline solution made from wood ash.[139] The idea that households in this period only attempted their laundry 'once or twice a year' has little foundation amongst the elite.[140] Anne Stafford, a fifteenth-century gentlewoman, paid her washerwoman for weekly laundry.[141] The Le Stranges employed a local washerwoman from 1606 to 1612 before they had an adequate live-in staff. Alice Chant was paid quarterly for her washing, at a rate of 6s rising to 8s quarterly, suggesting that she undertook regular washes. In 1615, forty-eight purchases of 1 or 2 lbs of soap were made during the year, with each purchase perhaps representing one wash. While the Le Stranges were in London in 1620–1, they paid 'for a woman for washing 1s and for 2 pound of soap 6d', indicating that this was the quantity of soap needed for each wash.

There were two main types of soap in the seventeenth century: hard white soap, which originally came from Castile but was manufactured in England from the late

---

[133] Thomas, 'Cleanliness and godliness'; A. Van Herk, 'Invisibled laundry', *Signs* 27:3 (2002), 893–900; S. Vincent, *Dressing the Elite: Clothes in Early Modern England* (Oxford, 2003), 52–4.
[134] Lee, *Cambridge*, 150.
[135] Hole, *The English Housewife*, 109–12; A. Sim, *The Tudor Housewife* (Stroud, 1996), 44–60; U.A. Robertson, *The Illustrated History of the Housewife 1650–1950* (Stroud, 1999), 74–80.
[136] L. Mascall, *A Profitable Book declaring dyvers approved remedies to take out spottes and staines in silkes, velvets, linnen and woollen clothes* (London, 1583); J. Partridge, *The Treasury of Commodious Conceites and hidden secrets. Commonly called the Good Huswives closet of provision . . . gathred out of sundry experiments lately practised by men of great knowledge . . .* (London, 1584); H. Plat, *Delightes for Ladies* (London, 1608).
[137] J. Thirsk, *Economic Policy and Projects: The Development of a Consumer Society in Early Modern England* (Oxford, 1978), 53–4, 83–92
[138] TNA PROB 4/3988.
[139] Sim, *The Tudor Housewife*, 52.
[140] G.E. Fussell and K.R. Fussell, *The English Countrywoman: A Farmhouse Social History* (Ely, 1955), 26.
[141] Woolgar, *The Great Household*, 168; Sim, *The Tudor Housewife*, 50.

sixteenth century onwards, and soft 'black' soap, which was sometimes homemade.[142] White soap was the superior product and the main type used by the Le Stranges. The very occasional purchases of black soap were often noted 'for the horses'. In total, the household purchased between 50 and 70 lbs of soap a year, costing 3d to 5d a pound. Starch was also used in large quantities: usually between 25 and 35 lbs a year, costing 3d or 4d a pound. In addition 1 or 2 lbs of powder blue, used for whitening linen, were purchased each year for 1s 2d a lb. These products were quite standard in this period. The household of Robert Loder purchased all the same things, at similar prices but in smaller quantities: 37 lb of soap, 7.5 lbs of starch and 14 oz of powder blue, for one year in 1618.[143] Soap was occasionally used for cleaning the house: in London in 1620–1 the Le Stranges paid a woman 'for washing the house 6d', with 1 lb of soap. More usually, houses were swept with brooms. The kitchen accounts record large numbers of brooms being purchased, about twenty in 1620, for instance. Many of these were 'marram brooms'. Marram grass, which grows on sand dunes, was a local product and must have created a more delicate broom useful for dusting. Marram grass was also purchased by the sack, perhaps to strew on the floor like rushes.

The provision of light, fuel and cleaning products provides an example of the Le Stranges' consumption strategies in microcosm. They followed a pragmatic approach, using local, renewable resources from their estate where possible, but were also open to novelties such as Castile soap, starch and coal when it proved convenient. Some items, such as the bundles of wood and gorse, were produced by their own workers, but they were also happy to subcontract work such as the production of tallow candles. Apart from their use of coal, which was in part a consequence of their geographical location, their consumption patterns were very similar to that of the middling household of Robert Loder in Berkshire. What differed was the scale of their consumption.

CONCLUSION

How had patterns of everyday consumption changed since the late medieval period? In the early seventeenth century, the Le Stranges were eating turkey for Christmas, drinking beer, using coal for heating and cooking and white soap and starch for their laundry: all innovations that had appeared in the sixteenth century. They consumed large quantities of sugar, predating the surge in sugar consumption that took place after the mid-century.[144] They partook in newly fashionable forms of food consumption: planting cherries, peaches, nectarines and artichokes in their garden and purchasing banqueting stuff such as comfits to celebrate their children's

---

[142] On black soap, see Sim, *The Tudor Housewife*, 53; on white soap, see Thirsk, *Economic Policy and Projects*, 54, and Clay, *Economic Expansion*, vol. II, 210.
[143] Fussell, *Robert Loder's Farm Accounts*, 152–3. His soap cost 4d/lb, starch 4d/lb, and powder blue 1.5d/oz.
[144] Mintz, 'The changing roles of food', 265.

christenings. They owned a collection of printed medical texts that added to the advice given by medical practitioners and passed down by women within families. Many of these changes fitted easily with established forms of behaviour. Turkeys were added to geese, and only partially replaced them, as poultry enjoyed at Christmas time. Beer replaced ale, but was brewed at home and consumed at the same times and in the same quantity as ale had been. Coal was used alongside the more traditional fuels of wood and charcoal. Coal required adjustments to fireplaces and chimneys in order to be burnt effectively without creating smoky rooms—this was easier for the gentry than other classes. The basic constituents of the diet remained very largely the same for the gentry, based around large quantities of beef and bread and supplemented by a wide variety of other meats and fish. As in the medieval period, imported spices, sugar and dried fruit were an important form of flavouring. Houses were lit with tallow candles. Despite the momentous religious changes, Lent and 'fish-days' continued to be observed, although in a more relaxed fashion. The most noticeable change to the basic diet was an increased consumption of cheese: a quiet revolution of English diet in the sixteenth century.

How did consumption vary with status? Gentry diets were marked by the variety of animals consumed, including wild birds and fish, by the quantity of beef, sugar, spices and dried fruit, and by the special meat of venison, which only they could afford to rear and hunt. Wealthy yeomen like Robert Loder also enjoyed plenty of meat, though usually mutton and pork or bacon rather than beef, and not the wild game and variety of fish that the gentry enjoyed. This solid diet was also enjoyed by servants in gentry households. In the absence of household accounts, the diet of labouring households is more speculative. It certainly contained less meat, and probably less cheese too: classic pottage is based on grain and garden herbs and vegetables, with meat used for flavouring. The poor did not necessarily eat what they produced or caught. Chickens were more likely to be exchanged for cash than eaten in any quantity by labourers. Catches of wild birds and fish may also have had cash values when sold to the gentry that exceeded their calorific value in a labouring family's cooking pot. The gentry had access to a wide range of medical advice, care and medicines that were beyond the reach of ordinary villagers. However, this care was extended to servants employed in the household and was offered by Alice Le Strange to the local community. The gentry and yeoman class enjoyed a degree of cleanliness and domestic convenience that was also denied to poorer households. They owned plenty of linen and could afford the convenient water supply, heating and soap to wash it regularly and thoroughly. Their houses were likely to be warmer, less smoky and better lit. Cookery books and contemporary commentators like Harrison exaggerate the richness of English diets. Variety was a marker of status for the gentry, but the quantities of exotic foods consumed, such as oranges and dates, remained limited even in wealthy households like that of the Le Stranges. There were strong similarities across social groups too. Grain was the mainstay for every class: more as fine white bread for the wealthy, and more as pottage for the poor. Everyone drank beer. Everyone aspired to consume beef, sugar and dried fruit on special occasions.

5

Material Culture

> *Also I give and bequeath unto the said Dame Anne Lestrang my greate band chest with all the linnen therein except one paire of three breadth sheetes of fine holland, one suite of Diaper and one sute of Damaske wrapped in a Cloth in the same Chest which I will and bequeath unto Dame Elizabeth Spring my daughter.*[1]

William Harrison, in his *Description of England* (1587), famously noted '[t]here are old men yet dwelling in the village where I remain which have noted three things to be marvelously altered in England within their sound remembrance': the addition of chimneys to houses; a great 'amendment of lodging' involving the replacement of straw pallets with flock and featherbeds; and the exchange of wooden 'treen' vessels for pewter.[2] The history of early modern consumption has stressed the significant changes in material culture that occurred after 1650, such as the spread of coffee and tea, cotton, china and clocks as common items of consumption. Harrison reminds us that Elizabethans also perceived themselves as living in a period of rapid change. All the changes he highlighted are well evidenced in the Le Strange accounts alongside other novelties, including precursors of late seventeenth-century changes in consumption, such as cotton cloth and clocks. Studies of early modern consumption have concentrated on material culture, particularly of the durable household goods listed in inventories. Probate inventories recorded the movable goods owned at death: as a source they have two great advantages. They survive in thousands for the early modern period across a wide region of north-west Europe and north America, representing households of a broad middling section of society. They often recorded goods in situ, locating them in particular rooms and in relation to other goods, providing evidence of how they were used. On the other hand, probate inventories also have two major disadvantages for the study of consumption: they only provide a snapshot of what was owned, rather than a record of expenditure and ownership over time, and they contain little detail about clothing or food, two of the most important categories of consumption. This chapter explores the material culture that clothed the body and furnished the home in the early seventeenth century using household accounts as its main source, but also taking evidence from inventories.

---

[1] The will of Alice Le Strange, 1656: TNA Prob/11/262.
[2] W. Harrison, *The Description of England*, ed. G. Edelen (New York, 1968). Harrison lived in Essex.

In her pioneering study of probate inventories, Weatherill found that despite their wealth the gentry were not the most innovative consumers in the period 1675–1725. Members of the 'dealing trades' adopted new goods more quickly and more uniformly than the gentry.[3] A larger sample of inventories studied by Overton et al. confirmed that, rather than the gentry, people working in 'professional services' were the first to adopt items associated with new ways of eating and cooking, such as tea and coffee utensils, saucepans and forks in the period after 1650. Yet this pattern did not necessarily apply across the whole of the early modern period, or for all types of material culture. Overton et al. revealed that in 1600–50 the gentry *were* the most innovative group, the first to adopt new items such as mirrors, jacks, chests of drawers and upholstered furniture in their homes.[4] Weatherill's study found that the gentry led in adopting clocks and were more likely than other groups to own books and mirrors in 1675–1725.[5] Neither Weatherill nor Overton et al. set out to study gentry consumption patterns. Their samples of probate inventories exclude those registered at the highest church court in southern England, the Prerogative Court of Canterbury (PCC), where most of the inventories compiled for the wealthy gentry were registered.[6] While a good number of the parish gentry registered probate with local courts, those of the knightly class, such as the Le Stranges, did so very rarely. Instead, the consumption habits of the English elite have been studied from a rather different perspective, which might be described as 'the V&A school', as many of its publications originate from London's Victoria and Albert Museum of art and design. Its focus is primarily on fine examples of surviving objects from the period, carefully put in context with the use of inventories, family papers and fine art.[7] This leads to concentration on royalty and those who moved in courtly circles: the super-rich of the English elite, rather than the county gentry. Despite their income of over £2000 a year, the Le Stranges' wealth and spending habits did not approach that of well-known courtiers, such as the Duke of Buckingham, who is said to have spent between £1500 and £3000 a year on clothes alone in the 1620s.[8]

Following eighteenth-century thinkers such as Steuart and Montesquieu, de Vries has suggested that a new form of luxury emerged as a product of 'the

---

[3] L. Weatherill, *Consumer Behaviour and Material Culture in Britain 1660–1760* (London, 1988), 184.
[4] M. Overton, J. Whittle, D. Dean, and A. Hann, *Production and Consumption in English Households, 1600–1750* (Abingdon, 2004), 166.
[5] Weatherill, *Consumer Behaviour*, 184.
[6] Few PCC inventories survive for the period before the mid-seventeenth century.
[7] For example: G. Beard, *Upholsterers and Interior Furnishing in England 1530–1840* (New Haven, 1997); R.J. Charleston, *English Glass and Glass used in England, c.400–1940* (London, 1984); P. Glanville, *Silver in Tudor and Early Stuart England: A Social History and Catalogue of the National Collection 1480–1660* (London, 1990); D.M. Mitchell, '"By your leave my masters": British taste in table linen in the fifteenth and sixteenth centuries', *Textile History* 20(1), 49–77; M. Snodin and J. Styles (eds.), *Design and the Decorative Arts: Britain 1500–1900* (London, 2001); P. Thornton, *Seventeenth-Century Interior Decoration in England, France and Holland* (New Haven, 1978).
[8] L. Stone, *The Crisis of the Aristocracy 1558–1641* (Oxford, 1965), 565.

commercial and urban societies that Europe possessed by the sixteenth century'.[9] Old luxury, the luxury of the ruling classes, was based on the consumption of 'grandeur or exquisite refinement', which could not be replicated by other social groups.[10] It took its fashions from the royal court, served to mark the status and authority of the ruling class, and thus maintained the existing social order. As such it relied on excess and display, for instance in clothing and architecture, to make its point. de Vries argues that a 'new luxury' first became evident in the seventeenth-century Dutch Republic. New luxury strove to promote comfort and enjoyment rather than de-mark status. Thus, it was more concerned with linen underclothes and domestic interiors than the outward displays of old luxury. Its fashions were generated by urban society rather than the court, and were available to a larger portion of society. It was made possible by new forms of production, which offered 'populux' goods. Goods such as Delft tiles and Dutch paintings were produced on a large scale and in gradated quality, and were acquired by a high proportion of households. Other examples of new luxury goods not so specific to the Dutch Republic were household and personal linens, upholstered furniture and mirrors.[11] In outlining these two forms of luxury it is possible that de Vries is mistaking different historiographical traditions for change over time. Old luxury with its 'exquisite refinement' is well illustrated by the V&A school and remained dominant in courtly circles well into the nineteenth century. New luxury with its emphasis on comfort, cleanliness and convenience was evident amongst wealthy urban consumers and sections of the gentry from at least the fifteenth century, as evidenced by probate inventories and wills. The Le Stranges' consumption habits, and presumably those of the bulk of the gentry, were closer to new than old luxury. This chapter explores three areas of domestic material culture: textiles and clothing, beds and furnishings, and dining and kitchen ware. The final section of the chapter examines the extent to which it is possible to reconstruct the meanings of these objects for the Le Strange family.

TEXTILES AND CLOTHING

Cloth production was early modern England's most important industry, and expenditure on textiles was second only to food in household budgets of the period.[12] The analysis of textiles and clothing in this chapter is based on three sources from the Le Strange accounts: all the purchases of textiles recorded in the

---

[9] J. de Vries, 'Luxury in the Dutch Golden Age in theory and practice', in M. Berg and E. Eger (eds.), *Luxury in the Eighteenth Century: Debates, Desires and Delectable Goods* (Basingstoke, 2002), 43.
[10] J. de Vries, *The Industrious Revolution: Consumer Behaviour and the Household Economy, 1650 to the Present* (Cambridge, 2008), 44.
[11] de Vries, 'Luxury'; and *The Industrious Revolution*, chs. 2 and 4.
[12] C.G.A. Clay, *Economic Expansion and Social Change: England 1500–1700* (Cambridge, 1984), vol. 2, 13; on expenditure see Weatherill, *Consumer Behaviour*, 299; N.B. Harte, 'The economics of clothing in the seventeenth century', *Textile History* 22:2 (1991), 292; M. Spufford, 'The cost of apparel in seventeenth-century England and the accuracy of Gregory King', *Economic History Review* 53:4 (2000) 677–705; and Chapter 3.

disbursement accounts of 1610–25; selected extracts from the disbursement accounts of 1626–37 referring particularly to the clothes of Nicholas and Elizabeth Le Strange; and two detailed inventories drawn up by Alice Le Strange of beds and bedroom furnishings and household linen in 1632 and recorded in the account books.[13] The inventories and accounts make it clear that large quantities of textiles were used for furnishing. For instance, in the nine years between 1617 and 1625 the Le Stranges spent £22 8s 7d on holland, a fine linen cloth, for clothing, but £27 19s 0d on holland for household linen. Their total expenditure on household linens for that period was £105 6s 5d.[14] A four-poster bed with canopies and curtains used 54 yards of woollen and velvet fabric (not including linings) compared with 32 yards for an expensive woman's dress or 37 yards for a man's suit and cloak.[15] Household furnishings are discussed in more detail in the next section, but they are included here in the analysis of the range of textiles purchased by the Le Stranges.

The Le Stranges purchased at least sixty-two different types of cloth between 1610 and 1632. The delineation of cloth into different types is not a strict science, and the types listed here follow the descriptions found in the accounts and 1632 inventories. Some types given different names were in fact very similar, such as Welsh cotton and frieze, or perpetuana and sempiternum. On the other hand, the description 'cloth' was a catch-all for any textile whose specific name was not known or remembered, ranging from 'fine spanish cloth' at £1 2s a yard to the cheapest cloth of 2d a yard. Slightly less general but still encompassing many types were 'stuff', which usually referred to worsted cloth of various types, and 'broad cloth', which usually referred to a range of woollen cloths, but may also have been used for other types of fabric purchased in broad widths.[16] Even some quite specific names, such as damask and camlet, encompassed many variations. Damask could refer to silk cloth from Italy, linen cloth from Flanders or worsted imitations from Norwich.[17] The damask purchased by the Le Stranges ranged from 12s to 3s 4d per yard in price, and given its uses in the household was predominantly of the linen type. Camlet was another fine foreign cloth, properly made of angora or other special wools, but also made of worsted in Norwich from the early sixteenth century. The Turkey camlet purchased by Nicholas Le Strange for a coat for one of his wedding outfits was of the fine foreign variety, and cost 8s 6d a yard.

Of the quantifiable purchases of cloth in the accounts from 1610 to 1625, 54.7 per cent were made of wool, 42.6 per cent linen and 2.5 per cent silk. Silk cloth was consistently the most expensive. Satin was purchased for 16s a yard, velvet for 15s,

---

[13] Disbursement accounts in LEST/P6, P7; 1632 inventories are towards the end of LEST/P10.

[14] The accounts are more detailed about usage from 1617 onwards. Total figure includes all holland for household items, damask and diaper cloth, and sheets, pillowbears and napkins of unspecified cloth.

[15] Estimates based on the black bed, Elizabeth's black and yellow dress of 1630, and Nicholas' wedding suits, discussed below. On textiles in furnishings see D. Jenkins (ed.), *The Cambridge History of Western Textiles* (Cambridge, 2003); and L. Martin, 'The rise of the new draperies in Norwich, 1550–1622', in N.B. Harte (ed.), *The New Draperies in the Low Countries and England, 1300–1800* (Oxford, 1997).

[16] For example, broad cloth was sometimes purchased for sheets.

[17] Thornton, *Interior Decoration*, 113.

taffeta for 14s 5d, grogram for 14s and sarcenet for 8s. Plush, a luxurious silk velvet, cost 27s a yard. High-quality woollens could equal or exceed these prices. The most expensive cloth purchased was 'best scarlet', a woollen cloth that cost £3 5s a yard; broad cloth was purchased for 14s 4d, but most woollens were cheaper. Linens could also be bought for a great range of prices; generally, damask was the most expensive, followed by lawn, cambric, holland, diaper, canvas, twill and sacking. True cotton cloth does not appear in the accounts until the mid-1620s. The 'cotton' which is recorded is Welsh cotton, a type of woollen cloth with a cotton finish, which was used for blankets, linings and babies' things.[18] Calico, a true cotton imported from India, first appears in the accounts in 1623, when a calico border was purchased for one of Elizabeth's gowns at the cost of 8d. In 1630, 29 yards were purchased: high-quality white calico for Nicholas's shirts at 3s 8d a yard, cheaper green calico for a bed tester, blue calico for unspecified use, and calico to make window curtains. This change corresponds with increased imports of calico by the East India Company from 5000 pieces in 1613, when it first appeared as a regular item, to $c.120,000$ in 1630.[19] The inventory of bedrooms records two further types of decorative Indian cotton, nicanee and pintado: nicanee to dress a bed, and pintado as cupboard and table cloths. Pintado was a 'fine cotton cloth painted or dyed with patterns of flowers', first recorded in England in the late sixteenth century and imported by the East India Company in the early seventeenth century. Nicanee, 'perhaps a cheap striped calico', was also being imported through this route by 1625.[20]

Despite the East India Company's role in increasing imports of cotton cloth, it did not introduce calico or pintado to the English market. Calicos are first recorded in England in the early sixteenth century, and a Cornish shopkeeper's inventory of 1606 shows that it was stocked in large quantities and sold cheaply in south-west England by that date.[21] Historians of the 'consumer revolution' of the late seventeenth and eighteenth centuries have stressed the importance of cotton in transforming clothing. It was cheap, colourful, decorative and easy to wash, replacing a world of 'black, brown, dark green and blue' woollens that had existed previously and bringing fashion to the classes below the elite.[22] Yet this is to ignore earlier changes in textile culture: the diversification of textiles in the fifteenth century and the 'new draperies' of the late sixteenth and early seventeenth centuries. The sixty-two types of fabric purchased by the Le Stranges show the imprint of each of these

---

[18] E. Kerridge, *Textile Manufactures in Early Modern England* (Manchester, 1985), 19.
[19] K.N. Chaudhuri, *The English East India Company: The Study of an Early Joint-Stock Company 1600–1640* (London, 1965), 192–3.
[20] Chaudhuri, *English East India Company*, 199–200. The OED's first reference to nicanee is from 1682.
[21] Cornwall County Record Office: inventory of Robert Bennett of Tregony, shopkeeper, 1606 (with 145.75 yards of four different types of calico). For a summary, see C. North, 'Fustians, figs and frankincense: Jacobean shop inventories for Cornwall', *Journal of the Royal Institution of Cornwall*, new series II (1995), 55–6.
[22] Quotation from de Vries, *The Industrious Revolution*, 135, describing the mid-seventeenth century. See also B. Lemire, *Fashion's Favourite: The Cotton Trade and the Consumer in Britain, 1660–1800* (Oxford, 1991).

transformations. Some of the cloth purchased by the Le Stranges was very traditional, and had been available since at least the fourteenth century: broad cloth, blanket, say, serge and satin for instance.[23] Nearly as many were first recorded in England in the fifteenth century, such as damask, holland, lawn and russels.[24] The first half of the sixteenth century brought more innovation with baize, flannel, frizado, calico and cambric all appearing for the first time.[25] The majority of these fifteenth- and early sixteenth-century innovations were imported, largely from continental Europe. The value of English imports of linen from the Low Countries rose from £6000–7000 in 1390 to £66,666 in 1530.[26]

The later sixteenth century and early seventeenth century saw rapid innovation in English woollen, and particularly worsted, cloth production, much of it led by immigrant cloth workers from the continent. The new cloths that were developed, collectively known as the new draperies, often mimicked more expensive fabrics.[27] They were lighter, more colourful and more decorative than traditional woollen and worsted cloth, but much cheaper than silks and high-quality woollens. As such, they shared many qualities with cotton. It is true that they did not wash as well; however, woollen cloth does not need to be washed as often as cotton: it does not soak up dirt and oil and can be brushed clean. Woollens were worn with linen or calico underclothes that could be, and were, washed regularly. Nine types of cloth purchased by the Le Stranges in 1610–32 first appeared in England between 1550 and 1599, including buffin, grogram, pintado and mocado.[28] Most striking, however, are the further six which were only produced for the first time in the early seventeenth century, and appear in the accounts of 1610–30 or the inventories of 1632. These were all new draperies produced in England: jollyboys, paragon, peropus, perpetuana, philip and cheney, and sempiternum. A further three types of cloth could not be traced, two of which may have been new draperies: novela and waveretta.[29] Another innovation of the sixteenth century was lace. The Le Stranges used lace in large quantities to edge every type of clothing and much of their furnishings. Even close stools were trimmed with lace in the Le Strange household. Levey notes that lace first 'emerged from the Italian passementerie industry by about 1500', but that it was lace made from linen thread on bone bobbins, or bone lace, that led a 'spectacular development of technique in the late

---

[23] The full list is baudkin, blanket, broad cloth, buckram, canvas, fustian, kersey, satin, say, scarlet, serge, taffeta, twill, velvet: fourteen types in all. The dating of types of cloth in this section was undertaken using primarily: Kerridge, *Textile Manufactures*; N. Evans, *The East Anglian Linen Industry: Rural Industry and Local Economy 1500–1850* (Farnham, 1985); Jenkins, *Cambridge History of Western Textiles*; and *OED Online*.

[24] Bustian, camlet, damask, diaper, dornix, frieze, holland, lawn, poldavy, russels, sarcenet, tapestry all appeared in the fifteenth century: twelve types in total.

[25] Along with stammet and satin a bridges: seven types in total.

[26] A.F. Sutton, *The Mercery of London: Trade, Goods and People, 1130–1578* (Aldershot, 2005), 156.

[27] N.B. Harte (ed.), *The New Draperies in the Low Countries and England, 1500–1800* (Oxford, 1997).

[28] The full list is: buffin, grosgrain, mocado, penistone, pintado, plush, rug, shag, tuftaffeta.

[29] The third was 'cow tayle'. One further type of cloth, saggathy, could not be dated. Seven types were too general to date: cloth, coarse cloth, 'cotton', linen, loomwork, stuff and ticking.

sixteenth and seventeenth centuries'.[30] The majority of the lace purchased by the Le Stranges was described as bone lace, although they also bought galloon lace, lace of silver and gold, and silk lace in various colours.

For people of the Le Stranges' wealth, both clothing and textile furnishings were colourful and decorative in the early seventeenth century. Nicholas Le Strange got married in a suit of pearl and carnation satin, and his sister attended the wedding dressed in a gown of black and lemon yellow. The beds in the Le Stranges' house were dressed in black velvet and gold, green snake velvet, crimson damask, scarlet, green and yellow stuff, green silk grogram laced with yellow, as well as buffin, jollyboys, waveretta and nicanee. While velvet, damask and scarlet were expensive, many new draperies were quite cheap and their consumption was certainly not restricted to the gentry and aristocracy. Cheap grogram (probably a worsted version) was less than 3s a yard, as were peropus, novela and russels; philip and cheney was less than 4s. These fabrics made their way into the homes of those of middling wealth, yeomen, wealthy craftsmen and traders, who also liked to dress their beds well and were beginning to use upholstered furniture.[31] The Le Stranges had no hesitation in using these new fabrics, despite their cheapness. Buffin (which was very cheap), jollyboys and waveretta were used for beds; mocado for upholstery; philip and cheney, paragon and peropus were used for coats and suits; while the new woollens from the west of England, perpetuana and sempiternum, were used for gowns and coats.

Fashions in cloth were important, and more relevant to the Le Stranges as consumers than to the modern consumer, because they purchased the cloth and then oversaw the construction of clothing and furnishings.[32] Just as household accounts provide much better information about the types of foodstuffs used to make meals than the actual meals eaten, so they provide more information about the cloth and other items used for clothing than the actual clothes themselves. The clothing of Alice and Hamon Le Strange is particularly poorly documented. Alice purchased her own clothing with her allowance of £66 13s 4d a year, and does not record it in the main accounts. Hamon's accessories are quite carefully recorded in the accounts but details of his clothing are largely absent. He tended to make purchases through his London tailor, for which the accounts only record the bill. On the other hand, the children's clothes, as a result of being Alice's responsibility but also a household expense, are recorded in some detail. Purchases of clothing for the boys become obscure once they reach adulthood, much like their father's, although there are exceptions. Elizabeth Le Strange's clothes, however, continued to be recorded until she left the household on marriage in 1636.

---

[30] S.M. Levey, 'Lace in the Early Modern Period, c.1500–1780', in Jenkins, *Cambridge History of Western Textiles*, 585.
[31] Martin, 'New draperies in Norwich', 251–3, 262–3.
[32] Lemire makes the same point with regard to the late seventeenth century, *Fashion's Favourite*, 7.

Women's main item of dress in the early seventeenth century was the gown.[33] Confusingly this was typically a set of clothes consisting of a petticoat, waistcoat and sleeves, which were designed to be worn together. Next to the skin, women wore linen shifts or smocks. On the top half of the body this was covered with a bodice or waistcoat, which was stiffened with strong linen cloth, sometimes with the addition of whalebone or bents.[34] The term bodice does not appear in the accounts, which instead refer to 'a pair of bodies', highlighting the fact that the garment consisted of two halves, which met at the front and back, and were tied together with laces. In fact this garment was quite rare, only two appear in the accounts of 1610–30: one stiffened with whalebone purchased for six-year-old Jane Le Strange in 1618 when she first started wearing adult-type clothing, and one for sixteen-year-old Elizabeth in 1630. Instead, the typical garment for the upper body was a waistcoat, which was also stiffened with linings and sometimes bone. Sleeves were made, and sometimes purchased, separately from the waistcoat, to which they were attached by points, laces or hooks, just as the waistcoat was joined to the petticoat. The stomacher, a flat panel which was fixed at the front of the waistcoat to cover its front opening and give additional structure, was characteristic of women's dress from the Elizabethan period and the early seventeenth century. Stomachers were purchased for Elizabeth Le Strange from 1627 onwards, when she was thirteen, but were not an element of every gown. The sleeves and waistcoat were trimmed with separate cuffs and collars made of linen and lace. Collars came in many styles: ruffs, rebatos, pickerdells and bands are all mentioned, along with the newly fashionable gorgett, a large kerchief worn around the shoulders instead of a collar and fastened with a brooch.[35] Gorgetts do not appear in the earlier accounts, but two were purchased for Elizabeth in 1630. By the time she married in 1636 neckwear consisted of neck clothes and gorgetts, with ruffs, rebatos and pickerdells all out of fashion.

Waistcoats were normally purchased together with a matching or contrasting skirt. All skirts were referred to as petticoats.[36] Layers of skirts kept the wearer warm, and portraits of this period show women wearing gowns that displayed at least two layers of petticoat, with a front split in the outer skirt to display another decorative skirt below. Further protection for the legs was provided by knitted hose or stockings. An additional outer layer of clothing could be provided by a loose over-gown, known as a night-gown.[37] This was a sleeveless, full-length garment that was worn on top of a waistcoat–sleeves–petticoat set. Two were purchased for Elizabeth Le Strange—one in 1626 and another in 1627. An outfit was finished off

---

[33] For descriptions of the elements of women's clothing in this period, see S. Vincent, *Dressing the Elite: Clothes in Early Modern England* (Oxford, 2003), 23–9, and A. Ribeiro, *Fashion and Fiction: Dress in Art and Literature in Stuart England* (New Haven, 2005), 63–71.
[34] Bents were made of marram grass: J. Arnold, *Queen Elizabeth's Wardrobe Unlock'd* (Leeds, 1988), 147.
[35] For definitions and illustrations see Ribeiro, *Fashion and Fiction*, 9, 49, 64, 127; and Arnold, *Queen Elizabeth's Wardrobe*, 360–71.
[36] The old-fashioned term 'kirtle' for an outer skirt appears only once in the accounts up to 1636.
[37] Ribeiro, *Fashion and Fiction*, 67–71.

with shoes, gloves and a headdress. The enormous quantity of shoes and gloves purchased by the Le Stranges is discussed below. The nature of women's headdress is difficult to reconstruct from the accounts: contemporary portraits and descriptions suggest that there was considerable variety.[38] Cauls were purchased for the girls when they were young; caps, coifs and pinners for Elizabeth when she was older. These were typically worn together with, or trimmed with, lace and gauzy linen to create various effects which framed the face. The portrait of Alice Le Strange shows her wearing an embroidered caul or cap on top of her head, with a lace headdress coming down over her forehead, which matched, but was separate from, her lace ruff.

One noticeable aspect of the Le Strange women's clothing, and one that is typical of women's dress in the period, is the lack of garments suited specifically to outside wear. There were no cloaks purchased for Jane or Elizabeth, and only one mention of a hood. They did not wear brimmed hats or boots. Gloves were for wear inside as well as out. The one exception was masks, worn by women in this period to protect their face from the elements, which were fairly frequent purchases. In contrast, men's fashion turned outside garments such as hats, boots and cloaks into ordinary items for wear inside and out. In this way, clothing served to emphasize the stereotypical spatial division between men and women: with women's clothing suited to domesticity and men's to the outside. Women's domesticity was also reinforced by their habitual wearing of aprons and kerchiefs to protect their clothing. Gentlewomen are rarely depicted wearing these garments in portraits, but they certainly used them just as women of lower status did.[39] Elizabeth purchased linen and lace to make multiple sets in 1636 in preparation for her marriage.

A gown, in the sense of a new set of clothes, was purchased for the Le Strange girls roughly once a year from the age of six until the year after marriage. Twenty gowns are recorded, six purchased between 1618 and 1627 when the girls were aged between six and thirteen, and fifteen between 1628 and 1637, when Elizabeth was aged fourteen to twenty-three. Jane died aged eight in 1620, and Elizabeth seems to have worn her cast-offs until she surpassed that age in 1622, when she began to receive her own new gowns. Because acquiring a gown was a process rather than a single act, involving multiple purchases of cloth and trimmings, and payments to one or more tailors, it is not always possible to be exact about the number and price of the sets of clothing. The gowns purchased for the girls when they were less than fourteen years old cost between £1 17s and £5 16s: expensive in relation to the pay of a female servant, but cheaper than most of those purchased when Elizabeth was older. At the age of fourteen Elizabeth received her first dress costing more than £10, and between the ages of fourteen and twenty she had six dresses costing between £8 and £17 each, as well as five cheaper ones costing

---

[38] Ribeiro, *Fashion and Fiction*, 67.
[39] For an illustration of ordinary English countrywomen travelling to market wearing hats, ruffs, kerchiefs and aprons, see G. Braun and F. Hogenberg, *Civitates Orbis Terrarum*, vol. 5 (Cologne, 1598), plate 1.

Table 5.1. Elizabeth Le Strange's four most expensive gowns

Description	Cost
Black gown and lemon coloured waistcoat, July 1630	**£30 19s 10d**
Black tufted grogram (16 yards)	£5 4s
Black Florence satin (2 yards)	£1 10s
Black taffeta (0.5 yards)	£1 1s
Black lace (9 dozen)	£1 7s
Lemon-coloured satin (12 yards)	£9 16s
Silver bone lace (22.25 oz)	£5 12s
White silk thread (1 oz)	4s
Russet silk thread (1 oz)	3s 6d
Yellow perpetuana to border the petticoat (0.5 yards)	1s 4d
Tailoring, a roll and bents	£5 18s
Two gowns for her wedding, June 1635	**£81 13s 7d**
Silver grogram (12 yards)	£14 8s
Sarsenet for a petticoat and waistcoat (5.6 yards)	£2 7s 3d
A pair of bodies	8s
Pearl-coloured sarsenet (18 yards)	£13 11s 10d
Silver bone lace (28 yards weighing 32.25 oz)	£8 6s 8d
Black satin (20 yards)	£14 10s
Black whip lace (29 yards)	£3 2s 10d
Scarlet satin (8.5 yards)	£6 7s 6d
Silver bone lace (23 oz)	£5 18s 6d
Gorgett and cuffs of bone lace	£6 12s
Holland (15 yards)	£4 6s
Bone lace (2.5 yards)	13s
A pair of damask bodies	£1 2s
Tailor's bill not specified	
Plush and tissued grogram gown, April 1637	**£61 17s 10d**
Plush (12 yards)	£12
Brocaided tabby (6 yards)	£6 15s
Silver and gold tissued grogram (11.25 yards)	£36 10s
White taffeta sarsenet (5 yards)	£2
Silver lace (15 yards weighing 11.13 oz)	£3 6s
Tailoring	£1 4s
Transport from London	2s 10d

Source: Le Strange disbursement accounts; LEST/P7.

between £3 12s and £6 each.[40] In addition, there were four much more expensive dresses of £30–62 each, purchased for special occasions, as shown in Table 5.1. These included a yellow and black satin and grogram gown for Nicholas Le Strange's wedding in 1630; Elizabeth's own wedding dresses, one of silver and pearl and another of black and scarlet, in 1636; and a spectacular gown purchased for Elizabeth by the Le Stranges six months after her wedding, as a final gift. While

---

[40] The £1 dress was for cloth only and does not include tailoring, trimmings or lining.

Material Culture 127

Table 5.2. Elizabeth Le Strange's other gowns, purchased 1628–37

Date purchased	Description (with yards of fabric in brackets)	Cost
Summer 1628	Gown of crimson philizela (7), with watchet and yellow stitched taffeta (11) for petticoat, sleeves and stomacher; taffeta sarsenet (2), crimson taffeta sarsenet (1), ribbon (12), bone lace (10)	£13 4s
Summer 1628	Black tammel gown with kirtle and stomachers of stitched taffeta: Turkey tammel (11), ribbon (20), black edging lace (2 dozen), pearl-coloured stitched taffeta (5)	£8 18s
Summer 1629	Camels' hair stuff (8) for petticoat, calico (2) for border, silver lace (2 oz), crimson stitched taffeta (14); green stitched taffeta (5), carnation taffeta (1), for sleeves and stomacher	£9 18s
1629/30	For a gown: crimson tammel (18), white edging lace (8 dozen); white and red Norwich damask for a petticoat (9), galloon lace	£4 19s
March 1631/2	Tammel for a gown (16), satin lace (7 dozen and 10 yards), black taffeta lining (1)	£6
Summer 1632	Black taffeta (11) for a gown, black satin comparsed lace (21 dozen)	£16 12s
Summer 1633	Green watered taffeta for a petticoat and waistcoat (5), green sarsenet (1), silver lace (15 oz)	£10 8s
Summer 1633	Black China damask (14) for a petticoat and waistcoat	£3 12s
March 1634/5	Black princely (8) for petticoat and waistcoat, scarlet baize (3) for petticoat, lace	£3 13s
March 1634/5	Petticoat and waistcoat of watered sky-coloured taffeta with silver lace	£8 16s
October 1635	Petticoat and waistcoat of black silk-watered mohair (15)	£3 10s

Source: Le Strange disbursement accounts; LEST/P7.

the cost of these gowns was high, they did not approach the expense of clothing worn by royalty and those in courtly circles.[41]

By modern standards gowns were not purchased frequently: they were durable items that lasted a number of years and could be adjusted and remade. By the time Elizabeth was twenty-three and a newly married woman, she would have owned a collection of fifteen gowns in a range of colours, styles and expense, as shown in Table 5.2.[42] Probate inventories rarely record clothing in any detail, but the few examples that do suggest that this was a fairly typical collection of gowns for a wealthy woman in this period. For instance, the 1607 inventory of Gertrude Driland, a widowed gentlewoman of somewhat lesser wealth from Wye in Kent, listed: 'One broad cloth gown, one tuff taffata gown, one stuff gown, one broad cloth morning gown, one velvet kirtle, two satin kirtles, one taffata petticoat, one damask petticoat, one cotton petticoat, one pair of bodices, one scarf, one muff, two stuff petticoats, one velvet stomacher, three hoods..., one fan and one old gown.'[43] The value of clothing recorded in probate inventories, however, is significantly lower than that in the accounts. Gertrude Driland's apparel was valued

---

[41] Stone, *Crisis of the Aristocracy*, notes dresses reputedly costing £1500 in 1613 for court occasions. See also Ribeiro, *Fashion and Fiction*, 34, 75.
[42] Assuming all the dresses purchased since 1628 were wearable in some form.
[43] Centre for Kentish Studies, inventories of the archdeaconry court of Canterbury: probate inventory of Gertrude Driland of Wye, 24 November 1607; doc. ref. 10.44.259.

at a total of £13 6s 8d. In a selection of thirty-seven gentry inventories dating from 1585 to 1645, with values of £300 or more and household goods worth £30 or more, the average (mean) valuation given for apparel was £21 4s, the median was £13 and the maximum was £100.[44] Elizabeth's clothes cost £261 8s to purchase.[45] It seems that the degree of depreciation between purchase cost as recorded in the accounts and second-hand value as recorded in the inventories was steep.

Clothes were vital to Elizabeth's presentation to gentry society as a marriageable young gentlewoman, and were a significant investment which she took from her family to her new household at marriage. As her education cost virtually nothing, they were second only to her marriage portion as a category of expenditure on her by her parents.[46] How did this compare with the treatment of her brothers? Men's basic clothing was somewhat cheaper than women's, largely because it normally required less cloth. Men wore linen shirts next to their skin, which were very similar to the smocks worn by women. Their equivalent of a woman's gown was a 'suit'.[47] On the top half of the body this consisted of a doublet or waistcoat, sometimes worn with a sleeveless jerkin over the top, or with a coat or cloak: all these items appear in the accounts. Below the waist men wore hose. Confusingly this description was applied to a number of different garments that clothed the legs. Hose on the upper leg were made of cloth. They could be the short padded trunk hose popular in the late Elizabethan period or knee-length hose that became standard from the 1620s onwards.[48] On the lower leg men wore knitted hose or stockings, which could be made of wool, linen or silk. Both upper hose and doublet or waistcoat were well padded: typically, three different types of canvas or fustian for lining and stiffening were purchased to make each these garments, as well the outer cloth which was on show. An alternative to the doublet and hose combination was a long, looser gown.[49] Two gowns were purchased for Nicholas—one when he was eleven and another when he was fifteen years old—and one for Hamon junior when he was nineteen. The dress of the upper body was very similar for men and women: men wore the same type of linen and lace cuffs and ruffs or bands (collars) around the wrists and neck, and, like women, their main garments were trimmed with large quantities of lace and sometimes ribbon. One difference was the use of buttons: rarely purchased for women's clothing, these were essential elements of male upper body dress in the early seventeenth century, with between thirty-six and 144 buttons purchased for each garment.[50]

---

[44] Selection includes all eligible inventories in M. Wanklyn, *Inventories of Worcestershire Landed Gentry 1537–1786*, Worcestershire Historical Society New Series, Vol. 16 (1998); the inventory sample from Kent and Cornwall used in Overton et al., *Production and Consumption*; and the inventory of Francis Guybon of Sedgeford, gent, 1632: NRO MF/X11 DN/INV 37/176.

[45] That is the amount spent on her gowns from 1628 to 1637 as recorded in the household accounts. Total expenditure on her clothing was higher including linens, shoes and so on. She also received an allowance of £40 a year from the age of twenty-one for buying clothes.

[46] On her education, see Chapter 6: Education and adult children.

[47] For descriptions of the elements of men's clothing in this period see Vincent, *Dressing the Elite*, 13–23, and Ribeiro, *Fashion and Fiction*, 42–52.

[48] Ribeiro, *Fashion and Fiction*, 43–4.

[49] Ribeiro, *Fashion and Fiction*, 47–8.

[50] Stone, *Crisis of the Aristocracy*, 565.

Material Culture

Table 5.3. Clothing accessories, purchased 1610–25

	Shoes and boots	Hose and stockings	Gloves
Unspecified, 1610–25	106 (6.6)	89 (5.6)	90 (5.6)
Mr Strange, 1610–25	19 (1.2)	17 (1.1)	31 (1.9)
Nick, 1610–25	66 (4.1)	44 (2.8)	41 (2.6)
Ham, 1610–25	61 (3.8)	37 (2.3)	36 (2.3)
Jane, 1611–20	35 (4.4)	28 (3.5)	27 (3.4)
Bess, 1613–25	51 (4.3)	23 (1.9)	34 (2.8)
Roger, 1616–25	40 (4.4)	26 (2.9)	24 (2.7)
Total	378 (23.6)	257 (16.1)	283 (17.7)

Note: In brackets, the average number purchased per year when aged one or more.

Source: Le Strange disbursement accounts, 1610–25; LEST/P6, P7.

Suits and gowns for Nicholas and Hamon junior between 1611 and 1624, when they were aged between seven and nineteen, cost between £1 5s and £7 3s, averaging at £3 3s.[51] This was less than the cost of Jane's and Elizabeth's dresses, which, if we exclude the four most expensive, cost an average of £5 7s. However, there are a number of reasons why we should hesitate in concluding women's dress was more expensive. First, men spent more on various accessories than women, and, second, men's clothing was recorded differently from women's in the accounts. The sheer number of accessories, particularly footwear, leg wear and gloves, recorded in the accounts is striking, as shown in Table 5.3.[52] Normally, the accounts note who these were purchased for: those which were unspecified seem to have been very largely for Sir Hamon Le Strange. Most of these items showed little gender difference. Each child was bought four or five pairs of shoes or boots a year, between two and four pairs of hose or stockings, and two to four pairs of gloves.[53] Gloves were bought slightly more frequently for the girls than the boys. However, men standardly wore many accessories which were not used, or only very rarely used, by women: as Peck writes, 'accessories were key'.[54] These included boots, silk stockings, girdles (belts) and hats. Boots were never purchased for the Le Strange girls and women, but they constituted half the items of footwear purchased for Sir Hamon.[55] Boots cost 10s to £1 a pair, compared with 2s or 3s for adult shoes. Elizabeth's shoes never cost more than 2s 4d a pair. Silk stockings were also only purchased for men in the Le Strange household in the period up to 1630.

---

[51] An average of fifteen purchases.
[52] The number of pairs of hose may be slightly under-recorded owing to entries such as 'for knitting hose for the children'.
[53] Gregory King estimated every adult purchased two pairs of shoes a year in 1688, see Harte, 'Economics of clothing', 288.
[54] L. Peck, *Consuming Splendor: Society and Culture in Seventeenth-Century England* (Cambridge, 2005), 29.
[55] Assuming all the unspecified footwear was for Sir Hamon, those purchased for him comprised sixty-three pairs of shoes and sixty-two pairs of boots.

They cost between £1 5s and £2 10s a pair.[56] The most expensive pair of stockings purchased for Elizabeth cost 8s. Girdles or belts were also male clothing in this period. They could be quite plain, costing 1s to 3s as purchased for the boys, or more expensive. Sir Hamon Le Strange's girdles cost between 6s and £1 5s, and are described as embroidered, gold and silver. However, it is men's expenditure on hats that really stands out. Between 1610 and 1625 Sir Hamon purchased thirty-three hats as well as notching up unspecified hatters' bills of £16 5s, enough to buy a further twelve. Unspecified or felt hats cost an average of 11s 4d, but beaver hats, of which Hamon purchased at least eight, were much more expensive, costing an average of £2 13s.[57] Hats were decorated with bands; sometimes bands were purchased with the hat and sometimes separately so that the band could be matched with other items such as the girdle. Separately purchased hat bands cost an average of 13s, as much as some hats. Feathers were also used to decorate hats, costing between 2s and 16s. Thus a man dressed in silk stockings and a beaver hat, with a matching hat band and girdle, could have spent an extra £7 on his attire, whereas women's headdress and stockings rarely exceeded £1 in cost.

There is another important reason for suspecting that the cost of Nicholas' and Hamon junior's suits and gowns recorded in the accounts are not representative of the real expense of adult men's clothing. Once the boys reached the age of sixteen their tailors' bills begin to appear in the accounts, much as they do for Sir Hamon Le Strange. Sir Hamon patronized London tailors, first Mr Lock and then Lawrence Michael. As he also borrowed money from these men, and later invested in the East India Company through them, it is not always possible to distinguish how much he was paying them for clothes. In 1610 he paid Lock £30 for apparel, in 1611 £16 10s, and in 1612 £60. The boys' tailors' bills start off modestly, at £3 11s for Nicholas when he was sixteen, £16 18s for both boys when they were seventeen and sixteen and £12 10s for Hamon aged seventeen. However, by the time he was eighteen, Nicholas seems to be spending on the same scale as his father, with a bill of £34 2s that year. It seems certain that more expensive suits of clothes were purchased this way, and the items Alice recorded in more detail in the accounts were cheaper suits for which she purchased the cloth and arranged local tailoring in Norfolk. Once they reached adulthood either Sir Hamon, or the boys themselves, managed the purchase of 'best' clothes in London. It became a male affair between them and their tailors and the details were not available for the accounts. This is in contrast to Elizabeth's gowns, which, even when purchased in Norwich or London and made up by tailors there, were always carefully itemized or described in the accounts, probably because they were overseen by Alice herself. The one exception to this pattern were the clothes Nicholas purchased for his wedding in 1630, which offer a glimpse into the details and cost of high-status male clothing, as shown in

---

[56] The eight pairs purchased 1610–22 seem to have been for Sir Hamon.
[57] If the hatters' bills were spent the same way as the itemized entries, they would have allowed him to buy nine normal hats, three beaver hats and two hat bands.

Table 5.4. The three suits of clothes Nicholas purchased for his wedding with their accompanying accessories were considerably more expensive than Elizabeth's two wedding dresses, which cost £81 14s. It is possible that this is one reason why another expensive dress was bought for her six months later. With her accessories included, this brings her total very close to Nicholas', suggesting that men and women did spend approximately the same amount of money on clothing for special occasions, and perhaps in other circumstances as well.

Table 5.4. Nicholas' wedding clothes, purchased London 1630

Description	Cost		
To the tailor for making the pearl-coloured suit, the scarlet suit, the cloth suit and the camlet coat	£18	16s	
Tailoring subtotal	**£18**	**16s**	
19.5 yards of pearl-coloured satin for a suit, cloak and doublet	£14	2s	6d
6 yards of carnation satin to line the suit	£4	10s	
Silver bone edging and chain plate lace weighing 21 oz	£5	11s	8d
9.33 yards of carnation plush to line the cloak	£12	13s	
5 yards of crimson satin to line the doublet	£4	2s	6d
3 yards of fine Spanish cloth for doublet and hose	£3	6s	
14 yards of Turkey camlet for a coat	£5	19s	
Gold and silver lace weighing 35 oz for the suit and coat	£8	15s	
4.25 yards of best scarlet for cloak and hose	£13	16s	
9 yards of pearl-coloured plush to line the cloak	£12	7s	
4.75 yards of crimson satin to edge and line the suit	£2	3s	9d
Cloth and lace subtotal	**£87**	**6s**	**5d**
A diamond ring and earring	£16	12s	6d
Jewellery subtotal	**£16**	**12s**	**6d**
2 cloth work laced bands and starching them	£5	17s	6d
3 falling bands and 2 pair of boot hose and 6 pair of Flanders strings	£2	4s	6d
A ruff and a pair of cuffs	£1	10s	
A pair of silk stockings	£1	12s	
A black beaver hat, dressed and lined	£2	18s	
Eight pairs of gloves: 3 white, 3 cordovan, 2 unspecified		15s	6d
A falling band and band strings	£1	6s	
A silver hat band		7s	6d
A beaver hat and band	£3	14s	
2 pairs of boots	£1	3s	6d
1 pair of pumps and 1 pair of white shoes		5s	6d
A pair of spurs		2s	6d
A pair of garters (£4) and roses (22s)	£5	2s	
A silver and gold waistcoat	£5	13s	
A silver girdle and a gold and silver girdle	£2	4s	
20 gold and silver open points	£1	10s	
20 crimson and silver open points	£1	6s	8d
20 scarlet and silver open points	£1	5s	
Accessories subtotal	**£38**	**17s**	**2d**
Total cost	£161	12s	1d

Source: Le Strange disbursement accounts; LEST/P7.

BEDS AND LIVING ROOMS

The early modern period was perhaps the golden age of the bed. In poor and wealthy households alike, beds were typically the most expensive and decorative piece of furniture.[58] From humble origins as a straw pallet covered with blankets in the medieval period, by the early seventeenth century the wealthy were sleeping in four-poster beds with feather mattresses, pillows and bolsters. Thornton notes that 'the massive bed' reached its 'high point of evolution shortly before 1600'.[59] Beds were canopied and curtained to provide warmth and decoration, and dressed with linen sheets and pillowbears, blankets, coverlets and rugs. Just as the hearth was the symbolic centre of the medieval household, beds became the symbolic centre of the early modern household. They were the site of birth and death, and of the consummation of marriage.[60] However, unlike modern bedrooms, early modern bed chambers were also used for socializing. In middling households of the early seventeenth century the best bed was typically located in the best furnished room, which was also used for receiving guests—the parlour.[61] In the early seventeenth-century Le Strange household the best bed chambers contained a large number of upholstered stools and chairs.

There is no complete inventory or surviving plan of Hunstanton Hall, but the early seventeenth-century bed chambers are particularly well documented. Alice Le Strange drew up an inventory of these rooms in 1632, perhaps at the point when the house, greatly enlarged by her husband's building works during the 1620s, was finally furnished to their satisfaction. This inventory does not provide valuations, but the purchase of beds and other items can be traced in the household accounts. Only one probate inventory survives for seventeenth-century Hunstanton Hall; this inventory was made in 1675 and records the goods of Sir Nicholas Le Strange, the grandson and heir of Hamon and Alice, who had died in 1669. Although a complete document, it is far from complete as a record of Hunstanton Hall and its contents. For instance, it lists only nine beds and bed chambers, whereas Alice listed thirty-three beds in twenty-nine rooms in 1632.[62] The bedrooms described in 1632 can be divided roughly into three categories: the best rooms for accommodating high-status guests; rooms used by the members of the Le Strange family; and rooms used by servants. Rooms in the first two categories were mostly listed in pairs with a named room and then an 'inward chamber' to that room, each containing

---

[58] N. Rothstein and S.M. Levey, 'Furnishings, c.1500–1780', in Jenkins, *Cambridge History of Western Textiles*, 633; C. Shammas, *The Pre-Industrial Consumer in England and America* (Oxford, 1990), 170–1; F.G. Emmison, *Elizabethan Life: Home, Work and Land* (Essex, 1976), 12.
[59] Thornton, *Interior Decoration*, 154.
[60] J.E. Crowley, *The Invention of Comfort: Sensibilities and Design in Early Modern Britain and Early America* (Baltimore, 2000), 8–14; M. Howard, 'The great bed of Ware', in M. Snodin and J. Styles (eds.), *Design and the Decorative Arts: Britain 1500–1900* (London, 2001), 48.
[61] Overton et al., *Production and Consumption*, 132; Crowley, *Invention of Comfort*, 53–4; N. Cooper, *The Houses of the Gentry 1480–1680* (New Haven, 1999), 291–2.
[62] All the bedrooms listed in 1675 are recognizable in the 1632 list.

beds and furnishings, but the inward chamber being slightly less luxurious than its pair.[63]

The best rooms in Hunstanton Hall, the Tower Chamber, Hall Chamber and Parlour Chamber, were furnished to a high degree of comfort and convenience and were highly decorative. For instance, the Hall Chamber had 'a crimson damask bed with curtains and canopy', six upholstered seats (three chairs and three stools), a cupboard covered 'with a carpet of cross-stitch of cucumbers', and a mattress, bolster and two pairs of pillows all filled with down. The bed had four blankets, as well as a rug and a counterpoint, the last matching the bed curtains and seats. There was a fireplace equipped with brass andirons, a fire pan and bellows, and a warming pan for the bed. The walls were hung with five pieces of Arras tapestry. The inner chamber had another canopied and curtained bed, but of less expensive fabric, a feather mattress and bolster but down pillows, and was equipped with 'a tawny velvet close stool laced crimson'. This was typical: all the best main rooms had fireplaces and multiple upholstered chairs and stools (never less than five). They were furnished with at least one table or cupboard covered with cloth of pintado or carpets. The inner room was always provided with a close stool.[64] The beds themselves varied. The Tower Room had 'a black velvet bed embroidered with curtains and counterpoint of black gold grogram', but apparently no canopy. In its inner room was a bed with 'a green velvet canopy and sarsenet curtains'. The Parlour Chamber had a 'bed of green russels laced white' and its inner chamber a bed with 'a canopy of green and yellow stuff'. All the main beds had down mattresses, pillows and bolsters, while the inner rooms had featherbeds. The Parlour Chamber was hung with five pieces of Arras 'of the same suit as the Hall chamber', but the Tower Chamber apparently had no wall hangings. There is no evidence that these grand rooms were inhabited by family members, and the presence of close stools suggests that they were conveniently fitted out for the comfort and privacy of guests: people of the same status as the Le Stranges or higher.

The rooms occupied by members of the Le Strange family were furnished comfortably, but less luxuriously than the best rooms. These fourteen rooms also came in pairs, with one exception. Alice Le Strange names 'my own chamber' and that of her recently widowed older 'sister Yelverton' nearby. They may have shared 'the little parlour' listed between the two rooms, also containing a bed, as well as a fireplace and two wicker chairs. Nicholas Le Strange and his wife Anne seem likely to have occupied the only room of this standard that contained two beds, which had been decorated shortly before their marriage in 1630. Hamon Le Strange's room had no inward chamber, but was named next to a 'closet', which contained a fireplace and 'a little couch with a stool to it'. No room is named for their daughter Elizabeth or for their sons Hamon and Roger, suggesting they were all resident away from home at this time, although there were three further main rooms to

---

[63] On inward chambers see Cooper, *Houses of the Gentry*, 296.
[64] Howard describes how gardrobes were replaced by close stools in inner rooms after *c.*1500: 'Fashionable living', in Snodin and Styles, *Design and the Decorative Arts*, 101.

choose from. These 'family' rooms had either featherbeds or, in the case of Alice's room and the Pantry Chamber, down beds. Only half of the beds had curtains, and only four rooms had fireplaces. They contained less furnishings than the best rooms: all the main rooms had a table or a cupboard covered with carpets or cloths, but not the inward rooms, and there were fewer chairs and stools. Alice, for instance, had no seats in her bed chamber. Nor did these rooms have wall hangings.

The third category of bedroom, nine rooms in total, was occupied mainly by servants. It included 'the maids chamber', 'clerks chamber', 'falconers chamber', 'butlers chamber' and 'grooms chamber'. However, it also included rooms such as the 'closet chamber', 'buttery chamber' and 'porters lodge', which were furnished to a degree of comfort suitable for less exalted friends, relations and guests. There was only one room in this category which had an inner chamber, and three of the servants' rooms contained two beds. Seven of these rooms contained no furnishings other than the bed. None of the named servants' rooms had bed curtains or fireplaces; nonetheless, even the servants slept on featherbeds equipped with blankets and bolsters and a bedcover. The beds in the clerk's chamber and the butler's chamber each had an 'old tester' or canopy. These rooms would have housed all the female servants and male liveried servants. The male agricultural servants must have slept elsewhere 'beyond the moat', in the outbuildings used to store agricultural produce, equipment and livestock.[65]

The furnishings in the best rooms were costly. The black bed in the Tower Chamber was purchased in 1620, and cost over £50, with another £5 spent on transporting it from London, as shown in Table 5.5. The crimson damask bed in the Hall Chamber was even more expensive. The cost lay very largely in the quantity of high-quality fabric used. The 'valance, head cloth, posts, curtains, counterpoint, stools, chairs and little carpet' for the bed required 83 yards of red damask at 13s a yard. The French bedstead cost only 28s. The Arras hangings, which were bought second-hand at the same time as the crimson bed, cost £41 14s 6d and consisted of five pieces '10 foot high and 22 yards half in length'.[66] Other items purchased for the room were relatively cheap. A looking glass cost 10s, the frames for a 'great chair' and a 'low chair' 4s 6d, and the cost of having them upholstered, 7s 6d. All were bought in London. For beds of lesser quality, the fabric, frames and accessories were bought and put together in Norfolk. A bed of jollyboys fabric, purchased for Nicholas Le Strange in 1627 but found in Alice's room in 1632, used only 21.5 yards of fabric, which cost a mere £1 3s 3d. With all the linings, bed mats, thread and so on, as well as 'a chair out of Holland', the total cost came to only £3 4s 3d. They must have reused an existing bed frame. A mattress and bolster set cost between £9 and £10 for a featherbed, and around £15 for a down bed. Between 1612 and 1614 when the Le Stranges were expanding the size of their household, they purchased eight featherbeds.

---

[65] The inventory lists all the beds 'within the moat'.
[66] The accounts record payment to 'Mr Angell in Cornwell'.

Table 5.5. The cost of the black bed, 1620, and the crimson damask bed, 1628

Description	Cost
The black bed	
For 52 yards half quarter of stuff for curtains and covering the black bed at 11s	£28 14s 9d
For silk and gold fringe 67 oz 1 quart at 3s 4d the ounce for the black bed £11 5s and for alcamy fringe for the curtains 16 oz 1 quart for the curtains at 3s £2 9s and ribbon 2s and silk 3s 6d	£13 19s 6d
For a bedstead 26s and for painting and gilding it and for 4 knobs £7	£8 6s
For 2 yards of black velvet at 14s 8d	£1 14s 10d
To the upholsterer whereof for bayes to line the counterpoint and to make cases 45s and for making up the bed and packing it up	£4 14s 10d
For a box for the bed and for carriage	4s 1d
Total cost	**£57 14s**
The crimson damask bedroom	
For 6 ells and 3 quarters of crimson taffeta for the tester of a bed and inward valance at 14s	£4 14s
For 83 yards of crimson damask at 13s for valance, headcloth, posts, curtains, counterpoint, stools, chairs and a little carpet	£53 19s
For a fair looking glass	10s
For 6.88 yards of call fringe 5 inches deep crimson ingrain weighing 19.13 oz at 3s 10d, for 8.38 yards of fringe of the same depth weighing 12.5 oz, for 8 yards of Turkey top fringe 3 oz, for 27 yards of lighter top fringe weighing 7 oz less a dramme	£7 19s 1d
For 51 yards of small purled lace and 52 yards of fringed lace for curtains and counterpoint weighing 12 oz	£2 9s 1d
For silk to make up the bed 1.38 oz	4s 6d
For a rug	£1 4s
For a French bedstead 28s and 3 curtain rods 5s, for gilt melon cups at 2s 8d each 11s 4d	£2 4s 4d
For 11.5 yards of red buckram to line the valance and head cloth at 15d – 15s, for 4 ells of canvas to line the tester 5s 1d, for staples 1s and making the tester and posts 18s 6d	£1 19s 7d
For incle for the curtains 1s 2d, and for 14 dozen horn curtain ringles 3s 6d	4s 8d
For 16 yards of baize to line the covering £2, for 20 yards of calico to line the pentados £1 10s	£3 10s
For 20 yards of seaming fringe for chairs and stools weighing 10 oz	£1 18s 4d
For a great chair frame and a low chair	4s 6d
For girtweb and sackcloth to bottom them 3s, for felt for elbows and leather for backs 1s 6d, for 3.5 yards of tick for the chairs 7s, for feathers for the 2 chairs 10s, for nails and tacks for both 2s 6d	£2 4s
For making the 2 chairs 7s 6d and for a bed mat 16d	8s 10d
For 12.75 yards of yellow cotton for covers	£1 0s 5d
Total cost	**£84 14s 4d**

Source: Le Strange disbursement accounts; LEST/P7.

136　　　　　　　　　*Consumption and Gender*

Fig. 5.1. A bed chamber at Hunstanton Hall *c.*1926, showing seventeenth-century furnishings. Reproduced with permission from the *Country Life* Picture Library.

Beds were durable items, often bequeathed in wills. Alice received five beds from her father on his death in 1619.[67] Both Hamon and Alice bequeathed beds in their own wills. Hamon left Alice five beds: two of these were beds from the best rooms, the green russels bed from the Parlour Chamber, and the green velvet bed from the inner chamber to the Tower Chamber, with all their accessories including matching upholstered seats and carpets. He also left her his own bed, a blue bed which cannot be identified from the 1632 inventory, and two other lesser beds. Alice bequeathed six beds. Her 'serge bed lined with pintado' went to her grandson Nicholas, and four beds to her daughter-in-law, Anne, her son Nicholas' widow, including the two green beds, and the blue bed which she was now using. A further bed 'whereon the dairy maid lyeth' was bequeathed to Elizabeth Guybon, Alice's servant and relation. Early twentieth-century photographs of Hunstanton Hall taken for *Country Life* magazine show a heavy wooden bed of the type Alice and Hamon may have purchased for the house (Fig. 5.1); although dressed in late seventeenth-century crewelwork embroidery done by Ann Woodhouse, who was Lady Le Strange from 1686 to 1696, this demonstrates that at least one seventeenth-century bed in Hunstanton Hall survived to the early twentieth century. This attitude towards beds is expressed in another of Nicholas Le Strange's merry jests attributed to Alice Le Strange:

[67] 'Household stuff given me by my father at his death'; LEST/P10.

One Ask't old mother Stone how her husband did; very well I thanke you good Neighbour sayes she, but keepes his Bedde still: I am sorry for that sayes he; so Sir am not I by Gods body says she, for on my knowledge he has kept it these threescore yeares, and I should be hartily sorry to see him sell it now.[68]

Yet this durability was not quite what it first seems. The frequency with which the Le Stranges bought new fabric for beds suggests that beds were often remade, and, as Table 5.5 demonstrates, the fabric was by far the most expensive element. None of the beds inherited by Alice from her father in 1619 were recognizable as a set of bedroom furnishing in 1632, although individual items such as down beds, Arras coverings, 'an old turkey work carpet', and 'a carpet of pintado' appear in both and could well be the same items reused in new combinations. Two of the best beds from 1632 appear in Hamon's and Alice's wills, but none of the beds listed in 1632 is recognizable in the probate inventory of 1675. The speed with which fabric aged and went out of fashion must explain why probate inventory valuations of beds, their second-hand value, was so much lower than the purchase price. One of the best rooms, the Tower Chamber, had its furnishings, bed and all, valued at £12 in 1675: this was a room Hamon and Alice spent at least £84 furnishing in 1628. None of the other bed chambers exceeded this value in 1675.

Wooden furniture was relatively cheap and easily mended. 'A long table with drawers for the hall' was purchased for £1 11s in London in 1624, and another 4s 10d spent on transporting it to Hunstanton. Other tables were less expensive and made closer to home. In 1611, Stibbard, a local carpenter, was paid 5s 8d for 'turning posts for the Hall table' and 1s 4d for 'turning feet for a table'. In 1610, he was paid 2s 8d for mending old chairs and making a canopy frame for a bed. Broadhead, a joiner, was also employed regularly between 1607 and 1614. In 1611, he was paid for '2 chairs 6s and a stool 14d and livery cupboard 10s and for a livery bedstead 9s'. The cheapness of this furniture was in part because it was not designed to be shown off, but rather covered with carpets and cloths or, in the case of beds, with curtains and canopies. It was not until the later seventeenth century that decorative woods and fine cabinet-making became fashionable.[69] There was plenty of wood on display in a house such as Hunstanton Hall, but it was in wall panelling and floors.[70] Rugs went on beds, and carpets on tables and cupboards.[71] Some of these 'carpets' were pieces of lined fabric which matched beds, but the best rooms also had home-embroidered carpets and carpets of Indian pintado.[72] Less prestigious rooms had 'old Turkey carpets' and carpets 'of tapestry' which had fallen out

---

[68] N. Le Strange, *Merry Passages and Jeasts*, ed. H.F. Lippincott (Salzburg, 1974), 37.
[69] Overton et al., *Production and Consumption*, 94–7; G.W. Digby, *Elizabethan Embroidery* (London, 1963), 98–9.
[70] See Figures 5.1 and 5.2, and photographs in C. Hussey, 'Hunstanton Hall Norfolk, The seat of Mr Charles Le Strange', *Country Life* (1926).
[71] Rothstein and Levey, 'Furnishings', 631.
[72] 'Carpet of cross stitch of cucumbers', 'green embroidered carpet', 'carpet of taffeta', 'carpet of pentado' (twice), 'cupboard cloth of waveretta', 'crimson damask table cloth'. One of the best rooms also had chairs covered in embroidered 'thistlework cross stitch'. Digby, *Elizabethan Embroidery*, 98–9, lists three main types of table carpet: Turkish carpets; embroidered carpets; and fringed carpets of velvet cloth, 98–9.

138 *Consumption and Gender*

of fashion. The hall was furnished with long tables and benches, suitable for offering hospitality to large numbers of guests, but there was also a dining room for more select occasions. Constructed in 1623, this was furnished with a couch and upholstered chairs in 1628. Some rooms were also provided with window curtains, a rare addition in this period. Curtains were purchased for the hall window in 1629, and for the dining room and 'inward Hall Chamber' in 1630. Of all the bed chambers, only the Tower Chamber had 'curtains to the windows of serge' listed in 1632.

It was not unusual for walls to be decoratively painted, and the £1 12s paid 'to the painter for painting the study chamber and the inward chamber' in 1619 suggests something more than a simple whitewash.[73] More substantial works were carried out in the summer of 1626 when a painter was paid: 'for the freize in the tower chamber 24s; more for painting the tower roof: £6; more for 80 foot of the dining room freize at 12d the foot: £4; more for painting the escutchions being 19 in the dining room and writing under them £5 8s.' There were also pictures hung on the walls. The family portraits possibly hung together in the drawing room as they were still arranged when photographed by *Country Life* in the early twentieth

Fig. 5.2. Family portraits *in situ* in Hunstanton Hall *c.*1926; two portraits of Sir Hamon Le Strange (1583–1654) and one of Lady Alice Le Strange hang on the bottom row. Reproduced with permission from the *Country Life* Picture Library.

---

[73] J. Ayres, *Domestic Interiors: The British Tradition 1500–1850* (New Haven, 2003), 140–6; Howard, 'Fashionable living', 101.

Table 5.6. Household linen listed in the 1632 inventory

Type	Number	1631 and 1632[a]
Pairs of sheets	158	19 (12%)
Pairs of pillowbears	53.5	
Cupboard cloths	25	4 (16%)
Cushion cloths	7	
Towels	78	6 (8%)
Tablecloths (suits)[b]	17	1 (6%)
Tablecloths (single)	86	29 (34%)
Napkins	995	110 (11%)
Plate cloths	31	18 (58%)

[a] Noted in inventory as purchases 'of 1631' or 'of 1632'.
[b] Suits were matching sets that contained at least three tablecloths each.

Source: Inventory of linens, 1632; LEST/P10.

century (Fig. 5.2).[74] There were also other portraits: a painting of their friend and relative lord Hobart was purchased for £4 5s 8d in 1620. A set of four 'Dutch paintings' depicting 'The King of Bohemia, another of his Queen, another of the Prince of Orange and the fourth of the Marques Spinola' cost 36s each in 1625. Prints and maps were bought for as little as 6d, although they could be more expensive: a map of Bohemia cost 15s in 1620, while an unspecified map cost £1 16s in 1610. Looking glasses were beginning to be hung on walls. Three relatively cheap ones purchased between 1610 and 1625 and costing between 3s and 1s 4d were probably hand-held. However, one costing 7s in 1610 and another costing 10s purchased in 1628 for the red damask bed chamber may well have been wall mirrors. Window curtains, pictures and mirrors all became more popular in the homes of the middling and wealthy in the later seventeenth century, along with clocks.[75] The Le Stranges purchased their first clock for £4 10s in 1629.[76]

One final item of furnishing requires detailed discussion. The topic of linen spans all the subsections of this chapter. It was a vital item of clothing, providing underclothes that ensured cleanliness and comfort. It performed a similar function in the bed, with sheets and pillowbears covering the areas of the bed which were likely to come into contact with the sleeper's skin. In the dining room linen was on show, but again its function was closely associated with cleanliness.[77] The tablecloth provided a clean surface from which food could be served and eaten, while napkins allowed individual diners to keep clean while eating. Lady Alice Le Strange wrote an inventory of her household linens in 1632. The sheer quantity is striking: she listed nearly 1000 table napkins, more than 150 sheets and over 100 tablecloths (see Table 5.6). In Mitchell's study of table linen owned by great households in the

---

[74] Hussey, 'Hunstanton Hall', 588.
[75] Weatherill, *Consumer Behaviour*.
[76] See Chapter 7: Literature, music and science.
[77] M. Visser, *The Rituals of Dinner: The Origins, Evolution, Eccentricities and Meaning of Table Manners* (London, 1991), 156.

fifteenth and sixteenth centuries none approach this quantity. The most he found were the 312 table napkins owned by Sir Thomas Ramsey in 1590, and the forty-six tablecloths belonging to the Earl of Pembroke in 1559.[78] Certainly a large household required large quantities of linen: there were at least thirty-three beds in the house, and conventions of gentry hospitality required that large numbers of people could be fed and entertained. Linen came in a range of qualities. The best bed linen was made of 'very fine Holland', while those of lowest quality were described as 'coarse flaxen sheets'. The best table linen consisted of suits of fine damask with pictures woven into the cloth. There was one with 'the story of Joshua and Caleb', which had been purchased in 1612 for £15 2s, another of 'Judith and Holofernes', and one of fine flowered damask.[79] The conventions of table setting demanded that more than one cloth was laid over the table at any time—three being usual. While the top cloth might be very fine, those beneath were less so. Quality was also determined by age, particularly for ordinary linens. Alice was careful to mark those which were new purchases of 1631 and 1632, and distinguished them from those which were 'old'. The inventory corresponds closely to the purchases in the accounts, which record just over £57 spent on bed linen and table linen in the period between April 1631 and August 1632. This is considerably more than was spent on these items earlier in the accounts. In the nine years between 1617 and early 1626, an already substantial £105 was spent on linen cloth of various types. Table linen in particular must have been vulnerable to staining: the only sure way to maintain clean white linen was to keep making new purchases and accept a high turnover.

DINING WARE AND KITCHEN WARE

The Le Stranges purchased a wide range of objects for dining, cooking and food storage. These are indicated by Table 5.7, which records a single shopping trip to London in 1628.[80] Probate inventories usually provide little detail about the small items found in the kitchen or buttery, which tend to get lumped together as 'other old implements and trash about the house' or 'small things unnamed'.[81] Although accounts only survive for the wealthiest households, the Le Strange accounts demonstrate that such households bought many ordinary everyday items as well as expensive luxuries. For instance, in the five years between 1619 and 1624 they purchased more than 130 wooden trenchers costing between a farthing and 2d each, and forty-eight small pots of various kinds costing between 1d and 6d. This

---

[78] Mitchell, 'By your leave', 58.
[79] See Mitchell, 'By your leave', for illustrations, 63, 69. More examples of tablecloths of these patterns, all Dutch and Flemish in origin, are at the V&A; see museum items T.161–1964; T.106–1931, T.213–1963.
[80] See Chapter 3: Urban shopping.
[81] Quoting the inventories of Nicholas Page of Hunstanton, 1622, and Robert Bidden of Hunstanton, 1631: NRO MF/X9 DN/INV 31/123 and MF/X11 DN/INV 36/212.

Table 5.7. Dining, cooking and miscellaneous items purchased on a shopping trip to London, 1628

Items purchased	Cost
4 round bowl glasses	
4 other beer glasses	
2 chamber pot glasses	
2 cans	
2 caudle cups	
4 porringers	
2 wine glasses	
3 rough glasses with 2 ears	
1 glass plate with foot	
24 high Venice glasses	
A glass piece and trencher knife	£2 2s 6d
A strong Venice glass (2s)	
A glass for beer	
A very great glass like a churn	
2 cruets	
A glass to set water in	
6 glass boxes	£1 6s 6d
2 trencher knives (18d)	
6 hoops of wicker	4s 6d
A table basket (2s 6d)	
Little basket (14d)	3s 8d
2 great wicker baskets	
2 little wicker baskets	
24 round trenchers	
3 cheeseplates	7s 4d
A hand basket	8d
Baskets of fine wicker	5s
For earthen things: 12 white saucers	
12 little earthen melters	
2 perfuming pans	
12 drinking pots	
3 pipkins	
A great gally pot	4s 10d
A little jug	10d
3 bunches of squirrels' tails to sweep with	1s
A fine 'hayrin' brush (18d)	
2 coarse 'hayrin' brush (14d)	2s 8d
A smoothing iron	2s 8d
A sleekstone (4d)	
2 glasses for the capers (4d)	8d
4 water pots for the garden	15s
A long plate for 'pasty'	7s 6d
7 yards of chain for the spit	7s
7 posnets of several sizes weighing 54 lb at 9½d	£2 3s 4d
3 little pots weighing 43¼ lb at 8½d	£1 4s 3d
2 great brass skillets	8s
2 very little skillet pans	1s 7d

Note: In many cases, the price relates to a group of items, probably purchased from a single retailer.

Source: Le Strange disbursement accounts; LEST/P7, fol. 195v–196 (1628).

section looks first at luxury items: table settings, silverware and glassware, before moving on to examine everyday items made of pottery, base metals and wood.

A handful of late-sixteenth and early-seventeenth century English paintings depict dining in process. To modern eyes, the tables look relatively bare. Clean white linen tablecloths are on prominent display, but there are no cutlery settings or individual drinking glasses.[82] Table forks did not become common items on elite tables until the late seventeenth century.[83] Before that date people ate with a knife or spoon. It was polite to eat with one's fingers and then wipe them on the napkin. Ben Jonson's *The Devil is an Ass* (1616) features a comic economic project to produce forks in England, bringing them 'into custom here as they are in Italy' for the 'sparing o'napkins'. It is feared the project will be opposed by the linen drapers, who would lose business.[84] Forks were used for carving meat and toasting. There is only one purchase of forks (other than pitchforks for agricultural use) in the Le Strange accounts before 1626. Histories of dining note that guests often brought their own knife, while spoons were provided by the host.[85] The Le Stranges certainly purchased both knives and spoons, but not in matching sets. Glasses and drinking cups might also be shared, with diners calling a servant to provide a drink when they needed one.[86]

The most expensive dining ware was made of silver. Silver was a traditional marker of status, and one that persisted well into the modern era. It marked status overtly, often bearing the family's arms, and was commonly inherited and given as a gift between gentry families at christenings and weddings. It was also a means of storing wealth in the era before banking.[87] Dining provided the opportunity to display silverware to guests during the act of hospitality. Despite its tradition, however, silver was subject to fashion. Silver plate rarely survives from the period before 1650 precisely because gentry families frequently exchanged their silver for newer styles.[88] The Le Stranges undertook one such exchange in 1620, and another in 1628 as part of the shopping trip described in Table 5.7. In 1628 Alice Le Strange took 320.5 oz of old silver plate to the goldsmith Mr Warde, and got in exchange a silver basin and ewer, two livery pots, three bowls, a great salt and four trencher salts, paying a balance of £6 7s.[89] She then invested some recent bequests—'£3 5s given for a legacy by my uncle Bozen and £10 given by David Banyard for a legacy to Mr Strange and other money that I had of Mr Strange for a

---

[82] For example: 'William Brook, Earl of Cobham, and his family', reproduced in A. Sim, *Food and Feast in Tudor England* (Stroud, 1997); or '"Dining scene" from Sir Henry Unton's Memorial Picture' (c.1596), National Portrait Gallery, London.

[83] N. Elias, *The Civilizing Process: The History of Manners*, transl. Edmund Jephcott (Oxford, 1978), 126–9; Overton et al., *Production and Consumption*, 106.

[84] B. Jonson, *The Devil is an Ass* (1616), act v, scene vi, lines 15–30.

[85] G. Brett, *Dinner is Served* (London, 1968), 60–1; Elias, *Civilizing Process*, 91.

[86] Brett, *Dinner is Served*, 74; E.S. Godfrey, *The Development of English Glassmaking 1560–1640* (Oxford, 1975), 219.

[87] H. Clifford, 'A commerce of things: the value of precious metalwork in early modern England', in M. Berg and H. Clifford (eds.), *Consumers and Luxury: Consumer Culture in Europe 1650–1850* (Manchester, 1999), 151.

[88] Glanville, *Silver*, 12.

[89] For descriptions of these objects, see Glanville, *Silver*, 235–6; 266; 282, 295–7.

ring given by Doctor Rant'—and exchanged some spoons and a pepper box to buy further items, before making outright purchases of a chafing dish, six saucers, six porringers, a little saucer, 'a little preserving spoon with holes', a gilt basin and ewer, two gilt livery pots and two gilt trenchers. All the new items were then engraved with the family's arms. These acts of exchange were common enough to be the subject of humour. Nicholas Le Strange's *Merry Jeasts* includes an anecdote told by Sir Hamon Le Strange:

> Mr Abraham Vemat, that married the Lady Peyton, perswaded her to send all her plate and silver vessell up to London to change, for he told her it was Old, batterd, and out of fashion; and not fitt to appeare at her Table: she did so, and when he came downe [she] was very inquisitive, about the fashion of her plate, and what Armes he had sett on: For de Fashion, sweet Hert says he, dere is no Exception, it be of de best and newest Stampe; and for de Armes, it beare a better den dine or mine, for be Got it ha's All de Kings Armes on't; and so it had, for he had metamorphosd all into currant Coine.[90]

Silver and fine linen had been standard for elite tables since the medieval period. Fine glassware became common in the sixteenth century. In the early sixteenth century none was made in England and hardly any imported; but by the 1560s imports of glass tableware had grown significantly.[91] Glass was in many ways the opposite of silverware: its expense lay in its fragility. Single items of glass did not approach the cost of silver, but nor was it an investment for the future. Breakages made frequent replacements necessary. The most expensive items of glassware were 'venice glasses', which were either imported from Venice or made in imitation. These high-quality drinking glasses could be engraved and exquisitely shaped.[92] The Le Stranges purchased five Venice glasses for 10s in 1621, and another twenty-four in 1628, both times in London. Purchases of cheaper 'drinking glasses' costing between 2d and 9d were more frequent, roughly once a year. Other glass items such as cruets, bowls and plates offered a cheaper, attractive, but less durable, alternative to silver or pewter.[93] However, the majority of the purchases of glass objects by the Le Stranges was not dining ware but storage containers, most commonly 'water glasses' and 'preserving glasses'.[94] Godfrey notes that 'water glasses' were certainly not drinking glasses as water was rarely drunk at the table.[95] It seems likely that these were storage containers for distilled concoctions such as rose water and aqua vitae, the uses of which were both culinary and medicinal. Preserving glasses could have been used for pickles or fruit preserved in alcohol or sugar, such as the 'glass of marmalade' received as a gift in 1620 (marmalade normally came in boxes). Other glasses were bought 'to keep juice'. Both glass containers and the practice of

---

[90] Le Strange, *Merry Jeasts*, 86–7.
[91] Godfrey, *English Glassmaking*, 14; see also J. Thirsk, *Economic Policy and Projects: The Development of a Consumer Society in Early Modern England* (Oxford, 1978), 14, 52.
[92] Charleston, *English Glass*, plates 12–14.
[93] Even glass chamber pots were purchased.
[94] Between 1619 and 1624 the Le Stranges purchased fifty-one items of glass dining ware; in the same period, they purchased at least sixty glass storage items. Godfrey notes similar pattern of consumption from excavations, *English Glassmaking*, 223.
[95] Godfrey, *English Glassmaking*, 247.

preserving fruit and vegetables with sugar were relative novelties first adopted in the late sixteenth century and still restricted to the wealthiest households.[96]

Most of the population of early seventeenth-century England relied not on silver and glass for their food wares, but on the trio of pottery, base metals (particularly pewter, iron and brass) and wood.[97] William Harrison noted the replacement of 'treen' ware (wooden trenchers and spoons) with pewter in ordinary households.[98] Probate inventories reveal that by the mid-sixteenth century pewter was found in all but the poorest households.[99] Hatcher and Barker point out that 'an ounce of silver cost as much as half a dozen pounds of pewter' in the sixteenth and seventeenth centuries, thus only the wealthiest aristocracy could afford to eat off silver dishes. The lesser nobility and the gentry contented themselves with 'show' pieces made of silver, such as basins and ewers and salts, but ate off pewter.[100] The Le Stranges bought not only pewter eating vessels but also cheaper versions of objects they owned in silver. In a large purchase in 1612, they bought six dozen pewter plates, a basin and ewer, one 'spout quart', four candlesticks, a dozen porringers, two dozen saucers, a salt, three basins, one 'piece', and two chamber pots for a cost of £13 3s 4d. They bought another large set of pewter items in 1620 for just over £5. Like silver, pewter could be 'changed' with old items replaced with new, and the Le Stranges changed some of their pewter every couple of years. It appears to have held little sentimental value: although sometimes bequeathed it was not used as gifts amongst the gentry. As it was not heavily ornamented little was lost by having old items melted down and new ones purchased in their place on a regular basis.

Pottery was rarely listed in any detail in probate inventories because it was so cheap, yet archaeological evidence shows that it was a ubiquitous and diverse product, and often imported.[101] While earthenware was produced in England, stoneware was generally German in origin. Pottery appears regularly in the Le Strange household accounts. For instance, in the five years between 1619 and 1624, there were twelve purchases of pottery, accounting for at least thirty-four items. These included earthen pots and pans, and 'stone' jugs, bottles and pots, as well as two purchases described as china. It is likely that many more of the items purchased were actually pottery, such as the fifty-four unspecified storage pots purchased in the same period, and a number of unspecified bottles, jugs, pans and dishes. Apart from unusually large items such as two 'great earthen pans', which cost 1s 2d each, and 'a great jug' for 1s 6d, most of these items were cheap, costing less than 6d each. The *Oxford English Dictionary* cites the first use of the word 'china' to describe pottery as 1634, but Allan has shown that Chinese porcelain was

---

[96] J. Thirsk, *Food in Early Modern England: Phases, Fads, Fashions 1500–1760* (London, 2007), 51–2.
[97] Overton et al., *Production and Consumption*, 98–108.
[98] Harrison, *Description of England*, 201.
[99] J. Hatcher and T.C. Barker, *A History of British Pewter* (London, 1974), 92–5.
[100] Hatcher and Barker, *British Pewter*, 107–9.
[101] S. Jennings (ed.), *Eighteen Centuries of Pottery from Norwich*, East Anglian Archaeology 13 (Norwich, 1981); J.P. Allan, *Medieval and Post Medieval Finds from Exeter 1971–1980* (Exeter, 1984); D. Crossley, *Post Medieval Archaeology in Britain* (Leicester, 1990), 243–89.

present in Exeter from at least the 1590s.[102] 'China' is first mentioned in the Le Strange accounts in 1617, when '8 porringers, a basin, 3 saucers and 2 pots of coarse china metal' were purchased for 10s. The cost and description suggests that this 'china' was actually Dutch tin-glazed ware, which was produced in imitation of Chinese porcelain from the last quarter of the sixteenth century onwards.[103]

Despite Harrison's suggestion that 'treen' ware had disappeared by the late sixteenth century, the Le Stranges bought wooden trenchers in large quantities, always by the dozens.[104] Even these cheap items existed in a range of qualities. The most expensive were maple trenchers, which cost 2d each, while the cheapest trenchers were less than $\frac{1}{2}$d each. It seems likely that servants and labourers ate from these plates, and that they were used in the kitchen when preparing food. Other wooden items could be surprisingly expensive. A great bucking tub cost 12s, and a little bucking tub 11s, both purchased from the cooper. Ordinary barrels, firkins, tubs and keelers cost between 1s and 3s. These wooden containers were staple possessions of rural households, used for washing, brewing and dairying. The Le Stranges also possessed larger copper kettles, often just referred to as 'coppers' in their dairy and brew-house. Three copper kettles weighing 60 lb were purchased for £3 17s 6d in 1612. Both the coppers and the wooden containers were strong durable items, partly because they could be easily mended. The cooper and tinker made regular visits to the household to fix wooden and metal items: the cooper six or more times a year, and the tinker two or three times. Large cooking pots made of iron ('pot metal') or brass were even more durable and thus irregular purchases. Like wooden tubs, nearly every household owned at least one of these cooking pots in this period; the Le Stranges simply owned more of what were common household objects.[105]

THE MEANINGS OF GOODS

Despite being packed with detail about the nature of material culture, household accounts contain little obvious information about the meanings attached to objects. This section follows three lines of investigation to explore the meanings that clothing and domestic goods held for the Le Strange family. The first is turnover.

---

[102] Allan, *Finds from Exeter*, 105.
[103] Crossley, *Post Medieval Archaeology*, 259–60.
[104] Emmison found treen ware being used in conjunction with pewter: *Elizabethan Life: Home, Work and Land*, 24.
[105] N. Cox, '"A flesh pott, or a brasse pott or a pott to boile in": changes in metal and fuel technology in the early modern period and the implications for cooking', in M. Donald and L. Hurcombe (eds.), *Gender and Material Culture in Historical Perspective* (Basingstoke, 2000); S. Pennell, 'Material culture of food in early modern England, 1650-1750', in S. Tarlow and S. West (eds.), *Familiar Pasts? Archaeologies of Later Historical Britain 1500-1800* (London, 1999), 40–1; S. Margeson, *Norwich Households: The Medieval and Post-Medieval Finds from Norwich Survey Excavations 1971–1978*, East Anglian Archaeology report 58 (Norwich, 1993), 235; Emmison, *Elizabethan Life: Home, Work and Land*, 25–7.

McCracken argued that the sixteenth- and seventeenth-century elite expressed their status partly through the patina of their goods. Patina was the quality whereby age, revealed by physical appearance, increased the value of goods. Not until the eighteenth century and the rise of fashion was the importance of patina undermined.[106] The second is the evidence provided by wills. Wills are the only personal document to survive in large numbers for the period before 1650. The will-maker decided which goods to give as bequests and to whom, as well as giving descriptions they felt appropriate in order to identify the goods. However, the degree of choice and self-expression found in wills has to be balanced by an appreciation of the legal process and conventions of will-making and inheritance to which they belonged. The third line of investigation is to examine gendered attitudes to goods: gender differences in bequests and in more general attitudes to clothing and linen are considered.

McCracken notes that status in early modern England came not only as a result of wealth but also as a result of the length of time a family had been wealthy. Those with old wealth sought ways of distinguishing themselves from the newly wealthy and found a solution in patina: goods that not only displayed wealth but also age. The consumption patterns of the Le Strange family, old established members of the Norfolk county gentry, provide an appropriate case study with which to test McCracken's theory. The only example he provides of patina-displaying goods is silverware.[107] This is not well chosen—as we have seen, the Le Stranges, like other gentry families in the early seventeenth century, frequently exchanged their old silver for new: silver did not bear patina. Wooden furniture was durable. However, the decorative, expensive, and status-displaying element of domestic furnishings was provided mainly by textiles: textiles such as cupboard cloths, linen tablecloths and bed curtains were all renewed on a regular basis. In fact, the opposite to a system that valued patina is demonstrated by the inventory of bed chambers: older items were found in less prestigious rooms and the newest items in the best rooms. Some older possessions were clearly valued by the family. Family portraits dating back to the first half of the sixteenth century were carefully preserved. Wills reveal that particular silver objects and items of embroidered needlework were kept and passed down the family. Yet it is unclear that they were valued for their patina, described by McCracken as objects becoming 'minutely dented, chipped, oxidized, and worn away'. Portraits displayed family history in much more overt manner. Particular silver objects and embroidery seem to have embodied sentimental values connected to family and gender rather than display and status, as discussed below. None of these goods gained value with age in the period under discussion. Newness appears to have been valued more than patina.

If the Le Stranges did not assert their status through the patina of goods, how did they display it? The short answer is that they did so through expenditure. Material goods were used to reinforce and enhance social status by embodying wealth. All

---

[106] G. McCracken, *Culture and Consumption: New Approaches to the Symbolic Character of Consumer Goods and Activities* (Indiana, 1988), 31–2.

[107] McCracken, *Culture and Consumption*, 31.

the most expensive objects—the silverware, glassware, fine linen, expensive foods, finely furnished bed chambers and beds—were on regular display to high-status guests. There were also more subtle means of displaying status, through fashion, taste and novelty, all of which were present, but are less easy to prove. Fashion and a love of novelty were not new in the eighteenth century. The Le Stranges followed fashions in interior furnishings and dining ware as well as in clothing. This was surely the motivation for exchanging silverware for new styles and refurnishing the best beds with new textiles. Nor did they display any hostility to novel and less durable items, such as glassware, tin-glazed chinaware, new draperies or cotton. Status was projected through many other means as well as via material goods, such as sources of wealth, political office, education, leisure and cultural interests, to name a few.[108] Yet there is no getting away from the importance of wealth in the Le Stranges' consumption patterns. It was quite possible to buy a bed fairly cheaply if it was purchased second-hand and dressed with colourful but cheap new draperies, and the Le Stranges were not averse to doing this if it was going in one of the lesser bed chambers. But for their best chambers they were quite happy to spend the cost equivalent to the building of a farmhouse on a single bed, with the majority of the expense going on non-durable textiles.

Wills have long been used as evidence of attitudes to religious belief; more recently, the work of Howell, Berg and Richardson has shown their rich potential for examining gendered attitudes to material culture.[109] Here our analysis is confined to only three wills: those made by Alice's father, Richard Stubbe, in 1617–19, Sir Hamon Le Strange in 1652–3 and Alice Le Strange in 1656.[110] All made lengthy and detailed wills. Each of these three wills appears true to the maker's character: Richard Stubbe, a professional lawyer, produced an unusually long and complicated will that was largely concerned with real property. Hamon Le Strange used his will to express his religious ideals and design his own funeral monument complete with motto. Alice prioritized her brewing equipment as well as making careful bequests to a wide circle of female relatives and friends. Yet in behaving in these ways, all three followed convention. Richard Stubbe's will is typical of a man with extensive landed property and no sons. Hamon's is a will of a man who had already settled the inheritance of his real property and wealth by other means, and was confident of his eldest son's ability to take his place. The will is thus concerned with 'extra' bequests and funeral arrangements. Alice's will follows a pattern observed in women's wills as far apart as late medieval Douai and eighteenth-century Birmingham, with its concern for domestic objects and female beneficiaries.[111]

---

[108] See Chapter 7.

[109] M. Howell, 'Fixing movables: gifts by testament in late medieval Douai', *Past and Present* 150 (1996), 3–45; M. Berg, 'Women's consumption and the industrial classes of eighteenth-century England', *Journal of Social History* 30:2 (1996), 415–34; C. Richardson, *Domestic Life and Domestic Tragedy in Early Modern England* (Manchester, 2006), 64–104.

[110] Both Richard Stubbe and Hamon Le Strange added codicils to earlier wills just before their deaths.

[111] Howell, 'Fixing movables'; Berg, 'Women's consumption'.

All three made bequests of silverware, jewellery, furniture and books. Hamon and Alice also both mentioned linen, pewter, clothing and a coach. Alice and her father both bequeathed brewing equipment. Livestock was only mentioned by Richard Stubbe; musical instruments, weapons and coins only by Hamon; and cabinets only by Alice. Richard Stubbe gave bequests of specified goods to nine people: his two daughters, one of his sons-in-law, five of his grandchildren, and a former maid servant. Hamon Le Strange had a similarly limited range of eight specified people: his wife, daughter, one daughter-in-law, one son-in-law, three of his grandsons, and two of his male servants. Alice gave bequests of specific goods to fourteen people: her daughter, two daughters-in-law, two grandsons, two granddaughters, a nephew, two nieces, a female cousin, the wife of a local clerk, a vicar, and a female servant. In each case, the 'residue of goods', all those things which were not specified, went to the executors of the will. Richard Stubbe's will was executed by his eldest daughter, Dionisia, and her husband, Sir William Yelverton; Hamon's executor was his eldest son, Nicholas; and Alice's her eldest surviving son, Hamon junior. These individuals were all excluded from the specified bequests, with the exception of Dionisia Yelverton, who was given a specific piece of silverware by Richard Stubbe. As not all children, grandchildren or servants were given specific bequests of goods, we can argue that goods were bequeathed for particular reasons. Some bequests, most obviously silverware, jewellery and coins, were an alternative means of transferring wealth, but they meant more than just money, embodying sentiment and, in the case of silverware, tradition. Other bequests, such as furniture, linen, pewter, brewing equipment, livestock, coaches and weapons, were practical. They might be given according to need but also as an acknowledgement of the receiver's inclination or aptitude towards a particular activity. Specific bequests communicate something about the giver, about the receiver (and in the case of bequests to children, their parents), and about the object given.

One piece of silverware, a Magdalene cup, appears in all three wills. Richard Stubbe described this as 'my magdelen box of silver' and bequeathed it to Alice. Glanville notes Magdalene cups, sometimes described as boxes, 'were treasured personal drinking vessels, frequently specified in wills', and largely restricted to the gentry and noble ownership.[112] This cup was not particularly valuable—Alice notes its value as £2 in the inventory of bequests from her father. Hamon bequeathed the same 'silver magdalene cup with a cover' to Alice in his will thirty-five years later, along with various other pieces of silverware noting that 'most of which [were] her own before marriage, but that I think fitt to express them to prevent question'. This is a reminder that even those items bequeathed to a married woman legally belonged to her husband. Alice in turn bequeathed the cup to her daughter-in-law Judith Le Strange, the second wife of Hamon junior. The complications of married women's property rights also mean that at least one set of items bequeathed by Richard Stubbe to Alice were gifts from Alice's mother, who pre-deceased her

[112] Glanville, *Silver*, 272–4.

husband. Stubbe gave Alice 'one cupboard carpet of needlework, one carpet of green cloth fringed with guards of velvet and six needlework cushions'. Hamon Le Strange repeated the bequest of at least two of these gifts to Alice, describing them as 'six cushions of needlework which [were] her mothers' and 'the green broad cloth cupboard cloth embroidered about the skirts with orange tawny silk twist upon purple velvet'. Embroidery such as this was typically the work of gentlewomen and thus can be seen as a very personal mother–daughter gift. Again, their monetary value was not particularly high, given as £6 13s 4d in Stubbe's inventory. Not all bequests of goods were given or received with strong sentiments. Alice copied an inventory of goods she received from her father into her account book. The inventory suggests that Alice was concerned with the monetary value of the gifts from her father as much as anything else. She noted elsewhere in the accounts that her inheritance was worth more than £1000 less than her sister's and this clearly mattered to her. Richard Stubbe's bequest to Alice of his brewing equipment was not overtly sentimental either, but it was perhaps a recognition of his daughter's skills and interests in practical housewifery. In fact, the equipment was valued at £10, more than the silver or embroidered furnishings. The importance of such things to Alice is emphasized by the fact that she also bequeathed her brewing equipment, making it the first bequest in her will.

Bequests from parent to child were significant and loaded with multiple motivations and meanings. A lack of a bequest was notable too. Neither Sir Hamon nor Alice bequeathed any goods to their youngest son, Roger. This was surely as significant as the gifts given to his siblings.[113] Gifts to grandchildren were perhaps more straightforward. Richard Stubbe had eight grandchildren. He gave Alice's five children forty sheep each, a gift aimed at training them in the management of foldcourse sheepflocks, as he had trained Alice. Only two of his grandchildren, Alice's eldest sons, Nicholas and Hamon junior, received personal items, each getting a piece of family silverware (valued in total by Alice at £38), and Hamon junior one of his rings. This favouritism can be explained by the fact that Nicholas and Hamon junior were living in Stubbe's house at the time of his death, along with their tutor, who ran a small school there. Likewise, Sir Hamon gave goods to only three grandsons out of a total of nineteen grandchildren. These were the older boys who had shared his interests before he declined into ill-health. It is likely that their widely differing gifts reflected their personalities: Nicholas' son and heir, Nicholas, received Sir Hamon's 'great English bible with gilt leaves', while his brother John received a bass viol and music books as well as a gun: the 'biggest birding piece standing in the parlour'. Their cousin William Spring junior received an 'ear ring set with diamonds'. All three of these boys, but not any of their siblings, were also given gold coins by Sir Hamon. Alice favoured a different set of grandchildren but was equally selective, making small gifts of jewels or embroidery to Dorothy Spring, Elizabeth's daughter, and Dorothy and Hamon Le Strange, the children of Hamon junior.

[113] Alice gave Roger £40; Hamon did not mention him at all.

Alice, although following a female form of will-making by favouring women and making gifts to a wide range of people, also demonstrated her belief in the importance of the Le Strange patrimony by making her largest bequests to her grandson Nicholas junior, who inherited Hunstanton Hall in 1655, and to Anne Le Strange, his widowed mother. Nicholas junior received a set of things that Alice had perhaps borrowed during her widowhood to set up her dower house in Sedgeford: brewing equipment, shelves, planks and tables from a boulting house and dairy, a washing copper and milk copper, as well as tables and cupboards from the parlour and dining room, and a complete set of bedroom furniture. Anne received those things suitable for an independent widowhood. These seem to have been more carefully chosen by Alice and carried greater meaning, as one would expect between two women who had shared the running of Hunstanton Hall for over twenty years and now shared a state of widowhood. Anne was given four beds, three chests of linen, a set of six embroidered stools, selected items of pewter and silver, and serving plates, as well as Alice's coach and harness. In her study of late eighteenth-century wills, Berg found that women were more likely than men to give bequests of clothing and of new consumer items.[114] Alice displays both these tendencies. She made two bequests of 'cabinets', small cupboards with compartments which were used for displaying curiosities, a fashion of the mid-seventeenth century.[115] Her 'black cabinet' went to her daughter-in-law Judith Le Strange, and her 'cedar cabinet' to her cousin Margaret Fisher. Both these women were also given clothing—Judith received a 'green silvered grogram petticoat', and Margaret a riding coat, 'two fine holland shifts' and 'two fine holland petticoats'. Alice gave all her 'ordinary apparel' and the residue of her wearing linen to Elizabeth Guybon, described in the will as her servant, but who was also a cousin. She also received a bed.

Howell describes wills as 'fixing movables', seeking to create in goods the properties of heirlooms, keepsakes and sentiment, to make them immovable, long-lasting and meaningful in opposition to the growing culture of constant circulation and commodification created by capitalist markets.[116] Wills are one of the few sources in which we can observe people using their goods to create meaning: they show how goods were used to reinforce social relationships and to discriminate between recipients. Material culture also plays an important role in constructing gender identities. Will-making followed different patterns for men and women. In part, this was because of property laws which gave married men complete control over all the property owned by a married couple. As a result, married women could not make wills without special provision and such wills were rare.[117] Most men who made wills were married men: their wills were dominated by provision for their wife's widowhood and their children's inheritance. The women who made wills tended to be in a rather different situation, which led to different priorities. Single women had no direct family to provide for, while widows often found that their husband had

---

[114] Berg, 'Women's consumption', 428.
[115] Peck, *Consuming Splendor*, 166–73.
[116] Howell, 'Fixing movables', 35–43.
[117] A.L. Erickson, *Women and Property in Early Modern England* (London, 1993), 24–6.

already provided for the children. On the other hand, the combination of property laws and customs of inheritance meant that women were less likely than men to own real property. As a result, women often had little to give other than cash, domestic goods, clothing and jewellery, and fewer dependants to provide for. This in itself would tend to lead to a situation in which men concentrated on real property and close family, and women gave more detailed descriptions of goods and distributed them more widely. However, these gendered tendencies persisted in different circumstances. Thus, even women with real property tended to give detailed descriptions of their movable goods, bequeath clothing and distribute widely;[118] and even men who had no family obligations and little real property to dispose of tended not to behave this way. Thus, we might argue that women expressed their femininity and concern for good housewifery in describing their domestic possession with care in their wills, as well as expressing the importance of female companionship and support by distributing these possessions widely, and more often to women than men. Howell notes that many men saw women's concern for the details of domestic goods and clothing as 'frivolous' and the distribution of gifts outside the immediate family as 'irresponsible'.[119] In other words, the culture of will-making was gendered in ways which went beyond the restrictions of property laws.

The expression of gendered attitudes to material culture was not restricted to wills, but it is often hard to separate real differences from stereotypes. de Vries has argued that the balance of spending between men's and women's clothes has varied over time from roughly equal amounts in the late seventeenth century to women spending more in the late eighteenth century, back to rough equality in the late nineteenth century and then to women spending more again in the late twentieth and early twenty-first century. He relates these changes to women's earning patterns: when women earn an independent income they tend to spend more on clothes, while men spend more on alcohol.[120] The importance of dress and fashion to women is a constant historical theme that was evident in the early seventeenth century, as in the eighteenth century and late medieval period.[121] One of Nicholas Le Strange's *Merry Jeasts* notes that when 'diverse gentlewomen, being mette together' they enter into 'serious discourse upon varietie of Dresse, and Apparrell, (the common Theames for women)'.[122] Puritan sermons commonly admonished women, rather than men, for vanity and expenditure on dress.[123] Women were more likely than men to bequeath items of clothing in their wills.[124]

---

[118] In Berg's sample 47 per cent of women bequeathed real property, but they still treated their goods in this way, 'Women's consumption', 419–21.
[119] Howell, 'Fixing movables', especially 28.
[120] de Vries, *The Industrious Revolution*, 141–3, 234–5, 262.
[121] Howell, 'Fixing movables', 28; J. Styles, *The Dress of the People: Everyday Fashion in Eighteenth-Century England* (New Haven, 2007), 182–3.
[122] Le Strange, *Merry Jeasts*, 51.
[123] Vincent, *Dressing the Elite*, 86. See also I. Warren, '"Witty offending great ones"? Elite female householders in an early Stuart Westminster parish', *The London Journal* 32: 3 (2007), 213.
[124] Samples of wills from F.G. Emmison, *Elizabethan Life: Wills of the Essex Gentry and Merchants* (Chelmsford, 1978), and N. Evans (ed.), *The Wills of the Archdeaconry of Sudbury 1630–1635*, Suffolk Record Society, vol. 29 (Woodbridge, 1987).

As Nicholas Le Strange's wedding clothes demonstrate, early seventeenth-century male clothing was no less flamboyant or expensive than women's. It had not undergone the 'great male renunciation' of the eighteenth century that led to men's fashion being plainer, less colourful and more uniform than women's.[125] Early seventeenth-century gentlemen appear to have followed fashion just as closely as women. Their frequent trips to London allowed them to observe and shop for fashions.[126] It is evident from the accounts, and from his portraits, that Hamon Le Strange cared deeply about his clothing. His trips to London on matters of business always resulted in purchases of dress. A package of things he sent up from London in September 1619 included the following purchases for himself: a pair of silk stockings (£2 10s), a dozen silver and gold points (15s), a scarf of gold and silver and silk (£4 15s), a ruff and cuffs (£1 6s), a new beaver hat and band (£2 10s), and a pot to dry ruffs on (2s), as well as two quires of paper (2s 4d), some musket moulds (1s 4d), two proclamations and three books (14s 9d). In fact, Hamon made as many bequests of clothing in his will as Alice, describing his clothes with equal care. He left his 'gray cloak lined and open at the arms with flat buttons ash colour and tawny' to one male friend, and his 'old shagge bayes gown' and 'black figured satin suite' to another. On average, however, men entered such descriptions in their wills less often than women, and thus we have to agree with Berg's conclusion that 'despite recognition of the detail and style of clothing, as well as the value of these goods, few men appear to have attached personal identity to their clothing significant enough for them to make individual bequests of apparel.'[127]

Not all clothing was treated in the same way: underclothes, even for the men of the house who purchased their own hats, jackets, waistcoats or hose, were purchased and often sewn by their wives, mothers or other female relatives.[128] Weatherill notes that 'women were traditionally responsible for the household linen, and it is recorded more often in their inventories.'[129] The importance of linen in displaying personal cleanliness and the fact that laundering linen always fell to women made clean, high-quality linen a sign of good housewifery as well as a mark of status.[130] In many parts of Europe, a trousseau of linen was an essential precursor for a respectable marriage, and bequests of linen passed between women for this purpose. Elizabeth Le Strange's careful preparation of an extensive collection of personal linens before her marriage had no equivalent in her brothers' wedding preparations. There is no evidence that the ownership of linen was restricted to

---

[125] D. Kuchta, 'The making of the self-made man: class, clothing and English masculinity, 1688–1832', in V. de Grazia (ed.), *The Sex of Things: Gender and Consumption in Historical Perspective* (Los Angeles, 1996), 54–78; D. Kuchta, *The Three-Piece Suit and Modern Masculinity: England, 1550–1850* (California, 2002).

[126] Vincent, *Dressing the Elite*, 105.

[127] Berg, 'Women's consumption', 424.

[128] Vincent, *Dressing the Elite*, 54; A. Vickery, 'His and hers: gender, consumption and household accounting in eighteenth century England', *Past and Present* supplement 1 (2006), 29–31.

[129] L. Weatherill, 'The meaning of consumer behaviour in late seventeenth- and early eighteenth-century England', in J. Brewer and R. Porter (eds.), *Consumption and the World of Goods* (London, 1993), 211, 224; also Vickery, 'Women and the world of goods', 282.

[130] Mitchell, 'By your leave', 56.

women in England, but gendered attitudes to ownership are often hard to discern in the documents as a result of men's legal right to married women's property. When Alice Le Strange wrote the inventory of household linen in 1632, a few weeks after the inventory of bed chambers, she titled it 'an inventory of all my linen', whereas the earlier inventory was merely 'an inventory of all the bedding and furniture to lodging chambers'. Next to some sets of table linen she noted in the margin 'these were mine' (meaning that she had brought them into the marriage) and that she had given them to 'her daughter Ham', the newly married wife of her second son. However, Sir Hamon also regarded the linen as his. He left Alice 'the half part of all myne household linen' in his will. Nonetheless, it was Alice who paid the most detailed attention to linen in her will. In her widowhood she had taken possession of four of the linen chests listed in the 1632 inventory and she divided them and their contents carefully between her daughter and two daughters-in-law.

CONCLUSION

Material culture has been the most intensely studied aspect of early modern consumption. However, existing approaches have left some significant gaps in our knowledge, gaps this chapter has tried to fill. The concentration on evidence from probate inventories has downplayed the importance of textiles as an area of expenditure, an element of furnishings, and as something that required regular replacement. Probate inventories record the second-hand value of goods, the money that could be raised when goods were auctioned off after a person's death.[131] Household accounts record the purchase cost of new goods. For items made of wood, such as tables, cupboards and tubs, and items made of metal, such as iron and brass pots, pewter and silverware, there was relatively little difference between these two values. For instance, pewter in inventories was valued at 60–70 per cent of the purchase price of new pewter.[132] However, for clothing, bed furnishings, upholstered furniture and linen, the difference could be significant. With use, textiles became worn, faded and stained, and as a result suffered a steep depreciation in value. In a selection of thirty-seven gentry probate inventories from 1600 to 1660, none had household linen valued at more than £65 and the average was £26, a fraction of what Alice Le Strange spent on these items. Textiles were purchased in many different grades of quality, but age also affected quality. In a gentry household, sets of bed furnishings were gradually moved to lesser chambers, from the guest rooms to the rooms of family members, and then down to the servants. Clothing suffered a similar fate. There was little waste in this system, but that does not mean that there was little turnover. Linen was purchased regularly to ensure that smart white tablecloths and napkins were available for best use; the

---

[131] M. Overton, 'Prices from probate inventories', in T. Arkell, N. Evans, and N. Goose (eds.), *When Death Do Us Part: Understanding and Interpreting the Probate Records of Early Modern England* (Oxford, 2000), 124.

[132] Overton, 'Prices from probate inventories', 131.

gentry purchased new clothes regularly to keep up with fashion and ensure that they had sufficient variety to wear.

The effect of comparing probate inventory studies of ordinary households with studies of exquisite objects owned by the elite has led to the misapprehension that there were two quite different material cultures in England in this period. In fact, upper gentry households such as the Le Stranges' provide a missing link, demonstrating that early modern England possessed a common material culture despite important regional and status differences. For the most part, studies of the material culture of ordinary households have been undertaken by economic and social historians and have used probate inventories as their document base. Studies of elite material culture have grown out of art history and political history, and have taken their evidence from objects, paintings, literature and personal papers. These two quite different approaches rarely cross paths, but those who have attempted to make sense of this dichotomy, such as McCracken and de Vries, have suggested sharp contrasts between the elite and the ordinary.[133] Households of the upper gentry such as the Le Stranges bridged this gap in the early seventeenth century. They were not part of courtly culture, but had cousins who were. They were not urban merchants, and were well above the parish gentry in wealth and status, but they had cousins who belonged to these groups as well. Members of the family went to London and Norwich a few times a year. Their consumption patterns reflected these social and geographical links.

The Le Stranges shared a basic material culture with their poorer neighbours. All the types of items listed in the inventory of Richard Wix, the local thatcher who worked regularly for the Le Stranges and who died in 1628, also appear in the Le Strange accounts.[134] The repertoire of furnishings was the same: beds for sleeping, tables for eating and working, cupboards and chests for storage, large metal vessels for cooking, large wooden vessels for processing foodstuffs and washing. In both households the bed was the single most valuable item of furniture. The Le Stranges owned more things of the types the Wixes possessed, such as a larger house, more beds and more tables, and the things the Le Stranges owned were more expensive and better quality. The sons and daughters of local families worked as servants in the Le Strange household: they slept in the featherbeds, looked at the paintings, polished the silver, laundered the linen and prepared the food. To be sure, Hunstanton Hall contained many movable goods not found in the Wix household. Some of these, such as tapestries, cushions, carpets, chairs, armour and silverware, were the traditional status markers of gentry consumption, common to gentry households since at least the fifteenth century. Others, such as upholstered seats, co-ordinated furnishings, pictures, window curtains and items made of glass, were more novel forms of consumption.

---

[133] McCracken, *Culture and Consumption*, 11–16; de Vries, 'Luxury', and *The Industrious Revolution*, ch. 2.
[134] Probate inventory of Richard Wix of Heacham: NRO MF/X10 DN/INV 34/173. See Chapter 8: The Le Stranges and the local community.

It is easy to overlook the novelties of the sixteenth and early seventeenth centuries as they look so 'traditional' to modern eyes. Linen went from being a home-made product in the medieval period to an international commodity in the fifteenth and sixteenth centuries. Pewter was adopted as the preferred form of tableware in the sixteenth century. Lace became a vital accessory for all 'best' clothing and many furnishings after the mid-sixteenth century, only falling from favour in the eighteenth century. New draperies offered more colourful and lighter clothing and furnishings from the late sixteenth century onwards. New forms of furnishing, ornamentation and household ware, which became more widespread in wealthy and middling households later in the century, were evident in Hunstanton Hall by the 1630s. These included upholstered furniture, window curtains, pictures, mirrors, a clock, tin-glazed earthenware and glassware. Unlike the novelties of the later seventeenth century, the new goods of the early seventeenth century were overwhelmingly European in origin, and, from the late sixteenth century, increasingly made in England too. The Le Stranges used the quality and expense of their goods to assert their status, but also to make their house and person more comfortable and pleasing to the eye.

6
Family Life Cycle and Consumption

Allowed to Mr Burward: for churching of myselfe: and for Baptizing and Burying John Le Strange and for our selves and our servantes Receiving of the Sacrament at Easter 20s.[1]

Alice and Hamon Le Strange's household accounts run from four years after their marriage to Hamon's death in 1654. This long run of accounts presents a rare opportunity to investigate consumption patterns across the family life cycle of an early seventeenth-century household. The chapter begins by looking at the size and make-up of the Le Strange household in comparison with expenditure, income and debt. This reveals that there was no strong relationship between household size and expenditure; instead, expenditure and debt varied according to life cycle stage and external events. The second section focuses on births, deaths and marriages as consumption events. Following Cressy's pioneering research, it examines how these events were organized and celebrated and the expenses involved.[2] The third section considers the evidence provided by accounts on the nature of childhood, looking at wet nursing, toys and clothing. The fourth section examines patterns of education and expenditure on the children as adults, their marriage portions, inheritance and allowances, and compares expenditure on the Le Stranges' four surviving children across the whole run of accounts. Household accounts have not been used previously for detailed study in any of these fields and offer a fresh perspective on existing debates. The themes of the chapter raise a number of important gender issues. Particularly informative are the comparisons between the childhood experiences and education of Jane and Elizabeth Le Strange and their brothers. From the age of six or seven the treatment of children became sharply differentiated in clothing, toys and education. The Le Strange boys were sent away to school while Elizabeth, the only daughter to survive to adulthood, was educated entirely by her parents at home. Arrangements for marriage were also strongly gendered. This applied not only to the exchange of wealth and property but also to the responsibilities of organizing and paying for a wedding ceremony. Despite the many complaints about the size of daughters' marriage portions in the seventeenth century, an analysis of the overall cost of sons and daughters in the Le Strange family shows

[1] Alice Le Strange, receipt accounts 1619; LEST/P6.
[2] D. Cressy, *Birth, Marriage and Death: Ritual, Religion and Life Cycle in Tudor and Stuart England* (Oxford, 1997).

that the allowance paid to Nicholas, the heir-in-waiting, was almost double the cost of Elizabeth's marriage portion. Family relationships, childhood and gender differences are all highly emotive experiences—household accounts are a blunt tool for studying them. Yet patterns of expenditure reveal the practicalities of family life in the early seventeenth century and illuminate some underlying motivations.

LIFE CYCLE AND EXPENDITURE

Compared with gentry households of medieval and sixteenth-century England those of the seventeenth century were smaller, more purely domestic and more feminine in their personnel.[3] It was nevertheless still typical for resident servants to outnumber family members, and this was the case in the Le Strange household. The size and make-up of the household between 1610 and 1654 is shown in Figure 6.1. It is not always easy to determine who was resident. Members of the family have been counted as resident if they were still being supported by the family. In fact, babies were cared for by local wet nurses until around two years of age. The boys left home to be tutored from as young as seven, before progressing to Eton, Cambridge, and the Inns of Court. Hamon Le Strange junior had his own income from the age of twenty-one onwards, so has been excluded from that time onwards. On the other hand, his brother Roger has been counted as resident from his birth onwards: he was certainly absent in prison and then in exile from 1644 onwards as a result of his Royalist activities during the Civil War, but he continued to receive an allowance and had no significant independent income or alternative home. Servants receiving annual wages have also been counted as resident,[4] despite the fact that, occasionally, older and senior male servants lived in their own homes. While these judgements err on the side of over-counting, the household almost certainly contained further people who were neither members of the direct family nor paid servants; these people have not been included in Figure 6.1. For instance, in the late 1610s, William Guybon, the son of Alice's cousin Francis Guybon of Sedgeford, acted as a servant but received no salary. During the trip to London in 1620, Alice notes the presence of a 'gentlewoman' who needed board along with family members, but does not give her name. In 1632, Alice's recently widowed elder sister, Dionisia Yelverton, was living in the household and had her own room. In addition, although they did not normally lodge in the household, agricultural labourers and building workers were paid partly in food, adding to household costs.

The direct family grew in size over time. In 1606, four years after their marriage, it consisted of Alice, Hamon and their two young sons Nicholas and Hamon junior, born in 1604 and 1605 respectively. Dorothy, born in 1608, died nine months later, while Jane, born in 1612, died in 1620. The next two children, Elizabeth and Roger, born in 1614 and 1616 respectively, both survived to

---

[3] K. Mertes, *The English Noble Household 1250–1600: Good Governance and Politic Rule* (Oxford, 1988), 188–91.
[4] With the exception of shepherds who lived out.

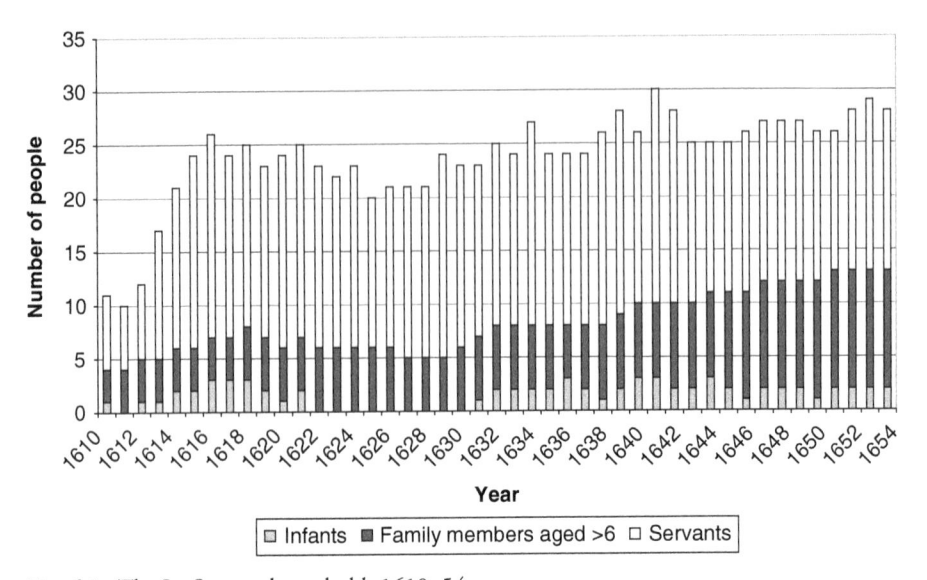

Fig. 6.1. The Le Strange household, 1610–54.
Sources: Le Strange disbursement and receipt accounts; LEST/P6–P11.

adulthood, while the last two, John and Mary, born in 1618 and 1621 respectively, did not live beyond a year. In 1630, Nicholas married and brought his wife, Anne Lewkenor, to live with him and his parents at Hunstanton Hall. This practice of creating a 'multiple family household' containing more than one married couple was not unusual amongst the wealthier sections of the gentry.[5] Their first child was born in 1631, and over the next twenty years Anne had a total of nine children. Only one, a daughter Anne, died as a baby. While this third generation was steadily adding to the family, Nicholas' siblings left home: Hamon junior by 1627 and Elizabeth when she married in 1636. Roger, as we have seen, remained dependent on the household and did not marry until the 1670s. The number of servants did not grow in relation to the size of the family. In the first few years for which servants are systematically listed, between 1610 and 1612 seven or fewer were employed annually; this increased to twelve in 1613, before rising to fifteen in 1614. The number employed then varied between thirteen and twenty for the rest of the period up to 1654, averaging sixteen or seventeen before declining slightly to fifteen in the last decade of the accounts.

From the 1620s onwards, the Le Stranges' annual expenditure averaged over £2000, matching their income. As the receipts and disbursements record real rather than anticipated income and expenditure, comparing them is not particularly

---

[5] L. Stone, *The Crisis of the Aristocracy 1558–1641* (Oxford, 1965), 634; M. Dawson, *Plenti and Grase: Food and Drink in a Sixteenth Century Household* (Totnes, 2009), 44; F. Heal and C. Holmes argue otherwise, *The Gentry in England and Wales 1500–1700* (Basingstoke, 1994), 69.

informative.[6] They matched each other closely over any twelve-month period, as only money in hand could be paid out. More informative are the size of new loans and levels of ongoing debt, shown in Figure 6.2. Loans were the means by which the gap between expenditure and income was met. Alice recorded all loans and outstanding debts from 1630 to 1654 in the back of her final account book.[7] This is supplemented by records of loans extracted from the receipt accounts from 1606 to 1626, leaving only a short gap in 1627–9, when no receipt accounts survive. The accounts demonstrate that the Le Stranges took out frequent loans from both relatives and professional lenders. Heal and Holmes have argued that the gentry were reluctant to pay or charge interest both on religious grounds and because it was seen as 'corrosive of ideals of friendship and neighbourliness'.[8] Despite being deeply religious and thoroughly neighbourly, the Le Stranges even paid interest on loans within the family to Alice's father, their children and grandchildren.

Figures 6.1 and 6.2 demonstrate that there was no strong correlation between household size and expenditure. However, income and expenditure were related to the family life cycle. Building works only began in earnest once Alice and Hamon came into possession of their full property and income from 1620 onwards, following the death of Alice's father. Most large property transactions were associated with the marriages of the Le Strange children. On the other hand, the family's continued indebtedness through the 1640s was largely due to an extraneous factor, the Civil War. Table 6.1 shows a breakdown of the Le Stranges' expenditure into five broad categories. Domestic expenditure is discussed in Chapter 3. The other four relate to the maintenance of the family and estate as a

Table 6.1. Average expenditure per year

Expenditure	1610–19	1620–9	1630–9	1640–9	1610–53
Total minus loans, interest and land purchases	£926	£1813	£2723	£2126	£1898
(a) *Amounts (£)*					
Domestic	523	895	992	758	770
Family finance	244	297	865	510	491
Political and legal	15	63	128	413	182
Estate	75	228	403	282	239
Building works	56	317	318	152	205
(b) *Percentages (%)*					
Domestic	56	49	36	36	41
Family finance	26	16	32	24	26
Political and legal	2	3	5	19	10
Estate	8	13	15	13	13
Building works	6	17	12	7	11

Note: The five categories do not add up exactly to the totals owing to some small payments which could not be assigned.

---

[6] In contrast to the accounts described by A. Simpson, *The Wealth of the Gentry 1540–1660: East Anglian Studies* (Cambridge, 1961), 3–10.
[7] LEST/P10.   [8] Heal and Holmes, *The Gentry*, 125.

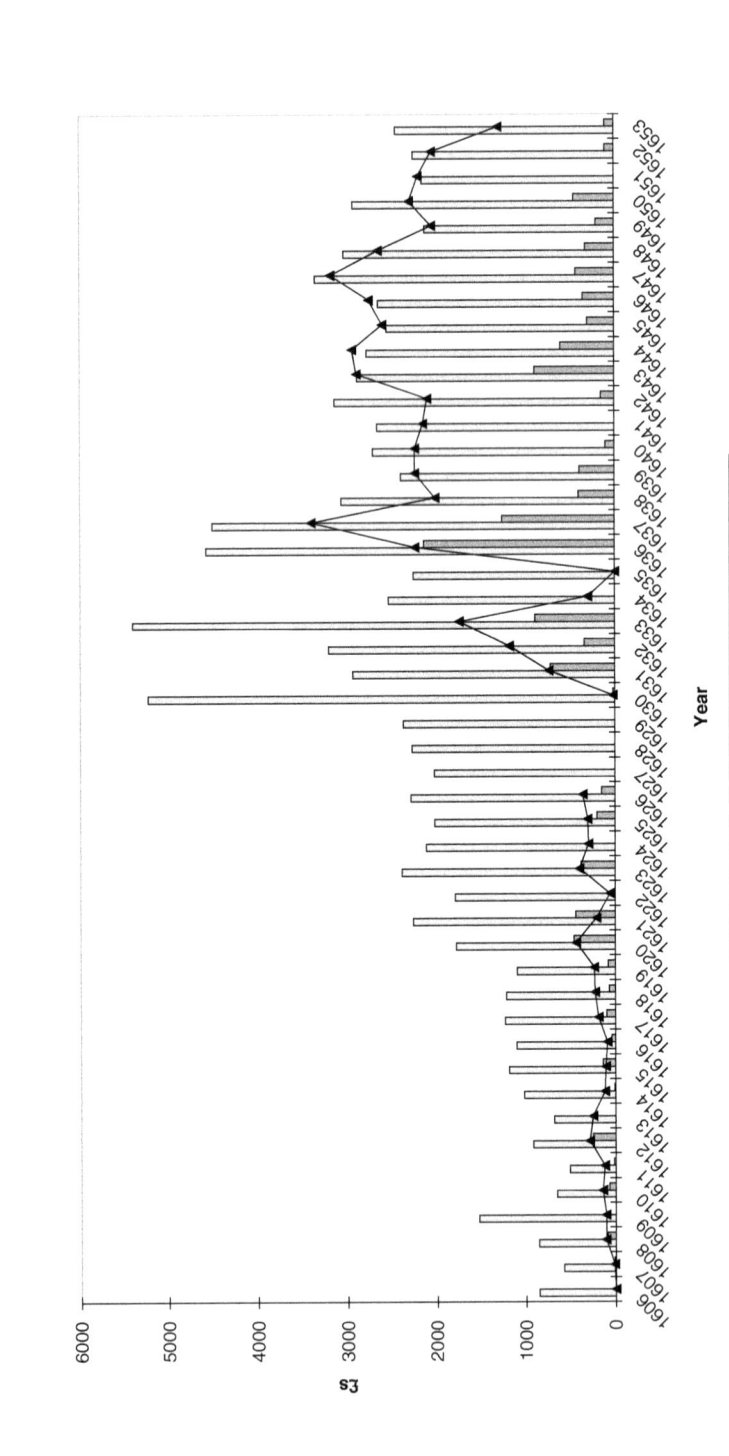

Fig. 6.2. Annual expenditure and money borrowed, 1606–53.
Sources: Le Strange disbursement and receipt accounts; LEST/P6–P11.

dynastic and business enterprise. The largest of these was 'family finance', which included Alice Le Strange's own allowance of £66 13s 4d a year, allowances and dowries paid to adult children, and annuities paid to a wider circle of relatives. These accounted for 26 per cent of the spending in the period 1610–53, outstripping expenditure on the estate and building works. Political and legal expenses, which included taxation, poor rates and the cost of office-holding, accounted for 10 per cent. All these expenses fluctuated over time. Family expenses were particularly high in the 1630s, when the three oldest Le Strange children married. Nicholas Le Strange continued to be paid a large annual allowance for the rest of the period of the accounts, while he waited to inherit the estate. Political and legal expenses were insignificant in the 1610s at an average of £15 a year, but rose steadily, before ballooning in the Civil War decade to £413 a year, as the Le Stranges were hit by heavy taxation and requisitioning, as well as claims of loss against Sir Hamon Le Strange for his Royalist defence of King's Lynn. Expenditure on the estate and building works were cut back, having risen steadily through the previous decades.

Over Alice and Hamon's married life the family passed through a number of distinct phases of getting and spending. The years between their marriage in 1602 and 1621 were ones of establishing and stabilizing the family and the household economy. Assessing the family's financial fortunes towards the end of her life, Alice noted: 'my husband was left in debt by his father's executors with money due to his uncle Roger Le Strange: £1500. He was left neither household stuff nor stock and his chief house half built and all his farm houses in such decay so as he hath built most of them out of the ground.'[9] Hamon Le Strange's minority and wardship, despite a good relationship with his guardians, left the estate in poor condition. On top of this, it was some years before Hamon and Alice received the full income from their lands. Between 1607 and 1612 their average annual receipts from the estate were £593. In the five years for which receipt accounts survive between 1613 and 1619 this almost doubled to £1097 per year. They jumped again in 1621 when the death of Richard Stubbe allowed them to take possession of Sedgeford manor and a number of other smaller properties. Estate income rose to £1769 that year, and with investment in the estate infrastructure income exceeded £2000 a year from 1630 onwards. In the early years of their married life, Alice and Hamon lived modestly for members of the upper gentry, keeping within their relatively low income and taking out small loans, predominantly from Alice's father and 'Uncle Bozoun'.[10] They made one large property acquisition in this period, selling the manor of Fring and buying the more expensive manor of Heacham, closer to the heart of the estate, in 1609.[11] Until 1613, they kept a small household of servants. This can be explained largely by the state of Hunstanton Hall: sleeping quarters were limited and the service buildings were in need of repair. Investment in their house and buildings changed this: the beginning of Alice's kitchen accounts in 1613 marks the start of large-scale home production of

---

[9] LEST/P10.
[10] Before 1620, 'Father' provided fifteen loans and 'Uncle Bozoun' seven; only four were provided by other people.
[11] Fring was sold for £2140, and Heacham purchased for £4400; LEST/Q38 fol. 26.

bread, beer, cheese and butter, and coincides with the employment of a larger complement of servants. For Alice Le Strange this was also a period of frequent pregnancies. In 1621, the birth of her last child coincided with the receipt of her full inheritance and the first phase of the household came to an end.

The 1620s were a period of stability and prosperity for the Le Stranges. With an income edging up towards £2000, and no other pressing demands, Hamon set about significantly enlarging Hunstanton Hall. This was done without incurring any major debts, although with their larger income the Le Stranges now made more use of professional money lenders. They borrowed money from Hamon's London tailor, Lawrence Michael, and from the town of Lynn. The enlargement of the house made it possible for Nicholas Le Strange to remain resident at Hunstanton after his marriage to Anne Lewkenor in 1630. The marriage heralded not only the arrival of a new generation of the family into the household in the form of numerous grandchildren but also the start of a series of large financial transactions. Anne brought a marriage portion of £3500 to her new family. Elizabeth Le Strange married William Spring in 1636 with a portion of the same size, but the money was not transferred from one woman to the other. Anne's portion went into the purchase of Benacre manor in 1630 for £2550. Benacre was then sold in 1633 to buy West Winch for £1792.[12] This manor was settled on Hamon junior when he married in 1634.[13] To fund Elizabeth's portion, Alice and Hamon sold property in King's Lynn worth £1240 and borrowed £1900.

The bulk of this debt remained with Alice and Hamon for the rest of their lives. In times of peace and prosperity they would have paid it off without difficulty over the next decade, but the Civil War intervened. All of the Le Stranges were Royalists. When Sir Hamon organized an unsuccessful defence of King's Lynn against the Parliamentarian forces in the summer of 1643, he was certainly joined by his son Roger and possibly Nicholas and Hamon junior as well. Earlier that year, Hamon junior was reported as a 'delinquent' to Parliament in a separate incident, disrupting a committee in Norwich. In 1644, Roger Le Strange hatched another misguided plot to take back King's Lynn, and as a result was imprisoned for four years and later went into exile.[14] There is some disagreement as to when the Le Stranges' lands were sequestered by the Parliamentarians, but they had certainly been confiscated by 1649.[15] Despite the sequestration, their income remained steady, closely matching the expenditure shown in Figure 6.2 and Table 6.1. Between 1647 and 1653 they were paying off debts rather than becoming more indebted. There were losses, however, recorded by Alice in the accounts.[16] In 1643, they were

---

[12] Benacre was on the Suffolk coast; West Winch just south of King's Lynn.
[13] LEST/AA 13.
[14] R.W. Ketton-Cremer, *Norfolk in the Civil War: A Portrait of Society in Conflict* (Norwich, 1985). *ODNB* entries for Sir Hamon, Nicholas, Hamon jun., and Roger Le Strange.
[15] Ketton-Cremer, *Norfolk in the Civil War*, 217. M.A.E. Green (ed.), *Calendar for the Committee of Compounding: Part 4* (London, 1892). *ODNB* entry for Sir Hamon Le Strange. The accounts contain legal and other fees arising from this process in 1651.
[16] LEST/P10.

taxed £300 by 'the rebels', and 'were plundered by the rebels of 1,660 sheep, all our corn and diverse horses'. In 1644, they paid £200 to 'the advance of the Scottish rebels'. The remaining losses were all connected to Sir Hamon's actions in Lynn. Despite negotiating immunity at the end of the siege, he was later held personally responsible by Parliament for those who had suffered damages and ordered to pay reparations.[17] He was sued by the mayor of Lynn for 'pretended losses' of £226 in 1645, as well as by various men 'for pretended imprisoning'. Alice quantified his total losses from 'the unjust and tyrannical oppression of Mr Toll and others of his faction in Lynn concerning the siege' at £1088.

The Le Stranges reacted to the Civil War by cutting back expenditure on textiles, clothing and building work. Nonetheless, their wage bill rose slightly, and expenditure on food held steady, suggesting the same household economy remained in place.[18] The true difficulty of the family's situation is revealed by a loan of £2000 raised in May 1654, on the eve of Sir Hamon's death. Three-quarters of this came from the mortgage of Barrett Ringstead manor, taken out jointly by Sir Hamon and Nicholas, to be repaid by June 1657.[19] The accounts give no explanation, but other documents show that this money was used to compound the Le Strange estate, allowing Nicholas to regain control of his lands and receive rents.[20] Ketton-Cremer notes that the process of compounding was a long and messy affair for 'notable Royalists such as Sir Hamon Le Strange'.[21] Alice completed her accounts with a 'stock take' of her and Hamon's life, probably drawn up in the autumn after his

Table 6.2. 'Losses in my husband's estate'

Year	Description	£	s	d
	Lost by adventuring in the East Indies	500		
1632	Lost by John Creamer the bankrupt	400		
1638	Lost by Heacham Marsh about	600		
1639	Lost in a suit for our Irish lands	221	10	
	Lost by adventuring in Boston fens	500		
(1643+)	Made and spent in suit by the unjust and tyrannical oppression of Mr Toll and others of his faction in Lynn concerning the siege	1088		
	Recovered by Stileman in an unjust suit being over-powered by the times	385		
	Sum	3654	10	
	Beside our great loss when we were plundered of all our sheep and corn			

Source: Notes at back of LEST/P10.

---

[17] For Sir Hamon's own account of this affair see H. L'Estrange, *The Charge upon Sir Hamon L'Estrange together with his Vindication and Recharge* (London, 1649); also Ketton-Cremer, *Norfolk in the Civil War*, 216–18.
[18] See Tables 3.1 and 6.1.
[19] Money lent by John Rant of Grays Inn and F. Rowland of London, gent.; see LEST/BN9. The loans were taken out jointly by Nicholas and Sir Hamon. Despite their deaths it was paid off on time; see LEST/BN10.
[20] LEST/supple/25/iii/2/15.
[21] Ketton-Cremer, *Norfolk in the Civil War*, 303.

BIRTHS, DEATHS AND MARRIAGES

Of Alice and Hamon's eight children, the two eldest were born before 1606, but the arrival of the next six all left a mark in the accounts. Four of these children died and burials are also recorded, along with the funeral of Alice's father in 1619. The weddings of their eldest son, Nicholas Le Strange, in 1630 and their only surviving daughter, Elizabeth, in 1636 are also well documented in the accounts. Table 6.3 shows the children's baptism dates as recorded in Hunstanton parish register and payments to the midwife from the household accounts. Alice used the same midwife for the births of at least the last five of her children—'Goodwife Crisp'. The Crisp family came from neighbouring Sedgeford, where Alice grew up. It is likely that Goodwife Crisp was married to one of the two male Crisps who appear in the accounts—John, who was one of the Le Stranges' shepherds, or William, a wealthier tallow chandler. Goodwife Crisp was well paid for her work, her fee of £1 10s was a significant sum considering that a full-time female servant working for the Le Stranges was paid no more than £3 a year in this period. The fee would have been supplemented by gifts from the Le Stranges' family and friends at the christening, an occasion on which the midwife was traditionally present.[22] Hamon Le Strange gave gifts of between 4s and £2 4s to the midwife and wet nurse at ten christenings of friends and relatives he attended between 1606 and 1626. Goodwife Crisp also appears in the accounts as a regular giver of small gifts of food, such as chickens and fruit, indicating her ongoing relationship with the Le Stranges.[23] Cressy argues that 'in aristocratic households, where

Table 6.3. Baptisms and payments to the midwife

Child	Date of baptism	Payment to midwife
Dorothy	11 May 1608	12 May (£1 10s)
Jane	11 February 1611/12	26 March (£1 10s)
Elizabeth	17 March 1613/14	18 March (£1 10s)
Roger	27 December 1616	28 December (£1 13s)
John	22 October 1618	October (£1 13s)
Mary	11 October 1621	October (£1 13s)

Sources: Hunstanton parish register and Le Strange disbursement accounts; LEST/P6, P7.

---

[22] Cressy, *Birth, Marriage and Death*, 150.
[23] See Chapter 3: The acquisition of food.

childbirth was closely implicated with lineage and power, the selection of a midwife was almost as important as the choice of a tutor or a steward. Both male and female networks operated to secure the most renowned or most advantageous services.'[24] However, careful selection did not necessarily imply someone geographically distant or high status. Alice relied on her local knowledge rather than on gentry connections to choose a woman of humble status for this crucial task: her repeated use of the same midwife indicates that Goodwife Crisp was skilful and trusted.

Margaret Cavendish, Duchess of Newcastle, wrote of the 'care, pains and cost, in getting, making, and buying fine and costly childbed linen, swaddling clothes, mantles, and the like' among her friends preparing for childbirth in the Restoration period.[25] Alice made more modest preparations, purchasing cloth and clothing for the new babies. Some of these items were practical, such as the 5.25 yards of cotton for blankets purchased for Jane and swaddling bands for Elizabeth and Mary; some were luxury textiles for 'bearing cloths' (christening robes). Jane's required crimson taffeta, silk and silver lace, while Mary's used scarlet bays. Bearing cloths were not mentioned for the other children as they were normally reused. However, if a child died as a baby, it was buried in its bearing cloth: Dorothy died before Jane, and John before Mary.[26] Descriptions of childbirth in early modern England reveal that the actual birth was only one event in a series of occasions marked by sociability, feasting and gift-giving. During the birth, the woman was attended not only by the midwife and prospective wet nurse but also by female relatives and friends. The christening, a few days after the birth, was an occasion to invite a wider circle of relatives and friends, who were entertained with food and drink after the service. Godparents, rather than the mother and father, played the key roles in the service. The mother remained in bed during this time and her reappearance into normal society, usually about a month after the birth, was marked by her churching, another occasion for female sociability.[27]

Of all these events, it is christenings which leave the strongest mark on the accounts: both those of the Le Strange children and those of friends and relatives. Christening feasts were characterized by special selections of banqueting stuff, sugary foods not used by the Le Stranges at other times.[28] Christenings were also an occasion for gift-giving, particularly between godparents and the child. Mary was given a gilt cup by Sir Roger Townshend, almost certainly her godfather. This was a favourite high-status christening present. Hamon Le Strange gave a cup worth £8 12s to Sir Philip Knivett's child in 1611 and another worth £6 8s 6d to his cousin Mordant's child in 1615. Lower status families were given six silver spoons by the Le Stranges, which cost between £1 14s and £2.[29] There is no

---

[24] Cressy, *Birth, Marriage and Death*, 70.
[25] Quotation taken from Cressy, *Birth, Marriage and Death*, 51.
[26] Cressy, *Birth, Marriage and Death*, 163–4.
[27] Cressy, *Birth, Marriage and Death*, 215–29.
[28] Discussed in Chapter 4: The meanings of food.
[29] See P. Glanville, *Silver in Tudor and Early Stuart England: A Social History and Catalogue of the National Collection 1480–1660* (London, 1990), 281.

indication in the accounts of sociability at the time of the births, or even of Alice being 'out of action' for a period of time: they offer a continuous record in her normal neat hand.[30] However, she did employ her washer-woman, Alice Chant, for extra help, being 'my keeper when I lay in' at the births of Jane and Mary and 'for helping wash when I lay in childbed' after Roger's birth. Likewise, Alice Le Strange recorded payments to the local minister for 'churching me', but no other ceremony surrounding this event.

The lavishness of christening celebrations are all the more striking given the likelihood of the child dying soon afterwards. Three of Alice's children died as babies: Dorothy at nine months, John at four months and Mary at three months.[31] All were with their wet nurses when they died. John and Mary died so young that Alice Le Strange noted only one payment to Robert Burward, the vicar of Hunstanton, for baptizing and burying the child and churching herself, as quoted at the start of the chapter.[32] Dorothy's death, which occurred when Hamon was keeping the household accounts, is not recorded at all. For John and Mary, a last payment to each wet nurse is noted. The household clerk, Cole, was paid 16d for 'ringing [the church bell] and making the grave for John Le Strange'. Costen, the carpenter, was paid 3s 4d for 'Mary Le Strange's coffin'. Alice accounted 16s for 'bread and meat which was spent when Mary Le Strange was sick and the night that women did watch with her the night that she died'; otherwise, no medical care was recorded for these infants. Nor is there evidence for anything other than a simple burial service.

When Jane Le Strange died in September 1620 aged eight and a half, her funeral was rather different. Sir Hamon Le Strange wrote apologizing for his non-attendance at the quarter sessions that autumn: 'a late loss which I have received in one of my children kept me at home'.[33] Jane's grave was paved, the church bell rung and a dole of £5 10s was made to the poor of Hunstanton, Heacham, Sedgeford, Holme and Ringstead. The payment to two servants of 20s a piece 'because they had no mourning cloaks' indicates that the whole household dressed in mourning for the funeral, although the kitchen accounts contain no evidence of a feast. Given that no new purchases are recorded, it is probable that the family and servants reused the mourning clothes bought for the funeral of Alice's father, who died on 24 November 1619. At that time, £11 4s 2d had been spent on mourning clothes, in addition to purchases of black hats and gloves for the family, and black bridles, saddle covers and 42 yards of black cotton to cover the coach. This expenditure was quite modest in comparison with some Elizabethan funerals; for instance, the executors of Sir Nicholas Bacon spent £648 11s 45d on black cloth

---

[30] A century earlier, Lady Le Strange was attended by women of her own circle at the birth of a child in 1520, and afterwards received gifts from 'the wives of Heacham': F. Heal, *Hospitality in Early Modern England* (Oxford, 1990), 81.

[31] Hunstanton parish register.

[32] The cost was allowed against the rent of his house; thus, these entries appear in the receipt accounts.

[33] NRO Norfolk Quarter Sessions: C/S3/Box 22. September 1620, addressed to 'my loving friend Mr Oakes'.

for those attending his funeral in 1579.[34] Neither the will of Richard Stubbe nor those of Hamon and Alice gave any instructions about funeral arrangements. Those of both Hamon and Alice, however, gave instructions for burial. Hamon asked to be buried in 'the chancell of Hunstanton' church, and added: 'I desire to have a plain black marble stone laid over me and in a plate of gilded brass this graven: in terris peregrinus eram nunc incola coeli [on land I was a pilgrim now a resident of heaven], in heaven at home, oh blessed change, who while I was on earth was Strange.' Alice merely asked 'to be decently interred in the chancel of the church at Hunstanton . . . near the body of . . . Sir Hamon Le Strange my late dear husband.' Blomefield's eighteenth-century description of the monuments in Hunstanton church confirms that both these instructions were carried out.[35]

These descriptions demonstrate that the family had a gradated scale of commemorations of the dead. Babies were buried wearing their bearing cloths in wooden coffins, but without much ceremony. Eight-year-old Jane Le Strange was given a paved grave, but no permanent monument, and her funeral was attended by the household in mourning clothes, but probably not by a wider circle of relatives and friends given the lack of evidence of feasting at the time of the funeral. The deaths of adult members of the family were commemorated with funeral monuments amongst those of the many Le Strange ancestors in the chancel of Hunstanton church, and almost certainly warranted larger, more public, funerals. There is a hint of this in the '12 gallons of white wine bought at Lynn' and '24 pounds of currants at Norwich' which Alice purchased in the week of Hamon's funeral, but unfortunately no other details survive, probably because the funeral was largely organized by Nicholas Le Strange, as son, heir and executor.[36]

Was the cost of a funeral a measure of grief? Gittings has argued that parents felt less grief at the death of babies than at the death of older children, but that 'the burial ceremonies for babies were still decently observed'. Older children received 'burials similar to those of adults'.[37] However, as she does not compare babies, children and adults from the same family, this argument remains necessarily vague. Houlbrooke demonstrates that the cost of funerals depended on social status. In the late sixteenth and early seventeenth centuries, earls' funerals could cost £1000 or more, knights' funerals cost several hundred pounds, while the average cost for a Kent yeoman's funeral in 1581–1650 was £2 4s 8d. About two-thirds of the expense at elite funerals was mourning attire and black cloth, while much of the rest was spent on food.[38] It is possible to argue that the costs of funerals is in part a function of wealth—eight-year-old Jane Le Strange's funeral cost more than the average for a Kent yeoman—but that costs were also affected by status. As men and

---

[34] Cressy, *Birth, Marriage and Death*, 440.
[35] F. Blomefield, *An Essay Towards a Topographical History of the County of Norfolk*, vol. 5 (London, 1739–75), 1276.
[36] P10, section headed 'monies received by me which were due to my son Strange and other monies due from me'.
[37] C. Gittings, *Death, Burial and the Individual in Early Modern England* (London, 1984), 80–2.
[38] R. Houlbrooke, *Death, Religion and the Family in England 1480–1750* (Oxford, 1998), 267, 269, 275.

married householders had a higher status than children, their funerals were more costly. The relationship between grief and the nature of the funeral ceremony is complex: grief is better documented elsewhere, in diaries and letters that record the intense feelings of parents at the death of their offspring.[39]

Surprisingly little is written about gentry weddings, as opposed to gentry funerals or the weddings of ordinary people.[40] Cressy provides a few examples of weddings among wealthy townsmen and gentry in the sixteenth and seventeenth centuries, and the Le Strange weddings conform closely to these in terms of the importance of clothing, gifts and the length of feasting.[41] Nicholas' wedding in September 1630 and Elizabeth's in October 1636 both left a significant mark on the household accounts. Nicholas was married at St Gregory's in Norwich,[42] Elizabeth at Hunstanton.[43] Nicholas' wedding preparations were concentrated in the half year before his marriage. During that time, he purchased his wedding clothes, accessories and gifts in London, while Alice prepared his underclothes and linen, and furnished rooms for the newly married couple in Hunstanton Hall. At the same time, the legal agreements associated with the marriage were drawn up. The total cost of the wedding for the Le Stranges, not including the new furnishings, was £272, of which the largest single category of expenditure was Nicholas' wedding suits. He spent £161 12s 1d on three suits and clothing accessories for his wedding.[44] Multiple sets of apparel were desirable because celebrations typically lasted for more than one day.[45] Elizabeth began her preparations earlier, purchasing her wedding clothes in London a year and a half before the wedding. She had two expensive dresses prepared.[46] In the following year, Alice and Elizabeth concentrated on purchasing and making a quantity of underclothes, linen items and accessories, such as smocks, aprons, cuffs, neck cloths, cross-cloths, petticoats, waistcoats, handkerchiefs, pinners and coifes, all liberally trimmed with lace, to a total cost of £41 13s.[47] Some of these were certainly designed to be worn with her wedding outfits, but the majority were for later use: this was Elizabeth's wedding trousseau. A further £26 13s was spent on accessories such as shoes, stockings, gloves and ribbons. The total cost of the wedding, not including food, of which clothing was the great majority, was £247. For both weddings, the Le Stranges purchased gifts of silver for the married couple, or, perhaps as is suggested by the gendered nature of the objects, for the new members of the family. Anne Lewkenor received a silver skillet with cover, a silver ladle, a silver basin and a little silver candlestick, costing a total of £24 3s.

---

[39] Houlbrooke, *Death Religion and the Family*, 234–7.
[40] For instance, Cressy, *Birth, Marriage and Death*; and J.R. Gillis, *For Better, For Worse: British Marriages 1600 to Present* (Oxford, 1985).
[41] Cressy, *Birth, Marriage and Death*, 361–3, 370–1.
[42] The Mormon database notes the marriage registered at St Stephen's, but the accounts state that St Gregory's was decorated.
[43] Hunstanton parish register.
[44] See Table 5.4.
[45] Cressy, *Birth, Marriage and Death*, 370–1.
[46] See Table 5.1
[47] Pinners and coifes were both types of close-fitting caps worn by women.

William Spring received a silver salt with branches for three candles, and a round 'voyder' knife with a brazil wood handle, worth £36 14s 6d.

Comparison between the weddings shows that some costs fell to the groom and his family, and others were the responsibility of the bride. Nicholas purchased jewellery worth £18 10s: a simple gold wedding ring for £1, 'a pawnsey ring set with diamonds' for £14, 'an ear ring with 3 diamonds' for £2 12s 6d, and 'an enamelled ring with a hart' for 16s 6d. He was also responsible for providing the traditional wedding gifts for the guests and bridesmaids, spending £19 9s on gloves and points for the guests, and £2 on a pair of garters 'which were given to his two bridesmaids'. Nicholas paid for the music or 'waites', the bell-ringers, and the 'dressing up' of the church, none of which was expensive, amounting to a total of £2. There is little evidence of Alice or Hamon's involvement in Nicholas' wedding celebrations, although his then sixteen-year-old sister, Elizabeth, was provided with her first really expensive gown for the occasion.[48] The ceremony itself was carried out by a relative, the Le Stranges' 'cousin Stubbe', for which they paid a special licence. Elizabeth purchased no jewellery or gifts before her wedding, and there is no record of payments for entertainments or dressing the church other than silk fringe for '2 church cushions', so the groom's family must have footed these costs. In return, the Le Stranges hosted the wedding feast.[49] The feasting lasted for several days.

After the wedding celebrations, couples retired to their new home. Nicholas and Anne were to live with Sir Hamon and Alice in Hunstanton Hall. Increased food consumption in late September and early October 1630 suggest that they were received at the house with further celebrations. The major cost, however, had been fitting out a suite of rooms suitable for the couple. A total of £88 17s had been spent in the six months before the wedding for this purpose, mainly on three new beds. After her wedding, Elizabeth went to her husband's home at Pakenham in Suffolk, and it is likely this couple also began married life living with the groom's parents. Alice records 'the carters charges coming from Pakenham when they carried home my daughter Springes trunks' after the wedding. Elizabeth's parents initially came with her as shown by payments made to 'the keeper of the bowling ground at Pakenham', 'to the servants at Pakenham' and to the bell 'ringers at Pakenham' who welcomed the couple. Elizabeth returned to Hunstanton in the early months of 1637 for a visit, when she and her mother put together one last dress, an extravagant affair made of plush, brocaded tabby and silver and gold tissued grogram, possibly for a visit to court. The accounts record the ambiguity of Elizabeth's new status for her mother—in the margin, Alice writes 'Bess', as she always had done for purchases of her daughter's clothes, but in the body of text the fabrics are described as purchased for 'my daughter Springe'. The following February Elizabeth's first child was born, and £2 14s was given 'by Mr Strange to my daughter Springes nurse, midwife and keeper'.

---

[48] See Table 5.1.
[49] See Chapter 4: The meanings of food, and particularly Table 4.3.

CHILDHOOD AND CHILDCARE

The nature of early modern childhood has been hotly debated.[50] The dominant thesis of the 1960s and 1970s, put forward by historians such as Aries, Shorter, Plumb and Stone, was that children were treated with either indifference or harsh discipline, in sharp contrast with childhood in modern Western societies.[51] This view was revised in the 1980s by Pollock, Wrightson and Houlbrooke, building on earlier work by Macfarlane: they played down the extent of change over time, arguing that the majority of parents have always been loving and tender towards their children.[52] As Pollock points out, the differences of opinion stem largely from research methods, particularly the type of evidence used. Those arguing that parents were harsh and uncaring have relied on advice books, sermons, moral and medical tracts, and art, while the revisionists relied on personal documents such as diaries, memoirs and letters.[53] Household accounts have not been considered an important source for the history of childhood. Macfarlane was rightly scathing of Stone's use of account books to prove an absence of parental emotion: we should not expect to find overt statements of emotion recorded in accounts.[54] However, material culture has been used to support various arguments: Aries, Demos and Plumb all use evidence of children's clothing and lack of toys to argue that children were treated like adults before the eighteenth century.[55] Other topics on which household accounts shed light, such as wet nursing and educational practices, have been used to suggest that early modern child-rearing practices were harsh and uncaring.

In wealthy families, no sooner had the child's birth been celebrated with its christening than he or she was sent to live with a wet nurse. Alice Le Strange employed a nurse immediately after each child's birth. The children, if they lived long enough, were cared for by the nurse for two years or more: Nick for thirty-two months, Hamon and Roger for twenty-eight months, Jane for twenty-seven and Elizabeth for twenty-two months. Pollock, using evidence from four seventeenth-century diaries, found that children breast-fed by their mothers were weaned at between nine and nineteen months of age, averaging thirteen months.[56] The Townshends of Raynham had their children wet-nursed 'until they were a year

---

[50] Summarized in L. Pollock, *Forgotten Children: Parent–Child Relations from 1500–1900* (Cambridge, 1983), chs. 1 and 2.
[51] P. Aries, *Centuries of Childhood* (London, 1962); J.H. Plumb, 'The new world for children', in McKendrick et al. (eds), *Birth of a Consumer Society*; E. Shorter, *The Making of the Modern Family* (London, 1976); L. Stone, *The Family, Sex and Marriage in England 1500–1800* (London, 1977).
[52] Pollock, *Forgotten Children*; K. Wrightson, *English Society 1580–1680* (London, 1982); R. Houlbrooke, *The English Family 1450–1700* (London, 1984); A. Macfarlane, *The Family Life of Ralph Josselin* (Cambridge, 1970).
[53] Pollock, *Forgotten Children*, 22–3, 43–52.
[54] A. Macfarlane, 'Review of Lawrence Stone, *The Family, Sex and Marriage*', *History and Theory* 18:1 (1979), 116.
[55] Aries, *Centuries of Childhood*, chs. 2–4; J. Demos, *Family Life in a Plymouth Colony* (Oxford, 1970), especially 139–40; Plumb, 'New world for children', especially 65.
[56] Pollock, *Forgotten Children*, 220; V. Fildes, *Breasts, Bottles and Babies* (Edinburgh, 1986), 352–64.

old' in the 1620s and 1630s.[57] The Le Strange children were nursed for much longer. It seems that either weaning was delayed, possibly because of the health risks which accompanied complete weaning, or the children were cared for by the nurse for a time after weaning. Three of the children died while 'at nurse', and Roger Le Strange also appears to have had problems feeding. He was bought 'a sucking bottle' for 2d when he was ten months old and his nurse given money to buy him sugar, although he continued to be nursed for a year and a half after this episode.[58]

All the Le Strange nurses were paid 2s a week, or £5 4s annually, a very good wage for a woman in this period, although the Townshends were paying their nurses £10 a year by the late 1620s.[59] Nurses, like midwives, also received gifts of money at the child's christening. The Le Stranges gave their nurses an extra payment of between 2s and 10s when the child left to come home. In early modern thought a child's character was influenced by the person who provided their breast milk, making it important to choose a nurse carefully for her morals as well as for her ability to care for the child.[60] The high wage had a direct practical purpose of ensuring that the woman could eat well and produce plenty of milk. Private wet nurses typically came from the relatively comfortable households ranging from artisans to yeomen.[61] Campbell demonstrates that this was the case for the Townshends' nurses in the late 1620s and notes that three of their nurses who could be definitely identified were former servants.[62] The Le Stranges' nurses were identified in the accounts by the child's name, such as 'Roger's nurse', rather than their own, making them difficult to trace. However, four nurses appear making food gifts to the household between 1613 and 1626: nurses Longstraw, Cobbes, Costen and Lane. The Longstraws appear only occasionally in the accounts, but the Cobbes were Le Strange tenants at Barret Ringstead, while the Costens were carpenters resident in Sedgeford. Goodwife Lane was almost certainly the newly married wife of Thomas Lane. Thomas Lane was a Le Strange servant from 1616 to autumn 1619, when he married and became a substantial tenant at Hunstanton and Holme. The fact that Dorothy, John and Mary Le Strange, who all died while being nursed, were buried in Hunstanton indicates that the wet nurses employed by the Le Stranges were local.[63]

Stone and Shorter argued that wet nurses mistreated children and mortality among nurslings was high.[64] The Le Strange babies certainly experienced high mortality, but we should be cautious about attributing this to the quality of wet

---

[57] L. Campbell, 'Wet-nurses in early modern England: some evidence from the Townshend archive', *Medical History* 33 (1989), 364.

[58] Fildes, *Breasts, Bottles and Babies*, 309, notes that upright baby-feeding bottles first appear in the late medieval period.

[59] Campbell, 'Wet-nurses', 364.

[60] V. Fildes, *Wet nursing: a history from antiquity to the present* (Oxford, 1988), 73. See, for example, H. Bullinger, translated M. Coverdale, *The Christian State of Matrimony* (1575), fol. 82v.

[61] V. Fildes, 'The English wet-nurse and her role in infant care', *Medical History* 32 (1988), 150.

[62] Campbell, 'Wet-nurses', 362.

[63] London children who were nursed were usually buried at the parish of the nurse even if it was only 5 miles out of London: Fildes, 'The English wet-nurse'.

[64] Stone, *Family, Sex and Marriage*, 55; Shorter, *Making of the Modern Family*, 175–83.

nursing. Fildes has shown that wet nurses used by wealthy parents generally cared for babies well: misinterpretation comes from confusing these wet nurses with those who took in orphaned children for poor law authorities.[65] Campbell demonstrates that the wet nursing practices of the provincial gentry were rather different from those of the more intensively studied wealthy Londoners, a conclusion supported by the Le Strange evidence.[66] These children were nursed near their parents' home where they could easily be visited, and often by former servants who the mother knew and trusted. Such practices were in fact not far removed from the care of children in some modern households by a nanny, other than that the nurse was also providing breast milk. One of the few statements we have from the period stating the rationale behind wet nursing for gentry children was concerned about the emotional consequences for the mother of forming too strong an attachment to the baby. 'It breedeth much trouble to yourself and it would more grieve you if sucking your own milk it should miscarry, children being subject to many casualties', wrote Sir William Knowles to Dame Anne Newdigate, a gentlewoman who insisted on breastfeeding her own children.[67] Even if it did weaken the bond between mother and child, wet nursing did not amount to parental negligence.

In modern society the birth and early years of a child is accompanied by considerable expenditure on equipment, clothing and toys. In contrast, even a wealthy seventeenth-century family like the Le Stranges bought few things for their children. The only baby equipment was a new cradle purchased at the birth of each child, costing between 2s 8d and 6s. These cradles were given to the wet nurse as a precaution against the nurse overlaying or smothering the baby in her own bed.[68] There is no record of cots or special beds for children who had outgrown their cradles. A chair costing 1s was purchased for each of the girls—Jane when aged one year old and Elizabeth when almost two. Nor were there any significant purchases of toys. Roger was given a gig and whip (a form of spinning top) costing 3d when he was four or five years old, but otherwise toys for young children were passed down the family, home-made or received as gifts: they do not appear in the accounts. Purchasing toys may have been a role for doting grandparents: Hamon and Alice spent 3s 6d on 'toys for little Jack', Nicholas' five-year-old son, in 1641. There were purchases for the older boys: Nicholas and Hamon junior received bows and arrows when they were eleven and ten, respectively, and tennis balls, shuttlecocks and battledores, and sets of bowls, when they were sixteen and fifteen respectively. No toys were purchased at all for the girls.

Plumb argues that the widespread absence of purchased toys and children's books before the eighteenth century indicates a failure to understand the needs of children.[69] Interestingly, one of the first books for children, an edition of *Aesop's*

---

[65] Fildes, 'The English wet-nurse'.
[66] Campbell, 'Wet-nurses'.
[67] V.M. Larminie, *Wealth, Kinship and Culture: The Seventeenth Century Newdigates of Arbury and their World* (Woodbridge, 1995), 83–4. Anne's children were born 1595–1607.
[68] Fildes, *Wet Nursing*, 98–9.
[69] Plumb, 'New world for children', 66; see 87–90 for proliferation of commercially produced children's toys and games in the eighteenth century.

Fables, was published in 1692 by none other than Roger Le Strange, just as his children were growing up.[70] Despite modern parents' copious expenditure on toys, books and equipment for children, cross-cultural comparisons make it hard to argue that such material objects are necessary for the happy upbringing of children. The absence of purchased toys does not prove an absence of play. Plumb thought that seventeenth-century 'children and parents shared few pursuits together'.[71] Yet the few objects purchased for the Le Strange children show that the boys enjoyed hunting, playing bowls and music, like their father; while Elizabeth's mode of education meant that, from the age of two until marriage, she was rarely separated from her mother.

While equipment and toys occasioned little expense, clothing was a major cost. Tracing the clothing purchased for one child, Jane, in her first eight years, we can see how the expense was distributed, and how clothing changed as the child grew older. The total cost of Jane's clothes was £14 7s 2d or an average of £1 14s 6d a year.[72] Between the age of three months and fifteen months, hose or stockings, sleeves and petticoats were purchased. The following year, ribbon, laces and furred gloves were added; aged two, she began to wear a caul or tight-fitting cap, and her mother purchased linen sacking, woollen kersey and fustian to make her clothes. Costs in the first three years were close to the average because, although the items purchased were relatively cheap, many sets of clothes were needed to keep the child clean and neat. During the next three years, between the ages of three and six, clothing was surprisingly cheap at around half the average, and showed little variation from the earlier pattern. It was not until she reached the age of six that Jane had her first 'gown', something approximating an adult woman's dress, made of more expensive cloth containing silk rather than the cheap washable materials used in her younger years. Her gown was worn with a bodice and wire, which was used either for a ruff or to set her hair. That year, £4 13s 9d was spent on her clothing, not including shoes, roughly twice the average. Another similarly complex and expensive gown was made for her the next year, age seven.

The transition to adult-style clothes was particularly stark for boys, who went from infant dress of feminine petticoats to the male dress of hose and jacket. Nicholas' first suit is recorded in April 1611 when he was seven years old. The moment of transition is not recorded in the accounts for the other children, probably because clothing from the eldest boy and girl was reused. Historians of childhood such as Aries have stressed the significance of the age at which children were first dressed like adults, and argued that they were treated as adults too from this time onwards.[73] Seventeenth-century clothing practices for children do suggest that the age of seven was a significant milestone: children's clothing became strongly gendered, and boys were likely to begin their formal schooling at this age. In poorer families it was the age at which many children began to earn wages.

---

[70] Plumb, 'New world for children', 81. Roger's first child was born in 1678; see *ODNB*.
[71] Plumb, 'New world for children', 67.
[72] According to her inventory, Jane's apparel was worth £20 when she died: NCC INV/37/129B.
[73] Aries, *Centuries of Childhood*, 61; see also Demos, *Family Life*, 139.

However, this does not mean that children over the age of seven were treated like adults. In the Le Strange family, naming practices perhaps provide stronger evidence of parental attitudes to children: Alice ceased using childhood nicknames for her sons when they were aged thirteen to sixteen, and her daughter between nineteen and marriage, which suggests a later and more gradual transition to the 'end of childhood'.[74]

EDUCATION AND ADULT CHILDREN

In seventeenth-century elite families it was a mother's role to educate boys younger than seven and girls of all ages.[75] Alice Le Strange certainly seems to have taken charge of the children's early education: many years later, Hamon thanked her in his will for 'her most pious and painful care in the educacon of my children, those olive branches, wherewith God hath pleased to bless our table'.[76] A primer was purchased for each child to teach them to read: for Jane when she was four and a half years old, for Elizabeth when she was three years and ten months, and for Roger when he was just three and a half years old. The boys were also bought accidences (grammar text books): one for Nick when he was seven, and one for Roger when he was five and a half. Alice also bought Latin text books: 'a Cato and Puryhs for Roger', by the time he was 8. The boys entered formal education and a new phase of life when they were sent away to board with a tutor. As was typical for well-off boys, Nicholas, Hamon junior and Roger began formal education between the ages of seven and nine.[77] Sending boys away at this age was recommended by educational advice books as a way of instilling discipline and encouraging maturity.[78] Plumb cites the upbringing and education of Robert Walpole, born 1676, which was almost identical to that of the younger Le Strange boys, as evidence of harsh treatment, with Walpole 'rarely spending more than a few weeks at his Norfolk home' between the ages of six and twenty-two.[79] However, the detailed evidence from the Le Strange accounts demonstrates that the Le Strange boys were not exiled from their families during their education. Nicholas spent extended periods at home during his early schooling because of ill-health. Hamon junior had an unbroken education but was never far from Hunstanton. Mr Loades, who taught Hamon junior between the ages of eleven and sixteen and Nicholas from age thirteen to sixteen, in fact lodged with Alice's father in neighbouring Sedgeford. Girls were often not sent away at all.

---

[74] Larminie, *Wealth, Kinship and Culture*, 100, for similar practices in another gentry family.
[75] Houlbrooke, *The English Family*, 146–8; Heal and Holmes, *The Gentry*, 249–50. K. Charlton, *Women, Religion and Education in Early Modern England* (London, 1999), 203–19, for multiple examples of mothers as educators.
[76] The will of Sir Hamon Le Strange.
[77] Houlbrooke, *The English Family*, 150–1. H.M. Jewell, *Education in Early Modern England* (Basingstoke, 1997), 92–3.
[78] Houlbrooke, *The English Family*, 150–1.
[79] Plumb, 'New world of children', 66.

Family Life Cycle and Consumption 175

The Le Strange boys were provided with a model education typical of the 'educational revolution' amongst the English gentry and aristocracy of the late sixteenth and early seventeenth centuries.[80] It was designed not only to make them fit for political and legal offices of various kinds but also to develop them as cultured Renaissance gentlemen.[81] The boys progressed from their tutors in Norfolk to Eton, then to Cambridge, and, finally, to the Inns of Court.[82] Hamon junior praised his father fulsomely in the dedicatory passage of his first published work, *God's Sabbath*:

> I call the education you have bestowed on me almost peculiar to your self, because that whereas most parents are either sordid in their allowance, or negligent in instructing, or become lewd patterns to their children; you have in breeding me failed neither in purse, nor in precept, nor in example. I write not this to flatter you, but to manifest that I set due and just value upon your fatherly care....[83]

Figure 6.3 shows the educational phases the Le Strange boys passed through, reconstructed from the household accounts. None of the tutors employed by the Le Stranges lived at Hunstanton Hall. Initially, the two older boys were sent to different tutors. Nicholas was tutored by a Mr Sturges and boarded with Mr Norton, before moving on to Mr Briggs in Norwich. Hamon junior was taught by Mr Skelton and then Mr Wheelwright. While Hamon's education was continuous, Nicholas' was more patchy, interspersed with long periods of time at home. In part this was due to ill-health, but it is also likely that Nicholas' role as heir to the Le Strange estate made his formal education less important.[84] His notebooks show that he learnt much about account-keeping and estate management from his mother, so his time spent at home was not wasted.[85] The situation was different for the younger sons, whose future was less certain.

From 1617 onwards, when the two older boys were thirteen and twelve, respectively, their education followed a similar course. Nicholas joined Hamon junior with Mr Loades, who had already been teaching him for a year and a half. They stayed together with this tutor until 1620, when they were sixteen and fifteen years old, respectively. The codicil of the will of Alice's father, Richard Stubbe, makes it clear that Mr Loades lived and taught from Stubbe's house in Sedgeford: 'I the said Richard Stubb will and devise that Mr Philipp Loades shall have his lodging diet and washing for himself, Mr Nicholas Le Strange, Mr Hamond Le Strange and Mr William Bendish at my house at Sedgeford during half a year next

---

[80] L. Stone, 'The educational revolution in England, 1560–1640', *Past and Present* 28 (1964), 41–80.
[81] Heal and Holmes, *The Gentry*, 245.
[82] This pattern of education is identified in J.H. Hexter, 'The education of the aristocracy in the Renaissance', *Journal of Modern History* 22:1 (1950), 6.
[83] H. L'Estrange esq., *God's Sabbath before, under the law and under the Gospel briefly vindicated from novell and heterodox assertations* (Cambridge, 1641).
[84] See L. Pollock, '"Teach her to live under obedience": The making of women in the upper ranks of early modern England', *Continuity and Change* 4:2 (1989), 248–9, on the lesser importance of formal education for eldest sons.
[85] The notebooks of Nicholas Le Strange: LEST/KA6, LEST/KA9, LEST/KA10 and LEST/KA 24.

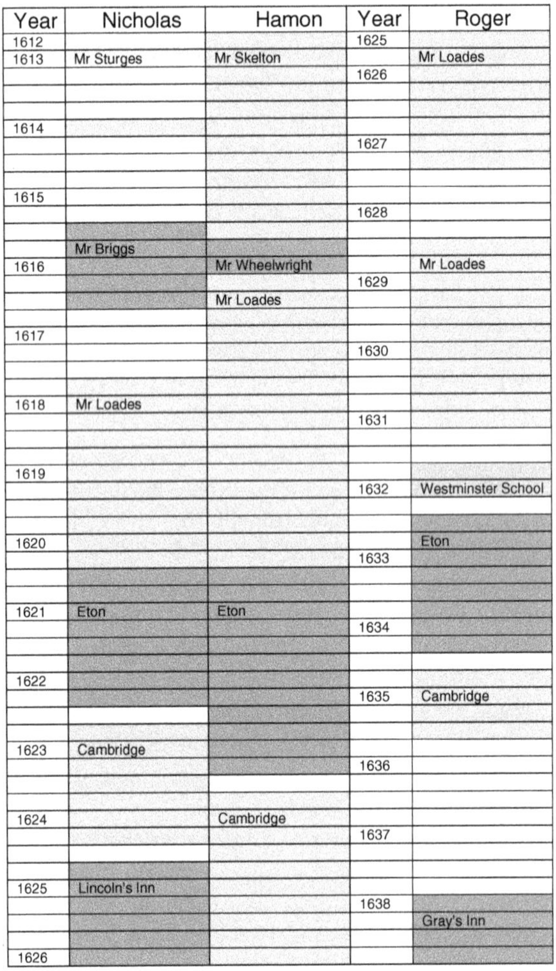

Year	Nicholas	Hamon	Year	Roger
1612			1625	
1613	Mr Sturges	Mr Skelton		Mr Loades
			1626	
1614				
			1627	
1615				
			1628	
1616	Mr Briggs	Mr Wheelwright		Mr Loades
			1629	
		Mr Loades		
1617				
			1630	
1618	Mr Loades			
			1631	
1619				
			1632	Westminster School
1620				Eton
			1633	
1621	Eton	Eton		
			1634	
1622				
			1635	Cambridge
1623	Cambridge			
			1636	
1624		Cambridge		
			1637	
1625	Lincoln's Inn			
			1638	
				Gray's Inn
1626				

Fig. 6.3. Phases of the boys' education.

Sources: Le Strange disbursement accounts; LEST/P6, P7.

after my decease at the onlie costes and charges of my executors.'[86] Both the will and codicil were witnessed by Loades. The provision was carried out: the boys remained with Mr Loades for six months after Stubbe's death, before their ages, and the family's increased income, made it a suitable time to send them to Eton College, where they were 'placed' on 18 May 1620.[87]

Eton was used as a finishing school for the Le Strange boys. Being tutored in Norfolk provided them with a sound intellectual education but limited social

[86] The will of Richard Stubbe: NA Prob/11/135.
[87] LEST/Q38, fol. 45.

interaction:[88] Eton allowed them to mix with a large number of boys of their own class. Not all their pursuits were intellectual: Nicholas took his viol with him to Eton, while Hamon had singing lessons. Eton was not cheap: a quarter year for the two boys cost £9 for board and washing plus further charges of between £1 and £3 for books, a study, and school rights, on top of transport costs for the boys, their trunks and bedding. In comparison, the Le Stranges had paid Mr Loades only £1 2s a quarter for both boys.[89] Nicholas stayed at Eton for two years, before moving on at the age of eighteen to Trinity College, Cambridge. Hamon stayed a further year, going up to Cambridge at the same age and entering Christ's College.[90] Nicholas left Cambridge in 1624 and was admitted to Lincoln's Inn in November that year. Hamon again stayed longer, spending three years in Cambridge, entering Lincoln's Inn in June 1626. Prest's study of the Inns of Court suggests that 'the accepted minimum cost of maintaining a student at the inns was £40 a year during our period', although it could be considerably more.[91] Nicholas spent £96 8s 11d during his time in London between November 1624 and April 1626, or approximately £64 a year. These figures do not include expenditure on clothing, as that was still managed mostly by his mother from home. Nonetheless, he does not seem to have been overly extravagant. A bill for books of £6 3s 5d and a doctor's bill of £5 were some of his largest expenses, although he was also given spending money which is not itemized.

Roger Le Strange, born in December 1616, was over ten years younger than his two brothers, and did not begin his formal education until 1625. His education followed a very similar pattern, as Figure 6.3 shows. The Le Stranges seem to have found a tutor they respected and trusted in Mr Loades: Roger, aged eight and a half, began his education with him and remained with Mr Loades until he went to Westminster School at the age of fourteen.[92] Westminster, an innovation for the family, was not a success: in less than six months, Roger became ill and returned home. A few months later, in April 1632, he was sent to Eton, where he seems to have got on better, remaining for just over two years. As with his brothers, Eton provided not only an intellectual education but also music lessons on the viol and, in Roger's case, an opportunity to act in a number of plays. In November 1634, just short of his eighteenth birthday, Roger went to Sidney Sussex College, Cambridge. He was there for less than a year before leaving in the summer of 1635, having been 'cut out of the buttery'. He left a string of debts behind him, including a pawned viol, which his parents called upon his brother Hamon to sort out. Given that the money owed amounted to only £11 3s 5d, it is unclear what lay behind this

---

[88] Stone, 'The educational revolution', 46. He gives examples of tutors and small schools in Norfolk sending boys directly to Cambridge University in the early seventeenth century.
[89] Mr Loades' charges had increased by the time he taught Roger to £2 15s a quarter, presumably because he was now paying for his own premises.
[90] The accounts do not record which college Hamon went to: the college name is provided by *ODNB*.
[91] W. Prest, *The Inns of Court under Elizabeth I and the Early Stuarts* (London, 1972), 27–8.
[92] An apparent gap in Roger's time with Mr Loades could be caused by two pages missing from the accounts of 1627.

episode. It was followed by a period spent at home, until, at the age of twenty-one, Roger was allowed to go to the Inns of Court, entering Grey's Inn in February 1638.

The contrast between the boys' education and that of their sister Elizabeth is stark. Girls of her status were typically educated in a domestic setting in this period, either in their own home or by lodging with another household of higher status. There is no firm consensus of what the 'typical' experience of a young gentlewoman would have been.[93] Nonetheless, Elizabeth's education seems to have been particularly sheltered. No books were bought for her other than her first primer, and, with one exception when she joined her brother Roger for singing lessons at Hunstanton aged twenty, she received no paid tuition. She certainly learnt to read and later to write: an inkhorn and knife were purchased for her as well as thimbles in 1623 when she was nine. A contrasting example of a girl's education is provided by Lettice Newdigate, born into an 'upper middling' gentry family in Warwickshire in 1604. Her brothers were educated in a similar fashion to the Le Strange boys. Lettice received private tuition for at least five years in her adolescence between 1616 and 1620, and later attended an academy in Deptford to learn French and other accomplishments at the cost of £22 a year.[94] Elizabeth did visit the houses of other Norfolk gentry. At the age of thirteen she visited Rougham with her eldest brother for a short time; she went to Bracondale for a while when she was seventeen, and Stiffkey when she was nineteen.[95] On the whole, however, Elizabeth appears to have been educated by her parents, probably very largely by Alice, who certainly had many skills to teach her daughter. The household had a large library which Elizabeth could have used.

While modern commentators criticize early modern parents for using wet nurses and sending boys away to school at a young age, one can imagine early modern parents of the gentry class being horrified by the lack of support accorded to adult children by parents in modern society. An early modern family's status was maintained by passing on the core of the landed estate to the eldest son, giving daughters large enough dowries to allow them to marry men of similar wealth, and providing younger sons with lands and allowances. The cost of these provisions far outweighed the expense of care, clothing and education for younger children. From the modern perspective, such strategies tend to be interpreted as overly 'controlling',[96] but it is likely that early modern families saw it as a sign of affection and respect for their children. Although resources were allotted unevenly to children, even younger sons received enough to live very comfortably by the standards of the day.

---

[93] The best introduction is Pollock, 'Teach her to live'; see also Heal and Holmes, *The Gentry*, 250–4, and A. Fraser, *The Weaker Vessel: Women's Lot in Seventeenth-Century England* (London, 1985), 133–52.
[94] Larminie, *Wealth, Kinship and Culture*, 120.
[95] Rougham was home of the Yelvertons, Alice's sister and brother-in-law. Tower House in Bracondale was the home of Richard Catelyn and his wife Dorothy, who was Anne Le Strange's aunt. The Townshends lived at Stiffkey.
[96] For example, Stone, *Crisis of the Aristocracy*, 594.

Discussions of gentry marriages in seventeenth-century England concentrate on arranged marriages and marriage settlements.[97] The household accounts provide no evidence of how Nicholas' or Elizabeth's marriages were arranged, although it seems certain their parents played a large role. The quantity of money and property exchanged in their marriage settlements dominated the overall finances of the Le Strange household from 1630 onwards.[98] Anne Lewkenor and Elizabeth Le Strange's portions of £3500 were higher than portions of some aristocratic women, although Stone notes that in 1624–49 the average marriage portion offered by peers was £5400:[99] Heal and Holmes found that £3800 'was seldom or never heard of for a knight' in the 1620s.[100] In both cases, the portion was paid very largely from parent to parent, and not to the married couple. The bulk of the sum was paid at the time of the wedding, with further instalments arriving later. The Le Stranges received £2700 from Lady Lewkenor, Anne's mother, on or just after the wedding, of which £50 was given to Nicholas. The final £800 does not appear in Alice's receipt accounts, so may also have been paid directly to Nicholas. At Elizabeth's wedding, the Le Stranges paid £2000 to Sir William Spring, the groom's father. A further £1200 was paid a year later, and the final £300 after that.

The dominance of parents in wedding arrangements was not universal; instead, it was characteristic of those children who were heirs to an estate or who were destined to marry an heir, as in Elizabeth's case. The arrangements surrounding the wedding of Hamon Le Strange junior, the second son, provide a contrast. Hamon junior had inherited property from Richard Stubbe. He received lands in Holme with a sale price of £1000, as well as Holme Parsonage, worth £70 a year, from his grandfather.[101] While Nicholas had to wait for his far more valuable estate, Hamon junior gained control of his inheritance at the age of twenty-one, in 1626. Hamon more or less disappears from the accounts at this date, just after he moved to London to attend Lincoln's Inn: Alice no longer purchased his clothes, as she did for the other children as unmarried adults. The fact that he appears in the accounts lending money to his parents between 1630 and 1634 indicates both that he was quite well off and that he remained on good terms with them. In July 1634, he married Dorothy Laverick, the daughter and heir of Edmund Laverick of Upwell in Norfolk.[102] This event caused barely a ripple of recognition in the Le Strange accounts: there is nothing recorded in the disbursement accounts, no gifts of silver, no evidence of other family members attending the wedding. The only entry relating to Hamon in that half year records the repayment of £200, which he had

---

[97] For example Stone, *Crisis of the Aristocracy*, ch. 11; J.P. Cooper, 'Patterns of inheritance and settlement by great landowners from the fifteenth to the eighteenth centuries', in J. Goody et al. (eds.), *Family and Inheritance* (Cambridge, 1976); J. Habbakuk, *Marriage, Debt and the Estates System: English Landownership 1650–1950* (Oxford, 1994); Heal and Holmes, *The Gentry*, 60–91.
[98] See above, Life cycle and expenditure.
[99] Stone, *Crisis of the Aristocracy*, 790. In 1600–24 £3800 was average among the peerage.
[100] Heal and Holmes, *The Gentry*, 142.
[101] LEST/P10 'lands and other gifts of Father'; the will of Richard Stubbe.
[102] Information from *ODNB*. The Lavericks were a minor family. It is not clear if they owned manorial property. The Bells, relatives of the Le Stranges, were manorial lords in Upwell, but the parish contained a number of manors.

lent his parents. Notes in the back of a later account book record that the manor of West Winch, which had belonged to Richard Stubbe but was inherited by the Yelvertons, was purchased in 1633 for £1796 and 'settled upon my son Hamon Le Strange'.[103] From the time of his marriage until 1649 Hamon junior received an annuity from the profits of West Winch, paid to him by his parents. Hamon lived on his property in neighbouring Holme after his marriage, styled himself 'esquire', and became one of the many friends and relatives who sent gifts of food to the Le Strange kitchen.[104]

Further evidence of the differential treatment of the children is provided by the payment of allowances. Nicholas received no regular allowance until he married. He was given occasional gifts of money, and his mother purchased his clothes and paid any bills he accumulated. After his marriage he received £200 a year, rising to £300 and £310 in 1635 and 1636. Hamon junior received £40 a year after his marriage, rising to £60 in 1638–48. Elizabeth, on the other hand, only received an allowance before marriage. From the age of twenty-one in March 1635, she received £40 a year 'for apparel', although her mother continued to buy clothes for her. This situation did not last long as she married in October 1636. After her wedding she received no further financial support from her parents. It is likely that instead she had an allowance from her husband, as was typical for married women. Alice Le Strange's allowance was set at £66 13s 4d a year throughout her married life.[105] Roger, with no significant property to inherit, was treated much like Elizabeth. He received an allowance of £30 a year sporadically from the age of nineteen onwards, although his parents also bought him clothes and paid off his debts. His allowance rose to £100 a year in 1648, when he fled abroad as a result of his Royalist activities during the Civil War. He did not marry until long after his parents died. He was not mentioned in his father's will, but other sources note that he received 'an inheritance sufficient for him to live "like a gentleman" in London' after Sir Hamon's death in 1654.[106]

So were sons or daughters more expensive? Erickson found that, for middling and poor families, there was no distinction in the cost of bringing up boys and girls.[107] Studies of the gentry, however, are littered with statements bemoaning the crippling cost of daughters' marriage portions to their families: Stone writes that 'the rise in the size of portions made girls particularly expensive and unwanted'.[108] The costs incurred by the Le Strange children are summarized in Table 6.4. Boys cost more to educate: Nicholas' education cost £144, Hamon's £138, Roger's £275, and Elizabeth's a little over £3, in total. Girls cost slightly more to clothe:

---

[103] LEST/P10.
[104] Before his death in 1660, Hamon junior married a second time, to Judith Bagnall of London, who is mentioned in Alice's will of 1656. He ended his life living in Pakenham close to his sister Elizabeth. See *ODNB* and will of Hamon Le Strange.
[105] For examples of wives' allowances, see J.T. Cliffe, *The World of the Country House in Seventeenth-Century England* (New Haven, 1999), 65–6.
[106] *ODNB*.
[107] A.L. Erickson, *Women and Property in Early Modern England* (London, 1993), 59.
[108] Stone, *Crisis of the Aristocracy*, 173; Heal and Holmes, *The Gentry*, 141.

Table 6.4. The cost of the Le Strange children from birth to 1654 (£)

	Education	Clothing	Allowances or marriage portion	Subtotal	Miscellaneous	Total
Nicholas	144	359	6860	7363	219	7582
Hamon	138	123	800 (+ 1792)	1061 (or 2853)	37	1098 (or 2890)
Roger	275	273	666	1214	565	1809
Elizabeth	3	423	3500	3923	127	4050

Note: Miscellaneous includes all costs assigned to that child in the account that do not fall under any other headings.
Sources: Le Strange disbursement accounts; LEST/P6, P7, P10.

up to marriage Alice Le Strange spent £423 on Elizabeth's clothing, compared with £359 on Nicholas'.[109] Hamon's clothing was cheaper because he bought his own once he reached the age of twenty-one, while Roger's was less than Nicholas' because he did not marry, with all the clothing expense that that entailed. It is true that Elizabeth's marriage portion constitutes one of the largest lump sum payments in the accounts, but the allowances paid to adult sons also added up to considerable totals. The allowance that Nicholas received after his marriage eventually amounted to almost double Elizabeth's portion. Younger sons were much cheaper.[110] It might be fair to add the cost of West Winch manor at £1792 to Hamon junior's total. This would make Roger the cheapest child, despite the cost of his education, and the frequency with which his parents had to pay his debts.

CONCLUSION

Alice and Hamon Le Strange were successful in many ways. Their estate was not greatly enlarged, but improved during their lifetime. They appear to have been a remarkably harmonious family: not only did Hamon and Alice enjoy a long and productive marriage, but all their children, with the possible exception of Roger, remained in close contact as adults. These contacts are evident in the loans of money that went to and from the parental household; in the book of jests compiled by Nicholas, which reveals their strong social contacts; and in other ways. Hamon junior lived at the end of his life in Pakenham, Suffolk, the seat of his sister Elizabeth's husband, Sir William Spring; he dedicated one of his published works to Anne, Nicholas' wife.[111] Alice and Hamon left many descendants, with Hamon listing fourteen grandchildren in his will (Figure 6.4). It was unlucky, therefore,

---

[109] There are problems with quantifying Nicholas' clothing expenses; however, see Chapter 5: Textiles and clothing.
[110] Cooper provides a summary of the treatment of younger sons in appendix 2 of 'Patterns of inheritance'. See also Heal and Holmes, *The Gentry*, 143.
[111] H. L'Estrange esq., *An answer to the Marques of Worcester's last paper*... (London, 1651).

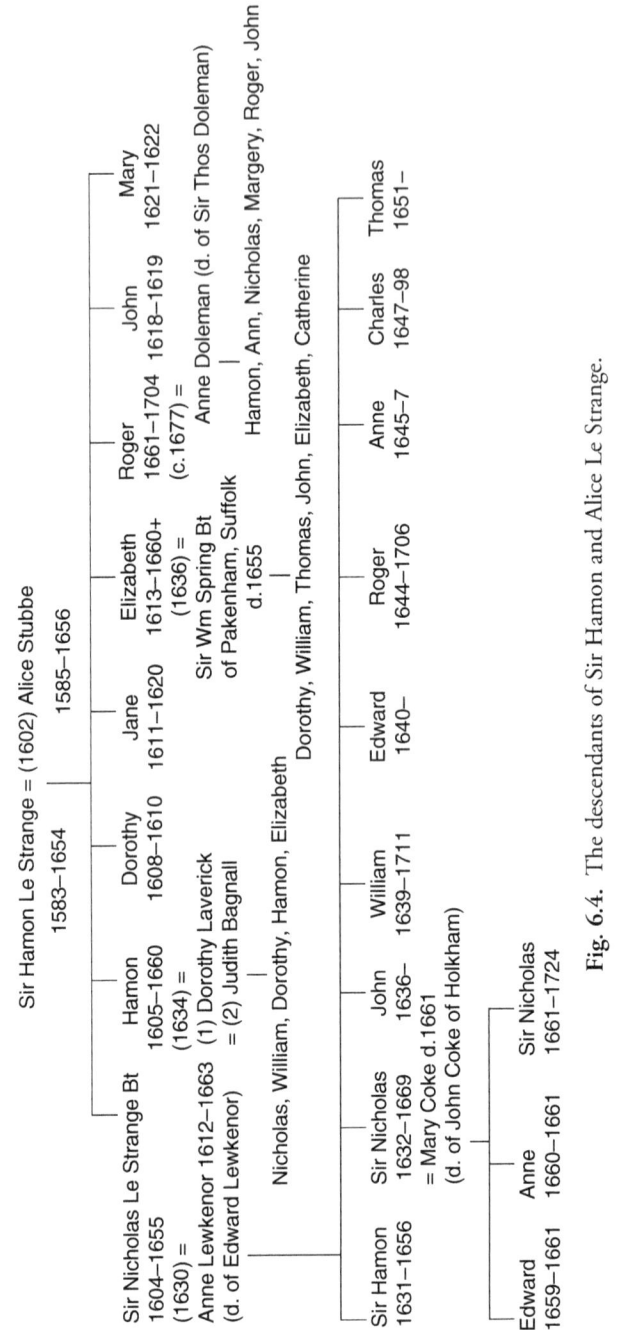

Sir Hamon Le Strange = (1602) Alice Stubbe
1583–1654   1585–1656

Sir Nicholas Le Strange Bt
1604–1655
(1630) =
Anne Lewkenor 1612–1663
(d. of Edward Lewkenor)

Hamon
1605–1660
(1634) =
(1) Dorothy Laverick
= (2) Judith Bagnall
|
Nicholas, William, Dorothy, Hamon, Elizabeth

Dorothy
1608–1610

Jane
1611–1620

Elizabeth
1613–1660+
(1636) =
Sir Wm Spring Bt
of Pakenham, Suffolk
d.1655
|
Dorothy, William, Thomas, John, Elizabeth, Catherine

Roger
1661–1704
(c.1677) =
Anne Doleman (d. of Sir Thos Doleman)
|
Hamon, Ann, Nicholas, Margery, Roger, John

John
1618–1619

Mary
1621–1622

Sir Hamon
1631–1656

Sir Nicholas
1632–1669
= Mary Coke d.1661
(d. of John Coke of Holkham)

John
1636–

William
1639–1711

Edward
1640–

Roger
1644–1706

Anne
1645–7

Charles
1647–98

Thomas
1651–

Edward
1659–1661

Anne
1660–1661

Sir Nicholas
1661–1724

Fig. 6.4. The descendants of Sir Hamon and Alice Le Strange.

that a period of demographic misfortune undid much of what they had achieved and took the family full circle. After Sir Hamon's death in 1654, Alice died in the autumn of 1656, predeceased by Nicholas in 1655 and his eldest son Hamon in early 1656. Anne Le Strange died in 1663, and her and Nicholas' son and heir, Nicholas junior, in 1669, leaving his son, another Nicholas, as heir at only eight years old.

Good quality household accounts studied intensively, as is possible with the Le Strange archive, provide a valuable contribution to understanding of early modern childhood and family relationships. Lacking any overt statements of emotion or feeling, they do not replace letters and diaries but complement them, providing a level of detail and accuracy about particular events not available from other sources. The spending of money is not disconnected from emotion, but we can only speculate about exact motivations for the spending patterns observed. The 'old school' of the history of childhood based its assumptions on an overly positive view of modern childcare and an exaggerated impression of the harshness of early modern childhood, creating a story of dramatic change over time. The revisionist school, in its efforts to correct these conclusions, has perhaps underplayed the extent of change over time in child-rearing practices. The Le Strange accounts demonstrate that childhood in an early seventeenth-century gentry family was quite different in many ways from that in modern England, but provide no evidence that the Le Strange children were not happy, or the parents uncaring. Patterns of education were strongly gendered, although it is impossible to judge the exact quality of the education received from the evidence in the accounts. Expenditure on children was gendered too, but, viewed over the parents' lifetime, the cost of a daughter's dowry was not as disproportionate as some commentators have assumed: elder sons could be much more expensive.

7

Elite Consumption

Payd to my brother Spelmans man to his m[ast]ers use for a Quadrant 14s, for Aristotles Ethickes 4s & for Vertagan 3s 6d.[1]

This chapter focuses on those consumption activities that were specific to the gentry and aristocracy. Although the gentry consumed food, clothing and furnishings in ways that denoted their wealth and status, these types of consumption were shared in different forms by those lower down the social scale. In contrast, the exercise of county-level political, legal and military offices; regular travel; certain leisure activities and cultural pursuits; and large-scale building works and estate improvement were largely the exclusive preserve of the elite. Education of the type received by the Le Strange sons also falls into this category. This education, itself an innovation of the late sixteenth century, fostered a distinctive lifestyle amongst the rural gentry of the early seventeenth century, one that combined a number of contradictory influences. Some were traditional. Just as in the medieval period gentry wealth and power rested on manorial landlordship, legal administration, political representation and military responsibilities, conspicuous leisure was spent hunting and hawking, offering and receiving hospitality, and playing games. Alongside these activities the cultural influence of humanist ideas and higher education gave rise to a new ideal—that of the Renaissance gentleman with his library, who took a learned but amateur interest in fine art, architecture, history, geography, literature, music and science. In the sixteenth century these strands were fused in works such as Thomas Elyot's *The Book named the Governor* (1531) and Sir Thomas Hoby's translation of *The Courtier* by Castiglione (1561), which set out the ideal education, behaviour and pastimes of a gentleman.[2] The most popular early seventeenth-century example of this genre, Henry Peacham's *The Complete Gentleman* (1622), was owned by Sir Hamon and placed its emphasis almost entirely on Renaissance learning rather than on the traditions of hunting, hawking and governance. A third and no less important influence was always present in this melting pot—religion. Sir Hamon, like many English gentry in the early seventeenth century, was a convinced Calvinist. While typically associated with the merchant class, Calvinism sat easily with the English gentry. The Calvinist idea of business with a social conscience accorded well with the model of the

---

[1] Disbursement accounts, 1608: LEST/P6.
[2] P. Burke, *The Renaissance* (Basingstoke, 1987), 41.

paternalistic landlord.[3] On the other hand, the Calvinist prescription of hard work and thrift appears to be in direct opposition to the gentry's need to display leisure and wealth as a mark of status. Sir Hamon displayed this apparent contradiction in his behaviour, combining devout religious belief with a love of hawking and hunting, bowls and cards.

What is less frequently commented on is the degree to which the display of gentry status through exclusive pastimes and spending patterns was largely a male preserve. Women were excluded from holding political, legal and military office. It is true that there were women who hunted and hawked or were experts in various forms of culture and learning. There were even more who designed their own country houses and improved their estates. But these pursuits were normal for gentlemen and unusual for women: there is ample evidence of participation by Sir Hamon from his notebook, library and the accounts. For Alice there is very little other than the recounting of 'merry jests', a form of entertainment that was not restricted to the gentry. Chapter 2 explained how Alice's activities accorded with those of the ideal housewife and concentrated on good management of the household and estate. This chapter shows how Sir Hamon aspired to the ideal of a Renaissance gentleman by displaying his learning, political competence and sporting prowess. Thorstein Veblen described wealthy women acting as vicarious consumers for their husbands. By spending generously on their own clothing and home furnishings, and through their leisure time spent in idle pursuits, women were the conspicuous consumers who displayed their husbands' status.[4] Historians have been slow to realize that this model of consumer roles, while perhaps an accurate description of the late nineteenth-century American business elite, does not apply to all elites in all places. In early seventeenth-century England the role of conspicuous consumption, of asserting elite status through consumption behaviour, fell predominantly to men.

POLITICAL AND LEGAL EXPENSES

This book is not about the nature of early Stuart government or politics. Those topics are covered elsewhere.[5] Instead, it views the costs of political and legal office, taxation and charity from the point of view of consumption. It might seem to be stretching a point to envisage the gentry 'consuming' political office, but in a way they did. Just as the buildings and leaseholds of an estate had to be maintained in order to keep or improve rental income, so political and legal offices had to be held to maintain or improve standing amongst the English elite. Office-holding incurred costs in the form of travel, accommodation, entertainment and hospitality.

---

[3] R.H. Tawney, *Religion and the Rise of Capitalism* (London, 1937), ch. 2 (iii); F. Heal and C. Holmes, *The Gentry in England and Wales 1500–1700* (Basingstoke, 1994), 360, 370–1.
[4] T. Veblen, *The Theory of the Leisure Class*, first published 1899 (Oxford, 2007).
[5] A.H. Smith, *County and Court: Government and Politics in Norfolk, 1558–1603* (Oxford, 1974); A. Fletcher, *Reform of the Provinces: The Government of Stuart England* (New Haven, 1986).

It provided opportunities of sociability as well as the exercise of power. For the county gentry, politics, law, taxation and charity were tightly intertwined. A place on the bench, as a Justice of the Peace (JP), was not only an important indicator of status but also an opening to involvement in tax assessment and a means of influence in legal cases. The social legislation implemented at the quarter sessions regulated the poor not deemed worthy of charity: setting wage rates, punishing vagrancy, apprenticing pauper children and maintaining houses of correction.

Sir Hamon quickly built on his wealth and status by taking up political and legal offices within the county. By 1606, at the age of twenty-three, he was already active as a JP. In 1608 he was appointed sheriff of Norfolk, and in 1613, 1620 and 1625 he was chosen as a Member of Parliament (MP). He served as a colonel of the militia, and was a Deputy Lieutenant for Norfolk from 1625. These offices were largely unpaid and brought onerous administrative duties. The ownership of a manorial estate entailed litigation over property rights in order to maintain that income. Wealth brought obligations in the form of taxation. In the twenty years between the start of the accounts in 1606 and April 1626, Sir Hamon Le Strange spent £161 19s 3d on expenses connected to political office, £195 2s 5d on private legal expenses and £187 9s 2d on taxes and local rates. This amounted to an average of between £8 and £10 a year on each category.

JPs were the judiciary of the quarter sessions, county courts held four times a year. The list of JPs for each county was an important indicator of rank. Smith notes that 'each justice sat on the Bench according to a strict order of precedence governed by his "placing" in the commission of the peace'.[6] In 1608 Sir Hamon Le Strange was placed thirtieth out of a total of fifty-nine JPs listed for Norfolk: below those with strong court connections and older members of knightly families, but above the esquires and a number of other knights. By 1636 he had risen to the rank of twenty-fourth out of sixty-two Norfolk justices.[7] Sir Hamon was active in Norfolk's northern division, for which courts were held at Fakenham and Little Walsingham. In 1606, for instance, the accounts record him travelling to at least two sessions at Fakenham, as well as another 'meeting of the justices there'. Attending the quarter sessions courts at Fakenham or Walsingham was not an expensive undertaking. It was rare for him to spend more than 10s 'laid out at Fakenham' and 'for horsemeat at the sessions', and 7s was typical. This covered food and accommodation for himself, a servant and their horses, but little else. It was paid for partly by the small allowance of 2s a day received by JPs for attendance at sessions.[8]

The more significant cost of being a JP was in time spent between sessions, taking examinations of accused parties, recording confessions and witness statements, signing recognizances and so on. Surviving quarter sessions papers from 1614–16, 1620–4 and 1627–32 show that Sir Hamon Le Strange was fully

---

[6] A.H. Smith, *County and Court: Government and Politics in Norfolk, 1558–1603* (Oxford, 1974), 60.
[7] J.H. Gleason, *The Justices of the Peace in England 1558–1640* (Oxford, 1969), 151–8.
[8] Smith, *County and Court*, 60.

involved in all these inter-sessional activities.[9] Some of these duties also appear in the household accounts; for instance, in 1618, 4s 8d was spent 'for horsemeat and Mr Strange his diet at Burnham and his 3 men when he went to bind out apprentices'. Inter-sessional duties often required JPs to work in pairs: Hamon tended to work with relatives—his father-in-law Richard Stubbe in the 1610s, his cousin Le Strange Mordaunt in the 1620s and his nephew William Yelverton in the early 1630s. He took his duties seriously. He wrote to his fellow JP and friend Sir Roger Townshend in 1636 noting: 'others will dispense themselves from the King's service to attend the humour of self pleasing privacy and leave us the anvil of the common troubles and disquiets of these parts, wherein have they erred against religion, reason and all moral and manly rule.' He proposed that they should lobby for more JPs for north-west Norfolk to ease their burden.[10]

Quarter sessions do not seem to have provided an occasion for much socializing, but the assizes were a different affair. Twice yearly assizes in summer and winter involved visits to the county by specially appointed itinerant royal justices to deal with more serious crimes. Whereas quarter sessions held at various locations around the county were normally attended by only a minority of the available JPs at any one time, all JPs were required to attend the assizes.[11] Norfolk assize meetings were held at Norwich and Thetford. The Le Stranges' regular summer and winter visits to Norwich were in part motivated by Sir Hamon's need to be present at the assizes. The fact that Alice accompanied him is a strong indicator of the social nature of these occasions. Sir Hamon's 'charges' at the assizes were normally between £2 and £4. Sometimes they were itemized. For instance, 'horsemeat and for our own mens charges & Mr Strange his ordinary at The Maids Head 5s during the Assizes' in Norwich in 1617 came to a total of 16s 11d.

In 1609, when Sir Hamon was Sheriff of Norfolk, the costs were of a different order. It was the sheriff's duty to organize feasts for the assize judges. The bill for August 1609 came to £84 19s 7s.[12] This was more than half of the total amount spent by Sir Hamon on office-holding in the whole of period from 1606 to 1626. The political and legal power of the sheriff had been much reduced during the sixteenth century but many administrative duties remained. The sheriff had to make the practical arrangements for all the quarter sessions, setting the dates and places and empanelling the juries, as well as overseeing the implementation of orders, judgments and decisions made by the JPs. He organized the assizes and entertained the judges, undertook administrative duties for the muster commissions and organized county elections.[13] While there is evidence that in some counties gentlemen tried to avoid the office of sheriff, Smith demonstrates that in

---

[9] NRO, Quarter sessions files C/S3/boxes 18–20, 22–4, 26–8.
[10] Quoted in Fletcher, *Reform in the Provinces*, 11 (from LEST/NF5). On Sir Roger's activities as a JP, see L. Campbell, 'Sir Roger Townshend and his Family: A Study of Gentry Life in Early Seventeenth Century Norfolk', Ph.D. thesis (East Anglia, 1990), 97–100.
[11] Smith, *County and Court*, 90; J.S. Cockburn, *A History of the English Assizes 1558–1714* (Cambridge, 1972), 157.
[12] Cockburn, *Assizes*, 54–5; Smith, *County and Court*, 153.
[13] Smith, *County and Court*, 139–41, 146.

Norfolk during the 1590s and 1600s there was competition for this office amongst a county gentry riven by factions, demonstrating that although the office was costly it still offered opportunities to exercise political and legal influence.[14]

Whether gentlemen were appointed or elected to office, costs inevitably arose. Sheriffs were appointed, and in 1608 Sir Hamon spent £4 8s 2d 'disbursed for the suing out of my commission for the Shreevalty'. MPs were elected. In 1613 Sir Hamon spent £5 3d 'laid out at Swaffham at the election of the Knightes of the Shire'. The costs of election in 1620 were more substantial: he spent £20 3s 4d 'laid out as appear by a bill of charges at the election of the Knights of the Shire', as well as 9s 'paid to divers messengers for bringing letters for the election'.[15] Attending Parliament required a prolonged trip to London, although Sir Hamon typically travelled to London at least once a year in any case. Parliament itself does not warrant mention in the household accounts, suggesting that no specific expenses were incurred, although the London journey and accommodation in the capital were certainly expensive.[16] For Sir Hamon, his duties as an MP, like his work as a JP, does not appear to have been a mere show of status. He kept a notebook in which he drafted possible bills for Parliament to remedy the problems he encountered as a JP and elsewhere concerning bastardy, brewers, unlicensed alehouses, the sale of corn, dove houses and settlement.[17]

The final set of county offices were connected to the militia and the defence of the country. Sir Hamon was a captain and then a colonel of the militia and Deputy Lieutenant for Norfolk from 1625. Fletcher describes the deputy lieutenancy as 'the pinnacle in the hierarchy of county offices'.[18] There were six deputy lieutenants under the leadership of the Earl of Arundel as Norfolk's Lieutenant. They were charged with organizing the recruitment and training of the local militia, which, given the need to secure Norfolk's long coastline, was a substantial body of men: 4744 in 1628.[19] This is one office that Sir Hamon tried to avoid. He wrote to Lord Hobart on the matter, claiming: 'The weakness of my body, obscurity of my situation and the great and contented fruition of myself at the plain labours of the plough (to which I have put my hand and will not pull back) make me say with Jacob I have enough.'[20] In reality he was preoccupied with extensive building works to extend Hunstanton Hall. Sir Hamon was appointed to the office nonetheless and was Deputy Lieutenant during a disastrous spell for Norfolk's militia when the whole organization almost collapsed.[21] These problems make no mark on the accounts. In the period when he was colonel Sir Hamon made various gifts to men at the musters: in 1618 Alice notes that he paid 'to my cousin Phillip Bell his

---

[14] Smith, *County and Court*, 147–9.
[15] For Hamon's role in county politics during the 1620s, see Campbell, 'Sir Roger Townshend', 81–90.
[16] See Chapter 3: Urban shopping.
[17] Fletcher, *Reform of the Provinces*, 362.
[18] Fletcher, *Reform of the Provinces*, 297; Smith, *County and Court*, 130.
[19] Fletcher, *Reform of the Provinces*, 289.
[20] Quoted in Fletcher, *Reform of the Provinces*, 298.
[21] This paragraph is based on Fletcher, *Reform of the Provinces*, 297–305.

man at the Musters 5s and the Drummer 18d and to 2 others there 2s', while in 1620 he gave £1 to Mr Patterson for mustering his company, and in 1624 paid 'for beer for the soldiers at the musters 5s 9d and the drummer 3s and to one that played on the pipe 6d and to Sallter for his horse and himself carrying the powder 18d in all 10s 9d'. Once appointed Deputy Lieutenant, Hamon recorded in his notebook a bulk-buy of weaponry in London in 1626, with twenty muskets purchased for his own use and ten for 'some of the Smithden band', the militia of Smithdon hundred. The muskets cost 15s a piece, but with accessories including bandoleers, musket moulds, scourers and worms, as well as the cost of transporting them by sea from London to Hunstanton, he calculated they cost 18s a piece. The muskets were then sold to members of the Smithdon militia, almost all Sir Hamon's own tenants, who bought either a whole musket or shares in one.[22]

Sir Hamon's financial costs for holding his various offices in the period 1606–26 were outweighed by money spent on private legal cases. For most of these there is little detail in the accounts. There were fees to lawyers and repeated payments for 'a bill', 'a brief' or 'a subpoena'. Legal costs were a simple fact of life for the gentry: the reason why gentlemen such as Sir Hamon and his sons all received legal training at the Inns of Court as well as a university education. Attendance at the quarter sessions and assizes provided further legal experience, not to mention the power to influence cases in some instances. The effect of losing legal and political office was felt painfully by the Le Stranges during the Civil War. Their Royalist sympathies left them isolated and losses from legal cases during this period dwarf those in the earlier period of accounts, as shown in Table 6.2.

It was no coincidence that their tax burden also increased significantly in the same period: Braddick records that Hunstanton paid £1158.93 in taxes of all kinds between 1639 and 1644.[23] Much of this was borne by the Le Strange household. Earlier in the century, Sir Hamon had taken an active part in the administration of taxation. He was already acting as a subsidy commissioner in 1606–7.[24] It is rare to be able to view taxation from the perspective of what a household actually paid.[25] Table 7.1 offers an overview of the taxes and rates paid by the Le Stranges in a twenty-year period from 1606 to 1626. It is not possible to be exact about all payments: some payments looked like taxes but are missing details necessary for identification such as a lump sum of £25 'paid which was due unto the treasury' in 1610. These are included in a miscellaneous tax category (Table 7.1, row 9). No payments of the fifteenth are recorded despite the fact that it was collected during this period. The overall figure of just over £187 given in the table is a substantial sum, but amounted to only 1 per cent of the Le Stranges' estate income in the period 1607–13, and 0.8 per cent in 1617–25. Taxation authorized by Parliament (the subsidy) was outweighed by royal taxes (purveyance and benevolences). Taxes

[22] LEST/Q38, fols. 89, 92.
[23] M.J. Braddick, *Parliamentary Taxation in 17th-Century England* (Woodbridge, 1994), 139.
[24] V. Morgan, E. Rutledge, and B. Taylor, *The Papers of Nathaniel Bacon of Stiffkey: Vol. V 1603–1607* (Norfolk Record Society Vol. 74, 2010), 271, 287, 289.
[25] M.J. Braddick, *The Nerves of the State: Taxation and the Financing of the English State, 1558–1714* (Manchester, 1996), chs. 4 and 5.

Table 7.1. Taxes paid, April 1606–April 1626

Type of tax	Amount paid	% of total of rows 1–8
1. King's provisions (purveyance)	£22 1s 1d	14.6
2. Subsidy	£34 9s 4d	22.8
3. Benevolence	£40 0s 0d	26.4
4. Rates for musters and poor soldiers	£7 5s 5d	4.8
5. Rates for bridges, havens, fortifications and houses of correction	£1 3s 10d	0.8
6. Unspecified constables' bills[a]	£3 4s 8d	2.1
7. Rates for church maintenance	£7 15s 0d	5.1
8. Poor rates to overseers	£35 0s 0d	23.2
9. Unspecified or unclear payments to treasury or undersheriffs or of rates	£36 9s 10d	–
Total	£187 9s 2d	99.8

[a] Constables were involved in the collection of all taxes in categories 1–5.
Sources: Le Strange disbursement accounts; LEST/P6, P7.

paid to central government and the crown dominated, but those levied by the county, hundred or parish made up a third of the total.

Poor rates, paid by the Le Stranges to the parishes of Ringstead, Sedgeford and Holme as well as Hunstanton, were already substantial. This had very largely replaced personal and voluntary charity by this date, although entries relating to small charitable gifts are scattered throughout the accounts.[26] Unnamed 'poor' who came to the door, or were encountered on journeys or visits to towns, were given a few pennies at a time. This amounted to only £2 for the period 1606–26, although it is likely not all these gifts are recorded. A further 13s 4d was doled out to poor soldiers, £1 10s 9d to those who had suffered losses by fire, and £3 11s 4d to strangers, travellers, Irishmen and Frenchmen, including £2 to 'poor exiled Frenchmen' in 1621. The poor economic conditions of the early 1620s seem to have prompted the Le Stranges to purchase cows for the poor. Six cows were purchased for the poor of Hunstanton, Sedgeford and Ringstead between 1620 and 1622 at a cost of £8 15s 7d. In his will Sir Hamon left £20 to the poor of the five north-west Norfolk villages that made up the core of his estate, and bequeathed 'at least half of the yearly profit' of a landholding which had escheated to him as a result of the tenant being hanged for murdering his wife to 'be yearly forever bestowed in some charitable way to the relief of poor people'. Alice left no charitable bequests in her will of 1656.

By modern standards, the proportion of income the Le Stranges paid in taxation before the Civil War was very modest. The proportion spent on private charity was even smaller. They spent, on average, as much on medical care per year as they did on political office or legal cases.[27] There were other less direct costs, however, such

---

[26] Tips paid to servants and workers are not included in this discussion; see Chapter 8.
[27] See Table 3.1(a).

as travel or the socializing necessary to retain political connections and support: these are considered in the next section.

TRAVEL AND LEISURE

Domestic travel was an essential part of gentry power, status and lifestyle in the seventeenth century. As a JP a gentleman had to travel to attend quarter sessions and assizes. As an MP it was necessary to travel up to London. Social visits required trips to county towns and the country houses of friends and relatives. As we have seen, London and Norwich were visited by the Le Stranges for business, pleasure and shopping several times a year in the early seventeenth century. Travel required horses. Horsemanship was an essential gentlemanly skill, a military and sporting asset as well as a practicality. As a result travel by coach was regarded as somewhat effeminate: suitable for women, the young, old or invalid.[28] Sir Hamon left a coach to Alice in his will and she in turn bequeathed it to her widowed daughter-in-law.[29] However, if coach travel was associated with women, the purchase of coaches and their accessories was the province of men. Early seventeenth-century coaches were a newly fashionable consumer good, first introduced to England from Pomerania in the reign of Elizabeth.[30] They quickly became an important indicator of status, largely restricted to the gentry in the first half of the seventeenth century. The notebook of Sir Hamon reveals that he was concerned with both the design and cost of his coaches, of which he purchased at least five.

Horses were bought and sold by the gentry. Between 1610 and 1625 the Le Stranges spent £329 5s 11d buying horses and sold horses worth £207. Coach horses could cost as much as £31, such as the 'two bay stone horses for the coach' purchased in 1624. In contrast 'a plough horse with a halter and a collar of bells' cost £6 3s 4d in 1617. Some were much cheaper, 'a horse from Lincolnshire' cost as little as £2 16s 8d in 1623. There were many ways of acquiring a horse. Some were purchased from tenants; others from friends among the Norfolk gentry; some were acquired in part exchange. Purchases were made at local fairs, at King's Lynn, and in Lincolnshire and Yorkshire. In 1606 Hamon Le Strange paid £22 12s 9d for two mares from Holland, and had them transported over to Norfolk at his own cost. Keeping a large number of horses also involved much expense, attention and organization. Horses had to be fed with hay and oats, shod, equipped and kept in good health. Hamon engaged a horse-keeper and a coachman to oversee this operation, and for guidance owned copies of Gervase Markham's books on horses: *The English Horseman* and *Markham's Masterpiece*.[31]

---

[28] J.T. Cliffe, *The World of the Country House in Seventeenth-Century England* (New Haven, 1999), 122; J. Crofts, *Packhorse, Waggon and Post: Land Carriage and Communications under the Tudors and Stuarts* (London, 1967), 109–10.
[29] The wills of Sir Hamon Le Strange and Alice Le Strange.
[30] Crofts, *Packhorse, Waggon and Post*, 112.
[31] See Chapter 8: Servants and the Le Strange library catalogue, LEST/NE1.

Edward Parker, a Le Strange servant from 1606 to 1608, graduated to become the local horse doctor and was paid for 'horse physic at diverse times' and 'for curing of horses' from 1613 onwards. Equipment consisted of stable ware, saddlery, harness, special clothing for horsemen and coaches. Saddlery was acquired locally, principally from Newman of Dereham, who presented a bill each year for mending and the making of new items. Between August 1609 and April 1626 these bills cost the Le Stranges £58 19s 11d. A detailed breakdown of the types of items purchased is shown by a bill recorded in Sir Hamon's notebook in 1629 from another saddler, Dawnay of Fakenham. He had supplied four saddles at 11s a piece, four bridles at 18d a piece, three white headstalls and reins for 3s each, four pairs of stirrups and leathers at 2s the set, four sets of girths at 12d each, four cloths at 20d per ell to a total of £5 3s 8d, and for 33s 4d a saddle of grey cloth, stitched with a cover, leathers and stirrups, cloth girths, bridle and snaffle.[32]

The Le Stranges' new coaches were purchased in London. Cliffe notes that coaches cost between £30 and £60 both before and after the Civil War.[33] Sir Hamon bought towards the cheap end of this scale. One purchased in 1606 cost £29. A second ordered in 1617 was not strictly a coach but a newly fashionable calash or caroche, a type of light carriage.[34] Sir Hamon recorded the agreement with the coach maker in his notebook:

> May 5 1617: agreed with Hyde of the Greene Dragon in Cowe Lane that he make me a new Caroch of Watchet Cloth of 12s and 12s 6d (to be chosen by my appointment) laced with watchet and yellow, and fringed so with a faire call fringe on the bootes and nailed with white nayles with furniture for horses of 9 straps on the back wth reines of lether to the same.[35]

It cost £36 10s, together with repairs to their old coach. They did not collect the caroche until 1620, when it was transported at further expense up to Norfolk. In 1623 they purchased again, this time from 'Perkins', at a cost of £38 'for a coach and harness for 4 horses'. In 1628 another coach, this time without harness, was purchased for £19 15s from 'Walker'. After ordering a fifth coach in 1631 Sir Hamon itemized the costs in his notebook, shown in Table 7.2. Purchase was not the end of the expense as coaches required frequent repairs. Barely a year passed without bills for mending the coach harness, leathers or wheels, not to mention the cost of oil, new wheels, bits for the horses and covers.

All this expense allowed the Le Stranges to travel in style, and travel they did. Unfortunately, records of Sir Hamon and Lady Alice offer no direct evidence of patterns of social visits, unlike the early sixteenth-century Le Strange kitchen

---

[32] LEST/Q38, fol. 118.
[33] Cliffe, *Country House*, 124.
[34] For 'calash' see Cliffe, *Country House*, 123; Henry Peacham, *The Coach and the Sedan* (1636), describes them as 'carouches'. Hamon Le Strange refers to the 'carsach' and 'caroch' in his notebook, and Alice Le Strange to the 'colasse' in the accounts. See also Crofts, *Packhorse, Waggon and Post*, 118, for 'carrosse' and 'caroache'.
[35] LEST/Q38, fol. 9.

Table 7.2. The cost of a new coach itemized, 1632

The upper lether which is the cover of a coach cost of the best about 26s or 28s, other hydes about 16s or 20s a piece	£1 – 8 – 0
Cloth about 7 yards at 12s	£4 – 10 – 0
In nayles about 40s	£2 – 0 – 0
In fringe and lace about 4 li the best	£5 – 0 – 0
Iron about the coach 10s	£0 – 10 – 0
Wheeles 4 li	£4 – 0 – 0
The body and carrage 8 li	£8 – 0 – 0
Paynting 40s	£2 – 0 – 0
Raynes, bets & harness for 4 horses 9 li	£9 – 0 – 0
	£36 – 8 – 0

Source: The notebook of Sir Hamon Le Strange; LEST/Q38, fol. 140.

accounts analysed by Heal.[36] Records of tips paid to servants at other households suggest that Sir Hamon—sometimes accompanied by Alice, sometimes not—was visiting at least nine other households each year in the twenty years between April 1606 and April 1626. Payments to people who found lost hawks or returned hunting dogs from these places provide some evidence of his motivations. Many visits combined business and pleasure. Two of the most frequently visited houses, Lady Sidney's at Walsingham and the Corbetts' at Sprowston, just outside Norwich, were convenient places to stay during the quarter sessions and assizes.[37] These were among the six households visited more than fifteen times in the period. Others were relatives or living on Le Strange manors. The Yelvertons, Alice's half sister and brother-in-law, were visited at least twenty-four times between 1606 and 1620. More distant relatives, cousin Sir Le Strange Mordaunt of Massingham and uncle Roger Bozoun of Whissonsett, were visited nineteen and seventeen times, respectively, throughout the period. Mordaunt was a fellow JP, while Uncle Bozoun, married to Hamon's father's sister, was an older relative relied upon to lend the Le Stranges money. When Philip Calthorpe leased the Le Stranges' manor house at Gressenhall, his household also became popular, with at least twenty-three visits between 1618 and 1625. These favourites were combined with less frequent visits to the Hares of Stow Bardolph, the Hobarts of Blickling and Norwich, the Townshends of Stiffkey and Raynham,[38] Sir Edmund Bell, Mr Stanton, Mr Edmund Drury and Mr Boyton, who were visited on five to seven occasions between 1606 and 1626. It is likely that all these people made return visits to the Le Stranges at Hunstanton, for which we have no evidence.

Sociable visits by gentry to the Le Strange household in the first half of the seventeenth century would have entailed good food, laughter and music. Evidence of laughter is provided by Sir Nicholas Le Strange's manuscript jest book,

---

[36] F. Heal, *Hospitality in Early Modern England* (Oxford, 1990), 59.
[37] Lady Sidney was Jane, widow of Sir Henry Sidney kt d.1612; F. Blomefield, *An Essay Towards a Topographical History of the County of Norfolk*, vol. 5 (London, 1739–75), 833–4.
[38] The Stiffkey kitchen books record that Sir Hamon Le Strange visited Sir Roger Townshend's household there three times 1622/3–7, Campbell, 'Sir Roger Townshend', 367.

the employment of fools, and even the ownership of an ape. Nicholas Le Strange's *Merry Passages and Jeasts* has been studied by H.F. Lippincott and more recently by Pamela Allen Brown.[39] They note that it is unusual in containing a high proportion of original anecdotes and jokes which refer to actual people. Nicholas recorded the source of his jests and this reveals that many, seventy-nine out of 611 jests, were originally told by women. A large proportion of these were told by 'my mother', Lady Alice, who contributed forty-three in all. She is outnumbered in the collection only by jokes from William Spring, Elizabeth Le Strange's husband and Nicholas' friend. Many of the jokes, including those told by Alice and other female relatives such as Aunt Catelyn and Dol Gurney, are extremely bawdy. They include explicit descriptions of sex, nudity and bodily functions. Everyone is fair game for a joke: from King James I, fellow gentry, pious ministers and worthy scholars to tenants, servants and the poor. As Brown observes, for effective telling, these jokes would have required a degree of mimicry and acting out.[40] This was a very different social world from the 'polite' society of the eighteenth-century elite.

A number of the jests concern professional comedians, or fools: Wiggett the fool features in five. An anecdote about him told by Alice makes it clear that fools were commonly present at the assizes when the judges were conducting private business over dinner, if not in the actual courtroom.[41] Three payments made by 'Mr Strange' to fools between 1608 and 1616 could have been at quarter sessions or assizes. The Le Stranges also had their own 'regular' fool: from 1615 to 1619 and from 1624 onwards a series of yearly payments were made to Randall the fool, who received between 5s and 2s 6d each time for his services. A rather different source of amusement was provided by apes. In 1610 one was sent from Sir Ralph Hare's household. A new ape was purchased in 1614 for £1 6s 6d, along with 'an ape's chain' for 8d, and 1s paid to the person who delivered it to Hunstanton; another was purchased in 1622 for £1 2s. Burton writes that 'many women kept monkeys as pets', so it is possible the ape belonged to Alice.[42]

A number of other professional or semi-professional entertainers were paid for their services. The Le Stranges were music lovers, and, as well as playing music themselves and patronizing composers, they also employed more humble musicians. Between 1612 and 1625 the accounts record sixteen payments to town waits, mostly of 4s to 6s. Town waits were small groups of musicians who played at civic functions, although from the Le Strange accounts it is clear that they also travelled to play at gentry households. Those who appear most frequently were the Newmarket waits, who were paid seven times between 1616 and 1625, followed by the Lynn waits paid five times from 1612 to 1624, and then the Yarmouth waits, Hadleigh waits and Cambridge University waits, who each received a single

---

[39] N. Le Strange, *Merry Passages and Jeasts*, ed. H.F. Lippincott (Salzburg, 1974); P.A. Brown, 'Jesting rights: women players in the manuscript jestbook of Sir Nicholas Le Strange', in P.A. Brown and P. Parolin (eds.), *Women Players in England 1500–1660* (Aldershot, 2005): the original book is in the British Library: Harleian MS 6395.

[40] Brown, 'Jesting rights', 309–11.

[41] Le Strange, *Merry Jeasts*, 19.

[42] E. Burton, *The Jacobeans at Home* (London, 1962), 302.

payment. In a number of cases the Le Stranges were visiting these places, but in others there is no evidence of travel. Sir Hamon first paid the Newmarket waits when travelling through on the way to London in 1616. But the following six payments, dating from 1621 to 1625, all suggest the musicians came to Hunstanton to provide entertainment. In 1612 the Lynn waits were paid while the Le Stranges were visiting Whissonsett to celebrate the christening of one of their cousin Bozoun's children. Seventeen further payments varying from 2s to 10s were made to unspecified musicians, paid both at home and at other houses and towns. Between 1619 and 1627 occasional visits were made by 'Anthony Dobbs and his company', who we can assume were travelling players. They received 5s a visit, or 10s in 1625. There is no evidence that the Le Stranges went to the theatre in London, although in 1622 Sir Hamon spent 1s 6d 'for going by water and seeing a bear baiting'.

Despite his religious beliefs, Sir Hamon was not averse to playing cards and other games, and gambling, although the sums he lost were always small. Between 1610 and 1626 Alice recorded 'lost by Mr Strange at cards' or words to that effect in the accounts twenty-two times. The most he lost was £2 14s 8d at Christmas 1619, but losses over £1 occurred only four times. He was also keen on 'tables' or backgammon. He purchased 'a pair of playing tables' for 4s in 1614, and 'a set of tablemen' for a further 10s in 1616. There are fourteen entries in the accounts from 1612 to 1622 of Sir Hamon losing at tables, although he never lost more than 6s. Alice does not record her own losses in the accounts: either she paid out of her personal allowance or she did not play these games. As well as cards and backgammon, Sir Hamon gambled at bowls, losing money at bowls nine times between 1606 and 1626, although he must have played more often than this. Apart from one occasion when he lost 16s 6d, the amount lost was rarely more than a shilling, so could easily have escaped the record. In 1629 Sir Hamon built his own bowling green, which stood to the south of Hunstanton Hall.

While all these activities provided diversions and occasions for sociability, both the accounts and Sir Hamon's notebook suggest that his real passion was hawking. He drew up a table in his notebook: 'A Catalogue of the number of Hawks, Falcons and Tercels which I have taken at the cliff from 1604 (when I came of age) with the months & days when they were taken.'[43] The list continues to 1649 and lists eighty-seven birds in total. Hunstanton was a good location for catching tercels, or peregrine falcons, which nested on the cliff there, but Sir Hamon also purchased birds. Between 1605 and early 1626 he bought eighteen birds at a total cost of £65 and sold birds worth £13. He commonly paid £4 for hawks, up to £7 for a falcon and in 1625 £10 for a lanner.[44] He bought, sold and exchanged birds with his gentlemanly friends, and received them as gifts. The training and keeping of hawks required the employment of a falconer, who in 1617 was Christopher Townshend, one of the senior liveried servants. He enjoyed a special relationship with Sir Hamon, with wages of £4 a year appearing in Hamon's notebook but not in the

[43] LEST/Q38, fols. 150–1.
[44] A lanner is a species of Mediterranean falcon, *Falco lanarius*.

household accounts. Special housing, hawks' mews, was built in 1616, and an extensive range of equipment purchased, including nets, flannel for casting, bells, hoods, muzzles, jesses, leashes, bags, lures and gloves. Hawks also needed regular supplies of fresh meat and occasional medicines; they frequently went missing and rewards were paid for their recapture. Between 1606 and 1626 the total spent on hawks, excluding wages and building, was £121.

Dogs were required for any sort of hunting, hawking and shooting, to retrieve birds, flush out quarry, find game, chase animals such as hares, foxes, deer and otters and dig them out when they went to ground. Sir Hamon built kennels for his hawking dogs and appears to have hunted them in couples. The accounts reveal no details about the type of dogs he owned nor is there any evidence of a pack of hounds. The principal activity at Hunstanton appears to have been wildfowling using guns or hawks. Hunting was a social activity for gentlemen, and one Sir Hamon shared with his sons, grandsons and other male relatives. In his will, Sir Hamon left his grandson John 'my biggest birding peece usually standing in the parlour'.[45] These activities, however, were not purely social; Sir Hamon and his friends supplied the household with a variety of birds, wildfowl and deer. For instance, an entry in the kitchen accounts for November 1619 reads, 'Killed by Mr Strange and William Guybon a curlew, a widgeon, 2 dozen of snipes, 4 blackbirds and 3 spowes'.

Other than coach travel, the activities described in this section were traditional: socializing, jesting, listening to music, playing games and gambling, hunting and hawking would all have been familiar pastimes to the gentry in the fifteenth century. Hawking, highly fashionable in the early seventeenth century, was experiencing its last gasp of popularity. By the late seventeenth century it had been largely replaced by shooting.[46] While he clearly enjoyed the good things in life, Sir Hamon did more than hold office, and 'eat, and drink, and play, and hunt, and hawk'.[47] Like many English gentlemen of this period he added a new set of activities to the gentry repertoire by taking a serious interest in forms of Renaissance culture and learning.

LITERATURE, MUSIC AND SCIENCE

An incomplete inventory of Hunstanton Hall, taken in 1675 after the death of Sir Hamon and Alice's grandson Nicholas in 1669, lists a library and a music room adjoining each other and close to the dining room. The music room contained '1 organ 1 pedal Harpeicon 3 presses with violls & musick bookes';[48] in the library there were 'Mathmatical instruments in the cupboard'. A catalogue of the Le Strange library dating from *c.*1700 lists 2659 printed volumes dating back to the

---

[45] LEST/AE8.
[46] Cliffe, *Country House*, 157.
[47] From Cliffe, quoting a sermon critical of those activities, 1657, *Country House*, 156.
[48] 'Presses' were cupboards. NA: PROB 4/3988.

sixteenth century.[49] The household accounts allow these interests to be traced back to Sir Hamon. For instance, between 1606 and 1609 Sir Hamon acquired at least ten books, which included a copy of Aristotle's *Ethics*; 'Vertagan', almost certainly Richard Verstegan's history of England *A Restitution of Decayed Intelligence: In Antiquities Concerning the most Noble and Renowned English nation* (1605); *De Horologiis Sciothericis Libri Tres* by Jean Voellus (1608), a study of sundials and their construction; 'Ortelius' or Abraham Ortelius, *An epitome of Ortelius his Theater of the world, wherein the principal regions of the earth are descrived in smalle mappes* (1601); and Robert Record's *Castle of Knowledge*, a study of mathematics and cosmography. He received a viol as a gift and paid 7s 6d for a new case; and purchased a pair of compasses and a quadrant.

Sir Hamon passed on his interests to all three of his sons. They all had music lessons as part of their education at Eton, Cambridge and the Inns of Court. There is evidence that both Nicholas and Roger were serious musicians and musical patrons. Nicholas used his knowledge of mathematics and surveying to drain the marshes of Hunstanton and Heacham.[50] Hamon junior was a published author of religious works and histories from 1641 onwards. Roger, who in his youth was a source of trouble to his parents, went on to become extremely influential in Restoration England after their death. Not only was he surveyor and licenser of the press, but he published extensively, both his own works and as a 'talented linguist and translator' of Spanish, Greek and French.[51] There is no evidence of the Le Strange women taking part in these activities. Ashbee's assertion that Alice played the viol is a misinterpretation of the accounts.[52] Elizabeth received singing lessons alongside Roger in 1634. Anne, Nicholas' wife, received a dedication in one of Hamon junior's works, suggesting she was a woman of serious religious thought, something that was likely given her parentage, but she left no writings herself other than sections of the accounts.[53] Alice bequeathed two books in her will: 'one Booke intitled Mr Greenhams workes' to a female friend; and 'Doctor Hawdens Booke' to William Waters, vicar of Sedgeford.[54] Her book-buying habits, like other personal spending, are hidden from the record by her personal allowance.

The presence of a specialist library room at Hunstanton Hall in 1675 is tantalizing. Country house libraries were rare in the first half of the seventeenth century.[55] Sir Nicholas Le Strange (1661–1724), the great-grandson of Sir Hamon

---

[49] NRO, L'EST/NE1. This is the number of books. There were a further 418 sermons and political papers, and thirty-seven manuscripts.
[50] LEST/KA6, LEST/KA9–10 and KA24.
[51] A. Dunan-Page and B. Lynch, 'Introduction', in A. Dunan-Page and B. Lynch (eds.), *Roger L'Estrange and the Making of Restoration Culture* (Aldershot, 2008), 1–5, quotation from 4.
[52] A. Ashbee, '"My Fiddle is a Bass Viol": Music in the Life of Roger L'Estrange' in Dunan-Page and Lynch, *Roger L'Estrange*, 149. The account entry 'for making a case for my viole', which he considers written by Alice in 1611, was made by Sir Hamon Le Strange in 1608.
[53] H. L'Estrange esq., *An Answer to the Marques of Worcester's last Paper*... (London, 1651).
[54] NA Prob/11/262. R. Greenham, *The Works of the Reverend and Faithful Servant of Jesus Christ M. Richard Greenham, Minister and Preacher of the Word of God, collected into one volume* (various editions, 1599–1612). We have not been able to identify Dr Hawden's book.
[55] Cliffe, *Country House*, 163.

and Alice, who almost certainly compiled the library catalogue, added a schedule of building works to Sir Hamon's notebook. It lists the date that each building on the estate, or, in the case of Hunstanton Hall, each part of that building, had been constructed or altered, but leaves a space beside the entry for the library blank.[56] A plan reproduced in *Country Life* (1926) places the library on the ground floor of the Elizabethan block of Hunstanton Hall, which burnt down in 1853.[57] If this was its location in the seventeenth century, its creation would have required fitting out an existing room with shelving and cupboards rather than anything more radical. In the codicil to his will of 1653, Sir Hamon asked his son Sir Nicholas to 'consider of his owne, and my library' and weed out duplicate copies to make gifts to local clergymen, but this most obviously refers to their collections of books rather than particular rooms. That each man possessed a substantial collection of books, and a private study in the first half of the century, is beyond doubt. In 1617 a 'desk to lay a book upon' was purchased for 4s 6d and in 1619 Hamon's study was newly painted at a cost of £1 12s.[58] This was before the enlargement of the house, so it is possible that it was the room later described as the library. 'Old Sir Nichs Studdy' appears in the inventory of 1675 near the kitchen and dairy, and was by then being used as a general storeroom. Cooper notes that 'the study is a room for work and for contemplation, for reading and writing and for the safekeeping of books and documents and other private treasures'.[59] While not as novel as a library, it was not a common addition to gentry houses before the mid-sixteenth century.

Sir Hamon must have owned well over 1000 books by his death in 1654. Of the 2659 volumes in the library catalogue 1670 (63 per cent) were published before 1655.[60] This would have made it one of the largest collections of books in Norfolk, on a par with Sir Thomas Knivett's collection of 1407 books in 1618 and well above the collections of Sir Roger Townshend and Sir Henry Spelman.[61] In the twenty years between 1606 and early 1626 the accounts record £88 spent on books, mostly making new purchases but also on bindings. Only occasionally are the titles given. The cheapest items were almanacs, often purchased two or three at a time, for 2d each. Books bought for the boys while they were children were rarely more than 1s each. Gervase Markham's books also retailed cheaply, the Le Stranges bought one for 1s in 1622 and another for 4d in 1628, neither was named. Most books cost between 1s and £1. Two copies of Xenophon were purchased, again presumably for the two boys, for 5s each in 1620. A dictionary cost 10s in 1617, and another 8s in 1620. 'Doctor Barrowe's Physick Book' (Philip Barrough, *The Method of Physic*) cost 2s 2d in 1621, and 'Dowlands introduction to song' (John

---

[56] At the front of LEST/Q38.
[57] C. Hussey, 'Hunstanton Hall Norfolk, The seat of Mr Charles Le Strange', *Country Life* (1926), 559.
[58] See Chapter 5: Beds and living rooms.
[59] N. Cooper, *The Houses of the Gentry 1480–1680* (New Haven, 1999), 300.
[60] The catalogue lists 440 items published before 1600; 1230 dating from 1600–54; 585 dating from 1655–98; and 404 which have no date.
[61] Cliffe, *Country House*, 164; R.J. Fehrenback and E.S. Leedham Green (eds.), *Private Libraries in Renaissance England* (New York, 1992).

Dowland, *The First Booke of Songes*) 2s 6d in 1629. The most expensive book purchased in the period up to 1630 was 'Speeds Chronacle' for £4 3s in 1629: no other books purchased cost more than £2.[62] Bindings could be more expensive than books. A copy of Chaucer, bequeathed to Sir Hamon by Richard Stubbe in 1619, was rebound in 1622 at a cost of 11s.[63] In March 1629, just a few months before his marriage, Nicholas was imitating his father's purchasing habits. A set of his purchases in the household accounts show him acquiring 'Burton's *Booke of Meloncholy*' for 10s and 'Record's *Arithmatick*' for 2s 6d,[64] as well as a new viol with a case for £1, a creance for his hawk, a set of a band and cuffs for 4s, two pairs of gloves for 2s 8d, and paying 3s 6d to the barber.

Sir Hamon Le Strange's book buying continued throughout his lifetime. Even the difficulties of the 1640s did not stop his acquisitions. In London in May 1648 'about [the] Linne mens busines' he took the opportunity to buy four books, and another two in Cambridge on the way home at a cost of 8s 9d. Whilst in London, Alice notes that Hamon also paid: 'To Mr Willson the Printer for printing of my Husbands vindication against falce Skandall raysed of him - £1'. This was Sir Hamon's first venture into print. The pamphlet was an attempt to justify his actions after the unsuccessful defence of King's Lynn for the Royalists.[65]

In the last years of his life, elderly and removed from county administration as a result of his Royalism, he found more time for literary pursuits, producing two more substantial volumes. In 1651 he published *Americans no Jewes, or Improbabilities that the Americans are of that Race*, a repudiation of Thorowgood's *Jews in America, or, Probabilities that the Americans are of that Race*, published the previous year. Thorowgood, a Norfolk clergyman, had sent a copy to Sir Hamon, who wrote in his own preface, 'I read the same with more diligence and delight for the Authors sake, but as I sailed through the discourse, I fell upon many sands and rocks of reluctance to my sense' and thus felt compelled to write a reply.[66] In 1652 Sir Hamon published again, this time a translation of Pierre Du Moulin's *Heraclitus, or, Mans Looking-Glass and Survey of Life*. Here the preface states: 'It is now above 40 years since I translated this piece out of French and laid it by in loose papers, intending to have published.'[67] Hamon junior was also publishing his own works during this period, with which Sir Hamon's are often confused.[68] His were a

---

[62] This most probably refers to John Speed, *The History of Great Britain*, which is a large book, but it may have been purchased in conjunction with John Speed, *Theatre of the Empire of Great Britain*, which is an atlas of maps and with which it shares pagination. Both were first published in 1611 but reprinted in the 1620s.

[63] NA PROB/11/135.

[64] Robert Burton, *The anatomy of melancholy* (1621); Robert Record, *The ground of arts teaching the perfect worke and practise of arithmeticke*, first published in 1573 but revised and reprinted in the early seventeenth century.

[65] Sir H. L'Estrange, *The Charge upon Sir Hamon L'Estrange together with his Vindication and Recharge* (London, 1649).

[66] H. L'Estrange, Knight, *Americans no Jewes* (1651), sig. A2.

[67] Sir H. L'Estrange, *Heraclitus* (1652), sig. A2.

[68] *Early English Books Online* attributes *Americans no Jewes* and *Heraclitus* to Hamon Le Strange junior.

mixture of Protestant theology and royalist history.[69] By the end of the century, their modest publications had been greatly exceeded by the output of Roger, which include '75 extant political books and pamphlets, two collected works, 13 translated works and 1,183 periodical issues', although Roger published nothing of book length until 1660.[70]

For all of the Le Strange men, literary pursuits were combined with a love of music, particularly the viol. The viol was the standard instrument for the domestic music in gentry households in this period. Henry Peacham advised in *The Complete Gentleman* 'I desire no more in you than to sing your part sure and at the first sight withal to play the same upon your viol'.[71] As we have seen, Hamon received a viol as a gift in 1608, although he certainly would have owned others by this date. In 1610 he purchased 'a little viol with wire strings' for £1 13s. The sixteen-year-old Nicholas had his own by 1620, when 2s 6d was spent transporting it to Eton for him. In most years from 1610 to 1626, between 1s and 6s was spent on new viol strings by the Hunstanton household. Music books were purchased, including 'a viol book' for 3s in 1614 and another for 5s 8d in 1616, a 'set of song books' for 4s 6d in 1620, and '2 music books' for 5s in 1622. Roger had viol lessons while at Eton in 1632–4, and Thomas Brewer was paid £1 to teach him and his sister Elizabeth to sing in 1634. Roger pawned his viol at Cambridge in 1635 before being thrown out of the university.[72] Nicholas left his musical mark on posterity by collecting 'fancies' or fantasias for the viol, the manuscripts of which survive, and by acting as patron to the composer of viol music, John Jenkins, who is believed to have stayed at Hunstanton Hall in 1644–5.[73] Thomas Brewer, the singing teacher, is described as 'my mus[ic] Servant', in Nicholas' *Merry Jeasts*.[74] Roger Le Strange was acknowledged as 'an expert violist' by Roger North, playing the bass viol, and Ashbee documents his active participation in the musical culture of Restoration London.[75] Sir Hamon left his own bass viol with a case and books of viol lessons to his grandson John, then aged sixteen, in his will of 1652.[76]

Sir Hamon's book collection and publications provide one strand of evidence of his intellectual interests; another is provided by his purchases of scientific instruments, shown in Table 7.3. These were presumably the 'mathmatical instruments' still stored in the library in 1675. As Bennett notes, instruments 'played an important and ubiquitous role across the early modern mathematical arts...

---

[69] H. L'Estrange: *Gods Sabbath* (1641); *An Answer to the Marques of Worcester's last Paper* (1651); *The Reign of King Charles an History* (1655); *The Alliance of Divine Offices* (1659).
[70] G. Kemp, 'The works of Roger L'Estrange: an annotated bibliography', in Dunan-Page and Lynch, *Roger L'Estrange*, 181.
[71] H. Peacham, *The Complete Gentleman*, ed. V.B. Heltzel (New York, 1962), 112.
[72] See Chapter 6: Education and adult children.
[73] P. Willetts, 'Nicholas Le Strange and John Jenkins', *Music & Letters* 42:1 (1961), 30–43; A. Ashbee, 'A further look at some Le Strange manuscripts', *Chelys* 5 (1973–4), 24–41; I. Spink (ed.), *Music in Britain: The Seventeenth Century* (Oxford, 1992); A. Ashbee and P. Holman, *John Jenkins and his Time: Studies of English Consort Music* (Oxford, 1996).
[74] Willetts, 'Nicholas Le Strange', 38.
[75] Ashbee, 'My Fiddle is a Bass Viol', quotation from 156.
[76] John was the third son of Nicholas Le Strange: LEST/AE8, and NA, Prob/11/238.

Table 7.3. Scientific instruments acquired, 1606–30

Year	Description	Cost
1607	A pair of compasses	£2
1608	A quadrant	14s
1610	2 globes	£4 13s
1610	A pair of compasses	6s 6d
1610	A brass instrument called a theodolite	£5
1610	A 'Geodettal Staffe' and the box to put it in	£2 1s 6d
1611	A perspective	7s
1611	3 brass plates for dials	£1
1612	'to Mr Wallis' man for bringing an instrument from Mr Briggs'	1s
1615	For a nest of hour glasses	4s
1615	'to Wright for an instrument'	7s
1618	For mending the two watches	9s 2d
1618	'To Edward Wright of Norwich for an azimuthall circle, diagonally divided with a box & needle'	£3
1621	A weather glass	1s 6d
1621	'to Wright for instruments'	£1
1623	A compass	3s 6d
1629	A clock	£4 10s

Sources: Le Strange disbursement accounts; LEST/P6, P7.

applied to astronomy, navigation, surveying, warfare, and other practical activities.'[77] The development of scientific instruments was an important element of the European Renaissance, and can be observed here filtering down to England's rural gentry.[78] Sir Hamon's ranged from the relatively cheap, such as the weatherglass purchased for 1s 6d in 1621, to the expensive, such as the theodolite costing £5 in 1610. Eight of the instruments purchased cost between £1 and £5. Some were purchased in London, such as the two globes which were shipped to Hunstanton at some expense. However, from 1615 onwards, Edward Wright, a Norwich goldsmith, was a favourite source of instruments. Wright provided an 'azimuthal circle' and the Le Stranges' first clock as well as various unspecified instruments. The number and range of instruments that Sir Hamon acquired in these years suggest that he collected them. But, viewed alongside evidence from the Le Strange archive, it is also clear that this was more than a hobby based on accumulating interesting and curious objects: he also used the instruments and encouraged others to use them.

There were a range of instruments for measuring time. The three brass plates for dials purchased in 1611 were surely for constructing sundials, and, as we have seen, three years earlier he had purchased a copy of Jean Voellus' *De Horologiis Sciothericis Libri Tres*, a study of sundials and their construction. By 1630 Sir Hamon had at

---

[77] J. Bennett, 'The mechanical arts', in K. Park and L. Daston (eds.), *The Cambridge History of Science*. Vol. 3. *Early Modern Science* (Cambridge, 2006), 675.

[78] L. Jardine, *Worldly Goods: A New History of the Renaissance* (Basingstoke, 1996), ch. 7; G. L'Estrange Turner, *Scientific Instruments 1500–1900: An Introduction* (London, 1998); Bennett, 'The mechanical arts'.

least three other methods of telling the time: the traditional 'nest of hour glasses' purchased in 1615, but also a watch and a clock. Two watches, presumably one each for Alice and Sir Hamon, feature regularly in the accounts from 1618 onwards, with one or both of them being mended at least once a year. They had perhaps been received as gifts. Early watches were notoriously unreliable. The clock purchased in 1629 also required regular and frequent repairs or adjustments. There was also a weatherglass: a simple instrument for measuring changes in temperature which consisted of 'an upright tube filled with water, terminating at the top in a bulb containing rarefied air. The water sank or rose in the tube as the air expanded or contracted'.[79] Again, this was unlikely to have been particularly accurate. More accurate clocks and thermometers were developed later in the seventeenth century. The nature of a 'perspective' purchased in 1611 is unclear. 'Perspective' was the name used for a number of optical instruments using glass lenses: given its low cost and early date it is most likely to have been a magnifying glass.[80]

A number of instruments were related to the more complex measurements needed for astronomy and navigation. A quadrant was purchased in 1608, a compass in 1623,[81] and an 'azimuthal circle' in 1618. Its description suggests that this was an azimuthal compass, which was popular in the seventeenth century.[82] These were complemented by the two globes, presumably one terrestrial and one celestial, which Turner notes were 'regular furnishings in a library from the seventeenth-century onwards'.[83] Measuring and mapping closer to home is evidenced by the theodolite, a mid-sixteenth-century invention, and geodetical staff, both instruments of surveying.[84] Following the trends of the time, Hamon had his own estate surveyed and mapped between 1615 and 1630.[85] Finally, there were two pairs of compasses used for drawing circles purchased in 1607 and 1610. This ties in with his purchase of Record's *Castle of Knowledge*, which was particularly concerned with nature of the sphere. It also connects to Sir Hamon's interest in architecture. It is possible the more expensive pair of compasses was a proportional compass used for enlarging or reducing drawings to scale.[86] The intellectual and cultural pursuits of Sir Hamon and his three sons reveal the degree to which Renaissance learning had percolated into the everyday life of English country gentlemen by the early seventeenth century. The range of pursuits is notable, along with the degree to which they were not just passively observed or patronized but actually undertaken. They not only read books but wrote them. They played music as well as listening to it. Sir

---

[79] *OED Online*, entry for 'Weather-Glass'. See also A. Wolf, *A History of Science, Technology and Philosophy in the 16th and 17th Centuries* (London, 1935), 83.
[80] *OED Online*, entry for 'Perspective'. See also Turner, *Scientific Instruments*, 91–102.
[81] As it is in the singular, this was presumably a magnetic mariner's compass, which were relatively common by this date: Turner, *Scientific Instruments*, 34.
[82] Turner, *Scientific Instruments*, 34, 57.
[83] Turner, *Scientific Instruments*, 27.
[84] Turner, *Scientific Instruments*, 39, 42; *OED Online* entry for 'geodetical'.
[85] LEST/OA1: Hunstanton; LEST/OC2: Heacham; LEST/OC1: Sedgeford; NRO, MC 77/1; Hayes and Storr, no.72: Gressenhall.
[86] Turner, *Scientific Instruments*, 62, 81–2.

Hamon indulged in a love of new scientific instruments, but also applied them to the improvement of his house and estate.

BUILDING AND ESTATE IMPROVEMENT

A gentleman's estate was his source of wealth and status. His house was not only a place to live but also an expression of his taste and values. The majority of Sir Hamon's activities concentrated on Hunstanton Hall and its park, and buildings elsewhere on the estate. His notebook shows that he was personally involved, designing details and commissioning workmen himself. Between 1610 and 1653, 11 per cent of the Le Stranges' expenditure was on building work, peaking at 17 per cent in the 1620s when Hunstanton Hall was enlarged.[87] This meant spending several hundred pounds on building work each year throughout the period of the accounts. Much of Hunstanton Hall and many buildings of the surrounding estate survive to the present day as a testimony to these activities.

As Alice noted in her account books, Sir Hamon started from a low base, 'his chief house halfe built and all his farme houses in such decay so he hath built most of them out of the ground'.[88] Figure 7.1 shows the phases of building at Hunstanton Hall before the nineteenth century. The house inherited by Sir Hamon consisted of a moated site with fifteenth-century gatehouse facing the 'half-built' element which combined a medieval block with a larger 'Elizabethan Wing'. In 1616–17, Sir Hamon added an elaborate classical style porch, topped with an escallop and three spheres, and decorated with two pyramids standing either side of his coat of arms against a pattern of chequered diamonds. Fine stonework was carried out by Hans Weller, a Dutchman lodging in Southwark. In 1617, Sir Hamon recorded in his notebook: 'Agreed with Hans Weller (who finished my porch, the armes and eschallop) to make me 2 pyramids to be sett by the armes on each side, which pyramids he shall work and carve in very good freestone on 3 sydes outward that each pyramid according to the draught...'.[89] The cost of the pyramids and their transport to King's Lynn was £5. In total the porch cost more than £20 to construct. The Elizabethan wing was destroyed by fire in 1853, but the porch still survives as a free-standing ornament.

In the 1620s two large T-shaped wings to the house were built, joining on to the gatehouse and linking it back to the Elizabethan wing to create a courtyard. The wings were constructed of chequered flint and carstone edged with freestone, in contrast to the red brick gatehouse (Fig. 7.2). The resulting house was greatly enlarged, with the twenty-eight bed chambers recorded in Alice's inventory of 1632. The hearth tax returns of 1664 and 1666 reveal Hunstanton Hall to be one of only thirty-five houses in Norfolk with twenty or more hearths.[90] The enlarged

---

[87] See Table 6.1(b).   [88] LEST/P10.   [89] LEST/Q38, fol. 11.
[90] A. Longcroft, 'The Hearth Tax and historic housing stocks: a case study from Norfolk', in P.S. Barnwell and M. Airs (eds.), *Houses and the Hearth Tax: The Later Stuart House and Society* (York, 2006), 70–2.

	14th Century		1577
	c.1487		1620s

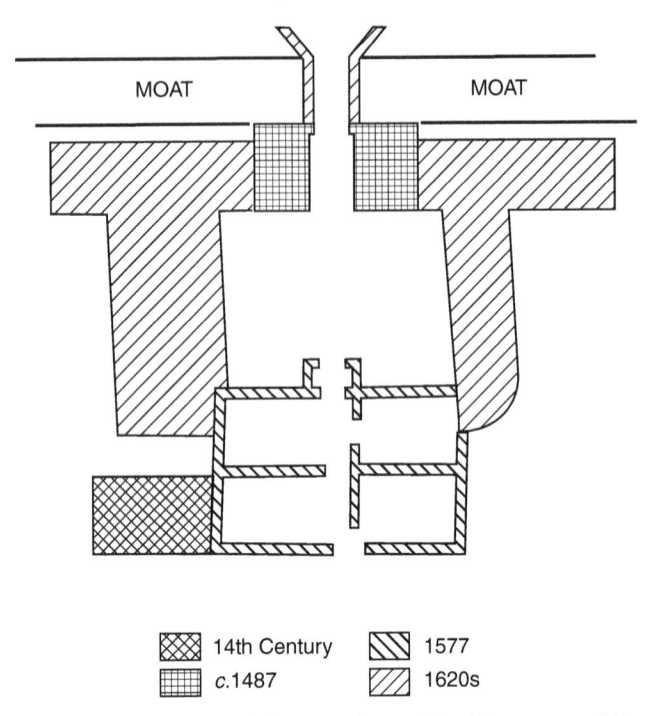

Fig. 7.1. A plan of Hunstanton Hall showing phases of building up to 1650.

house and its outbuildings were then enclosed with a wall. This allowed a grand entrance through 'the upper freestone gates', where lions, unicorns and a coat of arms sit astride a pure classical gate. Sir Hamon himself produced the sketches for the gates and the crenellations of the courtyard walls in his notebook.[91] Richard Russell, the architect who planned the extension to Hunstanton Hall and was paid £2 10s for 'drawing of a plot for the house' in 1620, remains obscure. The detailing and the execution of the plans seems to have been undertaken by Sir Hamon himself in liaison with the masons and other workmen he employed.[92] One of these men, William Edge, later became famous as the mason–architect who travelled to the continent with Sir Roger Townshend, and built early seventeenth-century Norfolk's most innovative house, Raynham Hall.[93] Edge worked first for Sir Hamon Le Strange, who paid him 10d a day in 1614, rising to 12d in 1618. He remained involved at Hunstanton Hall into the 1620s.

Sir Hamon's notebook reveals him sourcing many of the materials needed, recording contracts with a variety of skilled workmen. Freestone, the hard, good quality stone needed for edging and carving, was supplied by Mr Thomas Thorpe

---

[91] LEST/Q38.
[92] See Chapter 8: Craftsmen and specialist workers.
[93] L. Campbell, 'Documentary evidence for the building of Raynham Hall', *Architectural History* 32 (1989), 52–67.

Fig. 7.2. The front of Hunstanton Hall c.1926, showing the moat, fifteenth-century gatehouse, and new wings constructed by Sir Hamon Le Strange in the 1620s. Reproduced with permission from the *Country Life* Picture Library.

of High Cliffe, Northamptonshire. He was the father of John Thorpe, the noted architect, although there is no evidence he played any part in the overall design. Stone of this quality was also used for the upper 'freestone gates'; several hundred feet for the upper corbels and corbel tables on the north, south and west sides and the front of the house; ashlars, upper and lower, for below the vents; and miles of 'crests' for coping house walls, courtyard walls and garden walls. Costing at least £377 the freestone was all transported from Northamptonshire by water to Lynn, and thence to Hunstanton.[94] Glazing was provided by John Bateman of Lynn, glazier, with whom Sir Hamon agreed in 1623 'to glaze my house with good glasse, well leaded and bonded'. Edward Stanion of Gaywood, plasterer, made a chimney piece of artificial stone, with columns and pilasters, for the dining room, costing £25.[95] Robert Mason of Lynn, joiner, agreed to make a ceiling suitable for the dining chamber, 'at 20d yard square at 3 shillings the plaster, at 10d the freize ... And that he shall find the wainscot agreeable to that in the Parlour ... '.[96] Some materials and workmanship were procured from London, such as the carvings for the porch. In 1628 Sir Hamon noted information from his son, 'Nick ... upon his enquiry in London' concerning the price and availability of

[94] LEST/Q38, fols. 54, 70, 72.   [95] LEST/Q38, fol. 72.   [96] LEST/Q38, fol. 82.

marble; black was cheaper at 6s 8d a foot, two inches thick, compared with white at 10s.[97] Sometimes, it seems from his specifications that Hamon followed pattern books, and certainly insisted that written plans should be followed. For example, for the chimney piece in the small withdrawing room he referred to a 'prospect suitable to Dicen's book, pa 20'.[98] In 1629, he noted in his agreement with R. Stockden for 'the workmanship of the leaves for my outward stone gates, the worke to be made according to the moulding delivered in paper....'[99]

Architecture embodies cultural and personal values. Johnson has described the transition of elite houses from a 'feudal' to 'polite' style in this period.[100] Sir Roger Townshend's Raynham Hall, built at the same time that Hunstanton Hall was enlarged, is a strikingly modern Palladian-style house, a clear example of 'polite' architecture.[101] Despite being a cultured Renaissance gentleman, Sir Hamon made the decision to remodel his house in an old-fashioned style. He used mainly local building materials, retained a moat, and added crenellations and a courtyard: all features of late medieval elite architecture. While Townshend demolished his old house and built a new one, Sir Hamon incorporated older buildings into the modernized house. Classical-style houses such as Townshend's make no reference to farming, locality or local heritage. In contrast, Sir Hamon's house at Hunstanton emphasized the Le Stranges' rootedness in the locality through its use of local materials and the incorporation of older buildings and architectural references. The agricultural and service buildings at Hunstanton Hall were situated to the front of the house and encircled with an outside wall, giving them unity with the Hall (Fig. 7.3). Classical details were left to the two entrance ways, the porch and gateway, minor but prominent elements of the building. As such, Hunstanton Hall seems remarkably true to Sir Hamon's values.

The building programme was by no means confined to the main house. Service buildings had received attention before the main house was enlarged. The first substantial project was 'building the Dairy and altering the Brewhouse', which was provided with its own well, and cost just over £130. A still-house for distilling was glazed in 1615, a hawks' mew built the next year, followed by a hen-house, goose-house and coach-house. In the following decades barns, granaries, a coal yard, a wool-house, dove-house, bake-house, larder, apple chamber, slaughter-house, scullery and wash-house were added. The improvement of the buildings, particularly those of a functional nature, show Sir Hamon's interest in technology. In 1618, he designed a new brew-house and bake-house to be situated south of the dairy. It consisted of three rooms 46 feet long, divided into the bake-house, the cooler 'woortfatt', where the malt fermented, and the firehouse, copper and 'mashfatt'. 'The copper to stand on the east side and a cistern for draynes on the west'. At the

[97] LEST/Q38.
[98] LEST/Q38.
[99] LEST/Q38, fol. 123.
[100] M. Johnson, *Housing Culture: Traditional Architecture in an English Landscape* (London, 1993), 140–1.
[101] Johnson, *Housing Culture*, 140; M. Girouard, *Life in the English Country House* (New Haven, 1978), 122; Campbell, 'Documentary evidence'.

Fig. 7.3. The front of Hunstanton Hall *c*.1926 seen from the distance, showing the 'upper freestone gates', and the outer wall encircling service buildings to the front of the hall as well as the house itself. Reproduced with permission from the *Country Life* Picture Library.

same time, the dairy was equipped with pipes and pumps.[102] Nor were the Le Stranges' efforts restricted to Hunstanton Hall—they spent large sums building houses and farm buildings elsewhere on the estate. They were particularly active in Gressenhall, Heacham and Sedgeford. For instance, at Gressenhall a new manor house with a full range of service buildings was constructed. At Caly's manor, Heacham, the 'very ancient' house was improved, provided with new buildings and the watermill repaired. At Sedgeford, two principal farmsteads were constructed at East Hall and West Hall. At Ringstead, houses were built for the shepherds. This work was gradually taken over by Sir Nicholas. Between 1646 and 1652 at East Hall, Sedgeford, he extended the main house and built a new barn, dairy, yards and fence-walls, as well as undertaking building work in Hunstanton.[103]

The improvement of estate buildings combined a show of prestige with practical exigencies. Larger houses with better buildings indicated the presence of a wealthy landlord, but could also be let for higher rents. When it came to agricultural land, the Le Stranges were not aggressive improvers. Their two main projects during the first half of the seventeenth century were the improvement of the park and lands

[102] LEST/Q38, fol.29.   [103] LEST/KA9.

that surrounded Hunstanton Hall, and the drainage of marshes at Hunstanton and Heacham. Amongst Sir Hamon's first entries in his notebook is his description of the imparking achieved by his father in the 1580s; by purchasing 93.75 acres of strips he almost doubled the size of the park from 100 to nearly 200 acres.[104] Sir Hamon increased it further by acquiring 77 acres, where the park abutted West Field to the south. This new triangle of parkland extended the view from the new south wing of Hunstanton Hall. Against the new boundary, which rises up from the valley where the Hall stands, Sir Hamon erected palings and placed strategic plantings of trees screening the park from the open fields, and possibly protecting the house from the coastal winds.

The reclamation of the marshes at Hunstanton was Sir Nicholas' project, started in the early 1630s soon after his marriage. The enterprise can be seen as a self-contained venture for the young man eager to expand and develop his inheritance, working alongside his father and mother. He kept detailed notebooks, of which four survive, providing a run of his activities from 1631 to 1653.[105] The marshes at Hunstanton and Heacham harboured malaria in this period: their drainage was of general benefit to the local communities, although it is not clear whether either the Le Stranges or the local inhabitants realized this at the time. Sir Nicholas' motivations seem to have been twofold: to create new leasehold arable farms out of land that had brought in little income, and to provide planned areas for 'fishing, fowling and brooke-hawking' in the marshy land, and on the dunes between marsh and the sea at Hunstanton common, the aim being to make 'it handsome for gunne and hawke in'.[106] Drainage was a complex and labour-intensive business, a process outlined in detail in Sir Nicholas' notebooks, making it clear that there was at least one other consequence, the provision of plentiful work for the local population of smallholding labourers through the difficult economic years of the 1630s. The activities of Nicholas mimic on a small scale the attempts to drain the East Anglian fens at this date, something in which the Le Stranges invested and lost money: Alice recorded £500 'lost by aduenturing in Bosten fennes' in a summary at the end of her final account book. Sir Nicholas' activities were also costly; in the same note, Alice wrote 'lost by Heacham Marsh about £600'.[107]

CONCLUSION

A range of activities served to assert gentry status as expressions of wealth and lifestyle in this period: office-holding, travel, sociability involving house-visits, hunting, certain styles of music, the ownership of books, familiarity with the latest advances in knowledge, building large and impressive houses, and well-ordered estates. Aside from house-visits, gentlemen participated in all these activities more frequently than gentlewomen. Lady Alice owned some books, travelled in coaches,

---

[104] LEST/Q38; LEST/BK1; LEST/R9.
[105] LEST/KA6, LEST/KA9–10 and KA24.
[106] LEST/KA6.   [107] LEST/P10.

listened to music and told jests, but she was peripheral to many of the activities discussed in this chapter. The household economy rested on her careful management, and the family's status on her moral behaviour, but the promotion of the family's reputation and standing in the county community was undertaken by Sir Hamon. The accounts and Sir Hamon's notebook convey the strong impression that, in his pursuit of this aim, Sir Hamon spent money much more freely than his wife. His primary concern was status rather than good management. His particular interests—coaches, hawking, books, scientific instruments and house improvement—also show continuities across time in male patterns of consumption. These male consumption concerns of vehicles, sport, technology and house improvement are evident in the eighteenth and early nineteenth centuries, and remain important areas of active male consumption in the modern economy.[108]

Most of the forms of consumption discussed in this chapter revolve around activities rather than goods. Although the evidence provided by household accounts is not always perfect, they do offer evidence of ephemeral forms of consumption such as leisure, travel, sociability, games, sport, entertainment, music, learning and science, through equipment and fees paid to performers. Some of the objects associated with these activities were clearly fetishized, developing an attraction of their own beyond the activity they enabled or promoted, particularly coaches, books and scientific instruments. In a pattern that is familiar from the study of everyday consumption in Chapter 4 and material culture in Chapter 5, elite forms of consumption combined the traditional with the very new with little apparent tension. Newness was welcomed, enjoyed and respected in the form of books and scientific instruments, alongside traditional activities such as bawdy humour and hunting with hawks. This chapter has pushed the boundaries of what we might consider consumption to be: was holding political office and paying taxes really a form of consumption? If improving one's house and park were important forms of gentry consumption, what about improving other houses and lands on the estate? As with household management and the provision of food discussed in Chapters 2 and 4, the boundaries between production and consumption, work and leisure, duty and choice are indistinct.

---

[108] A. Vickery, 'His and hers: gender, consumption and household accounting in eighteenth century England', *Past and Present* supplement 1 (2006), 12; D. Hussey, 'Guns, horses and stylish waistcoats? Male consumer activity and domestic shopping in late-eighteenth and early nineteenth-century England', in D.E. Hussey and M. Ponsonby (eds.), *Buying for the Home: Shopping for the Domestic from the Seventeenth Century to the Present* (Aldershot, 2008), 47–72; J. Pahl, *Money and Marriage* (New York, 1989), 143–4; D. Miller, *A Theory of Shopping* (Cambridge, 1998), 22, 39.

8

The Employment of Labour

> *I agreed with Thomas Lane of Ringstead late servant to Richard Cademan that he shall enter my service at All Saints next, to be and continue with me in the office of bailiff of my husbandry, for the wages of £3 per annum, one livery, and to have 2 acres to sow with barley every year.*[1]

The employment patterns revealed by the Le Strange accounts demonstrate the close relationship between production and consumption in the early seventeenth century. Some workers provided services that were consumed directly by members of the family, such as barbers, musicians, tutors, coachmen, butlers, physicians and wet nurses. Others worked to maintain the Le Stranges' house and possessions: the tinker and cooper, who mended vessels in the kitchen; the chambermaids and washmaids, who cleaned the house and its contents; the carpenters, masons, thatchers, glaziers and plumbers, who maintained the fabric of Hunstanton Hall and its outbuildings; and the day labourers, who scoured the moat, cut back gorse and brambles, and hedged and ditched the estate. Then there were those workers who produced goods that were consumed directly and indirectly by the household, such as the agricultural workers, cook, tailors, knitters, weavers, apothecaries, silversmiths and building craftsmen. In the modern world the path from production to consumption is often a long and tortuous one, criss-crossing continents: reconstructing these relationships is seen as a primary aim for consumption studies by political economists such as Fine.[2] Only occasionally and out of necessity do we come into direct contact with the producers of what we consume: such as doctors, hairdressers, cleaners and builders, who provide direct services for our bodies and homes. In early seventeenth-century England it was normal and expected for producers and consumers to come face to face. People and objects who broke this direct link, traders and foreign goods, were still regarded with a degree of suspicion and curiosity despite being well entrenched in the English economy.

The lack of direct links between producers and consumers in the modern economy means that consumers typically have no understanding of how the goods they purchase were made, and do not have to confront the low pay, long working hours and poor living conditions endured by many producers. Differences

---

[1] Entry for 28 July 1616, the notebook of Sir Hamon Le Strange; LEST/Q38.
[2] The systems of provision approach in B. Fine, *The World of Consumption: The Material and Cultural Revisited*, 2nd edn (London, 2002), especially chs. 5 and 6.

of wealth were stark in early modern England but the rich and the poor remained in close contact. The Le Stranges had an income of over £2000 a year, while their servants earned annual cash wages of between £1 and £5, and labourers resident in Hunstanton village had an annual income of perhaps £10. The Le Stranges drew the majority of their income from rents, paid by the less wealthy households that lived around them in north-west Norfolk. One of the reasons these gross inequalities were tolerated is that landlords such as the Le Stranges not only took wealth away from local communities but also returned some of it. Their consumption patterns entailed the employment of large numbers of people. Thus, a detailed examination of the employment of labour is necessary both to offer a rounded view of consumption patterns in an elite household and to understand the social and economic consequences of consumption in the early seventeenth century. Consumption was not just about things in the early seventeenth century, it was also about social relationships.

In the ten years between 1615 and 1624 the Le Stranges employed a total of 274 named individuals as servants, labourers, craftsmen or specialists. Together these workers account for 4345 payments in the disbursement accounts and kitchen books. There was also work carried out by people described only by their occupation: the barber, cooper, tinker, sawyers, taskers, knitters and wet nurses, which account for a further 775 payments. Then there was work described by the task: digging up gorse, cleaning ditches, processing hemp, which together add another 282 payments. As a result of production and consumption being closely connected, payments for labour shade into payments for products. Servants rarely provided anything but their labour. Labourers sometimes provided tools, but little else. However, the work of craftsmen and specialists cannot always be clearly separated from the things they sold: a shoemaker was paid for the materials and labour it took to make boots, a silversmith for engraving and silverware, an apothecary for medicines and advice. These complexities make it hard to quantify the exact amount of labour employed, or the costs incurred. However, it is possible to describe the range of people employed and the tasks carried out, and suggest minimum numbers and range of day labourers, craft workers and specialists used by the Le Stranges. The close relationship between servants and the household means that they can be described in most detail, although the exact nature of their work often remains hidden.

This chapter follows a blueprint created by Smith in his classic articles on the labourers employed by Nathaniel Bacon of Stiffkey in the last two decades of the sixteenth century.[3] Stiffkey was just twenty miles along the Norfolk coast from Hunstanton, and Bacon was a gentleman of a similar wealth and status to the Le Stranges. Smith's aim was to examine 'the work patterns and life-styles of a group of labouring men and women', using Bacon's account books.[4] This led to a slightly different approach from that taken here. He discussed agricultural servants, but

---

[3] A.H. Smith, 'Labourers in late sixteenth-century England: a case study from north Norfolk', *Continuity and Change* 4:1 (1989) [Part I and II].
[4] Smith, 'Labourers' [Part I], 11.

not Bacon's other servants, who he considered primarily domestic workers. He concentrated on those workers who lived locally to Stiffkey and not the whole range of workers Bacon employed. However, he was able to put the lives of the workers he studied into a rich local context through the intensive reconstruction of late sixteenth-century Stiffkey and the surrounding villages using a range of documents. This chapter makes use of local parish registers, wills, probate inventories and the Le Stranges' estate rentals as well as the accounts, but does not attempt a full reconstruction of Hunstanton's village community. The chapter explores the relationship between the Le Stranges and their workers, looking in turn at household servants, day labourers, and craftsmen and specialists. The final section examines the relationship between the Le Stranges and the local community via case studies of particular families.

SERVANTS

Servants were intimately connected to the consumption patterns of the Le Strange household. They were themselves items of consumption that represented a significant regular expenditure by the Le Stranges. The male liveried servants in particular were employed and dressed as an overt show of status, part of the 'conspicuous consumption' necessary to maintain rank within the gentry. Servants produced, prepared and cared for items of consumption in the household: making food and drink, and maintaining the beds, linen, dining ware, house, garden, horses and coaches and other goods. In addition, they were consumers themselves: they ate, drank and slept in the house as well as working there.

Servant employment by elite households was transformed between the late fifteenth century and the early seventeenth centuries. Late medieval elite households were very large and dominated by men. Mertes observes that the average household of an earl 'numbered upwards of 200' people, the majority of whom were male servants.[5] These households were 'actively hostile to the presence of women'.[6] Large numbers of male followers in a household served to cement political ties of patronage and to provide a show of status and military force. With so many male servants, many of them single, women were seen as corrupting household order. The lady of the household and a few ladies-in-waiting kept as her companions made up the female contingent and were carefully separated from the majority of the men.[7] During the sixteenth century the role of the household and its servants in maintaining the political power of the aristocracy and gentry gradually waned.[8] Even in the early sixteenth century some gentry households were small: despite his wealth and court connections Sir Thomas Le Strange of

---

[5] K. Mertes, *The English Noble Household 1250–1600: Good Governance and Politic Rule* (Oxford, 1988), 187; also C.M. Woolgar, *The Great Household in Late Medieval England* (New Haven, 1999), 9–21.
[6] Mertes, *The English Noble Household*, 57.
[7] Mertes, *The English Noble Household*, 57–8; Woolgar, *The Great Household*, 34.
[8] Mertes, *The English Noble Household*, 190.

Hunstanton had a household of only seventeen people in the 1530s.[9] By the early seventeenth century gentry households had become more like those lower down the social scale: centres of production and consumption for a particular family. Elite households shrunk in size and the proportion of female servants increased.[10] Cliffe's survey of households with an income of £1000–3000 a year in the seventeenth century shows that most employed fewer than thirty servants, with only a few larger households of thirty to fifty people remaining in Yorkshire and Lincolnshire.[11]

Viewed from this perspective the Le Strange household as it existed between 1606 and 1653 was a modern establishment. It was small, with an average complement of sixteen servants; it contained no elite male servants paid more than £10 a year; and five of the servants employed at any one time were women. The servants were concerned solely with the production, consumption and leisure activities of the Le Strange family and had no direct political or military function. Employment of servants by elite households was still in the process of evolution, however. By the late seventeenth and eighteenth centuries, terms of employment were less stable, with servants rarely staying in a particular household for more than a year compared with an average of three years in the early seventeenth-century Le Strange household.[12] The social status of servants continued to decline over time. The Le Stranges' better paid servants came from the prosperous households of the yeomanry and lesser gentry. Service in a gentry household still conferred prestige and rewards that made it attractive to those of middling wealth. By the eighteenth century servants typically came from poorer households and the social distance between them and their employers had increased.[13]

In 1613 the Le Stranges expanded their household by increasing the number of live-in servants from around seven a year to twelve and then sixteen, which remained the average for the period up to 1653. The servants' names are listed in the disbursement accounts with their wages paid half yearly at Our Lady (Lady Day, 25 March) and St Michael (Michaelmas, 29 September), and occasionally quarterly at Midsummer and Christmas. In 1617 Sir Hamon drew up a list in his notebook of the servants employed, with their job descriptions (Table 8.1). The servants fell into three groups. First, there were the senior male servants, eight of whom were employed that year. These men received liveries as well as their wages. Hamon seems to have managed these servants himself: he purchased the liveries and sometimes recorded their contracts in his notebook.[14] They included senior household servants, such as the clerk, cook and butler, those in charge of the coach

---

[9] K. Wrightson, *Earthly Necessities: Economic Lives in Early Modern Britain, 1470–1750* (New Haven, 2000), 31.
[10] M. Dawson, *Plenti and Grase: Food and Drink in a Sixteenth Century Household* (Totnes, 2009), 47.
[11] J.T. Cliffe, *The World of the Country House in Seventeenth-Century England* (New Haven, 1999), 199–201.
[12] A. Vickery, *The Gentleman's Daughter: Women's Lives in Georgian England* (New Haven, 1998), 135; B. Hill, *Servants: English Domestics in the Eighteenth Century* (Oxford, 1996), 102.
[13] Hill, *Servants*, 5.
[14] LEST/Q38.

Table 8.1. Servants in the Le Strange household, 1617

Role	Name	Wage	Years employed
'my clerk'	Steward Trench	£3	4¼
'my falconer'	Christopher Townshend	£4	5
'my cook'	(John Reeve al. Cook)	£5	8¾
'my old servant and butler'	(Thomas) Ketwood	£3 (£4)	16
'my coachman'	(James Oldman)	£3 (£2 10s)	8¼
'my horsekeeper'	(Christopher Anguish)	£3 (£4)	3
'my bailiff'	(Thomas Lane)	£3	7½
(gardener)	(Rob Brasenets)[a]	(£4)	3
'all those person's before being household servants a livery a piece 8s'			
'a scullion'	(James Nightingale)	£1 16s	4½
'a boy to plow and cart'	(Cambridge)	£2 (34s)	5
'another to plow and cart'	(Bullward)	£2 (34s)	9¾
'a dairy maid'	(Anne Bower)	£2 (36s)	4¼
'a backhouse maid'	(Anne Willson/Anne Whittle)[a]	£1 10s	1 and 4¾
'a washer'	(Elizabeth Bride)	£1 10s	5¼
'two chamber maids'	(Margaret Lawes)	£2 10s	3
	(Margery Siborne)	£2	7½
		£40 6s	

Notes: Role, name and wage from Sir Hamon Le Strange's notebook; length of employment from disbursement accounts. Where names were not given in the notebook, and where wages in the accounts differed from those in the notebook, these are noted here in brackets.

[a] Brasenets left at Michaelmas 1617. Anne Willson left at Midsummer 1617, and was replaced by Anne Whittle, who began seven weeks before Michaelmas 1617.

Sources: Notebook of Hamon Le Strange; LEST/Q38. Disbursement accounts; LEST/P7.

and horses, and the bailiff of husbandry, who ran the home farm. The wages of the falconer, Christopher Townshend, do not appear in the disbursement accounts at all, although references in Hamon's notebook show that he was in employment for at least five years. Alice Le Strange oversaw the employment of the other two groups of servants, the female servants and the lower paid male servants, who included the kitchen boy and two or three farm workers. She also paid the wages. Comparison between the wages noted by Hamon and those in the disbursement accounts recorded by Alice show that although Hamon had a good idea of the overall wage bill, which came to £40, he was vague about what particular servants were actually being paid.

Comparison between the household servants employed by the Le Stranges and those of a wealthy yeoman, Robert Loder, and a minor gentleman farmer, Henry Best, demonstrate what was distinctive about the servants of the upper gentry. In 1615 Robert Loder of Harwell in Berkshire employed three men and two women. The men were a carter, a shepherd, and a boy who helped with the ploughing and other agricultural tasks. They were paid £3 10s, £2 8s, and £1 15s 6d, respectively, for their year's work. The two female servants were paid £2 and £2 5s. They malted barley, milked cows, picked and sold fruit from the orchard, and helped prepare food and clean for the other members of the household.[15] Henry Best, whose East Yorkshire farm was larger than Loder's, described the servants necessary for his farm and household in his memorandum book of 1642. He listed six male servants and two female servants. The male servants were all agricultural workers, stretching from the bailiff of husbandry, who was expected to be competent in all aspects of farm work and agricultural marketing and received £3 6s 8d a year, to a boy to help with the plough, who was paid £1. His two female servants, paid £1 4s and £1 8s, did 'washing, baking, milking and brewing', as well as cleaning the house.[16] Thus, we can see that lesser gentry and yeomen had no need for inside servants such as clerks, cooks, butlers and chambermaids; nor outside servants associated with travel and leisure, such as a coachman, horse-keeper or falconer. The work of female servants was less differentiated, mixing farm work with cleaning and cooking. The men concerned themselves with outside tasks. That said, the work of the Le Strange servants was not as specialized as first appears. The coachman, for instance, was also the brewer and was expected 'to dig at spare times in the garden', help at harvest time, and chop wood for Sir Hamon's chamber.[17] The bailiff in husbandry ran errands for the household, including travelling regularly to King's Lynn and occasionally to Norwich and London as well as doing farm work. And although the Le Stranges had a specialist dairymaid, at least one of the other female servants must have helped with milking the twenty cows twice a day in summer. Some gentry households employed more agricultural servants. Nathaniel Bacon of Stiffkey ran a demesne farm of 600 acres which employed between eight and ten male servants in husbandry each year.[18] The Le Stranges did not farm on this scale.

The Le Strange wage bill was low by the standards of the upper gentry. Their wages for equivalent employees were slightly lower than Robert Loder's, but higher than Best's Yorkshire wages. They employed none of the high-paid senior male servants that one would expect to find in a large household: there was no estate steward or household steward, who might be paid up to £20 a year.[19] Sir Hamon and Alice did this work themselves. And they kept quite a small household for their wealth. The twenty-five households with an annual income of between £1000 and £3000 in the period 1600–50 for which Cliffe provides details employed an average of twenty servants.[20] Wage bills varied from £97 to £200 a year, compared with the Le Stranges' £40–50.[21] The Le Stranges' highest paid servant was the cook on £5 a year. The bailiff of husbandry typically received £4. None of the liveried male servants received less than £2 10s a year. On the other hand, the kitchen boys and common servants in husbandry never received this much. The kitchen boys were

---

[15] G.E. Fussell (ed.), *Robert Loder's Farm Accounts 1610–1620*, Camden Society 3rd series, vol. 53 (London, 1936), 107.
[16] J. Whittle, 'Servants in rural England c.1450–1650: hired work as a means of accumulating wealth and skills before marriage', in M. Agren and A. Erickson (eds.) *The Marital Economy in Scandinavia and Britain 1400–1900* (Aldershot, 2005), 91–2.
[17] Coachman's contract 1632, in LEST/Q38, fol. 141.
[18] Smith, 'Labourers' [Part I], 12, 14.
[19] Cliffe, *Country House*, 114, and Chapter 2: Household and estate management.
[20] Cliffe, *Country House*, 199–201.
[21] Cliffe, *Country House*, 102.

the lowest paid workers. James Nightingale started work in 1613 receiving £1 6s 8d, raised to £1 14s in 1615. He supplemented his income by catching rats, for which Alice Le Strange paid him 2d each. Nightingale stayed for four and a half years. The next boy, Woodward, began on a wage of £1 10s in 1618, raised to £1 16s in 1620, and also stayed for just over four years. He was followed by Vincent, who received a mere £1 4s in 1623. He must have been poor as Alice paid to have his clothes made, with 3s spent on cloth and 1s 8d to the tailor to make them up. Two or three common servants in husbandry were employed each year 'to plow and cart' as Hamon put it. They received between £1 10s and £2 3s a year. Despite these relatively low wages, some stayed in the household for a long time, as can be seen from Table 8.1.

Female servants were, with a few exceptions, paid between £1 10s and £2 a year. When the household was first enlarged in 1613 Alice Le Strange attempted to employ five women at between £1 and £1 6s 8d a year: three stayed less than a year and none for more than eighteen months. From 1614 onwards female servants received at least £1 10s, the wage given to the scullerymaid or 'backhouse maid' and the washmaid. The dairymaid and chambermaids received £2 a year. Margaret Lawes, employed in 1616 for £2 10s, was the only female servant to receive more than this before 1627. She worked in the household for three years. Lawes was still single when she made her will in March 1624/5, showing herself to be a woman of some means. She came from neighbouring Sedgeford and owned a close of land and a stock of linen and furniture as well as £6 out on loan.[22] Wages crept upwards in the 1620s and in 1627 two women were employed for £3 a year. One, Anne Haymish, was the most productive dairymaid Alice engaged during this period but she stayed only a year.[23] Not all dairymaids arrived at the household ready trained. Some washmaids or scullerymaids graduated to this post. Anne Walker began work at the household in Michaelmas 1620 and became dairymaid in Spring 1622, with a pay rise of 6s to £1 16s. Elizabeth Harrold began work in 1625 for £1 10s a year. She became dairymaid for the summer of 1629, and was paid £2 for that year. Unlike Nathaniel Bacon, Alice Le Strange never employed married dairymaids.[24]

Despite the length of time many servants stayed with the Le Stranges, pay rises were not common. Of the eighty-nine different servants recruited between 1613 and 1628 only ten received pay rises during their period of employment. However, the majority of the payment received by servants for their work was not cash but payments in kind, primarily board and lodgings. Using calculations made by Robert Loder, the Berkshire yeoman, it is possible to show that 77 per cent of the cost of keeping servants went in food, drink and everyday consumables like fuel and candles.[25] The Le Stranges fed their servants plainer foodstuffs than they themselves ate but this still provided a good diet.[26] The inventory of bedrooms

---

[22] The will of Margaret Lawes of Sedgeford, singlewoman: NRO PRDC 1/2/5, fol. 280.
[23] See Chapter 3: The acquisition of food.
[24] Smith, 'Labourers' [Part I], 17.
[25] Whittle, 'Servants in rural England', 96.
[26] See Chapter 4: The meanings of food, particularly Table 4.4.

from 1632 shows that female servants and senior male servants slept in well-furnished featherbeds.[27] There were other types of payment too. The liveries worn by the senior male servants consisted of cloth suits and velvet capes edged with lace: these cost Hamon Le Strange £2 8s 5d to purchase for each man in 1616. Occasionally, servants' contracts record individually negotiated payments in kind. Thomas Lane received 2 acres of land to sow with barley each year. William Cox, a cook employed in 1625, received all calf-skins, rabbit-skins and lamb-skins. Henry Balls received a pig in addition to his cash wage each year.[28]

Further income was added by tips and gifts. In the later seventeenth century Sir Richard Newdigate gave his servants bonuses when he was pleased with them, but docked their pay for real or supposed misdemeanours.[29] The Le Stranges did not operate a similar system: no deductions or additions are recorded in the accounts, other than recurrent pay rises. However, high-status visitors to households habitually gave servants tips. We do not know how much was received by the Le Strange servants, but we can see how much Sir Hamon Le Strange tipped servants in other households. In 1617, not a particularly generous year, Hamon handed out over £4 in tips to servants in seventeen different households. On a trip to Norwich, for instance, he gave away £1 4s 8d in the houses at Rougham, Sprowston and Walsingham where he stayed. He gave Christmas gifts to the servants in Richard Stubbe's household: 'to Mary and Margrett at Sedgford 10s and to the Cooke 4s'. He gave 2s to Mr Corbett's footman, 1s to the shoemaker Sappe's man, and 6d to a horse-keeper at Massingham. Tips provided an addition to servants' wages but they also served as a reminder of the stark differences in wealth and status. A 5s Christmas gift to a female servant was about an eighth of her annual wage. The gentry could dole out these sums without much thought, while a senior female servant had to work for six weeks to earn as much.

Gifts were also given when servants left the household, and when household heads died. Twenty-one of the eighty-nine servants employed between 1613 and 1628 left with gifts of between 1s and £3 at the end of their service. All the servants who left to get married in Hunstanton or Heacham received gifts. Richard Stubbe and Sir Hamon and Alice each left bequests to servants in their wills. At his death in 1619, Stubbe gave bequests to four named servants, as well as smaller sums to all his 'household menservants' and 'maid servants'. Thomas Benwell, his 'trusty and faithful servant' who received a gift of £40, was probably his estate steward or clerk, as he was married and a tenant of the Le Stranges at the time. Stubbe's two senior female servants, Mary Burnell and Margaret Willson (the same two women Sir Hamon gave Christmas gifts to in 1617), received £15 and £6 13s 4d respectively. Sir Hamon left gifts for twelve of his servants in the codicil of his will, made three months before his death. All his clothing apart from velvet and furs was distributed amongst the male servants, one of whom also received a gift of £8.

---

[27] See Chapter 5: Beds and living rooms. Cliffe finds another example of this, *Country House*, 104.
[28] LEST/Q38, fols. 6, 7, 84, 140.
[29] S. Hindle, 'Below stairs at Arbury Hall: Sir Richard Newdigate and his household staff, c.1670–1710', *Historical Research* (forthcoming).

Margaret and Elizabeth Guybon, long-employed female servants, were given £5 each. The cook was given £2 and all other named servants £1. Alice left bequests to six servants, probably all those she employed at the time of her death.

Many servants worked for the Le Stranges for long periods of time. The average was three years, but of the servants first employed between 1613 and 1628 sixteen (18 per cent) stayed in the household for five years or more and only thirteen (15 per cent) stayed for less than year. The highest turnover was amongst female servants, who stayed at Hunstanton Hall for two and a quarter years on average. The low-paid male servants stayed longest: male servants with wages of less than £2 5s a year stayed for an average of four and a quarter years, while the liveried male servants stayed for three and a half years on average. This surely reflects the lack of alternative employment opportunities for labouring men in this difficult economic period, as well as the quality of food and accommodation offered by the Le Stranges. Servants arrived in the household and left again at all times of the year, as happened in Bacon's household at Stiffkey in the late sixteenth century.[30] The quarter days of Our Lady, Midsummer and Michaelmas were noticeable peaks, but plenty of servants arrived and left at other times, indicating that the Le Stranges relied on personal contacts rather than hiring fairs to recruit their workers.

What were the origins of these servants? A few, like the Guybons, were from the lesser gentry and were related to Alice Le Strange. A number came from local tenant families; some were the sons and daughters of labourers. Table 8.2 shows the origins of the eighty-nine servants recruited by the Le Stranges between 1613 and 1628, in terms of their family's previous contact with the household. The proportion who came from among the Le Stranges' tenants was quite low at 18 per cent. Tenants' sons most often became well-paid liveried servants. Typically these were the sons of yeomen farmers, lesser gentry or leaseholders taking on positions such as the bailiff in husbandry: men such as Thomas Banyard, Robert Bastard, Thomas Burnham, Thomas Cremer and Thomas Guybon fit this model. It was less common for the sons of smallholders to become ordinary servants in husbandry in the household; Bullward and Greenrod are the only examples in this period. Female servants came from the whole range of backgrounds: some, such as the Guybon sisters, Anne Rayner and Margaret Lawes, came from well-off tenant families. Others came from lower down the social scale. Margaret Mosse, Anne Bird and Alice Taftes were daughters of Hunstanton smallholders, taken on when the servant contingent of the household was expanded in 1613, but none of them stayed for long.

It was more common for servants to have connections other than land tenure with the household. Three female servants from the Chant family, Mary, Elizabeth and Frances, were almost certainly the daughters of Alice Chant, Alice Le Strange's former washerwoman, and her day labouring husband, who also worked for the Le Stranges.[31] We can imagine that they were trained to be washmaids like their mother. The Le Strange boys boarded with Mr Bust while at Eton from 1620 to

---

[30] Smith, 'Labourers' [Part I], 15.
[31] The Chants possibly came from Thornham (see will registers), they were not tenants.

Table 8.2. The origins of the servants employed, 1613–28

	Liveried male servants	Female servants	Non-liveried male servants	All servants
Same surname as a tenant	23%	17%	11%	18%
Others with same surname appear in accounts[a]	34%	53%	28%	40%
No known link[a]	43%	31%	61%	42%
Total	35	36	18	89

[a] Before the servant was employed. Other people with same surname appearing after the servant was employed have been assumed to result from the servant's employment. Hunstanton parish registers were also checked. None of the families which did not appear in the accounts, appeared having children baptized 1610–28.

Sources: Disbursement accounts and kitchen accounts; LEST/P6, P7, P8. Rentals and manorial accounts; LEST/EH 5; LEST/BK 15; LEST/BK7; LEST/DHI 16; LEST/EK5; LEST/OC1.

1623; his son William Bust went into service in the household in 1624. Mary and Lydia Waterman appeared in service in the household after Mr Waterman, the surveyor, had been employed by Sir Hamon. Widow Siborne was a seamstress who made sheets for the Le Stranges on one occasion in 1612; Margery Siborne was employed as a servant in 1615 and stayed for eight years before marrying a fellow servant. Sarah Waddelow is likely to have been the daughter of Waddelow the cooper, who regularly fixed the Le Stranges' tubs and barrels. Alice Benwell was probably the daughter of Thomas Benwell, Richard Stubbe's trusty servant. Once one sibling was employed, they were often followed by brothers or sisters. Nearly a quarter of the eighty-nine servants employed by the Le Stranges between 1613 and 1628 either followed or preceded a servant with the same surname.

The establishment of prior connections with the household seems to have been most important for female servants, possibly because some knowledge of family circumstances was desired as an indication of the servant's character. However, it was not essential and a third of the female servants employed had no previous links with the household that could be traced in the records. One of Nicholas Le Strange's merry jests told by Alice Le Strange relates to the pitfalls that could arise from this situation:

> A Wench came to my Grandmother Stubbe to seeke a service, and she entertaind her; so after she had been with her 2 or 3 dayes, sayes she, wench I forgott to ask the for a certificate or Testimoniall how you carryed your selfe where you were last: O Mistresse sayes she, I have one of those above in my Boxe; and up she runns, and for her Testimoniall, brings downe a very faire and formall warrant, signifying that she had lately had a Bastard, and was to be passed from Constable to Constable, to such a place.[32]

It is less easy to trace what happened to servants after they left the Le Stranges' employment. Occasionally there are glimpses of servants working their way up the

---

[32] N. Le Strange, *Merry Passages and Jeasts*, ed. H.F. Lippincott (Salzburg, 1974), 103–4.

occupational ladder. Sir Hamon noted that Thomas Lane, employed as a bailiff of husbandry, was 'the late servant to Richard Cademan', a freeholding yeoman in neighbouring Ringstead. Steward Trench, the Le Stranges' clerk from 1613 to 1617, left to serve the Hobarts, the Le Stranges' wealthy cousins. The longest serving employees effectively retired on leaving service: Hamon Le Strange's 'old servant and butler' Thomas Kettwood, who had been in the Le Stranges' employment since at least 1606 when the accounts begin, was set up with a leasehold farm in Hunstanton when he left their service in 1622. Others also appear to have used service as a route to land tenure. Thomas Lane held 33 acres by lease in Hunstanton in 1621. James Oldman, who was still in the Le Stranges' service, and William Cambridge, who had left service in 1620, shared a 4 acre lease in the same year.[33] William Cambridge, who had been a common servant in husbandry, became a day labourer for the Le Stranges immediately after leaving service. Other servants also remained in employment. Edward Spratt, a servant from 1606 to 1610, continued to act for the Le Stranges into the 1630s as a manorial steward and auditor. Edward Parker, servant from 1606 to 1608, became a farrier and horse doctor frequently used by the Le Stranges in the 1610s and 1620s. Abigail Towers, a servant from 1609 to 1614, became nurse to Elizabeth Le Strange in 1615 and was still making gifts to the household in 1621.

Other than a few senior male servants, such as the clerk and butler, the Le Stranges' servants were all young and single. At least eleven of the eighty-nine servants left the Le Stranges specifically to marry, and often they married fellow servants.[34] Robert Bastard, a bailiff in husbandry, married Barbara Fisher, a fellow servant, in Hunstanton church in 1616, both came from local families. James Oldman, a coachman, married Margery Siborne, a chambermaid, in 1622, after having both been in service with the Le Stranges for more than seven years. William Cambridge married Elizabeth Bride, a washmaid, at Hunstanton in October 1620 a week after leaving service. William Greenrod, another servant in husbandry, married Katherine Warner, one of the lower paid female servants, at Heacham in 1628. Anne Shilling, a Le Strange dairymaid, married John Boner in Hunstanton church in 1621. John was not a servant. A John Boner appears occasionally in the Le Strange accounts from 1610 onwards, doing odd jobs and presenting gifts of fish; goodwife Boner also made a gift in 1616.[35] The John that Anne married was either this man, recently widowed, or his son. John Boner continued to work for the Le Stranges thereafter, and present them with fish, and Anne Boner now made gifts of chickens, ducks and curlew. Twelve of the fifty-six servants who left the household between 1606 and 1623 later made gifts of food to the Le Stranges.[36]

---

[33] LEST/EH5.
[34] Traced via cash gifts given at marriage in the Le Stranges' accounts, and the parish registers of Hunstanton, Heacham, Ringstead St Peter and Sedgeford. The last two registers are badly damaged: legible entries recorded no Le Strange servants.
[35] It seems likely that he was a fisherman. One John Boner of Hunstanton died in 1625.
[36] See Chapter 3: The acquisition of food.

DAY LABOURERS

Day labourers had a looser relationship to the Le Strange household than servants. They lived in their own homes and had some choice about where to work and when. Yet, like servants, they were an important part of the household and estate economy. Labourers worked in agriculture, maintained the estate and did building work for the Le Stranges. Much of the household and kitchen accounts consist of a record of days worked by these people. The nature of day labouring, like service, changed over time. Rural Norfolk had possessed a large population of day-labouring smallholders since at least the fourteenth century, constituting around 20 per cent of householders in the late fourteenth and early sixteenth centuries.[37] Yeomen, large leaseholders and the gentry were regular employers of day labour, but many farms were still too small to require anything other than family labour. While real wages were pitifully low in the late sixteenth and early seventeenth centuries, many of those in the labouring class had sufficient resources to generate a mixed household economy. They rented smallholdings, and possessed livestock, fishing boats, tools and skills, which meant they were not wholly dependent on wages.[38] By the eighteenth century day labourers had increased as a proportion of the population and were much less likely to have access to income other than wages.[39]

The amount of day labour employed by the Le Stranges increased over time, reflecting their increased income. In 1613 the Le Stranges paid labourers and craftsmen for 719.5 days worked, and in 1617 for 1137.5 days. This jumped to over 3000 days a year in 1622, with over 5000 work-days paid for in 1623, falling back to 3684 in 1624. The number of days worked each year remained higher than that in the 1610s throughout the 1630s. However, after a gap in the kitchen accounts during the Civil War years, the amount had fallen back to a low level by the early 1650s. These figures do not account for all the work done by labourers: many types of work such as threshing, ploughing, hedging and ditching, and washing and clipping sheep were normally paid by the task and are not included in these totals. The Le Stranges were not arable farmers on the scale of Nathaniel Bacon or Henry Best. They employed at least two servants in husbandry each year to carry out their basic farm work. However, they did also, on occasion, employ workers by the day or task to plough and 'fellow',[40] to weed and scare birds from crops, to mow (harvest with a scythe) hay, barley, peas and oats, to shear (harvest with sickle) wheat and rye, and to thresh barley, peas, vetches, wheat, rye, mixtlyn

---

[37] J. Whittle, *The Development of Agrarian Capitalism: Land and Labour in Norfolk, 1440–1580* (Oxford, 2000), 227–52.
[38] Smith, 'Labourers' [Part II]; A. Everitt, 'Farm labourers', in J. Thirsk (ed.), *Agrarian History of England and Wales*. Vol. IV. *1500–1640* (Cambridge, 1967); below, The Le Stranges and the local community.
[39] K.D.M. Snell, *Annals of the Labouring Poor: Social Change and Agrarian England 1660–1900* (Cambridge, 1985); M. Overton, *Agricultural Revolution in England: The Transformation of the Agrarian Economy 1500–1850* (Cambridge, 1996), 178–82.
[40] To prepare fallow land for sowing.

and oats. Hemp was planted and then processed, by pilling, changing, riving, bunching and plashing, into rope. In 1622 a specialist hopman was employed to plant and tend hops, and by 1624 nine 'poore people' and 'divers boys & girls' were paid to gather them. Saffron was grown, perhaps experimentally, with 10s 2d paid for 'setting' or planting it 1616, and 2s 4d for 'gathering and picking saffron' in 1618.

Agricultural work shaded into estate maintenance, with agricultural labourers paid for mowing reeds and bracken as well as hay, and planting trees and cutting stakes for palings, as well as hedging and ditching. Trees were cut for timber and faggots, and gorse planted and then cut, also to make faggots for fuel. The estate provided the majority of the raw materials for the Le Stranges' building work. Clay and sand were dug and carted. Building stone was dug, gathered and broken. Lime, bricks and tiles were 'burned' using faggots gathered by the workers. Thatching was done with reed or straw from the marshes and fields. Despite this, the increased amount of workers employed in the 1620s was only partly the result of the large-scale building activities carried out by the Le Stranges in that decade. Most was agricultural and recorded in the kitchen books rather than the building accounts. Unfortunately, as the amount of work recorded in the accounts increased, the level of detail describing the tasks decreased.

Between 1615 and 1624, 103 named people carried out non-specialist wage labour for the Le Stranges, paid by the day or task. Ten of them were boys, two were women and there was one girl; the rest were adult men. One man, Bidden, appears over 300 times in the accounts, working regularly between 1615 and 1624. Four men, Taftes, Sallis, Wix and Moore, appear over 100 times in the same period. A further group of twelve, men such as Wesenham, and one boy, Wix's son, appeared thirty to ninety-nine times. Most of the workers, the remaining eighty-six, appeared only occasionally. Fifty-two were paid in the accounts fewer than five times. Thus, the majority of workers seem to have had a casual and occasional relationship with the Le Stranges. Even the regular day workers drew only a modest income from the Le Strange household in most years. Figure 8.1 shows the annual earnings between 1616 and 1624 of three day labourers, Bidden, Taftes and Wesenham, for day labouring and task work. Bidden made a reasonable income from his work for the Le Stranges, averaging just over £5 a year, although it dipped below £4 in 1620, and rose above £8 in 1622. Taftes' income was more variable. His earnings averaged just below £3 a year, but consisted of a mere 2s in 1616 and 8d in 1619, before exceeding Bidden's in 1623 and 1624 with earnings of almost £7 and over £10 in those years. Wesenham, a representative of those employed steadily but infrequently by the Le Stranges, averaged earnings of less than £1, ranging from 2s 8d in 1619 to £1 2s in 1621.

These workers carried out a mixture of tasks for the Le Stranges, including all three main types: agricultural work, estate work and building work. They were paid sometimes by the day, and sometimes by task. As task work is not always assigned to a particular worker in the accounts, they could have earned slightly more than shown in Figure 8.1, but not a great deal more. However, just because they carried out a range of tasks does not mean these workers were unskilled or unspecialized.

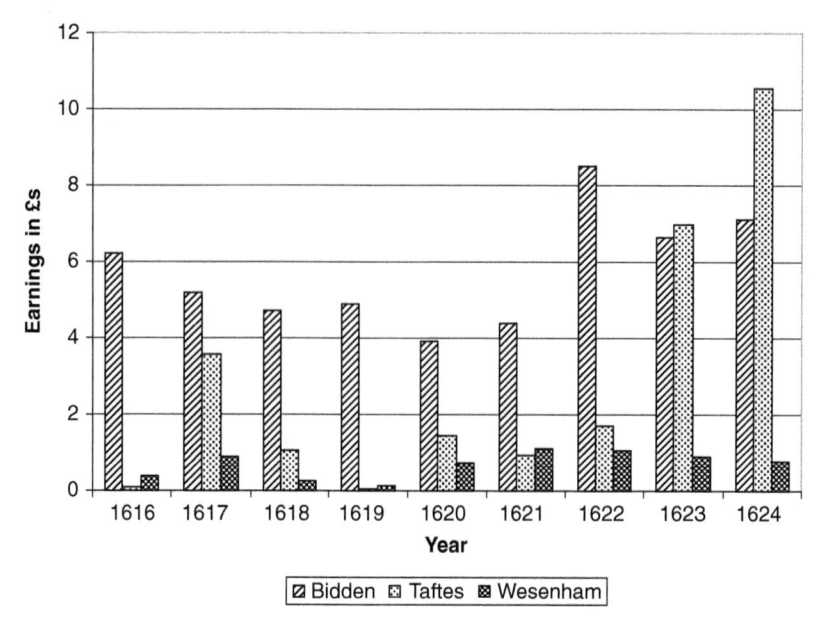

[Figure: bar chart showing earnings in £s for years 1616-1624 with three series: Bidden, Taftes, Wesenham]

Fig. 8.1. The annual earnings of three day labourers, 1616–24.
Source: Disbursement accounts, kitchen accounts and building accounts; LEST/P6, P7, P8.

Bidden, for instance, specialized in mowing and hedging and ditching, two well-paid labouring tasks that required skill and strength. Smith argues that hedgers and ditchers formed an 'elite group within the hierarchy of labourers'.[41] Certainly, Bidden very rarely worked for less than 6d a day, and normally earned 8d plus food and drink. Taftes specialized in working with gorse,[42] as well as threshing, although he also did hedging and ditching and on one occasion undertook the poorly paid task of weeding for 3d or 4d a day. His average daily wage was closer to 7d than 8d, although he was paid 10d a day for the strenuous work of digging gorse. The details of Wesenham's work tasks are rarely stated, suggesting he had no special skill. His average wage was 5d a day, and he was most commonly paid 4d plus food and drink—a low rate of pay.[43]

Nathaniel Bacon of Stiffkey frequently employed young unmarried women to work in gangs as agricultural labourers in the last two decades of the sixteenth century. These women did the weeding and the majority of hay-making, they sheared wheat, picked hops and gathered saffron. In 1593–4 labouring women worked 819 days compared with 662 days worked by non-specialist male labourers.[44] The picture for Hunstanton in the early seventeenth century is very different. Only seven female day labourers appear in the Le Strange accounts in the

[41] Smith, 'Labourers' [Part I], 22.
[42] For 'furze-making' in Langham, see Smith, 'Labourers' [Part I], 24.
[43] See Table 8.3 for comparisons.
[44] Smith, 'Labourers' [Part I], 28–30.

fifteen-year period from 1610 to 1624. The most 'regular' female worker was Margaret Wesenham, the unmarried sister of the male day labourer Wesenham, who undertook a total of thirteen days of agricultural work. She worked alongside her brother in 1613 for four days 'following the scythe', raking up the newly mown oats; and for another day alongside her mother, Widow Wesenham, binding the oats into sheaves. She followed the scythe again in 1614 for one day, and for three days in 1622, when she was paid 6d a day, the same as a male labourer. She also earned 6d a day in 1619 when she worked for four days alongside Godly, another male labourer from Hunstanton, perhaps at the same task. Margaret Wesenham was also Alice Le Strange's preferred choice when she needed extra help in the house. She earned 3s 6d in 1614 for 'helping my maids when I wanted a servant', and 1s 6d in 1617 for 'helping my maids when Anne had a sore hand'. The six other female day labourers who appear in the accounts between 1610 and 1624 appeared only once each, and none worked more than four days. They were all related to male labourers and craftsmen who worked more regularly for the Le Stranges and included three married women, two girls and one widow. They typically earned 4d a day, although Godly's wife, like Margaret Wesenham, was paid 6d, and Wix's wife 3d. It is possible that more female labour is hidden behind some general entries in the accounts where workers are not named, but the number of these entries is not sufficient to change the picture markedly. The impression that the Le Stranges rarely used female labour is underlined by the fact that they employed men to do tasks that were often done by women elsewhere. Smith writes that female day labourers 'weeded, sheared wheat, picked over corn, made hay, planted and harvested saffron, picked hops, sorted wool, and cut marram grass. Men, rarely, unless aged, did these jobs.... As far as these labouring families were concerned men's work and women's work was "sexually exclusive".'[45] On the Le Strange estate there is no evidence for this; instead, male labourers such as Bidden, Savage, Robinson, Wesenham and Wix made hay; and others such as Taftes, Breese and Makement weeded crops. Wesenham and Makement worked 'in the saffron'. All these tasks earned 4d a day, the wage also paid to women.

Hay-making and weeding was also occasionally done by boys for 2d a day, the same wage boys were paid for their other most common tasks, scaring birds from the fields and turning the spit in the kitchen at Christmas time. With the exception of the sons of craftsmen who worked as apprentices for their fathers, only one boy was employed regularly by the Le Stranges. Wix's son was employed from 1619 onwards, and did eighty-nine days' work for the Le Stranges in 1620, seventy-four days in 1621, and 109 in 1622, by which time he had started to earn the higher wage of 4d a day. He did a few days' work in 1623 but then disappears from the accounts, perhaps entering service in husbandry or an apprenticeship at that time elsewhere. The overwhelming reliance on adult male labour for day work was possible in the early seventeenth century because of the oversupply of labour. Yet the Le Stranges retained this pattern of employment in the early 1650s, when the

---

[45] Smith, 'Labourers' [Part II], 377. See also M. Roberts, 'Sickles and scythes: women's work and men's work at harvest time', *History Workshop* 7 (Spring, 1979), 3–28; Dawson, *Plenti and Grase*, 64.

Civil War had changed the situation significantly, and other employers were relying on female agricultural workers.[46] The kitchen books of 1650 and 1651 record no women employed in agricultural labour in Hunstanton: the Le Stranges' response to a reduced supply of male labour seems to have been to cut back the scale of their agricultural activities. In the 1650s regular male labourers were still doing weeding in the Le Strange fields as well as mowing, shearing, and hedging and ditching.

CRAFTSMEN AND SPECIALIST WORKERS

Many people in sixteenth- and seventeenth-century rural England worked not just in agriculture but also in a wide range of specialist occupations and crafts. For instance, a survey of men from rural Norfolk indicted at the quarter sessions between 1558 and 1592 revealed that 45 per cent were farmers, 28 per cent labourers and 27 per cent craft workers and specialists.[47] Using occupational descriptions from probate documents Patten found that 21 per cent of Norfolk's rural parishes contained tailors, 18 per cent carpenters, and 5 per cent smiths in the period 1600–49.[48] The picture of occupational diversity is confirmed by household accounts. Fifty-eight different occupations carried out by at least 120 different individuals are recorded in the accounts between 1615 and 1624. At least eight of the 120 were based in London, a further twelve were in Norwich or Kings Lynn and one in Eton.[49] Set against these were forty-one individuals who definitely lived in rural Norfolk. These included eight shepherds, five carpenters, five thatchers, three tailors, two masons, weavers, sluice menders, clerks, clergymen and nurses, and one each of occupations of brick-maker, tallow chandler, saddler, warrener, tutor, midwife and washerwoman. In Hunstanton itself during this ten-year period there were at least three thatchers, two clergymen, two clerks and two weavers, and one tailor, a knitter, a warrener and a shepherd. A similar range of specialists existed in the neighbouring parishes of Heacham and Sedgeford.

Some occupational specialists worked in agriculture. Eight shepherds appear in the accounts between 1615 and 1624. In the 1610s the Le Stranges kept sheep on their home farm in Hunstanton and on a foldcourse in Ringstead. The scale of sheep farming expanded from 1620 onwards, with the acquisition of Sedgeford manor. Alice Le Strange managed two foldcourses there, which, by 1625, contained 1400 sheep. In 1620 she employed three shepherds in Sedgeford: Woods was in charge of 477 ewes, Rose 270 ewes, and Corner 404 wethers. Woods and Corner were each paid £3 6s 8d a year and a livery payment of 6s 8d. Rose was not paid wages. He was a Sedgeford tenant and was allowed grazing

---

[46] See, for example, 'The account of John Willoughby of Leyhill 1644–6', in T. Gray (ed.), *Devon Household Accounts 1627–59, Part 1* (Exeter, 1995), 129.

[47] Total sample 773 people. Whittle, *Agrarian Capitalism*, 236.

[48] J. Patten, 'Changing occupational structures in the East Anglian countryside, 1500–1700', in H.S.A. Fox and R.A. Butlin (eds.), *Change in the Countryside: Essays on Rural England 1500–1900* (London, 1979), 111.

[49] See Chapter 3: The acquisition of clothing and furnishings.

rights for sixty of his own sheep at a value of £1 10s a year. It is possible that the rest of his wages were allowed in lieu of rent.[50] He and his wife made regular gifts of chickens and turkeys to the Le Stranges throughout this period. The Le Stranges paid their shepherds less than Nathaniel Bacon had in the late sixteenth century: he paid £5 a year along with the right to keep 100–120 of their own sheep, making by Smith's estimate a total payment of around £15 a year.[51] It is hard to estimate total income for the Le Strange shepherds. They certainly kept their own sheep: Crisp had 162 of his own sheep in the flock when they were clipped in 1622. Some were provided with cottages and land, and others, like Rose, were already tenants. Unlike labourers they were in continuous employment. It seems likely that the total income of the Le Strange shepherds was between £5 and £10 rather than £15: similar to the best paid agricultural labourers. Thomas Crispe, a Ringstead shepherd who died in 1630, was not well off; according to his probate inventory his movable wealth amounted to just £8 17s 2d. At that time he owned two cows, pigs and poultry, but no sheep.[52]

Other agricultural specialists included the warrener who leased the Le Strange rabbit warren. He was not paid for his work, but instead paid the Le Stranges £8 a year for the right to farm the rabbits. Between 1616 and 1625 he was making between 16s and £3 above his £8 rent from sales to the Le Stranges alone, and must have made more by selling the rabbits elsewhere. He was also a substantial tenant with 30 acres of leasehold in addition to the warren in 1621. The hopman, Johnson, was an itinerant specialist. Paid by the task for planting and tending hops, he arrived when needed. Johnson was well paid by agricultural standards, with board wages of 14d a day (equivalent to 8d a day with food and drink provided), and sometimes arrived with two 'men' or 'helpers' of his own. As such, his work patterns had more in common with those of rural craftsmen such as masons than day labourers. Craftsmen and specialists not only often held land but also occasionally worked outside their specialism for the Le Stranges. Francis Murton, a carpenter, did carpentry work, cut pales and did paling, and ploughed. Springall, a weaver, wove cloth, worked as a knacker killing cows and did unspecified day work. Richard Wix, a thatcher, regularly did thatching for the Le Stranges, but also undertook agricultural work such as mowing, reaping and threshing. Another thatcher, Giles Noke, had a similar pattern of work. All four of these men were Le Strange tenants in Hunstanton, although Wix actually lived in Heacham. Springall, Wix and Noke were smallholders. Murton was a more substantial tenant with 30 acres of land in 1621: he appears only five times as a worker in the accounts in 1615–16, perhaps before he acquired his full landholding.

Wix and Noke are among five craftsmen who appear more than 100 times in the accounts between 1615 and 1624. The others were Francis Costen, a carpenter, and James Horne and Warner, both masons. Thatchers worked alone with a single

---

[50] Sedgeford estate accounts; LEST/BK7. Sheep accounts in LEST/P10.
[51] Smith, 'Labourers' [Part I], 19.
[52] NRO DN/INV 36/230 Thomas Crispe of Ringstead, shepherd.

server or helper, who was sometimes their apprentice and sometimes a day labourer hired for the job. In contrast, carpenters and masons worked in 'firms' or 'companies' made up of master craftsmen, journeymen and apprentices and often based on close family ties.[53] Costen, Horne and Warner were all employed with companies of their own workers. Costen and his company and Horne and his company each appeared over 400 times in the accounts, while Warner and company, who only began working for the Le Stranges in 1618, appeared over 300 times. Francis Costen's company consisted of three generations of his family, and included at various times his father, 'Old Costen', his brother William and his son, as well as another apprentice and two 'men' or journeymen. A third brother, Thomas Costen of Heacham, was also a carpenter and made his will in 1616.[54] The complexity of their work patterns is indicated by two typical consecutive entries in the kitchen books for the week ending 8 December 1621: 'To Costen for 4 days at 8d and his man 6 days 3s and his boy 6 days 18d. | To Old Costen for 5 days at 8d and to his son for 4 days at 6d.' Thomas Costen had purchased land in Heacham, where he also held land by lease. Francis Costen leased land in Sedgeford, and by 1631 had a substantial leasehold of 39 acres rented from the Le Stranges.[55] The Costens first worked for the Le Stranges in 1614 and were still working for them in the 1650s. Carpenters carried out structural woodwork using large timbers. Finer and lighter woodwork such as making doors and furniture was done by joiners. Joiners appear less frequently in the accounts, but, as with carpentry, the Le Stranges had favoured individuals who they called on when needed. Broadhead, the joiner, was paid thirty-seven times in the accounts from 1607 to 1614 for making items such as furniture, troughs and ceilings; he was replaced with Charles Diser, who appeared seventy-four times in the accounts between 1615 and 1624.

Woodward comments on the lack of work available for masons in early modern England in comparison with the medieval period when building works constructing castles, cathedrals and parish churches had taken place. The construction of elite country houses was one of the few large-scale projects that persisted over time.[56] Ordinary houses were typically made of wood or clay, and increasingly of brick. In north-west Norfolk, substantial buildings in the seventeenth century and earlier relied on local materials: flint, clunch and carstone, sometimes edged with brick.[57] The Le Stranges employed masons to construct not only Hunstanton Hall and its outbuildings but also other houses on their estate and to repair parish churches. From 1610 onwards they employed Thomas and then James Horne as masons. Horne worked with his journeyman and two 'servers', who did the unskilled jobs. From 1618 onwards there seems to have been more work than Horne could manage alone, and the Le Stranges turned first to William Edge and

---

[53] Smith, 'Labourers' [Part I], 22; D. Woodward, *Men at Work: Labourers and Building Craftsmen in the Towns of Northern England, 1450–1750* (Cambridge, 1995), 25–7.
[54] NRO: NCC will register Sayer, 23.
[55] LEST/BK7.
[56] Woodward, *Men at Work*, 17.
[57] R. Lucas, 'Walling materials in parsonage houses, 1794', in P. Wade-Martins (ed.), *An Historical Atlas of Norfolk* (Norwich, 1994), 114–15.

his brother Robert, who worked for them from 1614 to 1618, and then to Warner. Warner's company typically consisted of six men: himself, his journeyman and his apprentice, and three 'servers'. From 1622 to 1624, at the height of building work extending Hunstanton Hall, it was necessary to employ a third company, Thomas and John Poynter, who appear seventeen times during those years. By this time, the Le Stranges were also employing a specialist stone-cutter, Ashley, to work the freestone they had imported from Northamptonshire to edge the buildings.[58]

The work of the masons and carpenters was supplemented by that of other craftsmen: a brick-maker, smith, glazier, plumber and tiler, but none of them worked on such a regular basis. Table 8.3 shows the wages paid to these craftsmen, their journeymen and apprentices by the Le Stranges, compared with agricultural wages and with the statutory maximum wages laid down by Justices of the Peace, such as Sir Hamon, at quarter sessions. The Le Stranges paid some masons and joiners as well as their gardener slightly more than these rates, but others, such as thatchers and apprentice craftsmen, slightly less. Most skilled craftsmen earned no more per day than an agricultural worker did for strenuous work such as mowing. However, unlike the agricultural day labourers, they received these wages whenever they worked, not just at harvest time. The Norfolk wage assessment of 1610 carefully specified different wages for summer and winter, allowing for variations in the working day. The Le Stranges did not observe these differences, paying their workers the same rate the whole year round. Normally, the Le Stranges' workers received food and drink with their cash wage. Those working away from Hunstanton in other parts of the estate received 'board wages', which were 5d or 6d higher per day for those normally paid 6d or more, and 4d higher for those on lower wages.[59] None of the masons held land from the Le Stranges. It is unclear where their families lived.

THE LE STRANGES AND THE LOCAL COMMUNITY

This final section assesses the impact of the Le Stranges' lifestyle and spending pattern on the local community as whole, and places the wages earned by particular workers in the context of their overall household economy. In his study of the Le Stranges and Hunstanton in the sixteenth century, Oestmann painted a picture of a small and stable community of around 250 people, the great majority of whom were manorial tenants. Between 1538 and 1597 England's population as a whole was growing at about 1 per cent per annum, but Hunstanton grew little, if at all.[60] Oestmann argued that there was little in- or out-migration and that Hunstanton was unusually self-contained: 'to a certain extent the community had closed itself

---

[58] See also Chapter 7: Building and estate improvement.
[59] J.C. Tingey, 'An assessment of wages for the county of Norfolk in 1610', *English Historical Review* 13 (1898), 522–7.
[60] C. Oestmann, *Lordship and Community: The Lestrange Family and the Village of Hunstanton, Norfolk in the First Half of the Sixteenth Century* (Woodbridge, 1994), especially 158–9, 161, 166–7.

Table 8.3. Examples of wage rates, 1610–30

Description	Statutory wages: Norfolk 1610	Statutory wages: Suffolk 1630	Paid by the Le Stranges 1615–24
Plumber, freemason, master joiner	9d summer 7d winter	8d	Plumber and freemason paid by task; joiner 12d or 10d
Master carpenter, rough mason or glazier	8d summer 6d winter	8d	Carpenter 8d; rough mason 10d
Mower of corn or grass, male reaper	8d with food 14d board wages	8d mower and reapers of corn, 6d mowers of hay	Mowing 14d board wages; 8d with food; reaping 8d
Thatcher, gardener	7d summer 5d winter	Thatcher 8d Gardener 6d	Thatching 6d or 8d; gardener 8d
Journeyman carpenter, rough mason, joiner	6d summer 4d winter	5d	Joiner 6d or 8d; carpenter 6d; rough mason 6d
Dyker/ditcher	6d summer 4d winter		Dyking 6d
Male hay-maker	6d		4d
Tailor, hedger, dawber	5d summer 4d winter	6d	Hedging 6d; tailor 6d; dawbing 6d
Female reaper, binder of corn, following the scythe	5d	4d	Following the scythe 5d and 6d; binding corn 4d
Thresher	4d summer 3d winter		Paid by task
Apprentice carpenter, rough mason, etc. under 18	4d summer 3d winter	4d	Apprentice joiner 2d or 3d; carpenter 3d; rough mason 4d
Woman labouring in harvest, female hay-maker	4d		None
'Women and such impotent persons that weed corn'	2d	2d	Adult men weeding corn 4d

Note: Statutory wage rates are for cash wages when food and drink is supplied by the employer.

Source: J.C. Tingey, 'An assessment of wages for the country of Norfolk in 1610', *English Historical Review* 49 (1898), 522–7; W.A.J. Archbold, 'An assessment of wages for 1630', *English Historical Review* 12 (1897), 307–11. Le Strange disbursement accounts, kitchen accounts and building accounts; LEST/P6, P7, P8.

off from the outside world, probably helped by the fact that the village was away from the main land travelling routes'.[61] Rates of baptism in early seventeenth-century Hunstanton remained similar to those in the late sixteenth century: in 1610–28 an average of 7.8 children were baptized each year, compared with 7.4 between 1578 and 1607.[62] In 1538–53 and 1561–70, 11 per cent of children were

---

[61] Oestmann, *Lordship and Community*, 167.
[62] Figures from Oestmann, *Lordship and Community*, 167, compared with Hunstanton parish registers, 1610–28.

baptized to non-landholding parents.[63] It is not possible to recreate Oestmann's methods exactly: he defined landholding families as 'the immediate family of the landholder, as well as associated members such as in-laws and servants'.[64] However, we can say that, between 1610 and 1628, 16 per cent of children baptized had fathers who were not manorial tenants and did not share a surname with a manorial tenant.[65] Having one child baptized in a particular parish does not prove that the parents were resident there: kin connections through the wife or godparents may have encouraged particular children to be baptized away from their place of residence. The baptism of two or more children does make residence likely. Only four men who were not manorial tenants in Hunstanton had more than one child baptized between 1610 and 1628, accounting for nine baptisms out of a total of 148. Two of these men, William Savage and Robert Greenrod, worked as labourers for the Le Stranges; Greenrod had also been a Le Strange servant.

These investigations demonstrate that, unlike many Norfolk villages, Hunstanton had virtually no subtenure. Almost all inhabitants rented land and houses directly from the manorial lord, the Le Stranges. This allowed the Le Stranges a degree of control over the community. This control was not necessarily negative. In many Norfolk villages, large tenants monopolized freehold and customary land, which enjoyed low rents, and leased cottages and smallholdings to subtenants at high rents. In Hunstanton it was the Le Stranges who leased smallholdings directly as manorial lords, a policy they had adopted in the 1560s.[66] By 1621 they were leasing twenty-three smallholdings of between 4 acres and 1 acre at a rent of 3s an acre. Only eleven of these tenants had other pieces of land in Hunstanton held by freehold or copyhold, and in some cases this was just a cottage. Despite Oestmann's assertion that the population of Hunstanton did not grow, it is evident that the number of tenants increased over time. There were forty-six tenants in Hunstanton in 1525, and thirty-six by *c.*1575. In 1621 and 1632, there were fifty-nine tenants. Nor can we agree that there was little in-migration. In the decade between 1621 and 1632, nineteen new surnames appeared amongst the tenants, representing a 43 per cent turnover. The Le Stranges certainly were not hostile to this process. They recruited the majority of their live-in servants from outside their estate and sometimes settled them with land in Hunstanton; they were happy to employ day labourers and craftsmen from neighbouring villages within and beyond their estate as well as those from Hunstanton. Of the 103 workers employed as non-specialist day labourers by the Le Stranges between 1615 and 1624, forty-three were not Le Strange tenants in Hunstanton, Heacham, Sedgeford, Ringstead or Holme.

Nonetheless, comparison between the household accounts and the lists of Hunstanton tenants reveals that almost every household in the village had

---

[63] Oestmann, *Lordship and Community*, 161.
[64] Oestmann, *Lordship and Community*, 160.
[65] Comparing Hunstanton parish registers with Le Strange rentals of Hunstanton for 1621 and 1632.
[66] Oestmann, *Lordship and Community*, 68.

economic and social connections with the Le Stranges other than paying rent. The fifty-nine tenants in 1621 had forty-four different surnames. Of these forty-four families, thirty-four had members who presented food gifts to the Le Strange household at some time between 1613 and 1627. Of those who did not, two were widows, but the other eight all worked as day labourers for the Le Stranges at some time between 1615 and 1624. In addition, five of the tenants were former Le Strange servants, and a further six families had provided a servant to the Le Strange household between 1613 and 1628. As discussed in Chapter 3, regular gift-giving was concentrated amongst the larger tenants. Those Hunstanton families who made ten or more gifts of food to the Le Strange household between 1613 and 1627 were tenants paying 30s or more in rent annually. This pattern was reversed for day labouring. Figure 8.2 compares rents paid in Hunstanton in 1621 with appearances in the Le Strange household accounts as a labourer between 1615 and 1624. It shows that while some of the larger tenants or their sons occasionally did a few days work for the Le Stranges, perhaps more as a favour than out of necessity, those working regularly as day labourers were clustered at the bottom of the rent scale. These were smallholders with 1 or 2 acres of land who needed extra income. For instance, Nicholas Page, a labourer who appears twenty-five times in the accounts, held 2 acres by leasehold for a rent of 6s and paid another 6d in bond rent, perhaps representing a further acre; Richard Wix, the thatcher who also did agricultural labouring, also held 2 acres of leasehold for 6s; Robert Taftes, a day labourer, paid 5s 8d in leasehold rent. Robert Bidden, the Le Stranges' most regularly employed and skilled agricultural labour, was an exception: he combined his labouring work with the tenure of a modest leasehold farm of 10 acres and a messuage for which he paid just over 30s a year.

The rest of this section examines the household economy of six tenant families, and their links with the Le Strange household. The examples are chosen to illustrate

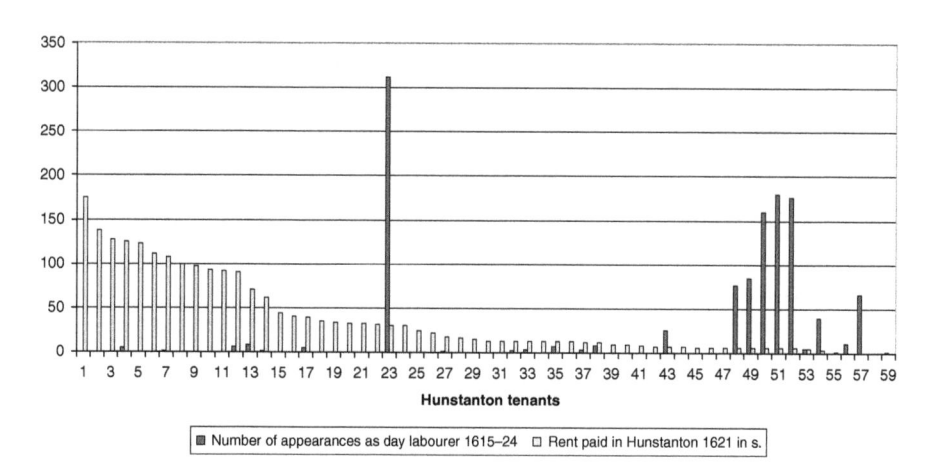

Fig. 8.2. Land tenure and day labouring in Hunstanton, 1615–24.

Sources: Hunstanton and Mustralls manorial rental 1621; LEST/EH 5. Disbursement and kitchen accounts; LEST/P6, P7, P8.

the full range of village society: the Guybons were a lesser gentry family; the Banyards and Gittings yeomen. Robert Bidden, as we have seen, was a labourer and husbandman; Nicholas Page a poorer labourer and smallholder; and Richard Wix was a thatcher and smallholder, whose wife and son also worked for the Le Stranges. Members of each of these families left inventories dated between 1621 and 1633, which are summarized in Table 8.4. In all cases these were predominantly agricultural households in which the value of crops and livestock exceeded that of domestic goods. The inventories reveal the mixed nature of the local economy in this period. Arable farming concentrating on barley and rye was combined with small-scale dairying and the keeping of pigs and poultry in all six households. The three larger farmers also owned horses and sheep, as did Nicholas Page. The two poorest households, as well as Eustace Banyard's, spun wool.

Francis Guybon of Sedgeford, gentleman, who died in January 1631/2, was the nephew of Richard Stubbe and first cousin of Alice Le Strange.[67] His property was primarily held by leasehold from the Le Stranges. He occupied 'the great farm' in Sedgeford and the house and site of the manor of West Hall in that parish. The farm comprised 153 acres of infield land, 106½ acres of enclosed ground and 300 acres of sandy breckland. In 1621 he paid a rent of £132 8s 9d to the Le Stranges, about 28 per cent of the total income they received from Sedgeford. The Guybons expanded their holding further in the 1620s, leasing the South Foldcourse in 1622 and East Hall farm and a close for £7 9s 6d in 1624. The Le Stranges bought and sold grain with Francis Guybon throughout the 1610s and 1620s, and in 1624 borrowed £140 from him. Gifts of chickens, ducks, turkeys, wild birds, pigs, veal and more rarely peacocks and cakes were sent from the Guybons to the Le Stranges: sixty-five gifts in total between 1613 and 1626, or an average of more than five a year.[68] Francis Guybon's probate inventory is sadly lacking in detail, with entries such as 'the bedding and furniture in the chambers and other rooms: £41 12s 8d'. Nonetheless, comparison with the incomplete Le Strange inventory of 1675, which lists domestic goods worth almost £350, compared with the Guybons' £102 in 1631, make it clear that, unlike the Le Stranges, most of Guybon's movable wealth was in crops, livestock and farm equipment. Thus, although very wealthy by local standards, they drew the great majority of their income from farming, and not from rents and the ownership of property as the Le Stranges did. After the death of Francis Guybon senior the Sedgeford farm was divided between his two eldest sons, William and Francis junior, who were both married and resident in Sedgeford by this time.

The relationship between the Le Stranges and the next generation of Guybons had already been firmly established. Francis Guybon senior left nine children—four sons and five daughters. William Guybon had been in the Le Strange household as

---

[67] The following two paragraphs rely on the inventory and will of Francis Guybon: DN/INV 37/176 and NCC will register Spendlove 191; Sedgeford parish register 1605–46 (but damaged in places); Sedgeford manorial rentals LEST/BK7; and the Le Strange household accounts.
[68] There were twelve full accounting years with records of gifts between 1613 and 1626; see Chapter 3: The acquisition of food.

Table 8.4. A summary of six tenants' probate inventories

	Nicholas Page of Hunstanton, 1622	Richard Wix of Heacham, thatcher, 1628	Robert Bidden of Hunstanton, 1630	Hamon Gitting of Ringstead, yeoman, 1633	Eustace Banyard of Heacham, yeoman, 1626	Francis Guybon of Sedgeford, gentleman, 1631
Total value	£12	£12	£29	£87	£146	£1050
Number of rooms	?	3	3	9	13	?
Number of beds	2	2	3	3	4	?
Value of apparel	3s 4d	15s	£2	£3	£2 13s 9d	£6 13s 4d
Value of best bedstead	16s	(£1)	£2	£4	£6	?
Value of domestic goods	£2 9s 5d	£3 13s 4d	£11 6s 4d	£24 5s	£37 7s 9d	£102 7s 3d
Value of crops	£3 10s	10s	£6 6s	£29 10s	£39 18s	£493 10s
Value of livestock	£6 0s 4d	£6 8s 8d	£6 3s	£22 12s	£37 15s	£258 4d
Value of debts and ready money	0	0	£4 10s	0	£19 10s	£128 17s

Note: '?' indicates that no information was given in the inventory. Figures in brackets are estimates made by disaggregating a combined value. Domestic goods are defined as all those goods inside the house, including apparel and plate, but excluding agricultural products in storage. Debts and ready money includes debts owed to the deceased, but not owed by him.

Sources: NRO: Page DN/INV 31/123; 'Wickes' DN/INV 34/173; Bidden DN/INV 36/212; Gitting DN/INV 39/70; Banyard DN/INV 33/249; Guybon DN/INV 37/176.

an unpaid servant between 1617 and 1620. He was trusted with handling money and making trips to King's Lynn, Norwich and London, and hunted wildfowl with Sir Hamon. In 1620 he married Dorothy Boyton, the daughter of another of the Le Stranges' friends, in Sedgeford church. Thomas Guybon, the youngest son, entered the Le Stranges' service in 1623. He remained with them for ten years. By the 1630s he was joined in the Le Strange household by two of his sisters. Francis Guybon senior's wife, Margaret, predeceased him, and their five daughters, Frances, Amy, Margaret, Anne and Katherine, were still unmarried when he died. Frances and Margaret immediately entered service with the Le Stranges at Our Lady 1632. Frances stayed for only a year, but Margaret remained for the next ten years. She was joined at various stages by her other sisters: Amy for a year in 1634, Frances returned in 1635–7, Anne in 1637–42 and 1644–7, and Katherine in 1641–2. When Anne left in 1647 the baton was immediately taken up by a new generation of Guybons. Elizabeth Guybon was in service with the Le Stranges from 1647 to 1648 and from 1652 to 1654, and another Margaret from 1649 to 1654.[69] They each received bequests of £5 from Sir Hamon Le Strange at his death. In the 1640s one of the Guybon women was employed as a wet nurse for the children of Nicholas Le Strange, and lent Alice Le Strange £40. Francis Guybon junior was Alice Le Strange's steward during her widowhood when she lived in Sedgeford, and his daughter Elizabeth was her servant. At her death in 1656 Alice Le Strange gave Elizabeth a bequest of £26, a bed, and all her ordinary wearing apparel. Here then were two families closely connected by mutually beneficial bonds which were no doubt strengthened by being close kin. The Le Stranges gained reliable leaseholders, business partners and servants; the Guybon men gained access to property, wealth and status; and the Guybon women a respectable role, earnings and, in some cases, gifts, before marriage.

Connections between the Le Stranges and their yeomen tenants were not as close as with gentlemen farmers like Francis Guybon. Nonetheless they were important and multifaceted. Yeomen dominated village society and developed dynasties of their own. The Banyard family was spread across the core manors in the Le Strange estate, holding land by leasehold, freehold and customary tenure in Hunstanton, Heacham, Sedgeford and Ringstead.[70] In Hunstanton, five of the fifty-nine tenants were Banyards, including Robert Banyard with a leasehold of 42 acres and freehold property, John Banyard with 36 acres of leasehold and a freehold messuage, and Robert Banyard, son of Thomas, with a lease of 23.5 acres and a small customary tenure. Between 1612 and 1627, fourteen children with the surname Banyard and

[69] Elizabeth, the daughter of Francis (junior) and his wife Anne, was baptized in Sedgeford in 1630.
[70] This paragraph uses the following sources in addition to the Le Strange household accounts: Hunstanton and Mustralls manorial rental, 1621 (LEST/EH 5); Hunstanton manorial accounts, 1632–53 (LEST/BK 15); Sedgeford manorial accounts (LEST/BK7); Heacham rentals and firmals, 1612–39 (LEST/DI 16); manorial accounts for Northall, Sedgeford, Barrett Ringstead and Gt Ringstead, 1632–53, summarized by Alice Le Strange (LEST/EK5); Hunstanton parish register; probate inventory of Eustace Banyard of Heacham, yeoman, 1626 (NRO, DN/INV 37/176); will of William Banyard senior, husbandman of Hunstanton, 1612 (NRO, NCC will register Coker, 119); will of Eustace Banyard, yeoman of Heacham, 1626 (NRO, NCC will register Mittings 369).

fathers named Robert or John were baptized in Hunstanton. In Heacham in 1620 Eustace Banyard was paying £4 14s 11d in leasehold rent for land in Heacham and Ringstead,[71] as well as freehold and customary rent. In Sedgeford in the 1630s Richard and Robert Banyard held substantial landholdings. Eustace Banyard's probate inventory shows him to have been a wealthy man by village standards. He supplemented his farming enterprise by dealing in timber, and appears in Sir Hamon Le Strange's notebook and the Le Strange accounts in that capacity as well as selling hay. His inventory typifies the modest comforts of yeomen's households in this period. His house had multiple chambers and service rooms, several beds, chairs with cushions, linens worth £5 10s, brass pots and pewter, but no silver plate. His household economy drew on multiple income strands: timber dealing, arable farming, cheese making, brewing, spinning wool, and keeping cows, sheep, pigs and poultry. Eustace's contacts with the Le Stranges were fairly minimal, but other Banyards developed strong links. One Robert Banyard of Hunstanton was bailiff for that manor, collecting the rents from other tenants. A Thomas Banyard worked as a senior Le Strange servant between 1619 and 1623. Between them, the Banyards made forty-seven gifts of food, mostly chickens, turkeys and fish, to the Le Strange household between 1613 and 1627. None of them performed day labour or craft work for the Le Stranges.

The Gittings were a family of similar status to the Banyards, mostly resident in Ringstead.[72] There, Thomas Gitting was manorial bailiff to the Le Stranges, a leaseholder and a freehold tenant. He sold sheep to the Le Stranges and ran errands for them in the early period of the accounts. Matthew and Hamon Gitting were brothers, and possibly brothers to Thomas also.[73] Matthew worked as a clerk for the Le Stranges between 1609 and 1624, and then became their warrener, taking over in this role from Thomas Gitting. He lived in Hunstanton with children baptized there in the 1610s. He leased 30 acres in Hunstanton from the Le Stranges, but also lands in neighbouring Ringstead. Thomas and Matthew Gitting and their wives made one or two food gifts to the Le Stranges each year of chickens, pigeons and the occasional pig or turkey. One Hamon Gitting entered the Le Stranges' service in 1623 for £3 a year and worked for them for five years. The Hamon Gitting who was buried in Ringstead in 1633, and whose probate inventory is described in Table 8.4, was either this man or the older Hamon Gitting who was Matthew's brother—probably the latter. The inventory shows him to be a yeoman of modest wealth. His possessions included a bible, a featherbed and three cushions, as well as a cheese press and brewing vessels.

In the manors owned by the Le Stranges each parish contained one family of gentry status like the Guybons or the Le Stranges themselves, and three or four families of the wealth and status of the Banyards and Gittings. Most inhabitants

---

[71] Probably for between 20 and 30 acres.
[72] Heacham rentals and firmals, 1612–39 (LEST/DI 16); manorial accounts for Northall, Sedgeford, Barrett Ringstead and Gt Ringstead, 1632–53, summarized by Alice Le Strange (LEST/EK5).
[73] Ringstead St Andrews parish register begins in 1570; Matthew son of Richard and Hamon son of Richard were baptized in 1572 and 1580, respectively.

were poorer. In Table 8.4 they are represented by Robert Bidden, Nicholas Page and Richard Wix. All these men were employed at some point as day labourers by the Le Stranges; Page and Wix also had sons who worked as day labourers while they were children, adding extra income to their parents' household. Their inventories reveal other sources of income. Their wives contributed actively to their household economies: spinning, cheese making and keeping poultry, activities restricted to women in this period, are all in evidence. In Nicholas Page's house there was 'one spinning wheel for woollen' worth 6d, as well as 'woollen yarn at the weavers' worth 6s 8d. In Richard Wix's house there was '2 stone of wool and a stone of hemp' worth £1 waiting to be spun. Anne Wix knitted hose for the Le Strange children: between 1619 and 1623 she appears six times in the accounts being paid between 7d for infants' hose to 20d for hose for the teenage Nicholas Le Strange. All three men owned one or two cows, as well as pigs. Evidence of dairying is provided by the butter churn in Nicholas Page's house; 'a stone of cheese and eight pounds of butter' worth 5s in Richard Wix's; and 'an old churn and a rack with small cheeses' worth 4s 4d in the house of Robert Bidden. Nicholas Page had '1 hen a cock and 4 chickens' worth 16d and Robert Wix '6 geese and 4 hens' valued at 4s. Page and Wix both leased smallholdings and had crops in store at the time of their death; Bidden had a more substantial holding. As was usual for day labourers in this period, Page and Bidden both owned their own tools.[74] Page had a scythe head worth 8d; and Bidden 'three scythes, a hook and hatchet spade' valued at 5s. Unlike larger farmers, however, none owned ploughs or carts, although Page had 'an old horse' worth 10s. Page and Wix appear to have lived in three-room cottages of the type also described for Stiffkey by Smith.[75] These consisted of one living room with a hearth, described in Wix's inventory as 'the firehouse', with a loft above and a small service room in the lean-to beside the firehouse. Bidden's wealth was reflected in the fact that he lived in a house with a parlour and a kitchen. Unlike the other two men, he had two featherbeds, a set of nine linen napkins and a pewter candlestick.

CONCLUSION

The effect of the Le Strange household on the local community was both positive and negative. On the negative side, they siphoned off thousands of pounds in rents. They used more than 250 acres of land-hungry Hunstanton for an ornamental deer park. They paid relatively low wages to their servants and labourers. There is also evidence that they occasionally entered into disputes with their tenants. One particular spat in the late 1630s ended up in the Court of Chivalry.[76] Robert Creamer, a gentleman copyholder in Heacham, supported by his uncle, Robert Stileman of Snettisham, accused Sir Hamon, Lady Alice and their manorial steward

---

[74] Smith, 'Labourers' [Part I], 17; Everitt, 'Farm labourers', 431–2.
[75] Smith, 'Labourers' [Part II], 374.
[76] www.court-of-chivalry.bham.ac.uk, case 372, 1638–40.

Roger Warner of tampering with his copies of the court roll. In return, Sir Hamon sued him for libel. Local inhabitants called to give evidence deposed one after the other that Sir Hamon was 'a very rich man and a man of worth and power in his country', which could be a good or a bad thing.[77] It was an accurate assessment, as Hamon won the case, despite considerable evidence in favour of Creamer's version of events. Many tenants had reason to be loyal to the Le Stranges. John Salter of Heacham, husbandman, aged thirty-seven, deposed that 'Sir Hamond Le Strange is a good landlord to his tenants in letting of his land at an easy and cheap rate, and did never knowe him wronge any of his tenants in his life'. Thomas Crampe of Heacham, yeoman, aged fifty-three, was perhaps more accurate when he stated that 'Sir Hamond is a good landlord to some, and letts his farmes to some at reasonable rents, but to others he rents his lands deare enough,' or as another Heacham yeoman, Edmund Jenner, put it, 'Sir Hamon doth lett to some of his tenants good pennyworths, but to other some he letteth hard pennyworths'.

The leasing of smallholdings of 1–4 acres to labourers and widows in Hunstanton at reasonable rents evidently benefited them. Leases of larger holdings of 10–40 acres to former servants, trusted employees like Francis Costen the carpenter and skilled labourers like Robert Bidden put their household economies on a sound footing. Large leases of manorial demesnes, like that held by Francis Guybon, provided a source of considerable wealth. All these tenants benefited from their connections with the Le Stranges. The wages recorded in the Le Strange accounts suggest that a significant number were also provided with income through this route. In the 1620s at least four agricultural labourers, three master craftsmen, six shepherds and a warrener drew the majority of their cash income from the Le Stranges. Then there were the sixteen or so mostly young people employed as household servants, who relied on the Le Stranges for their board and lodging, and were able save cash wages towards marriage. Many seem to have been successful in this goal, marrying and setting up households immediately after leaving the Le Stranges' service. But aside from those who depended on the Le Stranges, there were many more who benefited from their custom for goods, and occasional employment: the people who knitted, spun and wove cloth; the local tailors, the tinker, cooper, joiner and smith, who mended and provided household and farming equipment; and, perhaps most significantly of all, the local farming households, who provided poultry, eggs, pigs, veal, wild birds and sea fish for sale to the Le Stranges.

What would have happened if the Le Stranges had not been resident in Hunstanton? The Hall would have required some maintenance, and the farmland would have been leased to a large tenant employing some agricultural labour, but the amount of wealth leaving the estate and being spent elsewhere would certainly have been greater. The social links between the Le Stranges and the local community would have been broken. These are the concerns that lay behind the repeated royal proclamations ordering the gentry to leave London and reside at home on

---

[77] Quoting from the deposition of Thomas Clowdeslie of Cley next the Sea, gent, formerly of Walsingham, aged 67.

their country estates. The majority of these were concerned with the gentry keeping order and offering hospitality, but one from 1632 articulates a more sophisticated understanding of the economic consequences of the gentry's residence in London. It noted that while the gentry drew their income from the provinces it:

> is spent in the Citie in excesse of Apprell... and in other vaine delights and expences, even to the wasting of their Estates, which is not issued into the parts whence it ariseth, nor are the people of them relieved therewith, or by their Hospitalitie, nor yet set on worke as they might and would bee, were it not for the absence of the principall men....[78]

The proclamations were trying to hold back an unstoppable tide. Hamon and Alice Le Strange were unusually strongly rooted in the locality of their estate, even by early seventeenth-century standards. They had both grown up there, and their long, stable married life meant they knew two or three generations of many families of tenants and employees. The more general trend was away from close bonds between lords and tenants. The culture of food gifts was on the wane.[79] Relationships were becoming more strictly contractual. By the late seventeenth and eighteenth centuries, even gentry resident in the country were ordering an increasing proportion of purchases direct from London.[80] The work of the local joiner was replaced by fashionable furniture from London, the work of local weavers and knitters with ready-made town-bought purchases. The distance between production and consumption was widening, and the social bond between producer and consumer falling apart.

---

[78] J.F. Larkin (ed.), *Stuart Royal Proclamations*, vol. 2 (London, 1982), 351.
[79] F. Heal, 'Food gifts, the household and the politics of exchange in early modern England', *Past and Present* 199 (2008), 41–70; see Chapter 3: The acquisition of food.
[80] J. Stobart, 'Gentlemen and shopkeepers: supplying the country house in eighteenth-century England', *Economic History Review* 64:3 (2011), 885–904.

9

Conclusion

The early seventeenth-century household accounts on which this book is based are wonderful and frustrating documents. Wonderful because of the profusion of detail they contain about the realities of everyday life; frustrating because of what they lack. Alice Le Strange put her efforts into recording what had been purchased and what it cost; she rarely recorded who or where things were purchased from. Very rarely did she hint at the motivations behind purchases. Her personal spending from her annual allowance was omitted from the accounts. There are no letters illuminating the Le Stranges' attitudes towards consumption with which to interpret the accounts. Nonetheless, Alice Le Strange's records do leave us with a rounded view of the household's spending pattern: they allow a holistic reconstruction of consumption patterns and provide evidence of consumption as a process.

What do we gain from this holistic view? Contrasts are important: that second-hand furniture was acceptable to a gentry household but not second-hand clothing is revealing of both types of goods. But it is the parallels and connections between different types of consumption that stand out. For instance, the way medical care was accessed was remarkably similar to the way clothes were acquired. The household used medical practitioners and tailors of different status and expertise from London, Norwich and the vicinity of Hunstanton; some medicines and clothes were constructed at home from ingredients or cloth bought for the purpose. There were similar attitudes to novelty in both food and textiles: fashions changed and new foods and cloth were eagerly adopted, but any more profound changes in mealtimes or gendered differences in clothing met resistance. Social contacts rather than impersonal market relations were important in many different types of consumption such as food gifts, elite tailoring, wet-nursing, tutoring, building work and service. These reveal the inter-connectedness of different aspects of consumption: tailors who lent money; tutors who sent their own children to be servants; wet nurses who sold chickens; gentry friends who offered hospitality and sent garden seeds, hawks or books but not gifts of food; carpenters who rented land.

The holistic view of consumption surely offers a more fruitful vision of what consumption is. It is not just shopping or a set of objects owned. It is not just about luxury and pleasure. Domestic consumption is the process which starts with planning, moves on to acquisition by a variety of means, and finishes with appropriation and use of goods and services within the home. It encompasses tallow candles and pickled pigs' trotters as well as tapestries and clocks. It includes the work of servants, barbers, musicians, stone masons and featherbed drivers as well as furnishings and clothes. It is about cleanliness, leisure and household management as well as material culture. Consumption involves hard work and thrift as well as enjoyment and spending. The disbursement accounts with their seemingly endless lists of money spent edge the historian towards a vision of consumption as spending. We have tried to resist this as both too broad and too narrow. Not everything spent was connected to consumption. Large gentry households were businesses concerned with other things as well as consumption. Some areas of spending touched on in this book, such as legal fees and taxation, annuities to elderly relatives or the maintenance of houses and farm buildings on the estate, constitute a grey area. We have offered some insight into the sums and activities involved but have not dwelt on them. On the other hand, the kitchen accounts offer an antidote to the misconception that everything consumed was bought. They document in detail the complexities of home production and the importance of gifts of food.

Patterns of consumption in the period before 1650 are neglected in existing histories. Assumptions that later periods, such as the eighteenth century, experienced 'consumer revolution' need to be understood in the light of earlier changes. This study makes it clear that, in the early seventeenth century, as in other periods, consumption was in a constant state of change. Much of what the Le Stranges were doing between 1610 and 1650 was new. They bought Indian cotton, new draperies, a clock, window curtains and upholstered furniture. They educated their sons at university and the Inns of Court, travelled in coaches, collected a library of books and scientific instruments, preserved fruit with sugar in glass jars and decorated everything with lace. They ate turkey, artichokes, cherries, cabbage and sugar comfits, drank beer, washed with white soap and heated their house with coal. It is true that they also partook in 'traditional' forms of consumption—patterns of consumption that had existed since the late medieval period: they ate a diet heavy in beef and bread, enjoyed hawking and hunting, invested money in silverware, used the services of a local midwife, educated their daughter at home, and received gifts of food from their tenants. But all periods mix the old with the new and see practices fall out of use as well as adopting new ones. Perhaps the more important point to make is that there is no evidence of any hostility to novelty in the Le Stranges' consumption patterns. They tried new things; they appreciated things that were attractive and cheap, such as the new draperies, as well as things that were new and luxurious, such as beaver hats and books of printed maps. Sir Hamon Le Strange positively delighted in the latest inventions and devices such as pocket watches, theodolites and classical designs for his new porch, as well as showing a strong attachment to the past in the style in which he chose to enlarge his house. McCracken's idea of the gentry's attachment to patina—that goods gained value with age—is a red herring.[1] Even the gentry's silverware was periodically melted down to bring it up to fashion in the early seventeenth century.

If the period before 1650 has been neglected in the history of consumption, so has the gentry as a group of consumers. McKendrick emphasized Veblen's theory of

[1] G. McCracken, *Culture and Consumption: New Approaches to the Symbolic Character of Consumer Goods and Activities* (Indiana, 1988), 31–41.

emulation as the means by which new fashions of consumption were spread through England's relatively fluid ranks of society in the eighteenth century.[2] Leaving aside whether it is relevant for that period, it is hard to see how emulation could function widely in English society before 1650. As was emphasized in Chapter 1: in the early seventeenth century, to spend too little was to risk ridicule and lose status; to spend too much was to risk indebtedness, the sale of land and loss of status by another route. Rather than emulation, it is the transmission of knowledge that is more important. Contacts between social groups allowed knowledge of new forms of consumption to spread through society. Upper gentry households like the Le Stranges' provided an important link in this spread of knowledge. Relatives in court and frequent trips to London and Norwich provided them with information about new fashions and innovations. In turn, they spread these ideas to the parish gentry, to whom they were also related and counted as friends. Servants of lower status employed in these households experienced changes in consumption first hand. Social status was reinforced by the amount of money spent in ways that were obvious to observers: the size of houses, number of servants, quality of textiles in clothes and furnishings, variety of food, generosity of hospitality, the ownership of a coach, for instance. Novelties were adopted lower down the social order where they could be afforded, proved practical and were made attractive by other cultural changes. As William Harrison observed, pewter, featherbeds and chimneys spread through English society in the sixteenth century. There is no reason to see this as emulation. A yeoman was not aspiring to be a gentleman when he bought a featherbed and pewter platters. The gentry and ordinary households shared a common material culture: the objects common in ordinary households, such as wooden trenchers, earthenware pots and brass cooking pots, were also found in gentry households.

Consumption functioned differently in the early seventeenth century because it was intimately connected to other social relationships. Consumption was a social process that involved meaningful interaction between individuals and not just between people and things. Many goods were purchased directly from producers such as apothecaries, tailors, shoemakers, knitters, weavers, saddlers, clockmakers and coachmakers. These were often people with whom the Le Stranges had longstanding relationships and whom they made an active choice to patronize. Others were employed directly to carry out consumption work for the household: servants who cleaned, cooked and produced food; labourers who also produced food and maintained the gardens and park; building workers who enlarged the house and maintained its fabric. Many of these people also built up longstanding relationships with the Le Stranges. In different ways, food gifts and the choice of servants employed both reveal the strength of these connections. Food gifts were presented by friends, tenants and retailers of lesser status who aimed to reinforce their social and economic ties with the Le Stranges. The employment of servants shows one

---

[2] N. McKendrick, 'The consumer revolution in eighteenth-century England', in N. McKendrick, J. Brewer, and J.H. Plumb (eds.), *The Birth of a Consumer Society: The Commercialization of Eighteenth-Century England* (London, 1982), 15–22.

way in which they benefited: the Le Stranges provided employment and training for these people's sons and daughters. The length of time many servants remained in the households indicates that, despite low pay, service for the Le Strange household was an attractive option. So the purchase of goods and services involved not just issues of knowledge, quality, price and transport, but judgements about who to favour with patronage. Gentry families like the Le Stranges, who chose to remain resident on country estates and not to spend part of the year in London, strengthened their social links with the local community and supported its economy.

Both men and women took responsibility for aspects of consumption. In early seventeenth-century England men had ultimate control of household finances and women normally managed day-to-day consumption needs. There are strong continuities over time in these patterns. Sixteenth-century texts, just like those of the nineteenth and twentieth centuries, characterized men as producers and women as consumers. Shopping was seen as a feminine activity, and women's susceptibility to wasting time and money was criticized. Closer examination reveals that men as well as women were active purchasers. Men typically took responsibility for their own clothes, for the maintenance of the fabric of the house, and for modes of transport. Women were responsible for food, and their own and their children's clothing, and for keeping the house and clothing clean. Men took part in domestic consumption work if it constituted a full-time occupation: as cooks, tailors or tutors; but not if it was unpaid work for one's own family, when it fell to women. These patterns have held from at least the early seventeenth century to the late twentieth century. But these continuities should not blind us to changes that occurred over time. In elite households, household management passed from men (usually elite male servants) to women (wives or female servants) over the early modern period. Men in the early seventeenth century used consumption practices to uphold their family's status. It was Sir Hamon Le Strange and his sons who took part in elite leisure pursuits such as hawking, playing the viol and intellectual debate. Men's clothing was at least as ostentatious as women's. Sir Hamon seems to have spent money more freely than his wife: behaviour that was in keeping with his overriding concern with the family's status. Lady Alice Le Strange was a world away from the wealthy wives of late nineteenth-century American society described by Veblen who acted as vicarious consumers for their husbands, displaying the extravagant clothing and excess leisure that such men no longer indulged in.[3] Alice Le Strange's consumption activities were less directly concerned with the status of the family than those of her husband, and had more in common with the activities of women of lesser rank. Her consumption identity was dominated by the ideals of good management, hard work and thrift. While her husband's primary experience of consumption was pleasure and leisure, hers was primarily one of work: organizing the provisioning and maintenance of the household and directing the work of others.

---

[3] T. Veblen, *The Theory of the Leisure Class*, first published 1899 (Oxford, 2007), chs. 3, 4 and 7.

Select Bibliography

MANUSCRIPT SOURCES

The Norfolk Record Office, Norwich
NRO, Le Strange Collection

Household Accounts
LEST/P1–5: Household accounts, sixteenth century.
LEST/P6: Household accounts (disbursements, receipts, kitchen books), 1606–21.
LEST P7: Household accounts (disbursements), 1613–45.
LEST/P8: Household accounts (kitchen books, receipts), 1621–33.
LEST/P9: Household accounts (kitchen books, receipts), 1633–42.
LEST/P10: Household accounts (disbursements), 1645–54.
LEST/P11: Household accounts (kitchen books, receipts), 1650–3.
LEST/P12: Household book (Dame Catherine Calthorpe), 1652–62.

Notebooks and family papers
LEST/AA1: Marriage settlement of Sir Hamon Le Strange and Alice Stubbe, 1605.
LEST/AA66–73: Documents concerning the marriage of Sir Hamon and Lady Alice Le Strange.
LEST/AE8: Will of Sir Hamon Le Strange, 1652.
LEST/BN9–10: Mortgage agreement by Sir Hamon and Sir Nicholas Le Strange, 1654.
LEST/KA6; LEST/KA9–10; LEST/KA24: The farming notebooks of Sir Nicholas Le Strange, 1633–45.
LEST/NE1: Library catalogue *c.*1700.
LEST/P20: Letters of Sir Hamon Le Strange, 1641–54.
LEST/Q38: Memoranda Book of Sir Hamon Le Strange, 1613–37.
LEST/supple/25/iii/2/15: Letters and papers mostly concerning the Civil War.

Estate documents
LEST/BK3–9: Hunstanton rentals and firmals, 1611–55; LEST/BK7: includes Sedgeford account, 1621–35; sheep account, 1620–2.
LEST/BK15: Hunstanton estate rental and account, 1632–53.
LEST/DI 16: Heacham and Calys firmal, 1627.
LEST/DI 17: Heacham and Calys firmals and rentals, 1612–39.
LEST/DI 22 A: Heacham account, 1632–53.
LEST/EH4–5: Ringstead field books, 1620, 1621.
LEST/EK4–5: Ringstead accounts, 1632–53.
LEST/EK18: Rental of Ringstead and Holme, 1613.
LEST/R8–R10: Bailiffs' accounts.

Maps
LEST/OA1: Survey and map of Hunstanton, 1615, Thomas Waterman.
LEST/OB5, OB6: Map of Ringstead and Holme, undated.
LEST/OC1: Map of Sedgeford, 1631, probably by John Fisher.
LEST/OC2: Map of Heacham, 1625, attributed to Thomas Waterman.

NRO other

Inventories
DN/INV 31/123: Nicholas Page of Hunstanton, 1622.
DN/INV 33/249: Eustace Banyard of Heacham, yeoman, 1626.
DN/INV 34/173: Richard Wickes of Heacham, thatcher, 1628.
DN/INV 36/212: Robert Bidden of Hunstanton, 1630.
DN/INV 36/230: Thomas Crispe senior of Ringstead, shepherd, 1630.
DN/INV 37/176: Francis Guybon senior of Sedgeford, gentleman, 1631.
DN/INV 39/70: Hamon Gitting of Ringstead, yeoman, 1633.
NCC INV/37/128B: Jane Le Strange, 1630.

Wills
NCC, register Coker 119: William Banyard senior of Hunstanton, husbandman, 1612.
NCC, register Sayer 23: Thomas Costen of Heacham, carpenter, 1616.
NCC, register Mittings 369: Eustace Banyard of Heacham, yeoman, 1620.
NCC, register Jay 100: Richard Wickes of Heacham, thatcher, 1628.
NCC, original will 160: Robert Bydden of Hunstanton, 1630.
NCC, original will 216: Thomas Chrispe senior of Ringstead, shepherd, 1630.
NCC, register Spendlove 191: Francis Guybon senior of Sedgeford, gentleman, 1630.
PRDC 1/2/5 fol.280: will of Margaret Lawes of Sedgeford, singlewoman, 1624/5.

Parish Registers
PD 698: Hunstanton, 1538–1660.
PD 699: Heacham, 1558–1643.
PD 696: Ringstead St Andrew, 1570–1640.
PD 697: Ringstead St Peter, 1577–1640.
PD 601: Sedgeford, 1560–1640.

Quarter Sessions
C/S3/Boxes 18–20, 22–28: Norfolk Quarter Sessions files, 1614–32.

Map
MC 77/1; Hayes and Storr, no.72: map of Gressenhall, 1624, T. Waterman.

The National Archive
Prob/4/3988: Probate inventory of Sir Nicholas Le Strange of Hunstanton, 1675.
Prob/11/135: Will of Richard Stubb of Sedgeford, 1620.
Prob/11/238: Will of Sir Hamon Le Strange, 1654.
Prob/11/249: Will of Sir William Springe, 1654.
Prob/11/262: Will of Dame Alice Le Strange, 1656.
Prob/11/301: Will of Hamon Le Strange (junior), 1660.
Prob/11/479: Will of Sir Roger L'Estrange, 1704.

PUBLISHED DOCUMENTS AND PRE-1800 BOOKS

Blomefield, F., *An Essay Towards a Topographical History of the County of Norfolk* (1739–75).
Brathwaite, R., *The Good Wife: or, a Rare One amongst Women* (1618).

Bullinger, H., translated M. Coverdale, *The Christian State of Matrimony* (1575).
Cleaver, R., *A Godly Form of Household Government* (1598).
Collinges, J., *Par Nobile* (1669).
Emmison, F.G., *Elizabethan Life: Wills of the Essex Gentry and Merchants* (Chelmsford, 1978).
Estienne, C., *Maison Rustique, or The Countrey Farme* (1616).
Fussell, G.E. (ed.), *Robert Loder's Farm Accounts 1610–1620*, Camden Society 3rd series, vol. 53 (1936).
Gouge, W., *Of Domesticall Duties* (1622).
Gray, T. (ed.), *Devon Household Accounts 1627–59, Part 1* (1995).
Harrison, W., *The Description of England*, ed. G. Edelen (New York, 1968).
Hughes, P.L. and Larkin, J.F. (eds.), *Tudor Royal Proclamations*, vols. 1–3 (New Haven, 1964–9).
James I, *The Workes of the Most High and Mightie Prince* (London, 1616).
King, G., *The LCC Burns Journal*, in P. Laslett (ed.), *The Earliest Classics* (New Jersey, 1973).
Larkin, J.F. (ed.), *Stuart Royal Proclamations*, vol. 2 (London, 1982).
Larkin, J.F. and Hughes, P.L. (eds.), *Stuart Royal Proclamations*, vol. 1 (Oxford, 1973).
L'Estrange, H., esq., *God's Sabbath before, under the law and under the Gospel briefly vindicated from novell and heterodox assertations* (Cambridge, 1641).
—— *An answer to the Marques of Worcester's last paper* (London, 1651).
Le Strange, N., *Merry Passages and Jeasts*, ed. H.F. Lippincott (Salzburg, 1974).
L'Estrange, Sir H., *The Charge upon Sir Hamon L'Estrange together with his Vindication and Recharge* (London, 1649).
Markham, G., *The English Housewife*, ed. M. Best (Montreal, 1986).
Tingey, J.C., 'An assessment of wages for the county of Norfolk in 1610', *English Historical Review* 13 (1898).

SECONDARY SOURCES

Allan, J.P., *Medieval and Post Medieval Finds from Exeter 1971–1980* (Exeter, 1984).
Aries, P., *Centuries of Childhood* (London, 1962).
Arnold, J., *Queen Elizabeth's Wardrobe Unlock'd* (Leeds, 1988).
Ashbee, A., '"My fiddle is a bass viol": music in the life of Roger L'Estrange', in A. Dunan-Page and B. Lynch (eds.), *Roger L'Strange and the Making of Restoration Culture* (Aldershot, 2008).
Beard, G., *Upholsterers and Interior Furnishing in England 1530–1840* (New Haven, 1997).
Bennett, J., *Ale, Beer, and Brewsters in England: Women's Work in a Changing World, 1300–1600* (Oxford, 1996).
Bennett, J., 'The mechanical arts', in K. Park and L. Daston (eds.), *The Cambridge History of Science. Vol. 3. Early Modern Science* (Cambridge, 2006), 677–96.
Berg, M., 'Women's consumption and the industrial classes of eighteenth-century England', *Journal of Social History* 30:2 (1996), 415–34.
—— *Luxury and Pleasure in Eighteenth-Century Britain* (Oxford, 2005).
Berry, H., 'Polite consumption: shopping in eighteenth-century England', *Transactions of the Royal Historical Society* 12 (2002), 375–94.
Brett, G., *Dinner is Served* (London, 1968).
Brown, P.A., 'Jesting rights: women players in the manuscript jestbook of Sir Nicholas Le Strange', in P.A. Brown and P. Parolin (eds.), *Women Players in England 1500–1660* (Aldershot, 2005), 305–14.

Campbell, L., 'Documentary evidence for the building of Raynham Hall', *Architectural History* 32 (1989), 52–67.
—— 'Wet-nurses in early modern England: some evidence from the Townshend archive', *Medical History* 33:3 (1989), 360–70.
Carrier, J., *Gifts and Commodities: Exchange and Western Capitalism since 1700* (London, 1995).
Charleston, R.J., *English Glass and Glass used in England, c.400–1940* (London, 1984).
Chaudhuri, K.N., *The English East India Company: The Study of an Early Joint-Stock Company 1600–1640* (London, 1965).
Clay, C.G.A., *Economic Expansion and Social Change: England 1500–1700*, vols. 1 and 2 (Cambridge, 1984).
Cliffe, J.T., *The World of the Country House in Seventeenth-Century England* (New Haven, 1999).
Cockburn, J.S., *A History of the English Assizes 1558–1714* (Cambridge, 1972).
Connor, R., *Women, Accounting and Narrative: Keeping Books in Eighteenth-Century England* (London, 2004).
Cooper, J.P., 'Patterns of inheritance and settlement by great landowners from the fifteenth to the eighteenth centuries', in J. Goody, J. Tirsk, and E.P. Thompson (eds.), *Family and Inheritance: Rural Society in Western Europe, 1200–1800* (Cambridge, 1976), 307.
Cooper, N., *The Houses of the Gentry 1480–1680* (New Haven, 1999).
Corfield, P., 'A provincial capital in the late seventeenth century: the case of Norwich', in P. Clark (ed.), *The Early Modern Town: A Reader* (London, 1976), 233–73.
Cox, N., '"A flesh pott, or a brasse pott or a pott to boile in": changes in metal and fuel technology in the early modern period and the implications for cooking', in M. Donald and L. Hurcombe (eds.), *Gender and Material Culture in Historical Perspective* (Basingstoke, 2000), 143–57.
—— *The Complete Tradesman: A Study of Retailing, 1550–1820* (Aldershot, 2000).
Cressy, D., *Birth, Marriage and Death: Ritual, Religion and Life Cycle in Tudor and Stuart England* (Oxford, 1997).
Crofts, J., *Packhorse, Waggon and Post: Land Carriage and Communications under the Tudors and Stuarts* (London, 1967).
Crossley, D., *Post Medieval Archaeology in Britain* (Leicester, 1990).
Crowley, J.E., *The Invention of Comfort: Sensibilities and Design in Early Modern Britain and Early America* (Baltimore, 2000).
Davies, K., 'Continuity and change in literary advice on marriage', in R.B. Outhwaite (ed.), *Marriage and Society: Studies in the Social History of Marriage* (London, 1981), 58–80.
Davis, D., *A History of Shopping* (London, 1966).
Dawson, M., *Plenti and Grase: Food and Drink in a Sixteenth Century Household* (Totnes, 2009).
de Vries J., 'Luxury in the Dutch golden age in theory and practice', in M. Berg and E. Eger (eds.), *Luxury in the Eighteenth Century: Debates, Desires and Delectable Goods* (Basingstoke, 2002), 41–56.
—— *The Industrious Revolution: Consumer Behaviour and the Household Economy, 1650 to the Present* (Cambridge, 2008).
Digby, G.W., *Elizabethan Embroidery* (London, 1963).
Douglas, M. and Isherwood, B., *The World of Goods: Towards an Anthropology of Consumption* (London, 1996).
Dyer, C., *Standards of Living in the Later Middle Ages: Social Change in England c.1200–1520* (Cambridge, 1989).

—— 'Seasonal patterns of food consumption in the later middle ages', in C.M. Woolgar, D. Serjeantson, and T. Waldron (eds.), *Food in Medieval England: Diet and Nutrition* (Oxford, 2006), 201–14.
Elias, N., *The Civilizing Process: The History of Manners*, translated E. Jephcott (Oxford, 1978).
Emmison, F.G., *Elizabethan Life: Home, Work and Land* (Essex, 1976).
Erickson, A.L., *Women and Property in Early Modern England* (London, 1993).
Everitt, A., 'Farm labourers', in J. Thirsk (ed.), *Agrarian History of England and Wales*. Vol. IV. *1500–1640* (Cambridge, 1967).
Fildes, V.A., *Breasts, Bottles and Babies* (Edinburgh, 1986).
—— 'The English wet-nurse and her role in infant care', *Medical History* 32 (1988), 142–73.
—— *Wet Nursing: A History from Antiquity to the Present* (Oxford, 1988).
Fine, B., *The World of Consumption: The Material and Cultural Revisited*, 2nd edn (London, 2002).
Finn, M., 'Men's things: masculine possession in the consumer revolution', *Social History* 25:2 (2000), 133–55.
Fisher, F.J., 'The development of London as a centre of conspicuous consumption in the sixteenth and seventeenth centuries', in E.M. Carus Wilson (ed.), *Essays in Economic History*, vol. 2 (London, 1962), 197–207.
Fletcher, A., *Reform in the Provinces: The Government of Stuart England* (New Haven, 1986).
Fussell, G.E. and Fussell, K.R., *The English Countrywoman: A Farmhouse Social History* (Ely, 1955).
Girouard, M., *Life in the English Country House* (New Haven, 1978).
Glanville, P., *Silver in Tudor and Early Stuart England: A Social History and Catalogue of the National Collection 1480–1660* (London, 1990).
Glennie, P., 'Consumption within historical studies', in D. Miller (ed.), *Acknowledging Consumption: A Review of New Studies* (London, 1995).
Godfrey, E.S., *The Development of English Glassmaking 1560–1640* (Oxford, 1975).
Harris, B.J., *English Aristocratic Women 1450–1550: Marriage and Family, Property and Careers* (Oxford, 2002).
Harte, N.B., 'The economics of clothing in the seventeenth century', *Textile History* 22:2 (1991), 277–96.
Harvey, B., *Living and Dying in Medieval England 1100–1540* (Oxford, 1993).
Hatcher, J., *The History of the British Coal Industry* (Oxford, 1993).
—— and Barker, T.C., *A History of British Pewter* (London, 1974).
Heal, F., 'The crown, the gentry and London: the enforcement of proclamation, 1596–1640', in C. Cross, D. Loades, and J.J. Scarisbrick (eds.), *Law and Government under The Tudors* (Cambridge, 1988), 211–26.
—— *Hospitality in Early Modern England* (Oxford, 1990).
—— 'Food gifts, the household and the politics of exchange in early modern England', *Past and Present* 199 (2008), 41–70.
—— and Holmes, C., *The Gentry in England and Wales 1500–1700* (Basingstoke, 1994).
Herk, A. van, 'Invisibled laundry', *Signs* 27:3 (2002), 893–900.
Hill, B., *Servants: English Domestics in the Eighteenth Century* (Oxford, 1996).
Hole, C., *The English Housewife in the Seventeenth Century* (London, 1953).
Houlbrooke, R., *The English Family 1450–1700* (London, 1984).
—— *Death, Religion and the Family in England 1480–1750* (Oxford, 1998).

Howard, M., 'Fashionable living', in M. Snodin and J. Styles (eds.), *Design and the Decorative Arts: Britain 1500–1900* (London, 2001).
Howell, M., 'Fixing movables: gifts by testament in late medieval Douai', *Past and Present* 150 (1996), 3–45.
Hunter, L., 'Women and domestic medicine: lady experimenters, 1570–1620', in L. Hunter and S. Hutton (eds.), *Women, Science and Medicine 1500–1700: Mothers and Sisters of the Royal Society* (Stroud, 1997), 89–107.
Hussey, C., 'Hunstanton Hall Norfolk, the seat of Mr Charles Le Strange', *Country Life* (10 April and 17 April 1926), 552–9 and 586–95.
Jardine, L., *Worldly Goods: A New History of the Renaissance* (Basingstoke, 1996).
Jenkins, D. (ed.), *The Cambridge History of Western Textiles* (Cambridge, 2003).
Johnson, M., *Housing Culture: Traditional Architecture in an English Landscape* (London, 1993).
Kerridge, E., *Textile Manufactures in Early Modern England* (Manchester, 1985).
Ketton-Cremer, R.W., *Norfolk in the Civil War: A Portrait of Society in Conflict* (Norwich, 1985).
Kowaleski-Wallace, E., *Consuming Subjects: Women, Shopping and Business in the Eighteenth Century* (New York, 1997).
Larminie, V.M., *Wealth, Kinship and Culture: The Seventeenth Century Newdigates of Arbury and their World* (Woodbridge, 1995).
Lee, J., *Cambridge and its Economic Region 1450–1550* (Hatfield, 2005).
Lemire, B., *Fashion's Favourite: The Cotton Trade and the Consumer in Britain, 1660–1800* (Oxford, 1991).
Leong, E., 'Making medicines in the early modern household', *Bulletin of the History of Medicine* 82 (2008), 145–68.
Martin, L., 'The rise of the new draperies in Norwich, 1550–1622', in N.B. Harte (ed.), *The New Draperies in the Low Countries and England, 1300–1800* (Oxford, 1997), 245–74.
McCracken, G., *Culture and Consumption: New Approaches to the Symbolic Character of Consumer Goods and Activities* (Indiana, 1988).
McKendrick, N., 'The consumer revolution in eighteenth-century England', in N. McKendrick, J. Brewer, and J.H. Plumb (eds.), *The Birth of a Consumer Society: The Commercialization of Eighteenth-Century England* (London, 1982).
McRae, A., *God Speed the Plough: The Representation of Agrarian England 1500–1660* (Cambridge, 1996).
Mennell, S., *All Manners of Food: Eating and Taste in England and France from the Middle Ages to the Present* (Oxford, 1985).
Merritt, J.F., *The Social World of Early Modern Westminster: Abbey, Court and Community 1525–1640* (Manchester, 2005).
Mertes, K., *The English Noble Household 1250–1600: Good Governance and Politic Rule* (Oxford, 1988).
Miller, D., 'Consumption and its consequences', in H. Mackay (ed.), *Consumption and Everyday Life* (London, 1997).
—— *A Theory of Shopping* (Cambridge, 1998).
Mintz, S.W., 'The changing roles of food in the study of consumption', in J. Brewer and R. Porter (eds.), *Consumption and the World of Goods* (London, 1993), 261–73.
Mitchell, D.M., '"By your leave my masters": British taste in table linen in the fifteenth and sixteenth centuries', *Textile History* 20:1 (1989), 49–77.
Mui, H. and Mui, L.H., *Shops and Shopkeeping in Eighteenth Century England* (Montreal, 1989).

Muldrew, C., *The Economy of Obligation: The Culture of Credit and Social Relations in Early Modern England* (Basingstoke, 1998).
Oakley, A., *Women's Work: The Housewife, Past and Present* (New York, 1976).
Oestmann, C., *Lordship and Community: The Lestrange Family and the Village of Hunstanton, Norfolk in the First Half of the Sixteenth Century* (Woodbridge, 1994).
Overton, M., 'Prices from probate inventories', in T. Arkell, N. Evans, and N. Goose (eds.), *When Death Do Us Part: Understanding and Interpreting the Probate Records of Early Modern England* (Oxford, 2000), 120–41.
—— Whittle, J., Dean, D., and Hann, A. *Production and Consumption in English Households, 1600–1750* (Abingdon, 2004).
Pahl, J., *Money and Marriage* (New York, 1989).
Patten, J., 'Changing occupational structures in the East Anglian countryside, 1500–1700', in H.S.A. Fox and R.A. Butlin (eds.), *Change in the Countryside: Essays on Rural England 1500–1900* (London, 1979), 103–21.
Peck, L., *Consuming Splendor: Society and Culture in Seventeenth-Century England* (Cambridge, 2005).
Pelling, M. and Webster, C., 'Medical practitioners', in C. Webster (ed.), *Health, Medicine and Mortality in the Sixteenth Century* (Cambridge, 1979), 164–235.
Pennell, S., 'Consumption and consumerism in early modern England', *Historical Journal* 42 (1999), 549–64.
Plumb, J.H. 'The new world of children', in N. McKendrick, J. Brewer, and J.H. Plumb (eds.), *The Birth of a Consumer Society: The Commercialization of Eighteenth-Century England* (London, 1982), 286–315.
Pollard, S., *The Genesis of Modern Management: A Study of the Industrial Revolution in Great Britain* (Cambridge, Massachusetts, 1965).
Pollock, L., *Forgotten Children: Parent-Child Relations, 1500–1900* (Cambridge, 1983).
—— '"Teach her to live under obedience": The making of women in the upper ranks of early modern England', *Continuity and Change* 4:2 (1989), 231–58.
—— *With Faith and Physic: The Life of a Tudor Gentlewoman, Lady Grace Mildmay 1552–1620* (London, 1993).
Ribeiro, A., *Fashion and Fiction: Dress in Art and Literature in Stuart England* (New Haven, 2005).
Roberts, M., '"Words they are women and deeds they are men": images of work and gender in early modern England', in L. Charles and L. Duffin (eds.), *Women and Work in Pre-Industrial England* (London, 1985), 122–80.
Robertson, U.A., *The Illustrated History of the Housewife 1650–1950* (Stroud, 1999).
Rothstein, N. and Levey, S.M., 'Furnishings, c.1500–1780', in D. Jenkins (ed.), *The Cambridge History of Western Textiles* (Cambridge, 2003), 631–58.
Rye, W., *Norfolk Families* (Norwich, 1913).
Sambrook, P.A. and Brears P. (eds.), *The Country House Kitchen 1650–1900* (Stroud, 1997).
Serjeantson, D. and Woolgar, C.M., 'Fish consumption in medieval England', in C.M. Woolgar, D. Serjeantson, and T. Waldron (eds), *Food in Medieval England: Diet and Nutrition* (Oxford, 2006), 102–30.
Shammas, C., *The Pre-Industrial Consumer in England and America* (Oxford, 1990).
Shorter, E., *The Making of the Modern Family* (London, 1976).
Sim, A., *The Tudor Housewife* (Stroud, 1996).
Simpson, A., *The Wealth of the Gentry 1540–1660: East Anglian Studies* (Cambridge, 1961).

Slack, P., 'Mirrors of health and treasures of poor men: the uses of the vernacular medical literature of Tudor England', in C. Webster (ed.), *Health, Medicine and Mortality in the Sixteenth Century* (Cambridge, 1979), 237–73.

Smith, A.H., *County and Court: Government and Politics in Norfolk, 1558–1603* (Oxford, 1974).

—— 'Labourers in late sixteenth-century England: a case study from north Norfolk [Part I]', *Continuity and Change* 4:1 (1989), 11–52.

—— 'Labourers in late sixteenth-century England: a case study from north Norfolk [Part II]', *Continuity and Change* 4:3 (1989), 367–94.

Smith, W.D., 'Complications of the commonplace: tea, sugar and imperialism', *Journal of Interdisciplinary History* 23:2 (1992), 259–78.

—— *Consumption and the Making of Respectability 1600–1800* (London, 2002).

Smuts, R.M., *Court Culture and the Origins of a Royalist Tradition in Early Stuart England* (Philadelphia, 1987).

Spufford, M., *The Great Reclothing of Rural England: Petty Chapmen and their Wares in the Seventeenth Century* (Oxford, 1984).

—— 'Chimneys, wood and coal', in P.S. Barnwell and M. Airs (eds.), *Houses and the Hearth Tax: The Later Stuart House and Society* (York, 2006), 22–32.

Stone, L., 'The educational revolution in England, 1560–1640', *Past and Present* 28 (1964), 41–80.

—— *Ther Crisis of the Aristocracy 1558–1641* (Oxford, 1965).

—— *The Family, Sex and Marriage in England 1500–1800* (London, 1977).

Styles, J., *The Dress of the People: Everyday Fashion in Eighteenth-Century England* (New Haven, 2007).

Tawney, R.H., 'The rise of the gentry, 1558–1640', *Economic History Review* 11 (1941), 1–38.

Thirsk, J., *Economic Policy and Projects: The Development of a Consumer Society in Early Modern England* (Oxford, 1978).

—— *Food in Early Modern England: Phases, Fads, Fashions 1500–1760* (London, 2007).

Thomas, K., 'Cleanliness and godliness in early modern England', in A. Fletcher and P. Roberts (eds.), *Religion, Culture and Society in Early Modern Britain* (Cambridge, 1994).

Thornton, P., *Seventeenth-Century Interior Decoration in England, France and Holland* (New Haven, 1978).

Threlfall-Holmes, M., *Monks and Markets: Durham Cathedral Priory 1460–1520* (Oxford, 2005).

Trevor-Roper, H.R., *The Gentry 1540–1640, Economic History Review*, supplement 1 (1953).

Turner, L'Estrange G., *Scientific Instruments 1500–1900: An Introduction* (London, 1998).

Veblen, T., *The Theory of the Leisure Class*, first published 1899 (Oxford, 2007).

Vickery, A., 'Women and the world of goods: a Lancashire consumer and her possessions, 1751–81' in J. Brewer and R. Porter (eds.), *Consumption and the World of Goods* (London, 1993), 274–301.

—— 'His and hers: gender, consumption and household accounting in eighteenth-century England', *Past and Present* supplement 1 (2006), 12–38.

Vincent, S., *Dressing the Elite: Clothes in Early Modern England* (Oxford, 2003).

Wall, W., *Staging Domesticity: Household Work and English Identity in Early Modern Drama* (Cambridge, 2002).

Walsh, C., 'Shops, shopping, and the art of decision making in eighteenth-century England', in J. Styles and A. Vickery (eds.), *Gender, Taste and Material Culture in Britain and North America, 1700–1830* (New Haven, 2006), 151–77.

Warren, I., '"Witty offending great ones"? Elite female householders in an early Stuart Westminster parish', *The London Journal* 32:3 (2007), 211–28.

—— 'London's cultural impact on the English gentry: the case of Worcestershire, c.1580–1680', *Midland History* 33:2 (2008), 156–78.

Wear, A., *Knowledge and Practice in English Medicine, 1550–1680* (Cambridge, 2000).

Weatherill, L., *Consumer Behaviour and Material Culture in Britain 1660–1760* (London, 1988).

Whittle, J., *The Development of Agrarian Capitalism: Land and Labour in Norfolk, 1440–1580* (Oxford, 2000).

—— 'Servants in rural England c.1450–1650: hired work as a means of accumulating wealth and skills before marriage', in M. Agren and A. Erickson (eds.), *The Marital Economy in Scandinavia and Britain 1400–1900* (Aldershot, 2005), 89–107.

Willetts, P., 'Nicholas Le Strange and John Jenkins', *Music & Letters* 42:1 (1961), 30–43.

Wilson, A.C., *Food and Drink in Britain from the Stone Age to Recent Times* (London, 1973).

Woodward, D., *Men at Work: Labourers and Building Craftsmen in the Towns of Northern England, 1450–1750* (Cambridge, 1995).

—— 'Straw, bracken and the Wicklow whale: the exploitation of natural resources in England since 1500', *Past and Present* 159 (1998), 43–76.

Woolgar, C.M., 'Diet and consumption in gentry and noble households: a case study from around the Wash', in R.E. Archer and S. Walker (eds.), *Rulers and Ruled in Late Medieval England: Essays Presented to Gerald Harriss* (London, 1995), 117–31.

—— *The Great Household in Late Medieval England* (New Haven, 1999).

—— 'Meat and dairy products in medieval England', in C.M. Woolgar, D. Serjeantson, and T. Waldron (eds.), *Food in Medieval England: Diet and Nutrition* (Oxford, 2006), 88–101.

—— Serjeantson, D., and Waldron, T., *Food in Medieval England: Diet and Nutrition* (Oxford, 2006).

Wrightson, K., *English Society 1580–1680* (London, 1982).

Wrigley, E.A. and Schofield, R.S., *The Population History of England 1541–1871* (Cambridge, 1981).

Unpublished articles, Ph.D. theses and papers

Campbell, L., 'Sir Roger Townshend and his family: a study of gentry life in early seventeenth-century Norfolk', Ph.D. thesis (East Anglia, 1990).

Griffiths, E.M., 'The management of two east Norfolk estates in the seventeenth century: Blickling and Felbrigg', Ph.D. thesis (East Anglia, 1988).

Spicksley, J., 'Women, accounts and numeracy in seventeenth-century England', unpublished paper presented to the Economic History Society Annual Conference, Leicester 2005.

Websites

Oxford Dictionary of National Biography: http://www.oxforddnb.com
Oxford English Dictionary Online: http://dictionary.oed.com
The Court of Chivalry 1634–1640: www.court-of-chivalry.bham.ac.uk
The Perdita Project: http://human.ntu.ac.uk/research/perdita/index.html

Index

accounts *see* building; estate; household; kitchen
Akers, Thomas and Goodwife 72; *see also* specialist workers: bakers
alcohol, ale, beer, coffee, tea, wine *see* drinks
alms, charity and poor relief *see* family finance
Anguish, Christopher 69, 214; *see also* servants, male: horsekeeper
Anguish, Mr 68; *see also* merchants and suppliers: drapers
Anmer (Norfolk) 22
annuities and allowances *see* family finance
aristocracy, features of 15–16; *see also* gentry
Aristotle 197; *see also* books: Sir Hamon's library

Bacon, Anne *see* Lady Anne Townshend
Bacon, Sir Francis 45
    Nathaniel of Stiffkey 44, 189, 211–12, 215–16, 218, 221, 223, 226
    Nathaniel of Suffolk, artist 93
    Sir Nicholas 166
bailiffs *see* estate; servants, elite
Baillie, Lady Griselle 54
Balls, Henry 217; *see also* servants, male
Banyard family 66, 81, 83, 232–5
    David 142
    Eustace 232–5, 244
    John 234
    Robert 234–5
    Thomas 218, 235
    William 234, 244; *see also* estate: bailiffs, tenants; servants, male
Banyard, Widow 66; *see also* specialist workers: knitters
Barbican *see* Lady Jane Berkeley; London
barley, oats, wheat *see* grain
Barton Mills, Suffolk 60
Barrough, Philip 110; *see also* books: medical
Bastard family 83
    Robert 218, 220; *see also* estate: bailiffs, tenants; B. Fisher
Bateman, J. 205; *see also* craftsmen: glaziers
Beeton, Mrs 26; *see also* books: household
Bell, Dorothy *see* Lady Dorothy Hobart
    Mary *see* Lady Mary Le Strange
Bell, Sir Edmund 193
    uncle Bell, 82
    Philip 188
    Sir Robert of Beaupre Hall, Outwell (Norfolk) 19, 20
Bendish, Mr William 175
Benwell, Thomas 217, 219; *see also* servants, elite: clerks
    Alice 219; *see also* servants, female
Berkeley, Lord Henry 44

Lady Jane 14, 44, 45; *see also* Townshend family
Bidden, R. 140, 222–4, 231–3, 236–7, 244; *see also* tenants; labourers
Bird, Anne 218; *see also* servants, female
birds 18, 73, 81, 91–2, 221, 224
    game 77, 83, 94, 195–6
    hawks 13, 52, 61–2, 193, 195–6, 199, 206, 209, 239
    peacocks, hens 40, 79, 81, 232
    pheasants 79, 81–2, 94
    swans 78, 81, 99–100
    wild 77, 81, 83, 91, 95–6, 100, 116, 232, 237
    wildfowl 105, 196, 234
    see also foodstuffs; consumption activities; elite consumption; servants, male: falconer
Blickling Hall, Norfolk 45–6
Boner, John 220
    Goodwife 220
    Anne *see* Anne Shilling
books 7, 14, 25, 52, 54, 61–3, 84, 108, 118–19, 129, 152, 198, 202, 208
    account 24, 27, 33, 74, 99, 101, 120, 170, 203, 211
    advice and self-help 11, 27, 32, 37–42, 48, 65, 142, 170, 174, 184, 192, 200
    as gifts 148, 197–8, 239
    Bible 26, 36, 38, 110, 149, 235
    children's 172–4, 177–8, 198
    cookery 40–2, 48, 86–8, 103–4, 93, 116
    diaries 50, 108, 168, 170
    estate 22, 29–30
    gardening 93
    household 12, 23, 26, 28, 31, 51–2, 65, 80, 84, 113, 193, 211, 222, 225, 227, 244
    husbandry 39–42
    medical 88, 93, 106, 109–10, 116, 170, 191
    music 149, 200
    note 24, 34, 175, 208
    pattern 206
    Sir Hamon's library 197–200, 202, 240
    see also elite consumption; library
Boscawen, Margaret 108
Bower, Anne 214; *see also* servants, female: dairymaid
Boyton, Dorothy 234; *see also* Guybon, William
Bozoun family 82
    Hamon 19
    Uncle Roger of Whissonsett 19, 161, 193, 195
Brasenets, R. 214; *see also* servants, male: gardeners

Brathwaite, R. 38–9; *see also* bibliography: pre-1800 books
Brewer, Thomas 200; *see also* professionals: singing master
Breese 224; *see also* labourers
Bride, Elizabeth 214, 220; *see also* servants, female: washmaids; W. Cambridge
Briggs, Mr of Norwich 175–6; *see also* professionals: tutors
Broadhead 67, 137, 227; *see also* craftsmen: joiners
Buckingham, Duke of 118
building accounts 23, 29, 46, 51, 222–3
  work 9, 25, 28–9, 33–4, 45–6 49, 51, 74, 83, 112–13, 132, 134, 147, 159, 161, 163, 184, 188, 196, 198, 203–8, 221–3, 227–9, 239
  workers 3, 14, 51, 74, 157, 210, 227, 239, 241; *see also* craftsmen; labourers
buildings 2, 51, 74, 161, 185, 203, 206–7, 210, 227–9, 240;
  service 161, 206–7
Bullinger, H. 27, 38–9; *see also* bibliography: pre-1800 books
Bullward 214, 218; *see also* servants, male
Burnham, T. 218; *see also* servants, elite: bailiffs of husbandry
Burnham Ulph (Market), Norfolk 63
Burwood, Mr 82; *see also* professionals: clergymen
Bust, Mr at Eton College, Berkshire 218
  William 219; *see* servants, male

Cademan, R. of Ringstead, yeoman 210, 220; *see also* Thomas Lane
Calthorpe, Catherine *nee* Lewkenor 31, 243
  Philip of Gressenhall, 63, 193
calves, cows, sheep, pigs *see* livestock
Calvinist 184–5; *see also* Sir Hamon Le Strange
Cambridge, W. 214, 220; *see also* servants, male; E. Bride
Cambridge 60, 199
  University 114, 157, 175–6, 194, 197, 200
  Magdalene College 32
  Queen's College 21, 177, 194
  Sidney Sussex College 177
  Trinity College 177
Camoys, Lord, veteran of the Battle of Crecy, 20
Carey, Sir Robert 21
Cary, Lady 70
Catelyn, Aunt 194
  Richard and Dorothy of Bracondale, Norwich 178
Cavendish, Margaret, Duchess of Newcastle 165
Challoner, R. 108; *see also* books
Chant, Alice 99, 114, 166, 218; *see also* servants, female: washerwomen
Chapel Field, Norwich 57
  House 45–6
Chaucer, Geoffrey 199; *see also* books: as gifts

childcare 4, 8, 10, 31, 38–41, 48, 101, 105, 115, 123, 165, 170–3, 183, 234, 236, 242
childhood 106, 156–7, 170, 173–4, 183
children Le Strange 23, 25, 28–9, 59, 62, 157–8, 164–83
  clothing 66–8, 84, 129, 156, 168, 173–4
  education 156–7, 170, 172–8
  feeling for 166–8, 170
  gendered attitudes to 156, 173, 178, 180–3
  gifts to 82–3, 148–9, 195, 198
  grown up 150–1, 156–9, 161–2, 178–81
  of other families 44–7, 165, 170–1, 174, 234–6, 239
  pauper 186
  Rates of Baptism 219, 229–30
  wetnursing 156–7, 170–2; *see also* family; feasting and fasting
cleanliness 2, 86–7, 111, 113–14, 116, 119, 139, 152, 239; *see also* consumables; consumption activities: cleaning and washing
Cleaver, Robert 26, 37–9; *see also* bibliography: pre-1800 books
Clever, William 110; *see also* books: medical
Clifford, Mary, Countess of Cumberland 108
cloth *see* textiles
clothes 6, 8, 10, 12–13, 24, 31, 33, 41
  acquiring 62, 67–8, 71, 84
  cleaning 113–14
  different types of 118–20, 122–5, 128, 130–1, 151–2, 154, 165–9, 173, 179–80, 218, 239, 241–2; *see also* clothing; textiles
clothing 2, 3, 5, 7, 23, 25–6, 50–4, 61, 63–7, 70–1, 84, 111, 113, 119–31, 145–8, 150–5, 163, 168, 184–5, 192, 239, 242
  children's 156, 165, 170, 172–3, 177–8, 181, 242
  gendered attitudes to 12–3, 124, 129, 146, 173, 239
  men's 128–31, 139, 152
  women's 124–7; *see also* clothes; textiles; consumption activities
clothing accessories:
  boots, hose, shoes 61, 66–7, 125, 128–9, 131, 168, 173
  gloves, hats 13, 61–3, 66, 84, 125, 129, 130–1, 152, 166, 168–9, 173, 196, 199, 240
  haberdashery 6, 62–3, 68; *see also* merchants and suppliers: drapers
coal, charcoal, wood *see* consumables: fuel
Cobbes family 83, 171; *see also* specialist workers: wetnurses
Cogan, Thomas; *see also* books: medical
Coke, Sir Edward 45
Coke family of Much Marcle, Herefordshire 97
Coke, Mary *see* Lady Mary Le Strange
Cole 166; *see also* servants, elite: clerks
Collinges, Dr. John 32, 46–7; *see also* bibliography: pre-1800 books

Index

consumables, everyday 1, 3, 25, 86–7, 111, 216
  candles 62, 87, 111–12, 115–16, 169, 216, 239
  cleaning products 4, 7, 86–7, 111, 114–16, 131, 240
  fuel 1–3, 6, 20, 25, 51, 62, 74, 86–7, 111–16, 145, 206, 216, 222
  heating 86, 111–16
  lighting 25, 51, 111–12, 124; *see also* food; foodstuffs; medicines
consumer 2–4, 64–5, 123, 150, 246–51
  behaviour 4, 6–7, 11, 13, 26, 51, 54, 119, 139, 152
  boom 55
  culture 142
  gentry as 118, 240
  goods 4–5, 10, 12, 14, 55, 65, 240
  men as 191, 209
  Revolution 4, 6, 114, 143, 170, 241
  Society 4, 6, 143, 170, 241
  producers and 210, 238
  urban 119
  women as 185, 242; *see also* goods; gentry; consumption
consumption
  as a study, 1–8, 239–42
  as a process 24, 237, 241
  domestic 11–2, 23, 36, 28–9, 48–51, 53, 63–4, 73, 75–6
  changes in 7, 16, 117, 240–1
  gender and 8–13
  gentry and 14, 16, 17, 20, 48, 52, 55, 57, 118–19, 123, 132, 137
  identity 13, 16, 242
  management of 3, 24, 88, 242
  nature of 64, 74, 84
  patterns of 7, 16, 25, 102, 115, 146–7, 154, 211–12, 239–242
  practices 1, 4, 242
  production and 210–11, 213, 238; *see also* consumption activities; elite consumption; family; food; household; material culture
consumption activities, leisure 1, 3–4, 12–13, 17, 25, 57–8, 147, 184–5, 191, 213, 215, 239, 242
  eating and drinking 3, 5, 11, 86, 88, 96–7, 102–4, 115, 118, 139
  entertaining and dining 17, 56, 86, 142–3
  hawking and hunting 13, 18, 34, 52, 63, 92, 105, 173, 184–5, 195–6, 208–9, 240, 242
  purchasing 2, 5–6, 11, 13, 32, 49–50, 62–3, 84, 98, 104, 106, 115, 165, 168, 172, 199, 208
  shopping 1–2, 5–6, 8–11, 26, 55–7, 59, 61–2, 64, 84, 101, 140–2, 191, 209, 239, 242
  spending 3, 5, 8, 10, 13, 16, 26, 32, 39, 50, 54, 63, 85, 118, 130, 151, 161, 169, 174, 177, 183, 185, 197, 203, 228, 239–40
  visiting 9, 193, 195; *see also* birds; elite consumption; shops; visits
consumption activities, work 1–3, 12–3, 50, 242
  baking 12, 40–1, 112

brewing 12, 18, 20, 41, 69, 76, 90, 109, 145, 147–50, 215, 235
butter and cheese making 12, 40–1
cleaning 1, 11, 114–15, 215
cooking 1, 11, 87, 96, 99, 103–4, 109, 112–13, 115, 140–1, 215
dairying 18, 75, 97, 109, 145, 232, 236
distilling 12, 40–1, 109, 143, 206
gardening 12, 82, 109
laundering 152
milking 40, 42, 215
knitting 50, 66, 72, 129
preserving 41, 65, 111, 143–4
retailing 2, 5–7, 24, 63–4, 84
provisioning 11, 13, 38, 48, 242
sewing 12–3, 39, 62, 71
spinning 12–3, 39, 65–6, 72, 172, 235–6
tailoring 6, 13, 69, 126, 130–1, 239
tutoring 157, 175–6, 239
washing 65, 113–6, 145, 150, 154, 175, 177, 215, 221
weaving 13, 39, 65–6, 72; *see also* building work
consumption events, *see* feasting and fasting
Cooper, shipmate *see* Samuel Pepys
Cope, Sir Anthony 19
Cope, Lady Anthony 19, 22; *see also* Lady Anne Le Strange
Corbett family 60, 193, 217; *see also* Sprowston Hall, Norwich
Corner 225; *see also* specialist workers: shepherds
Costen family 83, 166, 171, 226–7
  Francis 166, 171, 226–7, 237
  William 227
  Thomas 227, 244; *see also* craftsmen: carpenters; specialist workers: wetnurses; tenants
county administration 15, 20–1, 56, 184, 186–8, 190–199
  families, gentry, gentlemen 7, 21, 23, 46, 118, 146, 186, 188
  society/community 16, 209
  towns 13, 17, 57, 191; *see also* elite consumption: office-holding
Courtenay, Thomas of South Pool, Devon 96
Cox, W. 217; *see also* servants, male: cooks
craftsmen 5, 14, 25, 34, 49–50, 67, 71, 84, 123, 210–12, 221, 224–8, 230, 237
  book binders 62
  brickmakers 225, 228
  carpenters 137, 161, 171, 210, 225–230, 237, 239
  coopers 145, 210–1, 219, 237
  farrier and horse doctor 106–7, 192, 220
  glaziers 109, 205, 210, 228–9
  glovers 63, 67
  goldsmiths 62, 142, 201
  hatters 63, 66–7, 130

craftsmen (*cont.*)
  joiners 69, 71, 227–9, 237–8
  masons, 204, 210, 226–9, 239
  plasterers, 205
  plumbers 210, 228–9
  printers 199
  saddlers 62–3, 69, 241, 192, 225
  sawyers 211
  shoemakers 51, 62, 66–7, 211, 217, 241
  silversmiths 210–11
  sluicemenders 225
  smiths 225, 228, 237
  tailors 6, 13, 49, 51, 62–3, 66–9, 71, 123, 125–6, 130–1, 162, 210, 216, 225, 229, 237, 239–42
  thatchers 68, 210, 226–9
  tiler 228
  tinker 145, 210–11, 237
  upholsterers 69; *see also* specialist workers; labourers; servants
Crampe, T., of Heacham 237; *see also* tenants
Creamer, John 163
  Robert of Snettisham 236–7; *see also* Robert Stileman
Cremer family 83
  Thomas 218; *see also* bailiffs of husbandry; tenants
Crisp family 164
  Goodwife, 83, 107, 164–5
  John 164, 226
  Thomas 226, 244
  William 111–12; *see also* merchants and suppliers: chandlers; specialist workers: midwife, shepherds

Dawnay of Fakenham 192; *see also* craftsmen: saddlers
dairy 29, 33, 37, 41–2, 74–7, 145, 150, 198, 206–7
  butter 12, 24, 28, 33, 40–1, 43, 73–5, 89–90, 92, 95–8, 100–2, 104, 162, 236
  cheese 12, 24, 28, 33, 40–1, 73–5, 79, 88–9, 92, 94, 96–9, 102, 104, 116, 141, 162, 235–6
  produce 76, 88–9, 92, 94, 96–7; *see also* foodstuffs; meat
Davison, J. 68; *see also* craftsmen: tailors
debts and loans, *see* family finance
diet 23, 25, 52, 60–1, 87–98, 101–4, 106, 110, 116, 175, 187, 216, 240; *see also* food; foodstuffs; feasting and fasting
Diser, C. 227; *see also* craftsmen: joiners
Dixon, Mr 66; *see also* specialist workers: knitters
Docking (Norfolk) 22
Dowland, John 198; *see also* books: music
Driland, Gertrude of Wye, Kent 127
drinks 6, 47, 50, 74, 90, 92, 101, 109, 142, 158, 165, 196, 212, 216, 223, 226, 228–9
  alcohol 12, 88, 90, 209, 143, 151
  ale 12, 41, 90–1, 96, 116
  beer 12, 20, 28, 41–2, 74, 76, 88–90, 94, 96, 98, 100–2, 115–16, 162, 189, 240
  coffee 117–18
  tea 5, 86, 117–18
  wine 6, 14, 20, 41, 62, 73, 77, 90–1, 99, 103–4, 141, 167
  see also consumption activities: drinking; household wares: dining and kitchen ware
Drury, Mr Edmund 193
Dye 68; *see also* craftsmen: tailors

East India Company 67, 121, 130
Edge brothers 204, 227; *see also* craftsmen: masons
Egerton, Lady Frances; *see* Lady Frances Hobart
elite consumption 7, 16, 25, 55, 118–19, 184–209
  coaches 13, 25, 52, 56–8, 61–4, 84, 148, 150, 166, 191–3, 196, 206, 208–10, 212–3, 240–1
  bowls, cards and games 52, 62, 173, 184–5, 195–6, 209
  clocks and watches 5, 63, 117–8, 139, 202, 239
  guns, muskets and weapons 13, 61, 84, 148, 152, 189, 196
  hospitality 13–4, 16–7, 55–6, 81, 99, 138, 140, 142, 184–5, 238–9, 241
  office-holding 184–191
  travel 26, 43, 46, 51–3, 56–60, 63, 84, 125, 184–6, 188, 190–2, 194–6, 208–9, 215, 229, 240
  scientific instruments 13, 25, 51, 61–2, 84, 196, 200–2; 209; *see also* birds; books; clothes; clothing accessories; consumption activities; county administration; furnishings; horses; militia
Elyot, Thomas 87, 93, 110, 184; *see also* books: medical
English Civil War 15, 21, 23, 25, 33, 63,77, 84, 97, 157, 159, 161–3, 180, 189–90, 192, 221, 225, 244; *see also* family finance
estate, Le Strange 18, 20–2, 28, 33, 35, 51, 91, 96, 161, 163, 175, 178–9, 181, 190, 203, 224, 227, 237, 240
  bailiffs 28, 30, 34, 40, 42, 83, 235, 243
  employment 210, 221–2, 228, 230
  foldcourse system 18, 21, 29, 149
  foldcourses 18, 65, 225, 232
  home farm 42, 72, 74–77
  improvement 9, 29, 34, 51, 114, 184–5, 198, 202–3, 207–9
  management 25–30, 34–5, 42–3, 50–1, 159, 175, 185–6, 189–90
  records 20, 27–30, 33–4, 212, 244
  resources 91, 96, 113, 115, 222
  tenants 14, 17–8, 24, 28, 34–5, 56, 77, 81–5, 99, 113, 171, 189, 191, 194, 218, 225–6, 228, 230–1, 233–8, 240–1

warren 40, 72, 91, 226
see also craftsmen; specialist workers; labourers; servants, elite, female and male
estates, wider 14, 16–7, 21, 27, 31, 36, 45–7, 56, 178–9, 217, 238, 240, 242
women and 24, 27, 30, 35–6, 41–8; *see also* Le Strange, Lady Alice
Estienne, C. 12, 39–42, 108, 110; *see also* bibliography: pre-1800 books
Eton College, Berkshire 59, 157, 175–7, 197, 200, 218, 225; *see also* children
Exchanges, New and Royal 5, 49; *see also* London
expenditure 1, 3–4, 23–5, 156–63, 166, 168, 172–3, 177
 domestic 50–5, 63–5, 85
 gendered attitudes to 8, 11, 13
 managing 28–31, 34–5, 46
 on consumables 86, 92, 99, 105
 on material goods 117, 119, 120, 128, 130 146, 151, 153, 202; *see also* family finance

Fakenham, Norfolk 62, 186, 192
Felsham (Suffolk) 22
family 1–3, 5, 11, 13–14, 17–21, 111, 145–6
 celebrations 164–9
 life-cycle and consumption 156–183
 maintaining the 50–1, 58, 60–3, 67, 71, 74, 82–3, 85, 87–8, 101–8, 116, 118–19, 128, 132–4, 138, 142–3, 146, 149–51, 154, 210, 213, 218–19, 221, 227, 230, 232–5, 242
 role of women in the 32, 35, 39, 41, 43–4, 46–7, 65, 209; *see also* children; feasting and fasting; family finance
family finance 160–4
 alms, charity, poor relief 17, 185–6, 190
 allowances 30, 46, 51, 63, 156, 161, 178, 180–1
 annuities 22, 161, 240
 debt 8–9, 14, 21, 23, 35, 44–9, 55, 74, 85, 156, 159, 161–2, 164, 177, 180–1, 233, 241
 loans 23, 33, 46, 51, 159–164, 181, 216
 taxation 25, 63, 161, 163, 185–6, 189–90, 203, 209, 240
feasting and fasting
 christenings 82, 99–101, 104, 116, 142, 164–6, 170–1, 195
 funerals 32, 147, 164, 166–8
 weddings 68–9, 99–100, 120, 123, 126, 130–1, 142, 152, 156, 164, 168–9, 179–180
 Christmas 4, 17, 64, 73, 77, 84, 91, 94, 96, 98–101, 115–6, 195, 213, 217, 224
 Easter 97–98, 156
 New Year 98, 100
 Lent 59, 72, 74, 92, 94, 97–8, 101, 116
 see also children; clothes; diet; family; food; gifts
fish, different types of 18, 73, 78–9, 88–9, 92, 94–5, 97–8, 101–2, 104, 240; *see also* foodstuffs

fishing, inshore 18; *see also* sea: fisheries, fish, food
Fisher, Barbara 220; *see also* servants, female; R. Bastard
Fisher, John 22; *see also* professionals: surveyors
Fisher, Margaret 150
food 1–2, 6–8, 24–5, 246–51
 acquisition 10, 18, 24, 28, 72–84
 consumption 4, 23, 28, 86–9, 91–2, 94–101, 104, 115, 169
 culture and diet 87–97
 expenditure on 52–5, 58, 85–6, 163, 167
 gifts 3, 17, 23, 50, 72, 77–84, 92–5, 99, 164, 171, 180, 220, 226, 231–2, 235, 238–41
 managing 10–1, 23, 28–9, 48, 51–2, 86–8, 140, 144, 157, 241–2
 meaning of 98–105
 payment in 216, 218, 223, 226, 228–9
 preparing 42, 50, 87, 145
 production of 2, 10, 23, 41–3, 47–51, 74, 76, 87, 93, 111–2, 139, 145, 154, 212, 215
 selling 77
 significance of 4, 7, 13, 17, 25, 96, 99, 115–7, 147, 165, 241
 see also household; foodstuffs
foodstuffs 2, 4, 10–1, 29, 41, 50–1, 73, 76–7, 87–8, 94, 96, 101–4, 111, 123, 154, 216
 bread 6, 14, 28, 42, 73–6, 88–90, 94, 98–102, 116, 162, 166, 240
 exotic 80, 92–3, 109, 111, 116, 222–4
 see also birds; dairy produce; garden; gifts; groceries; fish; meat; poultry
Fortescue, Bridget 108
Freke, Elizabeth 108
Fring (Norfolk) 22, 161
 fair 63
fruit, fresh, *see* garden; dried, *see* groceries
furnishings 3, 6, 13, 23–4, 42, 50–1, 61, 64–5, 67, 69–70, 84, 119–20, 122, 133–7, 139, 146–7, 149, 153–5, 168, 184–5, 202, 239, 241
 candlesticks 62, 111, 144, 168, 236
 carpets 70–1, 133–4, 136, 154
 curtains 64, 70, 120–1, 133–5, 137–9, 146, 154–5, 240
 cushions 68, 71, 149, 154, 169, 235
 pictures 138–40, 154–5;
 tapestry 122, 133, 137
 see also elite consumption; household wares; upholsterers
furniture, general 41, 65, 67, 69–70, 112, 118–19, 123, 132, 137, 148, 150, 153–5, 216, 227, 232, 238–40
 beds 3, 23, 25, 61, 67–71, 111–12, 117, 119–21, 123, 132–40, 146–7, 150, 153–4, 165–6, 169, 172, 177, 203, 212, 216–17, 232–6, 239, 241
 mirrors 111, 118–19, 134–5, 139, 155
 see also craftsmen: joiners; furnishings; gifts; linen

Index

game 91, 116
  fox, hares, otters 196
  deer 77, 91, 100, 196, 236
  rabbits 42, 72, 80, 89, 91, 93–6, 98–102, 217, 226; *see also* birds
garden 29, 40–2, 88, 92–3, 109–10, 115–16, 141, 205, 212, 215, 239, 241
  fruit, fresh 12, 41, 55, 73–4, 77, 81, 83, 92, 103–4, 164, 214
  honey 74, 80, 83, 104
  seeds 41–2, 73, 76, 82, 92–3, 99, 104, 239
  vegetables 6, 41, 50, 55, 73–4, 77, 92–3, 116, 144; *see also* groceries, food
Gaywood, Kings Lynn, Norfolk 63, 193
gender 1–2, 8, 32, 87, 146, 156–7
gendered attitudes, *see* children; cleanliness; clothing; consumption; goods; household management; identities, purchasing; shopping; wills and bequests
gentlemen
  definition of 15–18
  education 31–2, 36, 55
  English 196, 202
  elite 40, 46
  farmers 214, 232–3, 236, 241
  Norfolk 21, 211
  parish 7
  Renaissance 175, 184–5, 206
  role of 42–3, 57, 187–9, 191, 195, 200, 203
  social activities 13, 56–7, 75, 60, 93, 152, 175, 180, 196, 208, 234, 238
  see also elite consumption; gentry
gentlewomen 9, 12, 21, 24, 27, 47
  as housewives 27, 31, 67, 36–43, 64, 71, 84, 108, 125
  as managers 27, 32, 35–6, 43, 75
  as mothers 172
  clothing 125–8
  education 9, 27, 31–2, 37–8
  employing 60, 101, 157
  interests 63–4, 84, 149, 151–2, 208
  Norfolk 27, 43–4, 47–8
  skills 12, 71, 75, 108, 149; *see also* housewife; housewifery; housekeeping; women
gentry 1–2, 12–17, 26, 35, 37, 55–7, 66, 70, 99, 101, 103–4, 108, 116, 118–19, 123, 128, 132–3, 144, 148, 154, 158–9, 165, 168, 178–81, 184–5, 189, 191, 193–4, 196, 209, 212, 217, 221, 232, 237–9
  children 172
  county/rural 7, 64, 118, 146, 184, 186, 188, 201
  diet 55, 104, 116
  East Anglian 113
  English 14–15, 57, 175, 184
  Essex 12, 108, 151, 245
  families 18, 21, 97, 102, 142, 146, 174, 178, 183, 242

identity 105
inventories 128, 153
lifestyle 52, 168, 179, 191, 209
lower/middling 15, 17, 34, 45, 81–2, 213, 215, 218, 232
Norfolk 22, 178, 191
parish 15, 60, 118, 154, 241
provincial 57, 172
status 13–14, 113, 185, 191, 208
upper 1, 15, 17, 23, 34, 103, 118, 154, 161, 214–15, 241
see also consumption, gentlemen; households; houses; London
gifts 1, 3, 8, 28, 49–50, 61, 64, 77, 144, 147–51, 166, 179, 195, 198, 202, 220
  for children 171–2
  of money 17, 149, 164, 180, 188, 190, 217, 220
  wedding 168–9; *see also* food: gifts; wills and bequests
Gillbert 69; *see also* craftsmen: upholsterers
Gittings family 232, 235
  Hamon 233, 235, 244
  Matthew 72, 235; *see also* specialist workers: warreners; servants, elite: clerks
  Thomas 235; *see also* bailiffs; tenants
Glover, R. 46; *see also* servants, elite: accountants
Godly 224; *see also* labourers
Godwick (Norfolk) 22
goods 1–6, 12–13, 23–5, 31, 33, 39, 122, 132, 201, 209–10, 212, 237, 239
  acquisition of 1, 3, 24, 50, 52, 55, 59–60, 63–5, 69, 72, 86, 241–2
  bespoke 5
  consumer 4, 10, 12, 14, 65
  consumable 1, 86
  domestic 232–3
  durable 1–3, 25
  finished or ready made 5–7, 17, 72
  foreign 2, 7, 17, 84, 210
  gendered attitudes to 146–7
  homemade 6
  household 13, 86, 128
  locally produced 17
  luxury 48, 119
  meanings of 145–51, 155
  moveable 113, 154
  new/novel 2, 7, 17, 70, 118–19, 153, 155
  old/inherited/second-hand 4, 6, 24, 33, 70
  part or semi-finished 5–7; *see also* material culture
Googe, B. 39; *see also* books: husbandry
Gouge, W. 37–9; *see also* bibliography: pre-1800 books
grain 14, 42, 75–7, 88, 90, 92, 94, 101, 116, 232
  barley 18, 73–4, 76–7, 90, 210, 214, 217, 221, 232
  oats 74, 76, 97, 191, 221–2, 224
  peas 76, 78, 93, 95, 221

rye 76, 89, 90, 94, 221, 232
wheat 18, 72, 76, 88–90, 94, 223–4; *see also* drinks; bread
Greenham, Richard 197; *see also* books: as gifts
Greenrod, R. 230; *see also* labourers
Greenrod, W. 218, 220; *see also* servants, male; Katherine Warner
Gressenhall (Norfolk) 22, 35, 82, 113, 193, 202, 207, 243
Grey, Elizabeth, Countess of Kent 108
Grinell, cousin 61
groceries 62, 72–3, 77
  fruit, dried and preserved, 6, 14, 62, 73, 77, 92, 94–5, 99, 101–3, 116, 143–4, 167, 240
  oils 73, 92, 103–4, 108–9, 122, 192
  salt 92
  spices 7, 73, 77, 92, 102–4, 116
  sugar 7, 20, 55, 73, 77–8, 81, 86–7, 92, 99, 103–4, 115–16, 143–4, 171, 240
  vinegar 41–2, 73, 80, 92, 109; *see also* drinks; food; foodstuffs; medicines
Gurney, Anthony 182
  Dol 194
  Elizabeth 182
  Frank 61–2; *see also* merchants and suppliers
Guybon, family 21, 82, 218, 232–5; *see also* estate: bailiffs, tenants; servants, male
  Elizabeth, wife of Francis junior, 136, 150, 218, 234
  Francis, senior 60, 128, 157, 232–3, 237, 244, 232–3, 237
  Francis, junior 232, 234
  Margaret, wife of Francis senior 234
  Thomas 218, 234
  William 60, 73, 157, 196, 232; *see also* Dorothy Boyton
Guybon, daughters of Francis senior: Amy, Anne, Frances, Katherine, Margaret 218, 234
see also servants, female

Hamblyn, Mrs 32
Hans Weller, Dutchman 203; *see also* building work
Hares of Stow Bardolph 193
Hare, Sir Ralph Hare 82, 194
Harrison, W. 7, 15, 88. 90, 94, 97, 102, 116–17, 144–5; *see also* bibliography: pre-1800 books
Harrold, Elizabeth 216; *see also* servants, female: dairymaids
Harvey, Dr W. 106; *see also* professionals: medical practitioners
Hawden, Dr 197; *see also* books: as gifts
Haymish, Anne 216; *see also* servants, female: dairymaids
Heacham (Norfolk) 18, 22, 24, 30, 35, 92, 94, 154, 161, 163, 166, 197, 202, 207–8, 217, 220, 225–7, 230, 234–7, 243–4

health 87, 93, 105–6, 108, 110–11, 149, 171, 174–5, 191; *see also* books: medical; medical care
Heresbach, C. 39–40; *see also* books: husbandry
Heydon, Sir John 14, 70
Hobart family 24, 27, 43, 48, 74, 82, 193, 220
  Lady Frances (wife of Sir John 2nd Bt.) 31–2, 46–7
  Lady Dorothy 19, 21, 45–7; *see also* Dorothy Bell
  Sir Henry (uncle of Sir Hamon) 19, 21, 45, 46, 139, 188
  Sir John 2nd Bt. 22, 46
Hoby, Lady Margaret 108; *see also* books: diaries
Hoby, Sir Thomas 184; *see also* books: advice and self-help
Hocknell, Mr 82; *see also* professionals: clergymen
Hodgetts 62; *see also* craftsmen: book binder
Holme-next-the-Sea (Norfolk) 18, 73, 166, 171, 179–80, 190, 230, 243
Holme Parsonage (Norfolk) 20, 179
Horne, James and Thomas 226–7; *see also* craftsmen: masons
horses 25, 40, 52–3, 58, 62–3, 84, 109, 110, 163, 189, 191–3, 212, 214–15, 232, 236
  meat 58, 60, 80, 186–7; *see also* craftsmen: saddlers; elite consumption: coaches; craftsmen: farrier and horse doctor; servants, male: horsekeepers, coachmen
household
  accounts 1, 3–4, 9, 14, 19–21, 23–4, 26, 28–31, 46, 50–5, 63–4, 84, 87–8, 94, 96–7, 105, 116–17, 123, 132, 145, 153, 156–7, 164, 166, 168, 170, 175, 179, 183, 187–8, 196–7, 199, 209, 221, 225, 230–2, 234, 239, 244
  durables 117, 119, 120, 122, 128–9, 132, 134, 136, 139–40
  economy 161, 163, 209, 221, 228, 231, 235–7
  expenditure 51–4, 119, 123, 157–60, 189
  food 73, 75–7, 90–1, 93–103
  gentry 14, 17, 21, 48, 74, 193–4
  head of 8, 26, 31
  life-cycle and size 1, 4, 25, 156–9
  Le Strange 1, 3, 6, 10–12, 22, 24–5, 30, 48, 50–1, 58–61, 81–4, 87–8, 90–1, 100, 103, 111–12, 123, 154, 161–2, 167, 171–2, 178–9, 181, 189, 193, 200, 213–14, 221, 231–6, 239–42
  management 1, 8–9, 11–13, 20, 26–33, 34–5, 48, 185, 209, 242
  wealthy/large 4, 91–2, 94, 96, 101, 114, 212, 215
  women's role 1, 10, 12–13, 31–2, 36–9, 41–48, 87, 242
  working in the 65–70, 145, 210–18, 221, 236–7

Index

households 8, 13, 26, 35, 37, 49–50, 54, 65, 70–1, 101, 114, 119, 154, 171–2, 193–4, 213, 215, 217, 237
  aristocratic 17, 35, 92, 164, 212
  early modern 9, 31
  East Anglian 96
  elite 9, 13, 27, 50, 76, 212–13, 242
  English 2, 113,118, 249, 251
  farming 72, 232, 235, 237
  female headed 96
  gentry 1, 14, 17, 48, 74, 84, 99, 104, 116, 153–4, 157, 194, 200, 212–13, 215, 240–1
  labouring 116
  large 6, 27, 77, 139
  medieval 91
  middling 7, 77, 102, 112, 117, 132, 155, 171
  Norfolk 43
  Norwich 145
  ordinary 55, 77, 144, 154, 241
  poor 50, 112, 116, 144, 213, 232, 213, 232
  rural 7, 12, 51, 145
  urban 7
  wealthy 10, 27, 50, 81, 88, 91, 102, 116, 132, 140–1, 211
household wares
  brass 61, 70, 74, 87, 109, 133, 141, 144–5, 153, 167, 235, 241
  earthen and stone 14, 61, 144, 155, 241
  glass 52, 61–3, 141–4, 147, 154–5, 240
  kitchen and dining ware 70, 119, 140–5
  silver 52, 61, 142–3, 146–9, 153–4, 211, 240; *see also* furniture; furnishings; textiles
housekeeping 12–13, 48; *see also* servants, female: housekeeper
houses 87, 115–17, 193, 195, 203, 207–8, 217, 227
  ale 188
  Classical 206
  of correction 186, 190
  country 55, 185, 191
  dove 188
  elite 11, 206, 227
  farm 22, 29, 161, 203, 240
  gentry 2, 132–3, 178, 195, 198, 246
  improving 51, 209
  large 16, 114, 207–8
  multiple 46
  ordinary 227
  parsonage 227
  wash 114; *see also* buildings
housewife 1, 10–12, 26, 32, 36–43, 48, 65, 88, 93, 104, 108, 111–12, 114–15, 185
  wifery 11–13, 24, 26–7, 37, 39, 48, 87, 111, 114, 149, 151, 152
  work 8, 13, *see also* books; gentlewomen; women
Howard, Ann, Countess of Arundel 108
Howards, Dukes of Norfolk 20

Hunstanton (Norfolk) 1, 7, 14, 18–24, 29, 30, 35, 57–8, 60, 63, 71, 73–4, 76, 81–3, 92, 94–6, 105, 113–14, 137, 140, 162, 166–9, 171, 174, 178, 189, 190, 193–7, 200–2, 205–8, 211–13, 217–20, 223–6, 228–3, 233–7, 239, 243–4
  church 167, 220
  Hall 23, 24, 29, 34, 50–1, 69, 71, 74, 81–2,91, 94, 105, 113–14, 132–3, 136–9, 150, 154–5, 158, 161–2, 168–9, 175, 188, 195–8, 200, 203–8, 210, 218, 227–8, 237
  parish registers 164, 166–8, 219, 229, 230, 234

identities, gendered 8, 12, 150
identity 1, 3, 12–13, 42, 105, 152, 242; *see also* gentry; consumption
income 1, 9, 15, 22–3, 28–31, 34, 50–2, 85, 118, 156–9, 161–2, 164, 176, 185–6, 189–90, 208, 211, 215, 221, 232, 235
  of other families 12, 15, 22, 26, 31, 44, 46–8, 151, 211, 213, 216–17, 221–2, 226, 231–2, 236–8; *see also* expenditure; family finance
Inns of Court 17, 36, 55, 59, 63, 157, 175, 177–8, 189, 197, 240; *see also* London
inventories
  household 2, 110, 120–2
  probate 2, 7, 24–5, 65, 112, 117–19, 127–8, 140, 144, 152–4, 212, 232–3, 236, 244
  see also wills and bequests

James I, king of England (1603–25) 17, 21, 56, 97, 194, 245
Jenner, Edmund of Heacham, yeoman 237
Johnson 226; *see also* specialist workers; hopman
Jonson, Ben 142: *see also* books: advice and self-help
Justices of the Peace 15, 20, 34, 108, 186, 228; *see also* county: administration

Kervile, Sir Henry of Wiggenhall St. Mary, Norfolk 70
Kettwood, Thomas 66, 220; *see also* servants, elite: butlers; tenants
  sister of 66; *see also* specialists workers: knitters
King, Gregory 52, 54, 119, 129; *see also* books: advice and self-help
Kings Lynn (Norfolk) 6, 20,50, 58–60, 62–4, 68, 70–1, 73, 107–8, 113, 161–3, 194–5, 199, 203, 205, 215, 225, 234
kitchen 17, 25, 42, 50, 65, 73, 111–13 140, 145, 180, 192, 198, 210, 214–15, 224, 236
  accounts 23, 27–9, 31, 42, 50–3, 72–7, 80, 82–4, 86, 89, 92–5, 98–102, 105, 113, 115, 161, 166, 193, 196, 211, 219, 221–3, 225, 227, 229, 231, 240, 243; *see also* household wares: kitchen and dining; rooms and chambers
knights 15–6, 167, 186, 188; *see also* gentry

Index

Knivett family 82
  Sir Philip 165
  Sir Thomas 198
Knockin, Shropshire 18
Knowles, Sir William 172; *see also* children
Kytson, Sir Thomas of Hengrave Hall, Suffolk 113

labour 1–3, 14, 15, 18, 23, 29, 35, 39, 41, 43, 50–1, 68–9, 74, 81, 83, 99, 188, 210–11, 215, 219, 221–2, 224, 235, 237; *see also* labourers; labouring
labourers 25, 42, 51, 83–4, 101–2, 113, 116, 145, 157, 208, 210–12, 216, 218–26, 230–2, 236–7, 241
  day 83–4, 101, 113, 210–12, 221–6, 230–1, 236
  female 223–4; *see also* building workers
labouring, agricultural 231
  men 40
  women 12, 229; *see also* labour; labourers
ladies 9, 32, 35, 37, 114, 212, *see also* gentlewomen
land 15–16, 18, 29, 30, 33–5, 44–6, 50–1, 56, 76, 96, 113, 132, 145, 159, 161–4, 167, 178–9, 207–9, 216–17, 221, 226–32, 234–7, 239, 241
  tenure 16–18, 218, 220, 231
  holders 35, 82, 230
  holding 22, 30, 190, 226, 230, 235
  lord 184–5, 207, 237
  ownership 15, 179; *see also* estate; estates
Lane, Goodwife 83, 171; *see also* servants, female: wetnurses
Lane, T. 171, 210, 214, 217, 220; *see also* bailiffs of husbandry; servants
Langham, William 110; *see also* books: medical
Laverick, Dorothy, wife of Hamon Le Strange 179
  Edmund of Upwell, Norfolk 179
laundry 8, 12–13, 87, 114–15
  see also servants, female: washmaids; consumption activities: cleaning and washing
law courts *see* Westminster
Lawes, M. 214, 216, 218, 244; *see also* servants, female
Lemnius, Levinus 110; *see also* books: medical
Le Strange, Lady Ann, wife of Sir Nicholas 4th Bt., 71
Le Strange, Lady Anne, wife of Sir Thomas 30, 48
Le Strange, Lady Anne nee Paston *see* Lady Anthony Cope
Le Strange, Lady Anne, nee Lewkenor 31, 75, 150, 178, 182
Le Strange, Anne nee Goding *see* Anne Stubbe, mother of Alice, 19, 21
Le Strange, Lady Alice (1585–1656) 1, 9, 11–13, 15, 19–25
  accounting methods 27–37
  ideal housewife 41–9

acquiring goods 50–2, 58–65, 67, 69–77, 81–7
managing food 89, 93, 96–7, 99, 101
medical care 105–12
managing durables 116, 120, 122, 125, 130, 132–4, 136–40, 142, 147–53
wife and mother 156–7, 159, 161–9, 172, 174–5, 178–83
enjoying life 187–99, 202–3
as an employer 208, 214–19, 224–5, 234–6, 238–9, 242–3
Le Strange, Dorothy (1608–10) 164, 166, 182
Le Strange, Eleanor 19
Le Strange, Sir Hamon (1583–1654) 1, 9, 13, 15, 19–25
  sharing management 26–30, 32–5, 37, 43, 45, 47
  acquiring goods 48, 51–2, 59–64, 66–9, 74, 82, 84
  food and health 92, 96, 101, 105–6, 108, 110
  living space and material culture 123, 129–30, 132–3, 136–8, 143, 147–9, 152–3
  family man 156–7, 159, 161–9, 170, 172, 174, 180–3
  gentry life 184–93, 195–206, 208–10, 213–17, 219–20, 228, 234–8, 240, 242, 243
  see also bibliography: pre-1800 books
Le Strange, Sir Hamon 2nd Bt., (1631–56) 182
Le Strange, Sir Hamon, veteran of the Battle of Crecy, 20, *see also* household accounts
Le Strange, Hamon (1605–60) 59, 62, 105–6, 128–30, 133, 148–9
  author 197, 199
  childhood and education 157–8, 162, 170, 172, 174–7, 179
  marriage and money 180–2
  see also bibliography pre-1800 books
Le Strange, Hamon, brother of Baron Strange of Knockin (Shropshire) 18
Le Strange, Hamon (*c*. 1533–80) 19–20
Le Strange, Jane (1611–20) 164, 166, 182
Le Strange John (1618–19) 164, 166, 182
Le Strange, Judith 148, 150, 180, 182
Le Strange, Lady Mary 19–20; *see also* Mary Bell
Le Strange, Lady Mary, wife of Sir Nicholas 3rd Bt 182
Le Strange, Mary (1621–2) 59, 99, 100–1, 158, 164–6, 171, 182
Le Strange, Sir Nicholas 1st Bt. (1604–51) 15, 24, 31, 34–5, 42, 59, 62–34, 148, 167, 182
  author: jest book 42, 63, 67, 70, 75, 93, 136, 143, 151, 181, 193–4, 200
  childhood 173–7, 180–1
  clothes 120–1, 123, 126, 128–9, 130–1, 152, 236
  employer 234
  goods 132–4
  health 105–6
  money and marriage 149–50, 157–8, 161–4
  pastimes 197–200

Le Strange, Sir Nicholas 1st Bt. (1604–51) (cont.)
  projects 207–8, 219
  wedding 68–9, 168–9, 172, 179–80
  see also bibliography: pre 1800 books
Le Strange, Sir Nicholas 3rd Bt. (1632–1669) 182
Le Strange, Sir Nicholas 4th Bt. (1661–1724) 182
Le Strange, Sir Nicholas (1511–80) 19, 20–1
Le Strange, Sir Nicholas (1562–92) 19, 20
Le Strange, Sir Thomas (1490–1545) 20, 22, 212
Le Strange archive 24, 30, 32, 183, 201
Le Strange family 2–3, 18–23, 82, 101, 111, 119, 132–3, 145–6, 156, 174, 213
Le Stranges (as a couple) 1–2, 6–7, 10, 18, 20–5
  as household managers 27, 29–30, 34–5, 37–9
  acquiring goods 50–2, 54, 57–69, 71–4, 76–7, 81–4
  food and health 87–8, 91–8, 101–4, 106–7, 110–16
  material culture 118–23, 25–6, 133–4, 137, 139, 140, 142–7, 154
  as parents 156, 158–9, 161–5, 168–9, 171–2, 175, 177, 179
  lifestyle 187, 189–95, 198, 201, 203, 206–8
  as employers 210–27
  and the local community 228–32, 235–7, 239–42
Lewkenor, Anne see Lady Anne Le Strange
Lady 179
library, Le Strange 7, 24, 37, 48, 103, 110, 178, 184–5, 196–8, 200, 202, 240, 244; see also books; elite consumption; rooms and chambers
Lincoln's Inn 59; see also Inns of Court
Lingen, Blanche 35
livestock 18, 29, 50, 76, 134, 148, 221, 232–3
  calves 40, 75–6
  cattle 42, 76–7, 96
  cows 24, 29, 42, 74–5, 96, 190, 214–15, 226, 235–6
  pigs 29, 42, 40, 42, 72–3, 76–8, 89, 91, 95–6, 98, 100, 102, 217, 226, 232, 235–7, 239
  sheep 18, 21, 29, 33, 36, 41, 44, 65, 76–7, 96, 102, 149, 163, 221, 225–6, 232, 235
  see also foodstuffs; meat; poultry
Loades, Mr 174–7; see also professionals: tutors
Lock, Mr 49, 67–8, 130; see also craftsmen: tailors; professionals: moneylenders
Loder, Robert of Harwell, Berkshire 102, 112, 115–16, 214–16; see also books: diaries
London 2, 32, 118, 122
  as shopping centre 5–6, 17, 24, 55–6
  acquiring goods in 49–50, 52–3, 55, 60–4, 67, 126, 134, 137, 140–3, 168, 238
  buying specialist services 67–9, 71, 105–7, 111, 130–1, 163, 171–2, 225, 234, 238–9
  Barbican 44
  gentry links 7, 44–8, 57, 237–8
  growing attraction of 16–7, 55–6
  Highgate 45–6

Le Stranges relationship with 35, 43, 46–7, 57, 64, 84, 154, 237–8, 242
men's shopping in 9, 13, 130–1, 152, 168, 177, 179, 189, 201
staying and living in 63, 74, 101, 114, 180, 188
travelling to 58–60, 157, 162, 188, 191, 195, 199, 215, 241
women in 35, 56–7, 64, 84
see also Exchanges, Royal and New; Westminster; elite consumption; consumption activities
Longstraws 83, 171; see also servants, female: wetnurses
Lowther, Dame Mary 31

Makement 224; see also labourers
malaria see medical problems
Markham G. 12, 40–2, 65, 88, 93, 103–4, 108–10, 112, 191, 198; see also bibliography: pre 1800 books
Mary I, queen of England 20
Mary, queen of Scots 20
Mason, Robert of Kings Lynn, 205; see also craftsmen: joiners
Mason, Widow 83
Massingberd, Sir Drayner 32
Massingham, Norfolk 63, 217; see also Le Strange Mordaunt
material culture 1, 7, 16, 23, 117–55, 170, 209, 240–1
  see also clothing; elite consumption, furnishings; furniture; textiles
meat 14, 20, 37, 55, 72, 74, 76, 86, 88–9, 91–3, 96–9, 102–4, 116, 142, 166, 196
  bacon 29, 42, 74, 77, 91, 94, 102, 116
  beef 14, 28, 72–3, 76–7, 82, 88–9, 91, 93–4, 96–102, 116, 240
  lamb 29, 73, 78, 89, 91, 94–5, 217
  mutton 65, 74, 88–9, 91, 94–8, 100–2, 111, 116
  pork 29, 42, 74, 76, 88–9, 94, 102, 116
  sweet 62, 99
  tongue 72–3, 86, 91, 94, 96
  veal 73, 76, 78, 91, 94–5, 98, 232, 237
  venison 74, 80, 82, 94–5, 99, 116; see also poultry
medical care 12, 26, 51–3, 87, 105–11, 116, 166, 190, 239
  problems 105–6, 110, 171, 208
  practitioners see professionals; see also books: medical; health
  medicines 25, 41–2, 48, 52–3, 86–7, 105–6, 108–11, 116, 196, 211, 239
  apothecary stuff 62–3, 106
Mediolano, Joannes de 110; see also books: medical
Melton Constable (Norfolk) 44
merchants and suppliers 2, 7, 28–9, 35, 61, 72, 102, 154, 184
  chandlers 111–2, 225

drapers 63, 68, 142
mercers 62, 68, 122
moneylenders 67, 130, 159, 162–3, 179, 181, 193, 239
pedlars 2, 63, 84
retailers 2, 72, 74, 84, 241
shopkeepers 2, 5, 121, 238
Micheal, L. 67–8, 130, 162; *see also* tradesmen: tailors; professionals: moneylenders
Michell of South Creake 107; *see also* professionals: medical practitioners
Mildmay, Grace 12, 32, 108–9, 249
militia 13, 56, 186, 188–9; *see also* elite consumption: office holding
Molineux, Sir Edmund 37
Mordaunt family 82
Mordaunt, Le Strange 187, 193
mortality *see* medical problems
Mosse, M. 218; *see also* servants, female
Moore 222; *see also* labourers
Moulton, Thomas 110; *see also* books: medical
Murton, Francis 226; *see also* craftsmen: carpenters; tenants
music 25, 34, 139, 150, 169, 173, 177, 184, 193–7, 200, 202, 208–10, 239
see also books; elite consumption
musical culture 200
  instruments 148
  patrons 197
  waits 194–5; *see also* professionals: entertainers and musicians

Nevill, Lady 12, 75
Newcastle (Northumberland) 20, 165
Newdigate, Dame Anne of Arbury, Warwickshire 172
  Lettice 178; *see also* children
Newman of Dereham 192; *see also* saddlers
Nicholl, Mr 106–7; *see also* professionals: medical practitioners
Nightingale, J. 214, 216; *see also* servants, male
Noke, G. 226; *see also* craftsmen: thatchers; tenants
Norfolk 4, 14, 18, 20–4, 27, 35–6, 44–8, 59, 69, 72, 81, 94, 96, 101–2, 105–7, 113, 130, 134, 137, 146, 162–3, 166–7, 174–9, 185–93, 198–9, 203–4, 211, 221, 225, 227–30, 243–5, 248–51
Norton, Mr 175; *see also* professionals: tutors
Norwich (Norfolk) 13, 20, 24, 43, 45–6, 48, 50, 52, 57–60, 62–4, 67–8, 71–2, 84, 104, 107–8, 111, 120, 123, 127, 130, 144–5, 154, 162, 167–8, 175, 187, 191, 193, 201, 215, 217, 225, 227, 234, 239, 241, 246, 248
  Bracondale 178
novelty 4, 5, 8, 81, 93, 147, 239, 240, *see also* goods

Oakley (Bedfordshire) 22
Oldman, J. 214, 220; *see also* servants, male: coachmen
office holding *see* elite consumption; gentry
Ortelius, Abraham 197; *see also* books: Sir Hamon's library

Page, N. 140, 231–3, 236, 244; *see also* tenants
parish 2, 18, 29, 30, 35, 57, 151, 171, 179, 190, 225, 227, 230, 232, 235, 251
  registers 24, 164, 166, 168, 212, 219, 220, 229–30, 232, 234–5, 244
  see also gentlemen; gentry
Parliament 56, 59, 162–3, 188–9
  member of 15, 20, 34, 186
Parliamentarians 162
Parker, Edward 106–7, 192, 220; *see also* craftsmen: farrier and horse doctor
Paston, Anne *see* Lady Cope
Paston, Sir William 19
Peacham, Henry 184, 192, 200; *see also* books: advice and self-help
Pepys, Samuel 32
Peyton, Sir John of Doddington (Cambridgeshire) 20–1
Peyton, Lady 143
Pomarius, Petrus 110; *see also* books: medical
poultry 12, 72, 77, 83, 91, 94, 96–9, 116, 226, 232, 235–7
  capons, chickens and hens 12, 14, 72–3, 77–8, 81, 83–4, 89, 91, 95, 98, 100–2, 116, 164, 220, 226, 232, 235–6, 239
  ducks 73, 78, 91, 94–5, 100–2, 220, 232
  geese 40, 73, 78–9, 89, 91, 94–5, 98–100, 206, 236
  pigeons (doves) 40, 73, 77–8, 81, 91, 94–5, 235
  turkeys 4, 7, 78, 80–1, 84, 91, 94–102, 115–6, 226, 232, 235, 240
  eggs 6, 43, 72–3, 77–8, 80, 92, 97–8, 101–2, 237
  housing 188, 206; *see also* birds; food gifts; food items; meat
Powle, Nicholas 68; *see also* craftsmen: tailors
Powlett, Dame Frances 108
production *see* consumption activities
products *see* goods
professionals 13, 27, 35, 48, 72, 118, 147, 159, 162, 194
  clergymen 82, 198, 225
  lawyers 21, 36, 45, 147, 189
  medical practitioners 87, 91, 106–7, 110–11, 116, 143, 177, 197–8, 210–11, 239, 241
  midwives 83, 106, 164–5, 169, 225, 240
  musicians and entertainers 194–5, 197
  surveyors 22
  tutors and masters, 21, 149, 165, 174–7, 200, 210, 225, 239, 242

Ralph 66, 68
  wife of 66; *see also* craftsmen: tailors; specialist workers: knitters
Rant, J. of Grays Inn, London 163; *see also* professionals: moneylenders
Rant, Dr. W. 106–7; *see also* professionals: medical practitioners
Rayner, Anne 218; *see also* servants, female
Raynham Hall (Norfolk) 44–5, 204, 206, 246
Read family 83
  Christopher, John and William 83; *see also* local officials; tenants
Record, Robert 110, 197, 199, 202; *see also* books: medical; bibliography
Reeve, J. 214; *see also* servants, male: cooks
Reynell, Sir Richard of Forde, Teignmouth, Devon 98
  Lady Lucy 98
Ringstead (Norfolk) 18, 22, 30, 68, 166, 190, 207, 210, 220, 225,–6, 230, 233–5, 243–4
  St. Andrew (Barret or Little Ringstead) 24, 82, 113, 163, 171, 234–5, 244
  St. Peter (Great Ringstead) 24, 220, 234–5, 244
Robinson 224; *see also* labourers
rooms and chambers 25, 116–17
  bed and living 23, 25, 69, 71, 111–13, 121, 132–40, 146–7, 153, 168–9, 198, 216, 232–3
  best 61, 64, 71, 132–7, 146, 153
  dining 61, 69, 138–9, 150, 196, 205
  library 48, 103, 184, 196–8, 200, 202
  lodging 13, 17, 59–60, 69, 101, 153
  service 112, 206, 235
  study 177, 198; *see also* kitchen
Rose 225–6; *see also* specialist workers: shepherds; tenants
Rowland, F. of London 163; *see also* professionals: moneylenders
Rust and Sommers 67; *see also* craftsmen: hatters

Salter, John of Heacham, husbandman 237
Sander, G. of Snettisham 63; *see also* craftsmen: glover
Sappe of Norwich 62, 67, 217; *see also* craftsmen: shoemakers
Savage, William 224, 230; *see also* labourers
Sayer, Mr of Dickleborough, Norfolk 44; *see also* professionals: tutors
sea 18, 60, 94, 113, 189, 208
  fish 79, 81, 89, 92, 94–5, 97, 104, 237
  fisheries 18
  food 72, 83, 92; *see also* fish; fishing; foodstuffs
Sedgeford (Norfolk) 18, 21, 22–4, 28–9, 35, 60, 68, 72, 82, 103, 107, 113, 128, 150, 157, 161, 164, 166, 171, 17–5, 190, 197, 202, 207, 216, 220, 225–7, 230, 232–5, 243–4
  East and West Hall, manors of 207, 232
Segon family 83; *see also* estate: bailiffs

servants 3, 6–8, 12, 14, 25, 28, 34, 40–1, 45, 47–8, 50, 55, 61, 65, 70–1, 74, 84, 96, 101–2, 104, 106–7, 111, 113, 116, 132, 134, 145, 148, 153–4, 157–8, 161–2, 166, 169, 171–2, 190–5, 211–21, 230–1, 236–7, 239–242; 247–51
servants, elite 9, 17, 27, 31, 34–5, 92, 214, 242
  auditor 220
  bailiffs of husbandry 34, 210, 214–15, 218, 220
  butlers 34, 66, 134, 210, 213–5, 220
  clerks 34, 134, 166, 213–15, 217, 220, 225, 235
  receiver-general 46
  stewards 11, 27, 31–2, 34–5, 44, 46, 88, 165, 215, 217, 220, 234, 237
servants, female 10, 12, 34, 38–9, 60, 71, 75, 114, 213–20, 242
  chambermaids 34, 210, 215–16, 220
  dairymaids 24, 33–4, 74, 136, 214–16
  housekeeper 10, 27, 31
  washmaids, washerwomen 34, 113–14, 166, 210, 214, 216, 218, 220, 225
servants, male 9, 11–14, 17, 27, 34, 58–62, 76, 101, 134, 148, 157, 212, 214–15, 217–20
  brewer 215
  coachmen 34, 42, 76, 191, 214–15, 220
  cooks 34, 42, 76, 87, 93, 99, 104, 210, 213–15, 217–18, 242
  falconers 34, 134, 195, 214–15
  gardeners 42, 92–3, 214, 228–19
  horsekeeper 34, 191, 214–15, 217
  ploughboys 214
Sheriff of Norfolk 15, 20; *see also* county: administration
Shilling, Anne 220; *see also* servants, female: dairymaids; J. Boner
Shirley, Francis of Staunton Harold, Leicestershire 36
shops 2, 5–7, 9; *see also* goods; London; merchants and suppliers: shopkeepers; consumption activities: shopping
Siborne, M. 220; *see also* servants, female: chambermaids; J. Oldman
Sidney, Lady 82, 193; *see also* Walsingham, Norfolk
Sidney, Mary, Countess of Pembroke 108
Skelton, Mr 175–6; *see also* professionals: tutors
Smythe, John of Nibley 37
Snettisham (Norfolk) 22, 63, 236
Speed, John 199; *see also* books: Sir Hamon's library
specialist workers: 14, 25, 211–12, 221, 224–8
  barbers 199, 210–11, 239
  hopman 222, 226
  knacker 226
  knitters 42, 66, 210–11, 225, 238, 241
  shepherds 29, 157, 164, 207, 214, 225–6, 237, 244
  spinners 65

Index

warrreners 72, 225–6, 235, 237
weavers 42, 51, 66, 210, 225, 236, 238
wet nurses 25, 83, 157, 164–6, 170–2, 178, 210–11, 234, 239; *see also* craftsmen; labourers; servants
Spelman family 21, 60, 82, 184
  Dame Elizabeth 36
  Sir Henry of Congham (Norfolk) 19–20, 198
  Sir John 43
Spratt family 21
  John 67
  Edward 220; *see also* servants, elite: accountants; tenants
Spring, Sir William 93, 99, 162, 169, 181–2, 194, 216, 244
  Sir William, senior 179
  Elizabeth 117, 169
  William junior and Dorothy 149; *see also* Elizabeth Le Strange
Springall 226; *see also* specialist workers: weavers; knacker
Sprowston Hall, Norwich *see* Corbett family
Stafford, Anne 114
Stafford, Humphrey, Duke of Buckingham, 96
Stanion, E. of Gaywood 205; *see also* craftsmen: plasterers
Stanton Fair, Bury St. Edmunds, Suffolk 63
Stibbard 137; *see also* craftsmen: carpenters
Stiffkey (Norfolk) 18, 44, 102, 178, 189, 193, 211–12, 215, 218, 223, 236
Stileman, Robert of Snettisham 163, 236
Stonhouse, Sir William and Dame Elizabeth his wife, 37
Strange, Baron of Knockin (Shropshire) 18
Stubbe, Alice 19, 21, 28, 182, 243; *see also* Lady Alice Le Strange
Stubbe, Alice nee Richers 19, 219
Stubbe, Anne 19, 21
Stubbe, Dionisia 19; *see also* Dionisia Yelverton
Stubbe, Edmund (cousin to Richard Stubbe) 169
Stubbe, Richard of Sedgeford 19, 36, 82, 149, 217
  career, role and background 21–4, 187, 232
  will and bequests 24, 69, 147–9, 161, 167, 175–6, 179–80, 199, 217, 219
  see also professionals: lawyers
Sturges, Mr 175–6; *see also* professionals: tutors
Sydney, Phillipa Lady, (1st wife of Sir John Hobart) 46

Taftes, Alice 218; *see also* servants, female
  Robert 222–4, 231; *see also* labourers
Talbot, Aletha, Countess of Surrey, 108
Tasborough, Lady 70
textiles 13, 42, 50–4, 63, 66, 69, 84–5, 119–21, 146–7, 153, 163, 165, 239, 241
  cotton 117, 120–2, 7, 135, 147, 165–6, 240
  draperies, new 7, 120–3, 147, 155, 240

linen 12, 14, 23, 61–7, 71, 113–6, 118–22, 124–5, 128, 132, 139–40, 142–3, 146–8, 150, 152–4, 168, 173, 212, 216, 235–6
lace 61–3, 66, 68, 71, 122–8, 131, 133, 135, 155, 165, 168, 168, 73, 192–3, 217, 240
other types of cloth and fabric 120–3
woollen cloth 14, 63, 65–6, 114, 120–2, 173, 236
see also beds; clothes; clothing; furnishings
Thorpe (Suffolk) 22
Thorpe, John, architect 205
Thorpe, Mr Thomas of High Cliffe, Northamptonshire 204
Towers, Abigail 220; *see also* servants, female
Townshend family of Raynham 24, 27, 43, 82, 102, 165, 170–1, 178, 198, 204, 206
  Lady Anne *nee* Bacon (wife of Sir John Townshend) 14, 44–5, 47
  Lady Anne *nee* Spelman (wife of Sir Roger Townshend) 43
  Dame Eleanor 36
  Sir John 14, 44
  Robert 14, 44
  Sir Roger 1st Bt, (1595–1637) 14, 43–5, 187–8, 193
Townshend, Christopher 195, 214; *see also* servants, male: falconer
Trench, Mr 46, 214, 220; *see also* servants, elite: stewards
Trench, Stewart *see* Mr Trench
Tunstall, Thomas, Catholic priest 108; *see also* medical care

Verney, Ralph 37
Verstagen Richard 197; *see also* books: Sir Hamon's library
Vincent 216; *see also* servants, male
visits 59–61, 64, 74, 82, 84, 145, 187, 190–3, 195, 208; *see also* consumption activities: visiting
Voellus, Jean 197, 201; *see also* books: Sir Hamon's library

Waddelow 219; *see also* craftsmen: coopers
  Sarah 219; *see also* servants, female
wages 12, 28, 34–5, 41, 51, 53, 92, 101, 157, 173, 195–6, 210–18, 221, 225–6, 228–9, 236–7
  see also labourers; servants: elite, female and male
Walker, Anne 216; *see also* servants, female: dairymaids
Walpole, Robert 174; *see also* children
Walsingham, Norfolk 62–3, 82, 186, 193, 217, 237
Walton-on-Thames, Surrrey 44
Warde, Mr 142; *see also* craftsmen: goldsmiths
Warner family 82
  Roger 237; *see also* bailiffs; servants, elite: stewards

Warner, Katherine 220; *see also* female servants; William Greenrod
Warners 226–8; *see also* craftsmen: masons
Waterman, Thomas 22, 219, 243–4; *see also* professionals: surveyors
  Mary and Lydia 219; *see also* servants, female
Waters, William 197: *see also* professionals: clergymen
Wesenham 222–4; *see also* labourers
  Margaret 224; *see also* labourers, female
  Widow 224; *see also* labourers, female
Westminster 16–17, 56–7, 61, 151, 248
  Abbey 90, 95–6, 112
  School 176–7; *see also* London
West Winch, Norfolk 162,180–1; *see also* Hamon Le Strange
Wheelwright, Mr 175–6; *see also* professionals: tutors
Whitlocke, Bullstrode 35
Whittle, Anne 214; *see also* servants, female
widows 8–9, 14, 20–1, 32, 35, 44, 47, 60, 127, 133, 136, 157, 191, 193
  widowhood 36, 45, 83, 150, 153
  working 66, 219, 220, 224, 231, 237; *see also* gentlewomen; women
Wiggett the fool, 194; *see also* professionals: entertainers and musicians
wills and bequests 12, 24–5, 63, 69, 72–3, 119, 136–7, 142, 146–52, 190–1, 217–18, 234; *see also* gifts; inventories: probate
Willoughby family of Wollaton Hall, Nottinghamshire 88, 95
Willoughbys of Leyhill, Devon 97
Willson 68; *see also* craftsmen: tailors
Willson, Anne 214; *see also* servants, female
Willson, Dr E. 107; *see also* professionals: medical practitioners
Willson, Margaret 217; *see also* servants, female
Willson, Mr 199; *see also* craftsmen: printers

Wirsung, Christof 110; *see also* books: medical
Wisbech Castle, Cambridgeshire 108
Wivenhoe, (Essex) 44
wives *see* housewifery; housewife; gentlewomen; women
Wix, R. 66, 154, 222, 225–6, 231–3, 236, 244; *see also* craftsmen: thatchers; labourers
  Anne 66, 224, 236; *see also* specialist workerss: knitters; labourers, female
  'son' 222, 224, 236; *see also* labourers
Woods 225; *see also* specialist workers: shepherds
Woodforde, Parson 10
Woodhouse, Ann *see* Lady Anne Le Strange
Woodward 216; *see also* servants, male
women, and clothing 12–13, 66, 84, 120, 124–8, 131, 151–3, 173
  as gift givers 83, 147–51
  elite 36–7, 42, 47, 71, 179
  employment of 114–15, 166, 211–12, 214, 216–8, 222–5, 229, 234
  role and position 1, 8–9, 13, 27, 35–43, 47–8, 77, 87, 114, 152, 236, 242
  shopping and interests 9–10, 56–7, 64, 84, 185, 191, 194, 197
  skills 9, 12, 27, 30–2, 108–9, 111, 116
  types of 8, 10, 12, 24, 26, 36–7, 41, 44–5, 47–8, 101, 125, 151–3, 165, 171, 180, 236
  see also gentlewomen; housewife; servants, female; widows
Wright, Edward of Norwich 62, 201; *see also* craftsmen: goldsmith

Xenophon 198; *see also* books: children

Yelvertons of Rougham 178, 180, 193
Yelverton, Dionisia *nee* Stubbe 19, 21, 82, 133, 148, 157
  William of Rougham (Norfolk) 19, 21, 148, 187

Lightning Source UK Ltd.
Milton Keynes UK
UKHW010434091118
332016UK00008B/461/P

9 780199 233533